A New Science

A New Science

The Breakdown of Connections and the Birth of Sociology

BRUCE MAZLISH

New York   Oxford
OXFORD UNIVERSITY PRESS
1989

Oxford University Press

Oxford   New York   Toronto
Delhi   Bombay   Calcutta   Madras   Karachi
Petaling Jaya   Singapore   Hong Kong   Tokyo
Nairobi   Dar es Salaam   Cape Town
Melbourne   Auckland

and associated companies in
Berlin   Ibadan

Copyright © 1989 by Bruce Mazlish

Published by Oxford University Press, Inc.,
200 Madison Avenue, New York, New York 10016

Oxford is a registered trademark of Oxford University Press

Library of Congress Cataloging-in-Publication Data
Mazlish, Bruce, 1923–
A new science : the breakdown of connections and the birth
of sociology / Bruce Mazlish.
p.   cm.
Includes index.
ISBN 0–19–505846-1
1. Sociology—History.   I. Title.
HM19.M39   1989
301'.09—dc19   88-31952   CIP

2 4 6 8 9 7 5 3 1

Printed in the United States of America
on acid-free paper

Acknowledgments

Feelings run powerfully on the issues dealt with in this book. So do thoughts as to how these issues should be conceptualized. I have had to make controversial decisions as to procedure and perspective.

In these and similar decisions, I have been encouraged and discouraged by various of my friends, colleagues, and others, who have been kind enough to discuss the book with me. Among those who have read all or parts of the manuscript I want to thank Jean-Christophe Agnew, Julia Prewitt Brown, Peter Buck, Paul Fideler, Catherine Gallagher, John A. Hall, Thomas L. Haskell, Mark Hulliung, James Kloppenberg, Roger Johnson, Michael McGerr, Michael McKeon, S. Mike Miller, Arthur Mitzman, Katherine Newman, Robert Nisbet, James Paradis, Wolf Schäfer, Irene Tayler, and Saul Touster. An anonymous reviewer, generally out of sympathy with my overall approach, nevertheless pushed me to recognize places where I was expecting too much of the reader.

The Thomas Meloy Chair of Rhetoric at M.I.T., which I now hold, has also afforded me research assistance, and for this I am most appreciative.

Special acknowledgment should be given to my IBM PC XT S/N51562465160, which alternately helped and hindered me, but mainly helped.

Neva Goodwin not only guided me through the intricacies of the computer but contributed in all the more important ways that only she and I can know.

Contents

Introduction

Anyone who has thought much about the "Two Cultures" becomes increasingly aware that there are really at least three cultures: humanities, natural sciences, and social sciences. The latter stands awkwardly between the other two, trying to be "hard" like the natural sciences, and yet generally tumbling inelegantly "backwards" into the humanities. The humanities have had a long tradition of critical discussion, and much work has now been devoted to the philosophy and history of the natural sciences; much less attention (though there are some shining exceptions) has been given to the philosophy and history of the social sciences, perhaps a natural consequence of their late entrance on the stage of human knowledge.

In this book, I am attempting to further our understanding of the social sciences, in this case specifically sociology, and to do so by examining, historically, some aspects of its origins especially in relation to the humanities. On one side, then, I will look in sustained fashion at literary figures (the "humanists"). On another side, I will glance very briefly at the natural sciences. And in between, I will focus on the relation of economics—a "hard" social science—to the emergence of sociology. I will argue that a core concern, shared by literature, economics, and sociology, is what nineteenth-century contemporaries came to call the "cash nexus." The cash nexus referred to the omnipresent substitution of money for personal relations. Extrapolated, the metaphor came to stand for a profound sense of dislocation, a pervasive feeling that all connections other than the monied one between Man and Man (and between Man and

Nature, and between Man and God) had been broken.* I call this the "connections problem," and will treat it as central to the emergence of a "science" of society, that is, sociology. (It goes without saying that there are a multiplicity of factors involved in the development of sociology, and that I am focusing on only one.)

The issues involved transcend particular disciplines; and an interdisciplinary treatment has therefore been necessary. The main disciplines involved, as already implied, have been history, literature, and sociology, with gestures toward the history of science. Needless to say, I have been conscious not only of some of what I may have got wrong in specialized areas but of what has been underemphasized or left out. To anticipate some of what I will say in Chapter 1, one clear underemphasis has been on the earlier developments leading to a cash-nexus society. My colleagues, for example, who write on the sixteenth, seventeenth, and eighteenth centuries, especially in England, keep saying, correctly, "But that development is already present in ————," and name their favorite citation.

My response is that, while recognizing important continuities of theme with earlier times, I have legitimately focused on the breakdown of connections as occurring in a unique way in the nineteenth century, where, as a result of the confluence of the Industrial and French revolutions, this breakdown was characterized by an intensity and quality markedly different from anything preceding it. In short, it is modern.

In addition to the question of what I have left out and why (the book itself will speak, I hope eloquently, of what I have put in), there is the matter of the perspective that I bring. It is well to set this before the reader at the very outset.

I read human history as showing repeated breaks in our sense of connection. Such breaks in our sense of connection are what make possible forward motion. If there had been no breaks in the past, mankind would still be existing solely in terms of primitive societies (or whatever preceded them). As sociologists, historians, and philosophers have stressed, the development of society has been in

---

*I capitalize "Man," in order to indicate that I mean both men and women. While occasionally awkward, the use of "Man" keeps the pungency of the word, at the same time as it underlines its generic nature.

terms of widening circles of attachment and enlarged feelings of relationship. I share this "Hegelian" perspective.

Such constant breaking of connections and creating of new ones is always deeply disturbing to those undergoing the changes. Along with the break, there is always lament. No new sense of connection can come into existence without coming to terms with existing tradition. (The question of incorporating tradition is worth attention on its own, not given in this book; see, however, Chapter 4 for hints, in regard to George Eliot, as to how the problem can unfold.) While I hold firmly that traditions are important and must form part of any emerging new sense of connection, and in this sense then I sympathize with the lamenters, if hands must be counted I more often take my stand with the breakers.

Even the most ardent supporters of "community" are always arguing over *which* community they have in mind to which our loyalties are to be accorded. Early sociologists, such as Le Play, extolled the virtues of family. A religious group, the Mormons, extends the idea of family from living relations to all one's ancestors (and thus implicitly to all humanity). A utopian socialist, Robert Owen, opposed family, with its attachment to private property, as an impediment to his dreamed-of small communities and co-operatives. Modern reformers and revolutionaries, in general, have seen personal and family loyalties as potentially undermining the requirements of citizenship and of adherence to national or party identities. An economic development theorist, Gunnar Myrdal, speculates that developing countries cannot move forward while family, caste, and ethnic groups place their interests constantly above obligations to a larger secular community.

At a time when perhaps our most pressing need is to move to a sense of global community (and by this I do not mean world government)—to match our increasing interconnectedness in reality—I am on the side of the enlargers, who must, it seems, first proceed by breaking, that is, by transcending more limited loyalties. In this process, however, many of our traditional and limited communal attachments must also be preserved: as the bumper sticker has it, "Think globally, act locally."

The other side of enlarged community, however, must be expanded individualism. By this I do not mean expanded economic rapaciousness. Unfortunately, especially in America, there are those who use the rhetoric of individual, family, and local values to disguise their disdain for the real community of interest and feeling that must exist in a modern, multi-layered society. As I point out in what follows, Tocqueville over a century ago warned us against exactly such selfishness. By espousing individualism, I mean equally to espouse enlightened communitarianism, or, better still, connected-ness. My intent is to foster a spirit of creative interplay between the needs of individualism and community.

Other scholars have also tried to deal with this problem, especially in regard to America. While often suffused with laudable sentiment and a "Tocquevillian" sense of the issue, the work of some of these American writers suffers, in my view, from an insufficient understanding of the entangled historical roots of what I am calling the "connections" theme; such work thereby slips unconsciously into the threnody of the lamenters. In contrast, I have taken as my task a more long-range and interdisciplinary inquiry into the subject of the breakdown of connections, as perceived in the modern period, by some of those who underwent the experience. To this task I have brought, of course, my own perspective: a tilt in favor of the break-ers and enlargers. I have tried, however, to control my predilections by a scholarly commitment to the "facts" of history, with what success each reader, individually, will have to judge.

In retrospect, I realize that my interest in the connections problem had been running underground for a long time, before emerging in full stream in this book. In an earlier work, *James and John Stuart Mill: Father and Son in the Nineteenth Century*, I wrote, in passing, that "one of the key romantic complaints was that the new world of self-made men had broken all ties: with the past, with one another, with nature. The lament at the lack of 'connection'—'only [this word should have been "and"] connect the landscape with the sky,' Wordsworth implored—was omnipresent. Mediated through Car-lyle, the general theme passed into Karl Marx's accusation that the 'bourgeoisie had broken all ties between man and man except for the "callous" cash nexus!'"

My major concern, however, inasmuch as it was about connec-tions, was with generational connections, especially as mediated through father–son conflict in the nineteenth century. It was in these terms, then, that I touched on the connections problem, and wrote, for example, that John Stuart Mill "had taken Bentham's and his father's Utilitarianism and combined it with the new thought and feeling inundating the early nineteenth century: Carlyle, Saint-Simonianism, the Germano-Coleridgian school, Auguste Comte. Thus he 'connected' the eighteenth and nineteenth centuries, responding in this fashion to the desperate sense of alienation experienced by so many in his age, and epitomized by the Romantics."[1]

In fact, I paid only peripheral attention to the connections problem in the Mill book, being more concerned with the way psychology could be integrated with intellectual history; thus, I practiced what is called "psychohistory." This practice, in turn, was intended as part of an inquiry into the nature and meaning of the social sciences, seeking to understand more deeply how personality, like political, economic, or social dispositions, and along with them, entered into the construction of social theory. Thus, an examination of John Stuart Mill's "ethology," his projected social science, seen in these terms, marked the culmination of my inquiry.[2]

Subsequently, reading widely in the literature surrounding the period of the American and the French revolutions, and especially the Industrial Revolution, it slowly percolated into my consciousness that the thinkers and writers of that period were concerned, literally compulsively, with the "breakdown of connections," as I came to call the phenomenon. Yet, other scholars, my contemporaries, seemed not to recognize this absorption in the terms that I felt it deserved. I decided, therefore, to do a study of the breakdown of connections as a piece of intellectual history.

It quickly became obvious that the compelling metaphor of this subject was the "cash nexus." And the project became an account of how the idea of the cash-nexus society grew out of the concern with the breakdown of connections. In tracing this development, most of my sources, as it happened, turned out to be "humanist" ones, drawn from philosophy, poetry, and general literature.

Perhaps I should have stopped here. The result would have been a nice tidy one, conveniently fitting into a single discipline, that of intellectual history. Some of my sources were economists, but they were easily relegated to the sidelines.

Unfortunately, at least in terms of convenience, my interests in the nature and meaning of social science now surfaced again, for I became increasingly aware that the concerns of what I had come to call the breakers and lamenters were also those sounding in the work of the newly emerging professional sociologists. An undercurrent of feelings about the "breakdown of connections" was leading to the birth of modern sociology. A disjuncture in style and presentation was, in fact, based on a continuity of perspective, though not intention, about Man and society.

I could have written two separate books; after all, most humanists are neither interested nor versed in the social sciences, and most social scientists are uneasy about any cohabitation with their presumed less hard-headed neighbors. To do so, however, seemed to me to perpetuate exactly the false divide that has come to characterize the disciplines of the humanities and the social sciences. The result was that I pushed ahead with an "interdisciplinary" work, though recognizing its uncomfortable and even problematic character.

To compound my, and the reader's problems, I also came increasingly to realize how contemporary and polemical is the issue of connections. The subject is not a nice, placid, largely outdated one, a matter of only "historical" interest. It is alive and throbbing today. I had to decide, therefore, how explicit I should be about my own values. In the end, while trying to treat the historical materials as impartially as possible, I also decided to deal with the values issue in a more or less frontal fashion (a decision already reflected in the present Introduction). It is in this way that I have come to write a book that, starting with the historical problem of connections and the cash nexus, moves on to the origins of modern sociology, and to an evaluation of the values attached to these matters.

I

BREAKERS AND LAMENTERS

1

A Beginning

The Questions

Is human life better or worse now than it was in the past? Has any real change in the quality of life taken place since the Industrial Revolution? These are constantly debated questions today, as they have been in one form or another for the past two hundred years. This book is an examination of one set of answers to such basic human queries.

Man (I capitalize the word to show that I use it generically) is, in fact, a kind of "double Man." He is that peculiar being who can be conscious both of his self, with its individualistic needs, and also of the group or society to which he belongs. From this double nature flow both joys and despairs. In the course of Man's recent historical development he has become increasingly self-conscious at the same time as his conceptualization of society has become more acute and complicated. This "unsocial-social" creature, as the eighteenth-century German philosopher Immanuel Kant called him, has been pulled more sharply toward both sides of his nature and, in the judgment of many, made a more divided being in the modern period.

Questions about community, individualism, sympathy, altruism, sincerity, egoism, isolation, society, and the like animate Western discourse. They spill over quickly into concern whether community is really crowd, and whether solitude is a recoil from sociability, a desirable affirmation of the freedom to be alone, or a form of anomie. Man's split nature finds its echoes in dichotomies of rural and urban, organic and mechanical, traditional and modern, *Gemein-schaft* and *Gesellschaft,* (to use a more pretentious terminology), and other such polar opposites.

One term, connections, may allow us to link all of these themes into a single coherent whole. "Connections," of course, is a protean subject. It can refer to biological, racial, or cultural connections, for example. It can be expressed in terms of generations changing or in terms of persisting customs. It can concern Man's relations to God, to Nature, and to other humans; in the latter case, it concerns the nature of Society.

In the late eighteenth and early nineteenth century there was, even more than before, a general sense that the civilized societies of the West were undergoing powerful changes. Some saw these as changes for the better, and some saw them as for the worse; most agreed, however, on defining their nature as stemming from a breakdown in connections. In dealing with this sensed breakdown of connections, I shall try to follow the concerns of the people living then. Obviously, there seemed to be a vague but pervasive sense that *all* ties were coming undone, all attachments coming apart. Nevertheless, there was a special sense that Man's connection to the Godhead was being loosened under the impact of Enlightened and scientific thought. That the close relation to Nature was being threatened by the growth of mechanical civilization. And that the loyalties of Man to Man were shriveling in a cold cash-nexus society.

It is this last aspect of the connections problem, that of Man to Man, on which I will focus, though that focus must itself be seen against the background of the God and Nature questions. In dealing with this aspect, I will be talking about a range of polarities, which is the way both humanists and social scientists have dealt with the matter: polarities such as traditional and modern, primitive and civ-ilized, folk and urban, sacred and profane, mechanical and organic (or vice versa, as we shall see, in Durkheim's formulation), natural and unnatural, feeling and reason, and, closest to the terms I will be using, social and unsocial, society and individual, cooperation and competition, and altruism and self-interest.[1]

Sometimes the things we take for granted, like breathing, are what we notice least. I am arguing that an omnipresent concern with the breakdown of connections and the polarities listed above man-ifested itself in late-eighteenth- and early-nineteenth-century West-ern culture; yet, to my knowledge, no one has stood back from the connections phenomenon and sought to see it whole; nor to analyze the way one metaphor, the cash nexus, came to dramatize and polarize the subject (see Appendix). Nor to see how the "science" of sociology emerged from this disquietude over connections.

I shall also argue that, paradoxically, while many Continental thinkers, and especially sociologists, worried about what they saw as the disappearance of traditional society, or community, in England at the time of the industrial revolution, much of the problem was, in fact, the incompleteness of industrialization. Industrial capitalism, so to speak, had not yet done its job. Marx and Engels, for example, extolled capitalism's achievement—more was accomplished in a hundred years than was accomplished in the previous centuries—its abolition of all the old ties and structures, and especially its destruction of the idiocy of rural life (which Engels had first pictured, as we shall see, in his book, *Condition of the Working Class in England*); in fact, outside of perhaps England, they were citing hopes rather than describing realities. To put it summarily: the calamity that a number of sociologists claimed to have dealt with never really happened, at least in the terms they employed to analyze it.

The World of Cash Nexus

The themes I have mentioned, including the theme of connections, are not unique to the modern period. Indeed, most of them can be described as eternal questions about Man, everywhere and anytime. They can be found in all known cultures. In Western culture, they are clearly evident, for example, in Christianity. What else but the matter of our unsocial social being is Christ talking about when he exhorts us to love our neighbors as ourselves? We are also told to ignore the existing ties of family, friendship and community—as Christ enjoins us, "abandon thy father and thy mother and follow me"—in order to treat our fellow human beings equally and universally.

My task is not to give a history of these themes but to see how they take on a special quality and intensity in the modern period, which for my purposes I am defining as the last two centuries. Such intensity does not emerge all at once but is a slow gathering process. In the case of Europe, we see it first manifesting itself clearly from about the sixteenth century on. It is much affected by what has now come to be called the "scientific revolution," circling initially about Copernicus. It reorients inner space as seen in the writings of Montaigne, where individualism may be said first to declare itself fully. Some of its emergent features are also associated with, for example, the English Civil War, and even before that with the Protestant Reformation. In the realm of theory, there is the rise of classical economics. Taken together, such factors helped to provide a favoring climate for the growth of a market economy, and a society modeled on it. Its special expression can first be found in England, although it rapidly manifested itself in the rest of Western Europe, and then other areas as well. By the early and mid-nineteenth century the overall result was a changed world.

It was a world in which, as Karl Marx said, "All that is solid melts into air."[2] It was a world of modernism, in which the useful fictions of inherited authority—the veils and illusions—were flung aside in order to see—what? The scene disclosed, to the heightened imagination of many at the time, seemed to be one composed, so to speak, only of fragmentation and disconnection. It was a world of shifting forms, symbolized by money, or better still, by the only remaining connection, the *cash nexus*. First coined by Thomas Carlyle, this phrase was given extended currency by Karl Marx, who used it to indict bourgeois society for allegedly dissolving all other ties, loyalties, and attachments, thus leaving men isolated from one another and linked only by the payment of money.

Before, there had been *community*, which offered true and virtuous connection; or so the ideologists of the old or the opponents of the new would have it. Community itself was ill-defined, or defined in vastly varying ways, with nostalgia casting a glow over it that made analysis repugnant. Community, then, might mean family, or kinship group, or religious body, or political institution, with the possible conflicts between these attachments glossed over. Whatever else, however, it did mean bonds—connections—that were not merely those of money.

The alternative—a world tied together principally by money, or the cash nexus—was a world in which "value" was redefined, above all by the economists; and values, whether of commodities (as in exchange value), or of social position, were constantly changing. In a market-oriented society, status was being replaced by income as a measure of a man's worth, and class was displacing rank or estate as a means of social stratification. Settled connections were being broken, both materially and mentally. In the seventeenth century a prescient observer saw what was happening, when he declared that "Instead of Community therefore we now have commerce, which *Commercium* is nothing else but *Communio mercium*. . . . Money is an invention onely for the more expedite permutation of things. . . ."⁴ By the nineteenth century this observation had become a widespread conviction.

In the new world of the market, it was clear that Man was the creator of value. He made the commodities, and then he gave them their price, or value, in terms of the laws of exchange, that is, supply and demand. A cognitive view, such as this, quickly spilled over into the normative as well: values are not given eternally and from God, but are changing and shifting, as befits their creation by human beings.

Further, if values are Man-made, as, for example, economics teaches, then may not the society in which they function and whose institutions they animate also be seen as created, or even "manufactured," by Man? And, if this is so, cannot the actions of individuals, which taken together make up the community, that is, social relations, be both consciously described and ordered? It is at this point, as we shall see, that sociology arises to take its place next to economics.

A New Science

Once upon a time, the world existed without sociology. It is clearly a very young science. What difference does it make that we now have something we call sociology? Why does modern Man feel he needs it? If it is useful now, how did the world get along without it earlier—what social institutions performed sociology's role before it came into being? Or is it that modern circumstances are so different from anything that preceded them that the need for sociology simply didn't exist, that the modern world is so novel that it requires a new science to understand itself?

Certainly both the breakers and lamenters whom we shall be studying believed that unprecedented changes were occurring in their time. Such a belief could lead to the conclusion that something called sociology had not been needed for earlier times, but might be for the new world of modernism. In fact, many of the lamenters, as we shall see, resisted this conclusion, being generally hostile to something called "science," which they saw as more the problem than the solution; yet, as I shall argue, it is their work that played an essential role in the emergence of a science of society.

Society, itself, the core concept of sociology, was a relatively new notion.[5] It marked an awareness of the individual as intrinsically separate from the group—an awareness and self-consciousness that has come to be identified with the term "individualism." Conceptually, the sociologists tried to construct the idea of society in an almost Crusoe-like way, reintegrating the individual into a group for whose "making" he is also responsible, thus taking society not just as a "given" but as a human creation.

One aim for many sociologists has been to achieve a "positive" science, whose model is the natural sciences. Here, knowledge would be objective, verifiable, and certain. That effort, while perhaps laudable as to intention, has not been feasible in execution. More fundamentally, there are good grounds for believing that it is conceptually ill-conceived (and no longer even in accord with advanced thinking in the natural sciences). Is a human science, by nature, different from a natural one? This basic question animates all discussions in this area. Thus, in the course of what follows, I shall be touching on questions such as "What is meant by science?," "Why must knowledge for modern Man take on the form of science?," and "What have, in fact, been the results of the effort to create a science of sociology?"

We will not be addressing these questions frontally. Our inquiry will be historical, rather than philosophical per se. We shall be examining the passional roots, as mediated through ideology, that underlay the effort in the last two centuries at creating a science of society. We shall try to note the material circumstances that fostered the sociological approach to knowledge. And we shall seek to understand the historical experience of modern Man that led him in this direction.

The rise of sociology is a major focus of this book, with almost half of it devoted to chapters on the great classical sociologists themselves; in these chapters I shall be emphasizing their specific relation to the connections theme as constituting a fundamental inspiration for their effort at creating sociology. Most of the rest of the book is devoted to the breakers and lamenters who, I argue, opened up the way for the sociologists.

I have proceeded, in general, by focusing on individuals, not only for their own intrinsic worth but because they symbolize specific points I am trying to make, as well as embodying issues I want to discuss. To some of these figures I give a page or two; to others I devote large parts or the whole of a chapter. In no way, by this procedure, am I trying to write a history of sociology as such, or to offer traditional analyses of its subject matter. Instead, I am studying mainly the larger context in which the science of sociology emerged, that is, the shift in human perceptions, the sense of an almost total breakdown of connections in the modern period.

We will pay primary attention to these matters in terms of Western Europe. Here is where the sense of breakdown in connections first powerfully manifested itself. Here it took the form of an almost obsessive concern with the notion of cash nexus. I want to make clear, however, that in writing about a particular time and place, I have in mind a general phenomenon, characterizing all modernizing societies and extending to our own day. While the particulars may vary, as one might expect, the problems and reactions are more or less universal. Still, since the past colors and shapes our perceptions of the present, we will find it worthwhile to return to origins. There, too, we will find ourselves. Ecce Homo!

On Riding a Thesis

Let me state here as forthrightly as possible both what this book is and what it is not; or at least what it wishes to be. It is an extended essay, more of a "think" piece than a scholarly monograph. While I have tried to base my own work solidly on the existing scholarly literature, I have not tried to add to it by a magisterial summary or synthesis of such work.

I am, indeed, so to speak, riding a thesis; and in doing so am leaping over all sorts of briars and dividing walls. To put the matter another way, I am not trying to offer a definitive account of everything that could be said on the subject of connections and self and society. I have tried to immerse myself in the existing literature, primary and secondary, with what can be called an attitude of "free

floating attention." Out of that form of attention, I have then tried
to sense, and make sense of, the themes discovered running through
the materials. My thesis emerged out of this approach; I did not
come with it ready in hand, seeking to confirm or disconfirm it by
the "data."

The data themselves, as I first noted in the Introduction, are
interdisciplinary in nature. The number of books and articles on any
one of my subjects—sympathy, solitude, George Eliot, Max Weber,
the novel, sociology—might exhaust a scholar's life. Art is long, and
life is short. If one is to do interdisciplinary work, one must accept
a special order of limitations, and be resignedly aware that an
important treatment may have been overlooked and that a particular
scholar's favorite topic has been unwittingly ignored or insuffi-
ciently recognized. Such is my justification for not covering every
subject dear to the hearts of other scholars. On the other hand, the
problems of doing interdisciplinary work must never serve as an
excuse for sloppy scholarship or superficial theorizing; and I abjure
such an excuse here.

Because I am pursuing a thesis across disciplinary lines and
national boundaries—a sort of ideal type, to borrow a notion from
Max Weber—I have skimped on the actual historical changes
behind my literary and sociological figures. While I do make a limited effort toward establishing historical context, I recognize that I
have sacrificed details of the difference in background between, for
example, a Burke in the late eighteenth century and a George Eliot
in the mid-nineteenth, and between the latter and an early-twentieth-century Max Weber, where also the national difference enters.

Thus, a reader might ask, for example: why, in my discussion of
Durkheim, have I not placed him in the context of other French
sociologists? Why have I not dealt with Jane Austen as well as
George Eliot? Why have I short-changed the literature of economic
thought, as providing data on changed attitudes to the perceived
breakdown of connections attendant upon the coming of the industrial revolution?[6] And why, as already touched on, have I not paid
more attention to the origins of the cash nexus idea and to the reactions to it occasioned by eighteenth-century commerce, before the
coming of industrialism?

Even more specifically, a reader might ask why I have not spent
time discussing at length the so-called commerce (or "corruption")-
virtue debate, with its Machiavellian and neo-Harringtonian roots,

a central issue in the eighteenth century that is alleged to have set the stage for much of the argument over connection in the century following. Many of these issues have been brilliantly dealt with by J.G.A. Pocock, for example, in his controversial books *The Machiavellian Moment* and *Virtue, Commerce, and History*. For Pocock, Machiavelli is the source of the neoclassical concept of the republic, or what is called civic humanism, which was then developed by James Harrington and his followers—and the connection is rather convoluted—into a claim that republican virtue and the practice of commerce were incompatible.[7]

Why, also, have I not devoted separate attention to the Scottish Enlightenment (although I do deal in passing with Adam Smith) and such figures as Francis Hutcheson, Adam Ferguson, and David Hume? In the mid- to late eighteenth century, they stood, as Duncan Forbes comments about Ferguson's *Essay*, as a signpost at "a fascinating cross-roads in the history of ideas, with one arm pointing in the direction of Machiavelli, the other forward to the theme of 'alienation'—as much a commonplace in twentieth-century literature as corruption and luxury in the eighteenth. . . ." A key question in their work was: are civilization (with its attendant commerce) and corruption necessarily related? Moreover, their writings (and one should add John Millar's *The Origin of the Distinction of Ranks* (1771)) were early and fascinating efforts to establish a "sociology," though their emphasis was on a historical schema tracing the way man moved from hunter, shepherd, farmer and trader to manufacturer, according to laws of increasing division of labor and specialization.[8]

The answers to this series of scholarly questions, I trust, are implicit in what I have already said. It is evident that each of them could give rise to whole separate books: but they would not be the book I am setting out to write. My own interest centers in the acceleration of concern that originated at the time of the Industrial and the French revolutions, when the accumulated discomfort arising from earlier commercial, scientific, and political changes came to flood tide. (Pocock, himself, incidentally, acknowledges that "The great achievement of the Scottish school of sociological historians was the recognition that a commercial organization of society had rendered obsolete much that had been believed about society before it";[9] this is an admission that I am carrying beyond the commercial to the industrial world.) Indeed, I have already claimed that the concerns about self and society that circle about our theme of disconnection are more or less perennial and ecumenical. It is only in the nineteenth and twentieth centuries, however, in the West that it took on the special form of which I treat, and then spread out to the rest of the world.

Stated again in the briefest of terms, my thesis is that, manifesting itself especially around the late eighteenth and early nineteenth century, a traumatically acute sense of the making and breaking of connections came over Western Man and culture. A great tectonic shift seemed to be taking place under the hitherto apparently more settled continents of life and thought. It proclaimed itself in an omnipresent, even compulsive, concern with the snapping of ties, the unchaining of *all* established verities and social arrangements. Before this shift, Men felt more or less linked to God, Man, and the earth around them. They knew their "place." Afterwards, they knew only that the earth had moved, and, with it, everything upon it. To some, this was cause for celebration: new possibilities were opened up, old restraints gone. To others, it meant the falling apart of society and the self: an occasion for lamentation.

For those who lamented, the concern over breakdown was especially manifested in the social sphere and expressed first in the specific shape of what I shall be calling sympathy or sensibility. This form of expression, as it increasingly revealed itself to be inadequate and "out of sync" with the evolving culture, in turn laid the foundations for the development of a new science, sociology, when men and women came to realize that sympathy was not enough.

Signposts

I shall organize the story that I am telling in the following manner. First, we will be dealing with what I am calling the Break. Here the confluence of disconnections, or supposed disconnections, in the relations of Man to God and the Cosmos, of Man to Nature, and of Man to Man, all appear to come together. What had been dimly or disjointedly seen in the century or two before is now clearly evident. The *breakers*, according to their opponents, have smashed all existing links, leaving the world, both supernatural and natural, all in pieces, all coherence gone. To the eye of the breaker, however, things appear quite differently: what others have seen as connections, he has seen as chains; and in breaking the chains, he has prepared the way for freedom and independence, to be enjoyed by each individual.

What is more, the breakers would argue that they have established new connections, along with the new individualism. Adam Smith, following on Newton, believed that he had discerned original attractions holding together both the physical and the moral universe. Charles Darwin, going even further, struck off the shackles of the chain analogy completely, and put in its place the notion of a web of affinities, an ecological connection. In short, what opponents saw as a massive breakdown in connections, breakers saw as a breakthrough to modern society and its new, but no less valid, conceptions of cosmic and social life.

My treatment of the breakers will be short and suggestive, more to indicate what was happening than to describe it fully. I then turn to what I call the Lament. The *lamenters* are united in believing that an almost irreparable breakdown in connections has occurred; and that they don't like what they see. The lamenters are philosophers and poets, prophets and novelists. Though I treat them under a general term, they do differ in particulars: some mainly deplore the loss of an old, rural community, often idealized; others the coming of a new factory system. Some wish for a return to an earlier time; others accept the inevitability of industrialization, but wish to ameliorate what they consider its most vicious feature, the cash nexus.

By and large, I would argue, the lamenters came to dominate the cultural response to the changes of modernism, even though the breakers were more in tune with the actual transformations taking place.[10] Lamenters, such as Burke, Rousseau, Wordsworth, and Carlyle, operated in terms of a long tradition—eclogues lamenting rural displacements, and so on—and felt, in the main, estranged from the modern world. Their chosen weapon in the struggle was literary lamentation, not science. And their basic appeal was to sympathy, which they proffered as the new bond between people otherwise estranged by the cash nexus. Their most general hope was that the exercise of sensibility would solve, or remove, the problem of the breakdown of connections.

Was the breakdown in connections as sweeping and negative as the lamenters saw it? I attempt to explore the "fictions and facts" of the subject in concrete historical terms in Chapter 5, investigating recent work on whether it was actually the cash-nexus relationship or paternalism which was most prevalent in nineteenth-century England. My own conclusion, to anticipate, is that the cash nexus was the uncommon, not the common, tie.

In any case, by the second half of the nineteenth century, the effort to deal with the omnipresent sense of disconnection, whatever the reality, increasingly took the form, as I have already suggested, of an attempt at a new science, sociology. I will argue that the transition from sensibility to science is best understood first in terms of the work of Engels and Marx, whom I treat as revolutionary *sociologists*. They employed the methods of literary lamentation and sympathy as devices to establish a sociology that is both scientific (or so they would have claimed) and revolutionary. Their primary declared enemy was the cash-nexus society.

Following on Engels and Marx (and my ordering of them in this fashion is deliberate), we will see how the concern with community, caused by the threatened breakdown of connections, functions as the core element in the construction of the new "science," sociology. Literary lamentation is transformed into (presumed) scientific analysis. This is a transformation that has been little explored, but is fundamental;[11] I devote the rest of the book to exploring how this occurs in the work of Ferdinand Tönnies, Georg Simmel, Emile Durkheim, and Max Weber.

A Novel Genre

Inasmuch as the words sympathy and science occur frequently in what follows I should say something more about them here at the beginning. Before doing that, however, it is necessary to look at the characteristic form in which the appeal to sympathy was expressed. A brief excursus into the nature of literary genres, from our perspective, is thus in order.

For the evocation of sympathy, the novel became the chosen genre, although poetry and philosophy were also possible forms of expression.[12] Here was a genre perfectly suited to the emerging individualism and its carriers, the bourgeoisie (and I use the term in its most general meaning).

First of all, "novels" meant what the word said: they were "new." The sense of newness that took its rise in the Renaissance—when the old was given new birth—and then took on independence with the discovery of a "New World," stood at the birth of this novel genre. It corresponded with the victorious battle of the moderns against the ancients, with the novel becoming the true "book" of the former, displacing religious and classical texts alike (though not supplanting their primacy). By the mid-eighteenth century, the novel helped quench the thirst for commercial and other kinds of "news" of the ever-appropriating middle class, and symbolized their ambition unceasingly to expand into new domains, economic and social.

Novels also fulfilled the desires of new men and women to explore their interior emotions and changing life experiences in a fresh way. Novels primarily were to be read in private, alone. They were a splendid vehicle for exposing inner thoughts. Their central concern was characteristically the formation of the individual, the forging of his or her identity. The focus was thus on youth—many of the novels are *Bildungsroman*—and on moral and social choice.

The epistemological basis of these novels was individual experience. In this school of personal realism, the hero or heroine learns about him/herself. Part of such learning is also learning about others, for it is in relation to others that one best comes to know oneself. From its beginnings, the English novel especially was preoccupied with the structure of society; and even Defoe's *Robinson Crusoe* fits into this mold. *Par excellence*, the novel is the genre in which individual desire comes into conflict with the idea of an ordered and regulated society. In this contested knowing, of self and society, the notion of sympathy, as we shall see, becomes central.

Sympathy

Generally, sympathy is seen as being part of our Romantic heritage. It is the Romantic tradition, as David Marshall puts it, "that expects finely tuned sensibilities to enable one to imagine the feelings of another person."[13] But, as he also shows so well, behind the Romantic tradition lay the philosophies of sympathy of thinkers such as Shaftesbury and Adam Smith. Smith, in fact, had written his *Theory of Moral Sentiments* (1759) before his *Wealth of Nations* (1776), emphasizing the fundamental nature of what he called the "impartial spectator," and stressing the need for sympathy as the basis of morality.

There is quite a debate as to whether, when Smith came to write

Wealth of Nations, he put to one side the motive of sympathy and instead stressed that of self-interest; and I must pause over it a moment before making my own point. The debate is often referred to as the "Adam Smith problem," with a number of earlier German scholars claiming a dichotomy between the two books. More recent scholarship has been at pains to emphasize the unity. Thus, the editors of the excellent Glasgow edition of Smith's *Works and Correspondence* declare, in their most extreme statement, that "TMS and WN are at one"; and, as they point out, Smith himself thought there was no conflict, with WN being a fulfilment of TMS.[14] The matter is more complicated than this, however, for as one scholar points out, there are really two TMS: Smith rewrote for an edition in 1790, so that about one-third of his book was newly written, allowing him to change position and emphasis on a number of key issues.[15]

While I agree with the continuity interpretation of Smith—he certainly assumed his TMS moral philosophy as underlying his book on WN—I do not think it should cause us to overlook the very real differences between the two works; and thus the changing and developing nature of Smith's thinking from 1759 to 1776 (and again to 1790). As the authors of the Glasgow edition themselves acknowledge, "Sympathy is the core of Smith's explanation of moral *judgement*. The motive to action is an entirely different matter."[16] I would emphasize that in dealing with economic action, Smith, while recognizing a variety of motives, obviously stressed self-interest (which is different from selfishness).

Thus, while in both books, TMS and WN, and especially the latter, Smith speaks of the "invisible hand," in TMS he has in mind the rich being deceived by nature into wanting "conveniences," amassing them solely to gratify "their own vain and insatiable desires," and thus led by the invisible hand to provide a version of "trickle-down" to the masses. What a contrast, however, with WN, where, though similar images and phrases are used, Smith intends them for a very different service. In TMS, Smith is talking of landlords and an economy of luxury (he is undoubtedly influenced here by Mandeville); in WN, he is concerned with the division of labor, increased production, and the laws of supply and demand, by which is meant the precise scientific, economic form of connection covered by the metaphysical phrase "invisible hand." Without belaboring this argument, important and fascinating as it is, we can conclude that Smith's ideas, while closely related to one another, did evolve in the seventeen years between the publication of TMS and WN, with the latter taking on a distinct life of its own.

In any event, whatever Smith's assumptions about the relations of his moral and economic philosophies, his assumptions were missed, or dismissed, by most of his subsequent readers. Indeed, as one author has perceptively remarked, "Many students of Smith have found an exclusively economic argument for capitalism in the *Wealth of Nations*, in fact one of the most powerful cases for releasing economics from the traditional constraints of moral philosophy."[17] In any case, Smith's two books, divided as they are, have come strikingly to illustrate the bifurcation in attitudes that dominated Western bourgeois culture in the nineteenth century, and left Western man a "double Man." Smith was unable, in theory or in practice, to fuse convincingly the unsocial and social parts of Man, except through the invocation of an unpersuasive "invisible hand."

The poets and novelists who followed him, especially in England, attempted to achieve the fusion of sympathy with self-interest in a literary fashion. For example, Mary Shelley gave prototypical expression to the problem in *Frankenstein* (1817). Frankenstein's monstrous creature, otherwise nameless, promises that if a female companion is created for him, "My evil passions will have fled, for I shall meet with sympathy," and poignantly declares, "If I have no ties and no affections, hatred and vice must be my portion. . . . My vices are the children of a forced solitude that I abhor; and my virtues will necessarily arise when I live in communion with an equal. I shall feel the affection of a sensitive being, and become linked to the chain of existence and events, from which I am now excluded."[18] Here, in Mary Shelley's generally inelegant prose, we hear sounded many of the themes that obsessed her contemporaries.

In the works of other novelists who follow her, the theme of sympathy is given more conscious and formal expression, as we shall see in the case of Gaskell, Disraeli, and George Eliot. Without yet going into details, we can note here that their solution for the divided nature of both industrial society and nineteenth-century Man was not a reconstruction of society but a reconstitution of existing relations through the bond of sympathy. Their message was that if we can be awakened to a broader sensibility, a wider sympathy, by literary means, we can reach across to our fellow humans and establish attachments that go beyond merely that of the cash nexus.

Thus, Charlotte Brontë, in *Shirley* (1849), has her heroine rec-

ommend the reading of Shakespeare. The respondent inquires
whether it is, "With a view to making me better; is it to operate like
a sermon?" To which the heroine replies, ". . . it is to stir you; to
give you new sensations . . . read and discover by the feelings the
reading will give you at once how low and how high you are."[19]
Low and high are intended to indicate aspects of both our personal
and social nature, which sensibility permits us to perceive and
bridge within ourself and with others.

Brontë speaks of a "sermon"; her novel preaches a gospel of
sympathy. Elizabeth Gaskell spoke of a conversion experience, as
she envisioned the power of sympathy in her novels. Both authors
had religious backgrounds—Brontë's father and Gaskell's husband
were ministers—and they are clearly substituting the novel for the
sermon, and transmuting the Christian idea of love into the bourgeois notion of sympathy. Their work can be seen, therefore, as one
more link in the movement from religion to science.

Women

What must also be noticed is how many of the nineteenth-century
novelists were women. I have already mentioned Mary Shelley,
Charlotte Brontë, Elizabeth Gaskell, and George Eliot. One could
readily add the other Brontë sisters and Jane Austen, and innumerable others of lesser rank. One might also point out that among the
great early male novelists, Samuel Richardson wrote of women,
Clarissa and Pamela, and Daniel Defoe of Moll Flanders. The novel,
especially the English novel, gave women a prominence which they
generally lacked elsewhere.

Even in this domain, however, men ruled (not unexpectedly).
Many of our women novelists wrote under male pseudonyms; for
example, Charlotte Brontë published as Currer Bell, and George
Eliot was the pen name of Mary Anne Evans. In writing of connections, I have largely followed the male-dominated arguments of the
nineteenth-century Western culture. Hence, the reader is advised to
bear in mind throughout that another perspective can be brought to
bear on the materials.[20]

The women novelists were keenly aware of their problem, anticipating so much of what is obvious and even banal today. Brontë,
for example, felt acutely how devoid men were of sympathy for

women. As she remarks of one of her upright male characters, "He made no pretense of comprehending women." At another place, the heroine says to her kind but insensitive uncle, "'uncle, I wish you were less generous, and more—.' 'More what,' he asks. Sympathizing was the word on Caroline's lips," Brontë writes, "but it was not uttered. . . ."[21] In *Daniel Deronda*, Eliot has one of her characters declare, "No . . . You are not a woman. You may try—but you can never imagine what it is to have a man's force of genius in you and yet to suffer the slavery of being a girl."[22]

As we pursue our connections theme, we might remember, for example, that the family and its traditional ties extolled by the lamenters has as one of its consequences the subjection of women.[23] The maintenance of community in the form of the traditional family entails the maintenance of the household by the woman. A breaking of this connection may, from the woman's point of view, possibly be a form of individual liberation.

Indeed, much of the concern in the early novels of the eighteenth and nineteenth centuries is about marriage and family. For the first time, the possibility of their being freely and romantically chosen by the woman is publicly and widely mooted. Of course, most marriages were still arranged by the family, or through a marriage broker. Increasingly, however, individual choice, as in the tumultuous indecisions of *Clarissa*, comes into play. It is with sympathy that many of the novelists ask us to consider the issue. Richardson, for example, makes us think about the propriety and morality of his heroine's disobeying her family and breaking her ties and loyalties to it.

The arranged marriages are largely economic in intent, and, increasingly in the period under consideration, capitalistic in nature. And here in the heart and haven of capitalism, we are faced with a paradox. The chosen instrument of capitalist economics is, as we shall see further, the contract. The marriage contract is merely an intimate form of such a legal document. Yet, capitalism pushes toward individualism, and personal choice. Its bourgeois exponents thus face the dilemma of having to choose between the impersonal tie of money—the cash nexus, in short—which dominates the market, and the personal tie of affection, which may be an individual choice. Thus, the institution of marriage mirrors in itself the larger problem of connections that is so omnipresent in the period.

The cry of sympathy wrung from the women novelists for their

own plight is extended to the relation between classes of the industrial society. In *Shirley*, Brontë's charge against the male protagonist,
a mill owner, is that he "does not sympathize with his famished
fellow men."[24] In the novels of Gaskell and Eliot, which we will treat
at length later, numerous similar examples can be found. While men
are hardly immune to the feeling—Wordsworth, Carlyle, Disraeli,
and others, as we shall see, also call out vehemently for increased
sympathy—women seemed peculiarly sensitive to the issue, extrap-
olating from their own situation to that of the workers. Thus they
played a key pioneering role in the advocacy of sympathy as the
healing balm for the break in connections brought about by industrial society.

It was, of course, in the interest of the existing order to block and
to numb the feelings of sympathy. The division of classes, the very
geographical separation of the classes in cities such as Manchester,
were intended, consciously or unconsciously, to effect this isolation
of feeling. We can appeal again to Brontë's *Shirley* for an illustration,
when she has her heroine in a moment of unusual awareness say,
"People hate to be reminded of ills they are unable or unwilling to
remedy: such reminder, in forcing on them a sense of their own
incapacity, or a more painful sense of an obligation to make some
unpleasant effort, troubles their ease and shakes their self-
complacency."[25]

Without sympathy, the way is open to dehumanization of others.
At the end of that road can lie torture and extermination. As one
writer comments, "Torture cannot be surgically limited only to what
is necessary for some discrete goal, because once the taboo is vio-
lated the basis of all other constraints of civilization, which is sympathy for suffering, is destroyed."[26]

In fact, this is an extreme statement. Civilization is built on
blocking and numbing. We could not go on living if we were constantly aware of all the suffering, animal and human, around us. The
question is one of degree. One can sympathize, I believe, with the
bourgeoisie and their attempt to block feelings of sympathy that
would have ruled out much of the industrial development in which
they were engaged. (Of course, one can take the position that mankind would have been better off without such a development; I must
simply state my disagreement with such a sweeping opinion.) From
one point of view, the wonder is that the bourgeoisie were so vulnerable to the sympathetic cries of wives, ministers, and their own

ideology of humanitarianism. From another point of view, of course, one can wish that they had been even more open to the ties of sympathy.

A Science of Society

The problem with sympathy is that it was slow and unsure. Good intentions could go only so far. What increasingly seemed needed was knowledge, on which to act effectively. I have already suggested that Adam Smith bifurcated the problem when he left unconnected his treatment of sympathy in the *Theory of Moral Sentiments* and self-interest in the *Wealth of Nations*. One of his great successors, Alfred Marshall, claimed a resolution in his *Principles of Economics*, where he remarks that "economic studies call for and develop the faculty of sympathy, and especially that rare sympathy which enables people to put themselves in the place, not only of their comrades, but also of other classes."[27] In saying this, Marshall was promising more than his science of economics actually produced. It was the newly emerging field of sociology that tried to give concrete scientific form to the problem of sympathy or, more generally, to the problem of connections.

We will be exploring that effort in detail in the following chapters on sociologists. Here it is appropriate to introduce only a few general remarks on the subject of science as such. There is little question that science in the eighteenth and nineteenth centuries most frequently tended at first to be equated with the method and methodology of physics (although sometimes the equation was made with chemistry or biology); and both economics and sociology aspired, in many of their modes, to be like physics. Much of this aspiration took shape in the positivism of Auguste Comte, who first effectively coined the term "sociology." (In fact, Comte was much more subtle than many who followed in his name; he realized, for example, that the social sciences needed other methods than the mathematical, such as the comparative, to advance.)[28] Marxism, too, claimed to be a science, with laws equal in power to the physical (though, in addition, Marx also invoked the name of Darwin).

Another attempt at a science of society took the form of "natural history," as applied to Man. As we shall see, the biological model, in various forms, came to rival the physical. It is worth pausing here to notice a few of the considerations immediately relevant to this assertion. One comes from the field of physiology, which stands on the edge of both physics and biology. In the eighteenth century, there was a general concern with the question of how sympathy works—what are the nervous paths over which it flows? The answer was given by the great physiologist, von Haller, who in the mid-1750s argued that "sensibility," or "irritability," was the explanation for all human actions, voluntary and involuntary. Nerves, so to speak, were fate. The person of greater "sensibility," generally from the upper class, was also the person most gifted with "sympathy." Thus, sympathy was a mark of refinement—and of rank; it is worth noting that Adam Smith read Haller.[29]

When Auguste Comte came to found his sociology, however, in addition to enrolling Smith in his calender of saints, he relied on the work of early-nineteenth-century embryologists and physiologists, such as Bichat and Cabanis, and was especially aware of the emerging science of biology, which was being shaped by Lamarck and a few others (see Chapter 2). Thus, pre-Darwinian as he was, Comte nevertheless assumed the existence of an evolutionary biological science as a necessary precondition for the development of his new science of sociology. He, too, though in a different mode from Haller, perceived that feelings of community were rooted in the nervous system, from which arose impulses of sympathy. What distinguishes Comte's analysis from Haller's, however, was his recognition that while sympathy might be a component of social order, it was no substitute for a real science of society.[30]

As a result, after Comte, sociology, along with economics, stumbled forward, trying to establish itself in an independent way, though connected to biology (with Herbert Spencer being a key figure in this last regard). To complicate matters, a philosophical debate was concurrently taking place. Thus, in the late nineteenth century a contest was also being waged between those who saw no difference between the physical and human sciences, except of degree, and those who made a sharp division between what they called *Naturwissenschaften* and *Geisteswissenschaften*, that is, natural and moral sciences.

I do not propose to follow up these controversies. More germane to our purposes is the awareness that in the eighteenth century a number of thinkers had postulated that seemingly random and fractious qualities of the individual could be understood within the regularity and lawfulness of social action. Immanuel Kant did this in regard to history, where he instanced the regularity of marriage and population statistics in the face of individual choices. And Adam Smith, of course, did this in terms of his self-interested individuals conforming, without intending to do so, to a lawlike principle, that of optimum employment of resources. This way of thinking, as Reinhold Bendix points out, helped "to usher in a new view of the social world as an impersonal structure possessing attributes or principles of its own."[31]

Such a perception was a blinding one. It could lead to all sorts of excesses and misperceptions. One can see this in the most advanced of the eighteenth-century social sciences, economics, whose followers, envisioning a whole new world, blinded themselves to the fact that their theory was positing a one-dimensional, solipsistic "Man" with no social bonds: Man as mere commodity. It frequently led them, also, to ignore the fact that individuals did not always pursue their self-interest, and even when they did, did not do so in a perfect market with perfect information.[32] In short (although to give him credit, Smith was often aware of this feature), such perceptions too frequently ignored the test of reality. Understandable as was the exaltation, it made, finally, for flawed science.

Attention to the empirical arose in non-scientific guise from the poets and the prophets, who saw what was in front of them and not just in theory. It was mainly those such as Rousseau in France, Schiller in Germany, and Wordsworth and Carlyle in England who perceived that the gathering wealth of the nation did not always mean the improved condition of the average human being. They saw the reality of suffering, and sought to call forth the powers of sympathy to mitigate the problem. They perceived certain forms of breakdown in society, and brought the need for reconnections to the attention of those who were searching for law-like descriptions and formulations.

The sociologists who followed upon these literary seers drew heavily upon this tradition, even when not acknowledging it, or even when denigrating it. They, too, wrestled with the problem of connections, in all its various forms, only they tried to do so by offering science rather than sympathy as the solution. In considering Ferdinand Tönnies, Georg Simmel, Emile Durkheim, and Max Weber as our representational sociologists, we shall want to ask in the end whether, seeking science, they emerge only with myth, that is, a new form of literary rather than scientific expression. Or, is it that a science of society must necessarily resemble myth and metaphor more than it does equations and general laws?[33]

In saying this, I do not embrace the view expressed to me by my friend, the British sociologist John Hall, who in rather pixy fashion contends that sociology, or at least British sociology, is mainly a "literary" affair. I prefer David Beetham's view that "Sociology is not simply the modern intellectual's substitute for the novel as a means of self-expression."[34] While many of its roots are in the novel, as I have been arguing, sociology still aspires, and should, to be a new form of science.

The Chain and the Web

In reviewing the concerns already mentioned, through the eyes of our breakers, lamenters, and sociologists, it is important to highlight an overall shift in conception against which the controversy and analysis was played out. In different eras, different images attain a special ascendance. In the roughly eighty-five-year period from the late eighteenth to the mid-nineteenth century in parts of Europe and the Americas, the metaphor of a "web of interconnections" gradually replaced "the chain of being" as the image which summed up the way human beings thought of themselves in relation to God, Nature, and their fellow Men.

The earlier image—often specified as the Great Chain of Being—was the shorthand summary of a vision of a hierarchical world in which each species and each individual was related to all the rest as either "above" or "below."[35] This vision justified and explained the human world from the microcosm of parent-child, male-female, and master-servant relationships, to the macrocosm in which God had set humankind a little below the angels, and had given him dominion over all the animals. By analogy and resemblance, everything could have its place defined; thus, the relationship of a monarch to his/her subjects acquired awe from the analogy to God as ruler of the universe, and immediacy from the resemblance to a father as ruler of a household.

The slow but ever-moving shift from the hierarchical dominant image of a chain of being to the new image of a web of interconnections was mainly invisible, but it was so radical and pervasive a change that we look for large visible happenings to explain it. We have observed that the shift began with the rise of capitalism and the onset of the Industrial Revolution, and it took place over the span of time that included both the French and American revolutions. Adam Smith's *Wealth of Nations* in 1776 had provided a theoretical understanding of the new form of economic relationships. With Linnaeus, classification of the "economy of nature" extended across domains and undermined the simple linkages suggested by chains. In 1801-2 the term "biology" began to be used, to name a new way of studying life, defined as beings in a process of change. Darwin's *Origin of Species*, (1859) extended the sense of flux from the individual to the species—indeed, to the whole system of species to be found coexisting, mutually influencing one another's habitat and development. Politics and philosophy, science and technology, contributed to and were influenced by the passing of one era and initiation of another.

What was the character of the new era—the meaning of the image which replaced the Great Chain of Being? While that older idea defined all relationships, real and potential, in terms of "lower" and "higher," the new one had more to do with *process* than with *position.* It is, in effect, no longer a picture, at an instant in time, of the ladder on whose rungs every individual is positioned; it is, rather, a conceptualization of the infinite, dynamic interrelationships by which each being affects, and is affected by, all others.

Obviously, it was Charles Darwin who more than any other person gave a form and a substance to this idea (though George Eliot promoted it just as powerfully, as I will try to show). One might say that during the more than three-quarters of a century between the birth of Smith's political economy and that of Darwin's evolutionary biology there was a kind of hiatus, wherein the old image of how Mankind had fitted into the world had ceased to ring true, but no new one had appeared to take its place. Darwinism, and its often ill-applied caricature, Social Darwinism, may have come as a shock to old notions of a permanent, God-made order—already once shocked by Copernicus's revelation that the Earth was *not* the center about which the celestial sphere revolved; but it was nevertheless rapidly absorbed into the patterns of throught of a culture that had increasingly felt the lack of an explanatory image.

The "web of interconnections" is the image which persists through today (frequently expressed in terms of environmental

awareness and feedback mechanisms) as the dominant conceptualization to embrace the social and the natural sciences; to explain
how individual human beings fit into the interlocked worlds of society and nature. Just as the Great Chain of Being was, in its time, the
organizing principle behind all fields of thought, but was claimed as
the particular property of religious and philosophical theory, so,
today, the Web of Interconnections is widely accepted and assumed
in all fields, but most consciously expressed in terms of ecological
theory. Its origins, however, are to be found in the debate over connections, and their breakdown, in the nineteenth century.

Threads

My perception of the shift from the Great Chain of Being to the Web
of Interconnections emerged naturally and as no surprise from the
materials I set out to examine. I was not, however, especially expecting to stumble across two other assertions I have found myself making in the course of writing this book. The first started showing up
as a kind of thread weaving itself through the themes on which I
was concentrating. In treating the alleged breakdown of all connections into the single unconscionable one of the cash nexus, I found
myself aware of how often Engels and Marx and many of my novelists equated money with Jews, who are then associated with
strangers and sweatshops, and other alienating and repellent features of a market society. Perhaps this should not have come as a
surprise. But it was the particular link of this ethnic (or religious)
group with the connections problem, in the form of the cash nexus,
that seemed novel.

My next puzzlement was why my sociologists did not perceive
race as a powerful bond in society. The fact is that, in general, they
ignored it in favor of national or economic or religious ties. To a
post-World War II observer, it was clear what they were overlook-
ing. As the reader will see, it took two of the novelists, Benjamin
Disraeli and George Eliot, to recognize the potent force inherent in
racism (or perhaps it should be called racialism or tribalism), and to
deal with it specifically in the example of Judaism. Only with the
last of my sociologists, Max Weber, is the Jewish responsibility for
the cash nexus laid to rest, as he assigns the responsibility for capitalism and the dominance of money relations to the Protestant Ethic.

My other unexpected assertion can be dealt with here even more briefly. It is simply that the historical materials seem to show that it was not capitalism as such, but the insufficiency of capital that fostered the cash-nexus society. In the early years of the Industrial Revolution, it was the masters on the margin, those operating with a precarious investment, who were most likely to squeeze their workers and to treat them as disposable commodities. The larger manufacturers could frequently operate within the paternalistic tradition. It is ironic that often they did so with a bad conscience, for in large part their ideology told them that social relations *ought* to be carried out in terms of the impersonal market arrangement. In any case, the fact, or the myth, of the cash-nexus nature of capitalist industrial society turned out to be more complicated than I had suspected.

Myth and History

It is extremely difficult to distinguish myth from history; for much of history deals with myth, and is itself either a creator of myth or a form of myth-history.[36] Yet the distinction and the task is essential, if apparently Sisyphean. In dealing with connections and the cash nexus, I have tried to be guided by this belief. (So guided, I have also been acutely aware of the way my own values necessarily enter into my perceptions and judgments.)

Historical perspective is a prerequisite for keeping our values and judgments in touch with reality. It is essential in trying to comprehend large and powerful subjects such as the perceived breakdown of connections in the industrializing process. In order fully to answer questions such as those raised here, we should be able to reconstruct, for example, the economic and social world of eighteenth-century England, France, and Germany. What was rural life really like? Did the family actually provide emotional warmth and security, or was it too often a domestic despotism? Was the guild a useful protection against exploitation, or a coercive impediment to increased affluence? Were the church and state sources of ennobling attachment, or mainly constricting bands around individuals? Obviously, the responses will not be clear-cut—"some of each" will be the appropriate answer in most cases—and the weight given to them will depend on whether an individual experienced his or her situation as a connection or a chain. Given the most accurate description we can generate, we must then ask ourselves whether the resulting overall situation is one that we would wish to have brought about. Would we really wish to preserve or restore the "connections" of the past, with all the conditions that went with them before the coming of the Industrial Revolution? If the answer is no, as is mine, then historical imagination must take us back to the late eighteenth century and allow us to comprehend why a breaking of connections, in part achieved by the mallet blows of democratic aspiration, free enterprise, technological-industrial innovation, and scientific discovery seemed a good thing to many. Whether it went too far, of course, is another question immediately to be raised.

If, however, one's present-day life is colored by a prelapsarian myth, including the belief that there was once a just and organic society in which Men enjoyed comfortable lives, were happy with their work, satisfied with their economic sufficiency, and morally and physically uncorrupted by commerce and cities, then one will probably measure the coming of the Industrial Revolution by another standard. In my view, this would be to abandon both an historical and an evolutionary perspective in favor of a utopian aspiration, however consoling—and possibly inspiring—the latter may be.[37]

Once we recognize the human tendency to mythologize the past, and to see that past as somehow better, more natural, more human than the present, we can be on our historical guard. If we recognize that terrible and exploitive conditions existed in the early Industrial Revolution (whether they were the prevalent condition is another matter), we must also recognize that the poor in pre-industrial times composed the largest part of the population and lived in very severe deprivation. Even in good times, the poor man's diet absorbed 60 to 80 percent of his income. That income was low to begin with, and the purchase of a garment, for example, was a luxury generally out of reach. Poor housing and clothing, low life expectancy, high infant mortality, frequent sickness, and few comforts: these were some of the constant attendants of such a life.[38]

In sum, we must always try to make our judgments in terms of a broad historical perception. Such a perception must recognize the power of myths as they operate in people's lives, but not succumb to that power. By being conscious of our situation, as well as those of the subjects whom we study, we have a better chance of both comprehending adequately and dealing more realistically with the problems confronting us, now as in the past.

"A New Science: The Breakdown of Connections and the Birth of Sociology" necessarily touches on the most fundamental problems of the nature of humanity, the nature of society, and the nature of historical development; and thus arouses our deepest passions. Like the literary figures and sociologists we deal with here, we must take as our task the combining of passion with knowledge, in order to arrive at a better understanding of ourselves and of our societies. That is a major aim of this work.

2
The Break

The Cash Nexus

In 1839, in a chapter called "Laissez-Faire" of the book, *Chartism*, Thomas Carlyle introduced the notion that "Cash Payment has become the sole nexus of man to man!"[1] He was sufficiently taken with the phrase so as to repeat it in the next chapter ("Not Laissez-Faire"). By 1843, in *Past and Present*, Carlyle pleasedly quoted himself— "'Cash-Payment for the sole nexus'"—and then rings various changes on the phrasing in at least six other places in the book.[2]

The idea is then picked up by the young Friedrich Engels, in his 1844 review of Carlyle's *Past and Present*. Citing it as the only "work . . . worth reading" of all the "fat books and thin pamphlets" which had appeared that past year in England, Engels quoted a long passage in which the "Cash payment" phrase appears, and added his own observation that a "dissolution of the old ties of society" was occurring in England. Engels approved of Carlyle because "he has absorbed much that is German and is quite far removed from crass empiricism"; lamentably, though acquainted with German literature, Carlyle, according to Engels, "is not acquainted with its necessary corollary, German philosophy, and all his views are in consequence ingenuous, intuitive. . . ."[3]

Despite Carlyle's ingenuousness, and lack of German philosophy and science, Engels quoted his "Cash Payment is the only nexus" statement again in *The Condition of the Working Class in England* (1845). Carlyle had also spoken in *Chartism* of "the great universal under class" as being on one side of the nexus (with cap-

30

italists on the other side), and Engels extended this allusion to what he himself called the proletariat. Before the Industrial Revolution, Engels declared, the bulk of the English population was in a "patriarchal relation," growing up in "idyllic simplicity and intimacy with their playmates." Now, in 1844, hundreds and thousands of all classes and ranks crowd past each other, in "unfeeling isolation . . . each in his private interest." We witness, Engels tells us, "the dissolution of mankind into monads"; society has fallen into "a state of visible dissolution."[4]

By 1848, the "nexus" idea has come into the hands of Engels's collaborator, Karl Marx. He himself seems not to have been as impressed, at first hand, with Carlyle's work, but was quick to follow his friend's lead, and to give immortal form to Carlyle's phrase in "The Communist Manifesto."[5] Few will remember Carlyle's usage; but millions have read the sonorous lines as to how "the bourgeoisie, wherever it has got the upper hand, has put an end to all feudal, patriarchal, idyllic relations. It has pitilessly torn asunder the motley feudal ties that bound man to his natural superiors, and has left remaining no other nexus between man and man than naked self-interest, than callous 'cash payment.'"

These are powerful images; and I have already tried to suggest that there is a tremendous resonance, as well as sonorousness, to Marx's lines. For the particular notion that all ties binding Man to Man have collapsed into one, of cash payment, echoes the larger charge that all connection has ended, or frayed.

In our next chapter, on some of the lamenters, Wordsworth will prove to be important. His *cri de coeur*, "And Connect!," runs like a nervous pulsation through so much of nineteenth-century discourse: literary, political, economical, and so on, with the fields often crisscrossing (for example, Carlyle's cash nexus belongs to both literature and economics). If Wordsworth speaks of "The gravitation and the filial bond/of nature that connect him with the world," the Declaration of Independence speaks of dissolving "The political bands which . . . connected the colonists to Great Britain." In 1831, depicting "The Spirit of the Age," John Stuart Mill put the situation as follows: "It is felt that men are henceforth to be held together by new ties, and separated by new barriers; for the ancient bonds will now no longer unite, nor the ancient boundaries confine," and then he went on to say that some imagine "that because the old ties are severed mankind henceforth are not to be connected by any ties at all.'''[6] The sense of the new was epitomized in the Saint-Simonians's vision of the railroads as "connecting" the nations.

Overall, the pessimists appear, at least at this remove of time, to have been the dominant voices, deploring the breakdown of connections and the resultant cash-nexus society that had arisen. Thus, the trope, cash nexus, points to a fundamental sense of imminent breakdown (and renewal?) in the late eighteenth and early nineteenth century: a sense that bonds between Man and Nature, Man and Man, Man present and Man past have been frayed or broken.

The Great Chain

What was the presumed state of affairs before the fall into the cash society? The general picture given us by scholars is that pre-modern society perceived the world as both cosmologically and socially a chain of being, organically connected, and hierarchical. In this conception, everything is connected to everything, link by link, and everything has its place. In turn, society conceived of itself as a reflection of this model, with Shakespeare's wonderful lines about such a hierarchical structure, in *Troilus and Cressida*, catching its convictions:

> The heavens themselves, the planets, and this centre
> Observe degree, priority, and place . . .
> The primogenitive and due of birth,
> Prerogative of age, crowns, sceptres, laurels,
> But by degree, stand in authentic place?
> Take but degree away, untune that string,
> And, hark, what discord follows![7]

All was ranked, hierarchical connection, whether in court or countryside, guild or urban corporation.

Thus the first aspect to be looked at, briefly, of what I am calling the Break, is the snapping of belief in the Great Chain of Being, and the substitution for it of a Newtonian, for reasons that we shall see, and then, additionally, an evolutionary universe. Oddly enough, according to Arthur Lovejoy, the author of the classic work on the subject, the conception of the universe as a Great Chain of Being attained its "widest diffusion and acceptance" in the eighteenth century, although it had dominated Western thought since antiquity.[8]

Indeed, it had taken its rise in Plato and Aristotle—where the key principles of plentitude, continuity, and gradation were first given form—and then carried forward by Plotinus and the Neo-Platonists into the medieval period, which it permeated, thenceforth persisting into the Age of Enlightenment. Puzzlingly, Lovejoy offers no explanation of why it attained its widest diffusion in the eighteenth century.

In any event, we do see it accepted and drawn upon, in one form or another, by eighteenth-century thinkers as diverse as Addison, Bolingbroke, Bonnet, Buffon, Diderot, Goldsmith, Kant, Pope, Schiller, and Thomson. A bit earlier, for example, toward the end of the seventeenth century, Thomas Sprat, the first historian of the Royal Society, wrote of the need "to follow all the links of this chain"; and, in the middle of the eighteenth century, the *Encyclopedia* announced that "everything in nature is linked together" since "beings are connected with one another by a chain"; the art of the philosopher consists in "adding new links to the separated parts, in order to reduce the distance between them as much as possible."[9]

Probably the most famous expression of the concept is to be found in Pope's *Essay on Man.* Here, having pointed out "the ties,/ The strong connections, nice dependencies,/Gradations just," he expostulates, "Vast chain of being! . . . Where, one step broken, the great scale's destroy'd;/From Nature's chain whatever link you strike,/Tenth, or ten thousandth, breaks the chain alike." Edward Young, in his "Night Thoughts," echoes the commonplace notion, as he asks us to "Look Nature through, 'tis neat gradation all . . . The chain unbroken"; and these conceits are still to be found in the 1850s, elaborated by Victor Hugo, as he hymns the virtues of "L'échelle que tu vois," and asks, "crois-tu qu'elle rompe?"

But break it did; and, as Lovejoy points out, increasingly at the end of the eighteenth century. Implicit in its own principle of plentitude—the assumption of fullness, that is, that all possible things were already in God—was a temporalizing of the Chain of Being and a drift to Romantic evolutionism of the German type, epitomized by Schiller and the Schlegels. The previously immutable Chain, Lovejoy argues, was converted into a Becoming; and, what is more, God himself was now placed in, or identified with, this Becoming.

I shall not be following out the Lovejoy scenario—in the final analysis, he is primarily interested in the origins of Romanticism—

but will take it for granted that the general concept of the Great
Chain is now roughly clear to the reader. My interest is rather in the
way first Newton and then the evolutionary biologists prepared the
breaking of the chain.

In fact, as Voltaire first pointed out, Newton's work ran counter
to the concept of the Great Chain by, for example, demonstrating
the reality of a vacuum, thus undermining belief in the assertion that
"nature makes no leaps" and hence that every link in the chain is
full. So, too, the Newtonian mechanism, where Moon and Earth,
apple and tide, are connected by the laws of attraction, resolves the
Great Chain of Being into gears and levers.

Put as succinctly as possible, Newton's genius, while remaining
within the world of the chain metaphor, was to offer a major alternative conception to it. Thus he prepared the way for others eventually not only to chip away at links but to bring down the whole
edifice of enchained thought.[10]

Adam Smith: Newtonian

The chief point I want to make here, however, is that what is
involved in the Newtonian world-view is a new form of connection,
not a disconnection, though, clearly, it was felt by many at the time
as a complete breaking and breakdown. And I want to make the
point, not with Newton but with Adam Smith, an economist.

The fact is that Smith was not only an economist, the great shaping figure in back of the trope of "cash nexus," but the author as
well of a "History of Astronomy" (ca. 1746–48). He writes on this
topic in order to illustrate "The Principles Which Lead and Direct
Philosophical Enquiries." In this essay, the sentiments that lead us
to such inquiries are wonder, surprise, and admiration; and of these
it is wonder that most arouses his interest and enthusiasm. According to Smith, there is an inherent tendency in the human mind to
connect observed phenomena and to do so, generally, by classifying
them. "It is thus," he observes, "that all things endowed with a
power of self-motion, beasts, fishes, insects, are classed under the
general name of Animal."[11] Wonder arises when we cannot connect
a new phenomenon to our previous collection and classification. We
are unsettled, disturbed by the sentiment of wonder, which Smith
oddly enough describes as "that staring, and sometimes that rolling

of the eyes, that suspension of the breath, and that swelling of the heart, which we may all observe, both in ourselves and others, when wondering at some new object. . . ."

To assuage the sentiment of wonder, we seek to connect. "Philosophy," Smith informs us, "is the science of the connecting principles of nature." It represents "the invisible chains which bind together all these disjointed objects," and seeks to "introduce order into this chaos of jarring and discordant appearances, to allay this tumult of the imagination, and to restore it, when it surveys the great revolutions of the universe, to that tone of tranquility and composure, which is . . . most suitable to its nature." As Smith repeats, spurred by wonder, or curiosity, we seek "to find out those hidden chains of events which bind together the seemingly disjointed appearances of nature."[12]

I want to highlight a few elements here. The first is Smith's use of wonder, for we will find shortly a very different employment of that term by those, such as Wordsworth and Carlyle, whom I will classify as lamenters. The next is Smith's counter-use of "jarring" to, say, Shakespeare's: the great poet sees an enchained world, which must not be jarred; Smith sees a jarring chaos, which must be chained together.

The chaining agent is science, and specifically Newtonian science, which Smith refers to as "a system whose parts are all more strictly connected together, than those of any other philosophical hypothesis."[13] As Smith remarks, "Systems in many respects resemble machines." A system, in fact, "is an imaginary machine invented to connect together in the fancy those different movements and effects which are already in reality performed." In short, the universe is mechanistic, as Newton has shown, and our minds are so formed as to mirror, mechanistically, the actual connections of reality.

The language of Smith is almost compulsively of connection. When he turns his wonder to the world of economics, the compulsion is still with him. I have quoted his "invisible chains," and the reader will remember their rattle as we talked earlier about Smith's "invisible hand" in the *Wealth of Nations*. If we go back to the "History of Astronomy," we ought to note one particular example Smith offers as an additional illustration of wonderment. "When we enter the work-houses of the most common artizans," he informs us, "such as dyers, brewers, distillers; we observe a number of appearances, which present themselves in an order that seems to us very strange and wonderful. Our thought cannot easily follow it, we feel an interval betwixt every two of them, and require some chain of intermediate events, to fill it up, and link them together."[14] I do not think it too fanciful to advance the notion that here we find the seeds of Smith's analysis of the division of labor, which bear fruit in the great, fecund first chapter of the *Wealth of Nations*. Division in this case, paradoxically, is for Smith a consequence of connection.

I should like to suggest that this way of seeing the world, this manner of connecting all phenomena in a scientific chain, can best be described by employing the poetic image of "that other eye." I take the term from what might appear to some an unlikely source: Wordsworth; for he is often viewed as simply hostile to science. But the same Wordsworth who sometimes spoke of Newtonian-inspired science in harsh terms, epitomizing its analytic inclination in the famous lines, "Our meddling intellect/Mis-shapes the beauteous forms of things:—/We murder to dissect," and who preferred "a feeling of the whole," could also write:

> How different with those favoured souls who,
> >   taught
> By active Fancy or by patient Thought,
> See common forms prolong the endless chain
> Of joy and grief, of pleasure and of pain;
> But chiefly those to whom the harmonious doors
> Of Science have unbarred celestial stores,
> To whom a burning energy has given
> That other eye which darts thro' earth and heaven,
> Roams through all space and unconfined,
> Explores the illimitable tracts of mind,
> And piercing the profound of time can see
> Whatever man has been and man can be.[15]

It is "that other eye" that permitted Newton, and Smith and his contemporaries, to see how connected nature truly was and, tracing out its chains, to realize, for example, that heat and energy are connected to one another; indeed, that heat is a form of energy and is converted to it at a fixed rate of exchange. By the early nineteenth century, Sadi Carnot and others such as Rudolf Clausius, Julius Robert Mayer, and Lord Kelvin spelled out this insight in terms of laws of thermodynamics (the conservation laws), showing just how linked such phenomena are. In both society and the universe, the same "exchanges" seemed to reveal themselves to the eye of wonder, in the form of scientific systems.[16]

Evolutionary Theories

Smith's work, following on Newton's, dealt one blow to the Great Chain, though it stayed within its metaphorical grasp. The other blow came in the form of evolutionary theory. By substituting the new concept of "biology" for "being," it snapped the links that had formerly bridged the celestial and human worlds. Jean-Baptiste Lamarck is the key early figure in this development. It is he who, about 1800, was one of the first to coin the term "biology" to refer to that part of terrestrial physics that deals with the "origin and the developments of organization of living bodies."[17]

Lamarck was an odd, somewhat exasperating, and occasionally cranky figure who, when honored by his contemporaries, was honored as a gifted classifier in conchology, that is, shells. He is most famous in our time for his doctrine of acquired characteristics—that traits acquired by an animal during its lifetime (e.g., the stretching of a giraffe's neck as it reaches for higher leaves) is handed down genetically to its offspring. While this particular doctrine is largely discredited today (interestingly enough, it was not original with Lamarck, but a commonplace in his day), Lamarck is credited with pioneering an evolution theory of ascent.[18]

Lamarck came to his theory of evolution in fits and starts, and in a generally muddled fashion. He did not start out as a biologist, but as an ambitious savant of all the sciences: a "naturalist-philosopher" is how he fancied himself. In his practical work, however, he was first mainly a classifier, who connected natural phenomena by a system of shared names and families. In this, he followed Linnaeus, but claimed to do better. As he exclaimed at one point, "No one could deny that the class of worms of Linnaeus was a kind of chaos in which very different things were united."[19]

Lamarck brought order into the "chaos." In the process, he traced out what he perceived to be a graduated scale of complexity in the animal kingdom. What made Lamarck an evolutionist, starting around 1800, was his belief that the graduated scale represented organic change, as well as mere taxonomic arrangement. The more complex was linked to the more simple by genealogy. In short, they had evolved out of the latter over time.

This was Lamarck's great insight. It did not matter that he also believed in spontaneous generation and in acquired characteristics—a theory to which he came because he believed that living things, faced with changed circumstances, make their organization more complex. His genius was to realize that nature's Great Chain was dynamic; and that it moved to greater complexity, a progressive development that he labeled nature's "marche." Presented in sketchy and erratic fashion, at first retracted as often as advanced, Lamarck's theory, nevertheless, offered a new version of connection, what he himself described as "a truly general theory, linked everywhere in its parts . . . and applicable to all the known data."[20]

Starting with a version of the Great Chain of Being, Lamarck gave animation to his classifications, and emerged with a theory of evolution. It offered his contemporaries an alternate way of connecting the data of life. Most of them at the time rejected it, fearful of losing the old lifelines and suspicious—rightly so?—of the destabilizing effect of the new evolutionary conception. It would be another half-century and more before Charles Darwin made the theory itself relatively secure, crediting his predecessor with having performed "the eminent service of arousing attention to the probability of all change in the organic as well as in the inorganic world, being the result of law, and not of miraculous interposition."[21]

Toward the end of his life, Lamarck did one other thing of importance. Bitter and feeling neglected, he gazed out upon a world in which the old ties had ceased to restrain men in their pursuit of personal progress, and he joined the lamenters. An evolutionary Jeremiah, he cried out in 1817:

> By his egoism too short-sighted for his own good, by his tendency to revel in all that is at his disposal, in short, by his lack of concern for the future and for his fellow man, man seems to work for the annihilation of his means of conservation and for the destruction of his own species. In destroying everywhere the large plants that protect the soil in order to secure things to satisfy his greediness of the moment, man rapidly brings about the sterility of the ground on

which he lives, dries up the springs, and chases away the animals that once found their subsistence there. He causes large parts of the globe that were once very fertile and well populated in all respects to become dead, sterile, uninhabitable, and deserted.[22]

It is a note we shall hear sounded again shortly.

For the moment, however, I want to turn to his contemporary across the Channel who shared Lamarck's major insight about evolution, but lived amidst the "egoism" of the expanding capitalism decried in the passage above. Erasmus Darwin, grandfather of Charles, and an ingenious proponent of evolution, was the intimate of Josiah Wedgwood, mass producer of pottery, of James Watt, inventor of the steam engine, of Matthew Boulton, proprietor of the Soho Works where the new power was being given its metallic form, and of the other luminaries of the Lunar Society.[23] Philanthropic as were these gentlemen themselves, they nevertheless comprised part of the first wave of "egoism" that was perceived by some as destroying the old ties and, according to their opponents, leaving only a "cash nexus."

I shall not pursue that facet of Erasmus Darwin here, but concentrate briefly on his role in evolutionary theory. He presented his evolutionary ideas in strange garb: a sort of inspired doggerel, which he called "The Botanic Garden." A doctor, founder of the Lichfield Botany Society, leading figure in the advanced scientific thinking of his time, he was not a systematic or always coherent expositor, yet he managed to propound what some have considered the first well-rounded theory about the development of the living world. It was a matter of inspiration, not sustained empirical work. His contribution is well caught by one scholar's comment that

> ... Erasmus Darwin's grasp of the interconnexion of all things in nature, and his faith in the boundless perspectives of science, were most strikingly expressed when he wrote in explanation of his bold hypotheses: "Extravagant theories . . . in those parts of philosophy, where our knowledge is yet imperfect, are not without their use; as they encourage the execution of laborious experiments, or the investigation of ingenious deductions, to confirm or refute them. And since natural objects are allied to each other by many affinities, every kind of theoretic distribution of them adds to our knowledge by developing some of their analogies.[24]

Through classification, as with Lamarck, or analogies, as with Erasmus Darwin, the Great Chain of Being was first unwound as cosmology, and then new wound as science. Vague and troubling in 1800, evolutionary theory came in the hands of Erasmus Darwin's grandson Charles to be the new cosmological-biological framework of Man's being.

Charles Darwin

I shall not try to encapsulate Charles Darwin's achievement in a few paragraphs here, nor even to hint at the scholarly work on him; I shall attempt, instead, only to touch on the implications of his great work for our theme of connection.

It was during the course of the voyage of the *Beagle* that Darwin glimpsed the new world of evolutionary forms. He saw there "this wonderful relationship . . . between the dead and the living," and intuited an explanation of "that mystery of mysteries—the first appearance of new beings on this earth."[25] We all know the result: a theory of natural selection to serve as a mechanism for evolution and thus to explain how it took place; and the final substitution of genealogies for classifications, with descent originally for animals, "from at most only four or five progenitors" and for plants from an equal number, with both animals and plants "descended from some one prototype."[26]

To his contemporaries, by the time of publication of *The Origin of Species* (1859), Darwin had given the final rend to the fabric of nature, tearing it completely apart. They accused him of philosophical materialism, though he tried to bury his true beliefs in his Notebooks. What was left was a nature "red in tooth and claw," where the survival of the fittest echoed Hobbes's atomistic conception of nature, where each man warred against every other. Social Darwinism appeared to be a cosmic version of the "cash nexus"; that is, a view of nature and society as being at one in their disregard of human values other than the struggle to divide a fixed pie.

In fact, there was some justice in his contemporaries' accusations. Darwin had unreflectively imbibed much of the capitalist atmosphere of his time and class (the voyage of the *Beagle* was conceived in order to further Britain's trade possibilities; Darwin's wife was a Wedgwood; etc.). He was led to his theory of natural selection by the inspiration of Malthus, and, as importantly, though less known, of Adam Smith; it was the reading of Dugald Stewart's *Life of Adam Smith* some weeks before reading Malthus that prepared Darwin to be receptive to the latter's population theory. What took place, then, was a creative transfer of a theory in classical economics to the realm of biology.[27]

With evolutionary theory, Darwin did for animate matter what Newton had done for inanimate. Darwin is explicit about his model. He makes a clear analogy between the attack on Newton (as being subversive of religion) and the attack on himself. And he is clearly comparing his own achievement to that of the great cosmologist and natural philosopher, when he writes in the very last sentence in *The Origin of Species* of how "whilst this planet has gone cycling on according to the fixed laws of gravity, from so simple a beginning endless forms most beautiful and most wonderful have been, and are being evolved."[28]

As with the charge that Darwin lends himself to a selfish version of his theory, that is, to Social Darwinism, there is also partial truth in the religionists' accusations against Darwin. While, in principle, his theory of evolution could coexist with the traditional religious view, it potentially undermined the latter. The last link holding together the Great Chain of Being was snapped, and, where angels formerly held rank in the classifications, now only giant fossil birds flapped ancient leathery wings. Where before wonder called forth religion to fill the vacuum of broken and missing connections, now science stepped into the void. There seemed little left to tie Man to the heavens, or even to keep his feet solidly on a changing earth (for Darwin was a geologist as well as a biologist).

What Darwin's opponents did not see was that, in breaking one set of connections, Darwin was creating a new set. Cutting the Great Chain, he affirmed that "the real affinities of all organic beings, in contradistinction to their adaptive resemblances, are due to inheritance or community of descent."[29] Affinities and community, these are forms of connection. So, too, though an aspect of Darwin pointed in the direction of strengthening only the "cash nexus" (to the great glee of some who favored this version of Social Darwinism), the larger part of his work bore a different directional sign: to ecology. For the chain he was substituting a web of relationships. The phrase Darwin constantly used is "economy of nature" (he is not alone in this usage); but by it he meant what today we refer to as ecology, the most connected of all visions. Indeed, with his eye on the species rather than on the individual, Darwin also praised altruism as an evolutionary development of Man's nature (this he did in *The Descent of Man*) and implicitly decried a vulgar Social Darwinist interpretation of his theory.

Darwin is filled with the realization that all forms of life are connected to all other forms; that, to use the old language, nature is one chain of dependence—and thus interdependence (the new ecological perspective). He talks characteristically of how an old lady's keeping a cat affects the rats, who affect the bees, who affect the clover, which affects the crops, and so on *ad infinitum*. There is a kind of Rube Goldberg-contraption aspect to many of Darwin's explanations. Let one quotation stand for many. Speaking in *The Voyage of the Beagle* about the flora and fauna of the Tierra del Fuego, Darwin somberly remarks:

> I can only compare these great aquatic forests of the southern hemisphere, with the terrestrial ones in the intertropical regions. Yet if in any country a forest was destroyed, I do not believe nearly so many species of animals would perish as would here, from the destruction of the kelp. Amidst the leaves of this plant numerous species of fish live, which nowhere else could find food or shelter; with their destruction the many cormorants and other fishing birds, the otters, seals, and porpoises, would soon perish also; and lastly, the Fuegian savage, the miserable lord of this miserable land, would redouble his cannibal feast, decrease in numbers, and perhaps cease to exist.[30]

The aged Lamarck would only have nodded his head in agreement, though with an added frown. Yet, between them, Lamarck and Darwin had frightened their contemporaries into a suspicious anxiety that the world was no longer secure, no longer held together in trustworthy fashion. In spite of their truly connecting and ecological "other eye," Lamarck and Darwin, and their evolutionary theories, were perceived by many as subverters of the natural order, in the social as in the biological world.

Others, of course, felt free of unwanted restraints, ancient, traditional hamperings, and eager to follow, in wonderment, the possible new connections of an expanding, evolving universe, of which human society was one small mirroring part.

Crusoes of a New World

In tracing the break with the Great Chain of Being, and its substitution by the theory of evolution, I have run somewhat ahead of my main story, in an attempt to sketch some of the background of what I have earlier called the God and Nature questions about connection. Now, I want to return to my main focus, on human society rather than its cosmic and biological backdrop. I want to look at what is called "individualism," and to look at it as symbolized by Daniel Defoe's *Robinson Crusoe*. Here we shall see a fundamental break in society with past connection—a historical revolution in psychology and values.[31]

Robinson Crusoe is often thought to be a children's book; and so it is, in part. It embodies a child's fantasy of a world without adults. A closer look reveals a son's rebellion against his father, both in heaven and on earth, followed by guilt, punishment, and an acting-out of the desire both to eliminate fatherly presences and to suffer the consequences of being expelled from his presence. The result is a revolt against dependence, a growth and discovery of the individual self, and a subsequent ability to return out of isolation to the world of other Men.

On the simplest level, of course, *Robinson Crusoe* is an adventure story. It also picks up the persistent theme in seventeenth- and eighteenth-century European culture of the threat of solitude and isolation; as with the sailor Selkirk actually being marooned on an island; or as in Descartes's *Discourse on Method* where he imagines himself sealed in his mind, with all his senses deceived by a malevolent God, and thus thrown back entirely on his inner resources; or as with the wolf children, who are raised by nature, so to speak, unencumbered by, or deprived of, human society.[32] It then weaves out of this theme a young man's narrative of exploration and exploits.

It is important that *Robinson Crusoe* takes place on an island. Although we should not ignore the presence of God—for the island is a fitting place for Crusoe's constant dialogue with the Deity—the island is symbolic of the detached, isolated self that must develop by itself. There is a striking contrast with Defoe's fellow countryman, John Donne, who earlier wrote that "No man is an island unto himself."

Alone, Crusoe could construct his own world, largely out of his own resources (as we know, he does start out with some provisions from the shipwreck). He can do so, so to speak, from the ground up (although again we must add that he does so with memories acquired from his old world). It is no accident that Rousseau chooses *Robinson Crusoe* as the one book he will allow his fictional student, Emile, to read (who is otherwise to learn only from nature). In a phrase reminiscent of Descartes, Rousseau declares that "the surest way to raise oneself above prejudices, and order one's judgment on the real relationship between things, is to put oneself in the place of an isolated man, and to judge of everything as that man would judge of them according to their actual usefulness."[33]

Such a judgment, of course, is unconnected to the past. It takes place completely in the present. It questions all inherited notions. One of these notions is God and the father's wisdom. We all know of *Robinson Crusoe* as an adventure story; fewer of us realize that it is also a theodicy, or a questioning of the justification of God to Man. Crusoe is constantly asking, "Why has God done this to me? What have I done to be thus used?" His quick response—"My conscience presently checked me in that inquiry, as if I had blasphemed, and methought it spoke to me like a voice: 'WRETCH! dost thou ask what thou hast done? Look back upon a dreadful mispent life'"— only temporarily halts the debate.[34]

By steadily returning to a supposed state of nature, Crusoe seeks his blasphemous answer. Whatever his qualms of conscience, he is constantly implying that he is self-created. He does make just as constant obeisances to "the Invisible Power which alone directs such things," but he is moving toward a questioning of that invisible power more along Adam Smith's scientific lines than on traditional religious lines. The rhetoric links to the past:

> The whole transaction seemed to be a chain of wonders; that such things as these were the testimonies we had of a secret hand of Providence governing the world, and an evidence that the eyes of an infinite Power could search into the remotest corner of the world, and send help to the miserable whenever He pleased.[35]

But the actions are rooted in the present: Crusoe behaves as a self-reliant individual, master of his own fate.

The form and structure of the book mirrors its latent message. It is, first of all, written as an autobiography, that most characteristic and revealing of modern Western genres.[36] It is an "I" book. The titles of the first nineteen chapters, with one exception called "The Journal," all begin with "I." "I Go to Sea," "I Am Captured by Pirates," and so on. It is noteworthy that with the coming of Friday, the last eight chapters are mainly entitled "We . . . ," introducing a note of ambiguity as we shall see, though the last chapter reverts to "I Revisit My Island."[37] *Robinson Crusoe* is mainly, however, an inquiry into the nature of selfhood and individual development, initially outside of the "We" of society.

Karl Marx was right to see in Robinson Crusoe the prototype of capitalist economic character. As he remarked, ". . . in the island, we have one independent person, the only inhabitant. In Europe during the Middle Ages, all are dependent: serfs and barons, vassals and suzerains, laymen and priests."[38] Crusoe symbolizes, brilliantly, the individualism—the breaking of dependent ties—that stands at the threshold of modern Western development.

One Man's Connection Is Another Man's Chain

Robinson Crusoe carries to the farthest degree the sounding of the self, alone. It goes to rock bottom. Only then does it begin to climb back to humanity at large. It must be said, however, that Defoe's novel itself offers us an ambivalent message, for his concept of society in the book at the end is, explicitly, a patriarchal one. Crusoe prides himself that the affections of his subject Friday are tied to him "like those of a child to a father." He teaches Friday to call him "Master," and when he adds Friday's father and a Spaniard to his dominion likens himself to a "King" who is "absolute lord and lawgiver."[39] For our modern tastes, Crusoe alone seems preferable to Crusoe in society.

It is, therefore, only implicitly, and in terms of the questioning of the first part of the book, when Crusoe is alone and raises the theodicy issue, that the story brings to us the recognition that an increased sense and knowledge of our individualism has as its accompaniment an increased sense and knowledge of our isolation. The concept of society—and our alienation from it—arises as the pendant to the conceptualization of self.

Before the assertion of individualism and independence, dependence was taken for granted. Only after the latter is challenged can its features be examined, and new social ties imagined and constructed. With *Robinson Crusoe*, the novel precedes social science. In a brilliant analysis, Ian Watt reminds us that "the modern study of society only began once individualism had focused attention on man's apparent disjunctions from his fellows." As he points out, it is appropriate that

> the tradition of the novel should begin with a work that annihilated the relationships of the traditional social order, and thus drew attention to the opportunity and the need of building up a network of personal relationships on a new and conscious pattern; the terms of the problem of the novel and of modern thought alike were established when the old order of moral and social relationships was shipwrecked, with Robinson Crusoe, by the rising tide of individualism.[40]

Novel, of course, means "new," as was pointed out earlier, and it is only fitting that it is this new genre, as much as John Locke's philosophical *Essay Concerning Human Understanding*, which allows us, imaginatively, to posit a kind of human "blank tablet" on which new lines can be inscribed and new social relations, overturning the past paternal and paternalistic arrangements, can be laid out. Locke, in his *Two Treatises on Government*, had queried, "Who Heir?" and gone on to attack the divine right to rule, vindicating in its place self-rule.

Locke was questioning, in the most fundamental sense, the power of society over the self. "I am an individual, unto myself. What are the bonds, the connections, that should tie me to others?" This becomes the novel, modern question. In order to answer it, the old connections that have somehow or other grown up around the individual must be banished, in mind even more than in material life, in order for new ones to be forged, rationally.

This, certainly, was the attitude of many in the eighteenth century who surged forward in the movement I am calling the Break. In England, for example, individualism can be said to have faced off against "connection" in the most literal sense. One was born into (or out of) a web of connections and patronage, for the two were linked. It was one's relatives or one's "connections" who secured one entrance to the sinecures of government, to posts in the navy and army, to fellowships in university. It was one's patrons who helped in the same way, presenting one with a living in the parish church, protecting one from possible legal suits, and looking after one's interests (and their own) in a general way.

It was an "aristocratic" society, taken in the broadest sense. It was a world of social and intellectual connectiveness, embedded for us in amber by another novelist, about a century after Defoe, Jane Austen. The individual is trussed up in the family's roots and branches (where family "branches" are all important). As H. J. Perkin puts it so well:

> In the mesh of continuing loyalties of which appointments were the outward sign, patronage or 'vertical friendship' was the master-link of the old society, a durable, two-way relationship between an infinite series of patrons and clients which permeated the whole of society. It was a social nexus less formal and inescapable than feudal homage, more personal and comprehensive than the contractual relationships of capitalist "Cash Payment."[41]

For some it brought warmth and stability, a settled and satisfactory way of life. For others, the connections were chains, binding them down to a lowly position in society. Society, through its connections, made some and unmade others. The latter, if they were ambitious, had to try to make themselves, to become "self-made men." Such men, and sometimes their wives, saw themselves as part of a new "generation," needing to break with the past, and its old ways.

One was James Mill (who can stand as a symbol for many). A poor boy, out of Scotland, he came to reject his own past, as a preliminary to rejecting that of the aristocrats and their consequent claims to pre-eminence. James Mill was quite fanatical about the need to be independent, and not to play the game of connection (though he himself, in fact, constantly benefited from it).[42] "In the choosing of a line of life," he intoned,

> it is always a sign of an erect and *manly* character to choose those employments, however poor, which are least allied to *dependence* . . . where it is necessary for them to court the favour of others, and to dread the frown, which they must endeavor to escape by way out of submission and compliance. . . .[43]

It was only natural that a man such as James Mill would become a Utilitarian, following Jeremy Bentham in his attack on prerogative government and society, and grounding all authority and position on their "usefulness." To establish the latter, one worked out a calculus of pleasure and pain, which, in turn, could be converted into

the laws of supply and demand. Not social connection but utility—
in fact, another form of connection, as we shall see later—should
rule as the correct relation of Man to Man. Each man should make
himself; and laissez-faire should rightly prevail among equal individuals, all necessarily self-made.

It is from a number of sides, then, that we see a struggle going
on between those who cherish connections—by which they mean
the old connections—and those who detest them, as chains. The
new, thrusting men of the early industrial period saw the "cash
nexus" as liberating, not as a loss of sustaining connection. Their
alienation had been from aristocratic society, not from the new,
emerging industrial society, as Thomas Carlyle called it.

But what of the ordinary people, the rural and urban working
population that had formed the base of the stable connecting hierarchy described by Perkin? Certainly, in the eyes of the lamenters,
their lot was an unenviable one, exposed as they were to the callousness of the cash nexus. And so they were, in large part, victims
of a massive transformation of society. I shall speak much more of
this later. For the moment, though, it must be entered in the balance
that for many workers the dissolution of old ties and society opened
up a new world into which they *wanted* to enter. Economic historians debate how much was push or pull in the labor sector of the
early nineteenth century in England (and subsequently in all newly
industrializing nations). Whatever the exact resolution, one fact is
clear: some workers—how many is not clear—voted with their feet,
that is, entered the new towns because they were exciting, personally liberating, and, however precarious, often more rewarding
materially than the "place" from which they came.

This is not a side of the connections question to which lamenters
were wont to give much attention. Indeed, even the breakers tended
to keep their gaze on the successful few, the self-made partisans of
laissez-faire, as being the prime beneficiaries of the new system in
terms of personal liberation. While stressing that the workers might
benefit through increased affluence, men such as Adam Smith also
saw the price—personal degradation—resulting from the new division of labor. Thus, Smith joined the lamenters temporarily when
he spoke of laborers as a "commodity," like any other, and admitted
the deplorable fact that in the progress of the division of labor, the
worker "generally becomes as stupid and ignorant as it is possible
for a human creature to become."[44]

Smith's fellow Scotsman, Adam Ferguson, in his *Essay on the History of Civil Society* (1767), also acknowledged that in the modern "commercial state,"

> . . . man is sometimes found a detached and a solitary being: he has found an object which sets him in competition with his fellow-creatures, and he deals with them as he does with his cattle and his soil, for the sake of the profits they bring. The mighty engine which we suppose to have formed society, only tends to set its members at variance, or to continue their intercourse after the bands of affection are broken.[45]

A half-century later, Sir Walter Scott (and after him, Friedrich Engels) thought he saw the explanation for this development. Ferguson's "mighty engine" was, in Scott's view, Watt's power-driven machine. "Much of this [unhappy dislocation]," Scott exclaimed,

> is owing to the steam engine. When the machinery was driven by water, the manufacturer had to seek out some sequestered spot where he could obtain a suitable fall of water, and then his workmen formed the inhabitants of a village around him, and he necessarily bestowed some attention, less or more, on their morals and on their necessities, had knowledge of their persons and characters and exercised a salutary influence as over men depending on and intimately connected with him and his prospects. This is now quite changed; the manufacturers are transferred to great towns, where a man may assemble five hundred workmen one week and dismiss them the next, without having any further connection with them than to receive a week's work for a week's wages, nor any further solicitude about their future fate than if they were so many old shuttles.[46]

Whatever the exact cause, the "detached and . . . solitary being," who in Defoe's *Robinson Crusoe* was mainly seen as a cause of celebration, was now also seen as a claimant on our sympathy, suffering from a broken connection. Indeed, there is a nice link between Ferguson, who generally approved of the new, emerging society, and Carlyle, who didn't, which runs through the German writer Friedrich Schiller. Schiller had read Ferguson and admired him. Drawing upon the enlightened Scotsman, Schiller spoke of the individuals of the developing industrial society as "fragments," with "whole classes of men, developing but one part of their potentialities." As a result, "a mechanical kind of collective life" has ensued.

"State and Church," Schiller went on, "laws and customs were now torn asunder; enjoyment was divorced from labour, the means from the end, the effort from the reward," while, "everlastingly chained to a single little fragment of the Whole, man himself develops into nothing but a fragment."[47]

Carlyle, in turn, read Schiller (and in fact wrote a *Life of Schiller*, published in 1825). Inspired by his German mentor (and through him by his fellow Scotsman, Ferguson), Carlyle sought to view life whole, rather than in fragments. I have already quoted Carlyle's statements about cash nexus in *Past and Present*. Let me now add his comment that "Love of men cannot be bought by cash-payment; and without love men cannot endure to be together. . . ." It is love, and brotherhood, that are "deeper ties than those of temporary day's wages!" Then, with a direct thrust at the Robinson Crusoes of the new world, Carlyle thundered:

> Isolation is the sum-total of wretchedness to man. To be cut off, to be left solitary: to have a world alien, not your world; all a hostile camp for you; not a home at all, of hearts and faces who are yours, whose you are! It is the frightfulest enchantment; too truly a work of the Evil One.[48]

For Carlyle, in sum, the disconnecting industrial society was the work of the Devil, rather than of heroic individualism.

The Great Transformations

The Industrial Revolution marks a major transformation in the condition of Man, comparable only to the shift somewhere around 12,000 years ago when humans went from being hunters and gatherers to being members of settled agricultural communities. Though rooted in slowly developing pre-conditions—social, political, intellectual, economic—it had, and has, truly novel and awesome implications. The experience of industrialization, occurring first around 1760-1860 in England, and then spreading, however intermittently, to many other men and women, in all parts of the globe, was and is one of tremendously rapid and unsettling change. It gave a new dimension to the breaking of long-established connections, as well as conventions, that had been steadily acquiring force in the preceding century or so. It moved Men from the land to the city in unprecedented numbers; and it was accompanied, or partly caused, by a demographic revolution at large. It shifted the focus of work significantly from the farm to the factory, and changed the discipline of work drastically in the process. It speeded up the tempo of travel and communication—the railroad, the telegraph—in a quantitative way that soon become qualitative. And it helped to change the character of Man, as well as his condition: the individualist, the Robinson Crusoe-type Man, comes front and center on the Western stage.[49]

The great transformation brought about by industrialism was accompanied by major political revolutions, the American and the French. Taken together, the two types of revolution, the industrial and the political, make up what the historian Eric Hobsbawm has aptly called the "Dual Revolutions," thus emphasizing their relatedness. The strain on existing connections became even heavier. Earth itself seemed torn from its gravitational moorings, as in the song sung at the surrender of Cornwallis to the Americans at Yorktown: "The world turned upside down."

The new state of affairs was dramatically announced by the Declaration of Independence. It proclaimed, for all to hear, the right to independence. "When, in the course of human events, it becomes necessary for one people to dissolve the political bands [sic] which have connected them with another . . ." Most readers will not recall that the largest part of the document is filled with particulars, spelling out the details of how "the history of the present King of Great Britain is a history of repeated injuries and usurpations. . . ." What stands out is the universal right to dissolution and independence.

To emphasize one particular psychological perspective, until at least the 1760s the colonies had felt strongly dependent on George III—a paternal authority—and on Great Britain—a nurturant mother. The colonies were their "children." Such were the dominant images used by the actors at the time. Suddenly, a transformation in affections occurred, and George became a tyrant, and Great Britain a step-mother, denying rightful sustenance and freedom to her growing "Sons of Liberty." English laws regulating trade that had seemed protections, now became, as Samuel Adams put it, chains of "a bondaged state."[50]

Anger and resentment replaced the comfort of being dependent on Great Britain. Filial ties had now to be sundered. Whatever the anxiety at the prospect of separation, the idea of continued dependency had become even more tormenting than the dangers of independence. The bonds were dissolved, as we know. And in their place came new bonds: the union of the colonies in the United States of America.

In his Farewell Address of 1796, Washington repeatedly alluded to the new ties and bindings. He spoke of his own decision to retire from the presidency, that is, not to be a candidate for re-election, as being taken in spite of "the relation which binds a dutiful citizen to his country." He talked further of his "inviolable attachment" to his country; of his wish that his fellow citizens' "union and brotherly affection may be perpetual"; of "the unity of government" as "the edifice of your real independence"; and of the "Immovable attachment" and "sacred ties" which link together the new "Americans," one to another.[51] Independence *and* union cohere for Washington; one requires the other. Yet what remained dominant in Men's minds, when thinking of the American Revolution, was the imagery of dissolution and breaking of connections.

Thomas Jefferson, not Washington, symbolized the continued unsettling spirit of rebellion, the blank check drawn on the future. It was he who served as the principal draftsman of the Declaration of Independence; and it was as if the ink of that statement could not be rubbed off his fingers. He called for a rebellion, a dissolving of the political "bands," every twenty years, the span of a generation. He set generation against generation, declaring that "the Earth belongs in Usufruct to the Living," meaning that the present owed nothing to the past. And it was Jefferson's version of perpetual revolution that excited Men elsewhere even after the United States settled down into its new but persisting affections and attachments.

Jefferson, in fact, was in Paris as American Minister when, in less than a generation, the tree of liberty was watered anew. If the American Revolution sent a tremor through the Old World, the French Revolution was a violent shaking and remaking, changing the modern political landscape once and for all. In the *Social Contract*, in 1762, Rousseau had written that "Man is born free; and everywhere he is in chains." The events of 1789 unchained Men not only in France but in many other parts of Europe, and then, over time, had an effect in other parts of the globe. Whether it brought freedom is a matter of more debate.

The French Revolution was marked by what it was against at least as much as by what it was for. It was against the aristocracy, the privileged church, and the existing corporations. I shall not recite its well-known opposition to the first two, but concentrate on its less-known attack on the corporations. The attack was led by Turgot and the other Physiocrats, or *Economists* as they were called, who marched forward under the slogans "laissez-faire" and "laissez-passer."

In his edict of 1774, Turgot, as controller general, declared, "It will be free to all persons, of whatever quality and condition they may be . . .", to practice "whatever form of commerce or arts and crafts they wished." His attack, in the name of freedom, on the monopoly held by the corporations was answered in the language of connection. The Parlement responded that "Each manufacturer, each artist, each worker will regard himself as an isolated being, depending on himself alone and free to indulge in all the flights of an often disordered imagination. All subordination will be destroyed. . . ." Claiming that "a correspondence of interests united workers and masters," the Parlementary reply predicted anarchy and despotism, not true freedom, if the corporations were abolished. In a dire tone, the Parlement warned that the corporations were "a chain of which all the links are joined to the first chain, to the authority of the Throne, and which it is dangerous to break."[52]

The Parlement, of course, was absolutely right in its premonition, as the events of 1789 proved. However, what for them was a rightful chain and a harmonious hierarchy was for Turgot and his like a series of fetters, preventing the individual from exercising his natural right to freedom. The fall of the Bastille symbolized the snapping of the fetters. The individual stood free, liberated. He had broken with the old hierarchy—its privileges, ranks, and orders—and, so it seemed, with the entire weight of the past. "Bliss was it in that dawn to be alive," exclaimed a temporarily exuberant Wordsworth.[53] In the eyes of the youthful Hegel, a new epoch had dawned.

"Time" itself had changed, and to mark the decisive break that had occurred the revolutionists remade the calendar. 1792 became the Year One, thus showing that a totally new beginning had been made, equivalent to the coming of Christ. Even the months were renamed.

People, too, were remodeled. In place of the old hierarchies, a single equality prevailed, marked by the new, common form of address, "Citizen." Alongside "Liberty" stood the other slogans of

"Fraternity" and "Equality." The individual had broken his bonds to the old, but was now united in terms of the "Nation," to which all swore allegiance. All were brothers, bound together as the People; all intermediate loyalties were abolished. Rousseau was the voice of such sentiment, as we shall see in the next chapter. Such loyalties, as the revolutionists viewed them, were actually privileges whose sacrifice, as the Assembly declared on the famous night of August 4 which swept them away, was "necessary for the close union of all parts of the country."[54]

Prior to that night, the Abbé Sièyes had written in his famous pamphlet, "What Is the Third Estate?," that by itself the Third Estate was "a complete nation." Until privileges and the other Estates were done away with, however, the Third Estate was "like a strong and robust man with one arm still chained." After the unchaining—and one notices anew the ubiquity of such language—the "particular interest of each individual" must prevail, subject only to the "general interest." Between the individual and the general no other corporate bond may exist; it is for this reason, not hostility to workers as such, that the Assembly was led in 1791 to pass the Le Chapelier law, forbidding workers to form "coalitions," or unions.

In the light of subsequent history, we know the power of the one union, the Nation, that was permitted. The armies of the Revolution, carrying its ideas, swept into the rest of Europe.[55] Everywhere, the Revolution began to uncouple Men from their ancient connections, to call them into question. With Napoleon, the tide carried as far as Moscow, then receded. It was a temporary recession, as the revolutions of 1830 and 1848 show (even though they, too, were not immediately successful).

It was Napoleon who symbolized the tensions and contradictions inherent in the new order brought out of the disordering of the old. Here was the epitome of the new, self-made Man, now manifest in the political rather than the economic sphere. He seemed to come from nowhere, and to rise by his sheer charismatic individual qualities; to be attached to no place except the abstraction "France." He was the "little corporal" who rose to be the successor to kings, and who told his followers that each carried a "marshall's baton in his knapsack." Yet it was this same Napoleon who made himself an emperor, created a fresh corps of aristocrats, and tried to create a new hierarchical order out of revolution.[56]

Napoleon can be taken as the fulfillment both of a promise of freedom and of a prophecy of greater tyranny. Nevertheless, he is in many ways the culmination of the dissolving acids of both the American and the French revolutions, occurring as they did in the time of an industrial revolution. He embodies, in a vivid symbolic way, and in spite of his atavistic efforts at recoupling, the Break with inherited authority and connection. In the eyes of many anxious contemporaries, the American and the French revolutions, and the latter's Napoleonic aftermath, had broken all the ties of society and sent it spinning out into an equally unchained and unconnected world.

If one can view the capitalistic industrial revolution as reducing Men's connections to that of the cash nexus, the French Revolution and even its Napoleonic sequel, at least in its first phase, could also be seen as reducing all hierarchical ranges to the one flat plain of equality, in the nation state. To later, more historical eyes, both these epochal happenings, the industrial and the political revolution, do, indeed, appear to have marked a massive break—but also the establishment of powerful and enduring new bonds. To many contemporary observers, however, these happenings seemed only to be dissolving their society and world into isolated fragments, with all connection gone except the cash nexus, and perhaps the national tie; thus, the time was one fit only for lamentation.

3

The Lament:
Philosophers and a Poet

Lamenters

Those who lamented the breakdown of a connected world (as they perceived it) were not themselves a homogeneous, united group. Their reactions to the American and French revolutions were often mixed, generally ambiguous and sometimes marked by a shift from an initial enthusiasm to a fervid rejection. And, when the lamenters took up political positions, they often split into conservatives and revolutionaries, united only by their reaction to a perceived world of shattered ties.

Some of the lamenters whom I shall discuss were political philosophers, such as Edmund Burke and Jean-Jacques Rousseau; some were poets, such as William Wordsworth; others essayists and social critics, such as Thomas Carlyle; and others novelists, such as Elizabeth Gaskell, Benjamin Disraeli, and George Eliot. In many cases, they stepped over the boundaries of these classifications: Rousseau wrote operas and a novel; Wordsworth wrote an important essay (Preface to the *Lyrical Ballads*); and Disraeli became a practical politician, indeed a Prime Minister.

Most of them are figures mainly of the first half of the nineteenth century, with the novelists lapping over into the second half. Some of them, as a result, belong to different generations and even centuries—Burke was born in 1729 and George Eliot in 1819—and this clearly affected what particular phase of "breakdown" they experienced. Burke and Rousseau, unlike the others, were responding mainly to the commercial society expanding around them, though Burke was also experiencing the early stages of industrializing society, and, unlike Rousseau, also living through the French Revolution. A fuller treatment, as indicated earlier, would pay more attention to this changing background; but I am largely neglecting such social history.

In any event, I have chosen my figures primarily to illustrate the first wave of reaction to the "Dual Revolutions": the French and the Industrial. The collective voice of the lamenters, and that of others like them, deploring the breakdown of connections in various and sundry areas, but especially in the natural and social world, was not stilled in the latter part of the century—one thinks of a Ruskin or a Pugin—but was supplemented by a new sound, that of the sociologists. The philosophic, poetic, novelistic, essayistic response to the presumed sundering of ties was, I am claiming, itself "scientized" in the form of the new social science, sociology.[1]

First, however, come the early figures, who initially set the tone of the reaction, two of whom, Burke and Rousseau, more or less belonged to the same generation in the sense of being formed before 1789, and one, Wordsworth, who was responding in the next generation to the trauma of the French Revolution (which came in the name of Rousseauian precepts and ended by evoking a Burkean counterrevolution). By our going in some depth into the reality of their lives, we can see how the connections problem actually played itself out, often in a highly contradictory and agitated fashion missed by smoother accounts of their abstract positions.

Edmund Burke

Edmund Burke is important on two counts: he is a prime figure in turning the lamentation over the breakdown of connection into a full-fledged political philosophy, conservatism; and he is an excellent illustration of the complexity of such a reaction. The fact is that political revolution is a dramatic form of disconnecting; and yet Burke approved highly of both the Glorious Revolution of 1688–89 in Great Britain and the American Revolution of 1776. His alarm arose only with the coming of the French Revolution of 1789. It is that shattering event, and only that one, which occasioned his conscious elaboration of the doctrine of conservatism.

Burke approved of the Glorious Revolution because he viewed it as a restoration of the natural and historical rights of Englishmen— here the issue was simple. He accepted the American Revolution because it was on the same plan: a desire for "security to its ancient constitution."[2] He deplored the stupidity of George III, who insisted on the letter of the law instead of ruling by expediency and adherence to historically affirmed natural right. The American breaking of the "bands" that followed upon 1776 was, thus, in Burke's eyes the reaffirmation of more legitimate, primordial ties to the "ancient constitution."

The French Revolution was a wholly different matter. In his *Reflections on the Revolution in France* (1790), Burke spelled out the differences, as he saw them. His language shows us how central the notion of "connections" was to his new philosophy of conservatism. Society, for Burke, was a link of generations in time and a hierarchy in space. Woe unto him who turns against the fathers, the previous generation. In Burke's impassioned words, a man "should approach to the faults of the state as to the wounds of a father, with pious awe and trembling solicitude. By this wise prejudice we are taught to look with horror on those children of their country who are prompt rashly to hack that aged parent in pieces."[3] Society, Burke agreed, is a contract—but it is a binding one for all generations. Not for Burke was the every twenty-year annulment clause of Jefferson, who recommended dissolution. Instead, Burke intones, in a long and fundamental passage, that

> society is indeed a contract. Subordinate contracts for objects of mere occasional interest may be dissolved at pleasure—but the state ought not to be considered as nothing better than a partnership agreement in a trade of pepper and coffee, calico, or tobacco, or some other such low concern, to be taken up for a little temporary interest, and to be dissolved by the fancy of the parties. It is to be looked on with other reverence, because it is not a partnership in things subservient only to the gross animal existence of a temporary and perishable nature. It is a partnership in all science; a partnership in all art; a partnership in every virtue and in all perfection. As the ends of such a partnership cannot be obtained in many generations, it becomes a partnership not only between those who are living, but between those who are living, those who are dead, and those who are to be born.

At this point, Burke connects human society with the cosmos, of which it is a reflection, both having been created by the same God, who keeps them in place. Burke continues:

> Each contract of each particular state is but a clause in the great pri-meval contract of eternal society, linking the lower with the higher natures, connecting the visible and invisible world, according to a fixed compact sanctioned by the inviolable oath which holds all physical and all moral natures, each in their appointed place.[4]

Burke, in short, is one of the last spokesmen for the Great Chain of Being. Against revolution, he has opposed restoration, in short, his philosophy of conservatism.

The great enemy is abstract rationality, which eats away at the necessary hierarchical connection. It substitutes metaphysical, universal principles for historically established relations, that is, it undermines prerogatives established by long usage, what Burke calls prescription, the time-bound glue that holds society together. What Burke calls "this mechanic philosophy" has as its consequence that "nothing is left which engages the affections."[5] It levels all hierarchical attachments into a false equality; but, says Burke, "the levelers . . . only change and pervert the natural order of things."[6] Things would have been well, he says, if only the *philosophes*, who embodied learning, had kept their "proper place," and maintained thereby "their indissoluble union" with the nobility and clergy. As Burke reaffirms,

> To be attached to the subdivision, to love the little platoon we belong to in society, is the first principle (the germ as it were) of public affections. It is the first link in the series by which we proceed toward a love to our country and to mankind.

Instead of adhering to the natural connections of society and the cosmos (embodied in feudal society), the cold, mechanical thinkers have broken them apart, according to Burke. The result is, in Burke's telling words, that "the age of chivalry is gone. That of sophisters, economists, and calculators has succeeded. . . ." A "revolution in sentiments, manners, and moral opinions" is upon us. And at this point, Burke implicitly connects the political revolution with the

Industrial Revolution. He notices that at the opening of the Estates-General it had been said that all occupations were honorable. Admitting that no honest employment is disgraceful, Burke insists that

> in asserting that anything is honorable, we imply some distinction in its favor. The occupation of a hairdresser or of a working tallow-chandler cannot be a matter of honor to any person—to say nothing of a number of other more servile employments. Such descriptions of men ought not to suffer oppression from the state; but the state suffers oppression if such as they, either individually or collectively, are permitted to rule. In this you think you are combating prejudice, but you are at war with nature.

What Burke took for nature (and he never explained how, in fact, he knew what "nature" demanded), others—the sophisters, economists, and calculators—were claiming to be a matter of nurture, or rather mere social convention. In the age of Richard Arkwright, who had been a hairdresser, and of Benjamin Franklin, whose father was a tallow-chandler, Burke's was a tactless remark; it was also at odds with the shift in feeling and thought of those who saw the break in connection as a form of liberation.

It was at odds, too, with a substantial part of Burke's own attitude to commercial society. The fact is that Burke, in other contexts, supported the trading interests. He became, at one point, a member of Parliament for Bristol, the port heavily engaged in trade with the American colonies, and represented its interests. He was also a paid agent of the colony of New York. He, who spoke against speculators, mingled his own fortunes with his kinsmen, Richard and William Burke, who were speculators, often close to the margin of fraud. Moreover, Burke attacked the government's policy in India, while his family was speculating in East India Company stock. He tried to get positions for his relatives in government, which would help them in their financial schemes. Though Burke himself was scrupulously honest, he lent himself unreservedly to the speculative designs of those whom he loved.

What appears to be even more at odds with his professed conservatism is Burke's espousal of laissez-faire economic theory. In his *Thoughts and Details on Scarcity*, of 1795 (published five years after the *Reflections*), he put forth views similar to those of Adam Smith. Earlier, on the first appearance of Smith's *Theory of Moral Sentiments*,

Burke had written a handsome review of it for his periodical, the *Annual Register*. When Smith put out a sixth edition shortly before his death in 1790, adding some pages that seem to bear on the French Revolution and that comment in a critical tone on the "disorder of faction" and the fanaticism that wished even to "newmodel the constitution," we can easily surmise that Burke would have been pleased and perhaps even influenced (although it is not clear who influenced whom in this matter).[7] In any case, by 1795, he was supporting Smith's economic ideas as well, and we face the paradox that Burke, who decried the coming of economists, was nevertheless supporting their ideas.

How can we explain these paradoxes? Indeed, they go back to Burke's origins, where we find additional ones. The Burke who praised following fathers had himself rejected his father's desires: on becoming a lawyer, as his father was, Edmund Burke then rebelled, abandoned his legal studies, and became a professional writer. So, too, he who extolled settled place left his natal Dublin to follow his career in London. Once there, unable to earn a satisfactory living as a writer, he attached himself as a secretary to one figure and then quickly to another, the Marquis of Rockingham. It was as spokesman for the Rockingham Whigs, and their opposition to the King's American policy, that Burke first made his mark.

The fact is that Burke had entered the world of social "connections," which has been described earlier as characterizing eighteenth-century British society. He had acquired a patron, and his subsequent advancement and gain resulted from that tie. His conservatism, as it happens, also aimed at conserving the world of connections that had served him so well, while allowing him a great deal of independence.

There were two other sources, more fundamental even than Burke's connections, that impelled him to his philosophy. One was his religious commitment. Burke came from a mixed Protestant-Catholic family background, married a Catholic, and was constantly accused by his enemies of being a secret Papist. In fact, he was a loyal Anglican, and it was his heartfelt commitment to the Christian religion in this traditional form that caused him to be so vehement in his opposition to what he saw as the "atheistical" doctrines of the French Revolution. It was for this reason that he upheld so strongly "the great primeval contract" of the Chain of Being.

The other source was Burke's romanticism. Burke, we must

remember, had aspired to a literary career. It was only because of its precarious financial status that he turned to other work. As a literary person, however, at age twenty-seven he had written *A Philosophical Inquiry into the Origin of Our Ideas of the Sublime and the Beautiful* (1756), which revolutionized the aesthetic realm. In place of the Augustans' praise of beauty, which they saw as clear, measured, and reassuring, Burke exulted over the sublime, that feeling of shadowiness, wildness, and awe. Our experience of the sublime leaves us also, Burke pointed out, with a sense of loneliness, of what we today call *angst*.

Burke approached the writing of his *Reflections* with the same romantic enthusiasm he had vindicated in his *The Sublime and the Beautiful*. It is simply another paradox: his revolution in aestheticism was placed in the service of his attack on political revolution. The result was romantic conservatism, a glorification of "connected" society. To the objection that the connections, or prescriptive places, might have originated in ages of ignorance and violence, Burke replied: "Be it so;—it proves that they were made long ago; and this is prescription, and this gives right and title . . . that which might be wrong in the beginning, is consecrated by time and becomes lawful."[8] Of course, when Burke declared that "the whole organization of government becomes a consideration of convenience,"[9] he did not stop to consider "whose convenience?" To have done so might mean a rational, and even revolutionary, reconsideration of existing connections; and in this Burke was not prepared to engage. There is a final paradox in that Burke, who turned the connection question into political conservatism, was himself a precursor of the modern Man. He who extolled the tradition of the past became a romantic, who threw over the reigning settled conventions of aestheticism, and thus how we view the world. He who clung to a view of the world as a connected whole, and opposed the analyzing, dissecting view of the mechanical rationalists, was himself a highly fragmented being, with one part of him in the emerging new world and one part in the old and thus, as a fragmented being, symbolic of the character of the future.[10]

Jean-Jacques Rousseau

The person who, even more than Burke, symbolized the divided Man of modern society was Jean-Jacques Rousseau. Moreover, where Burke was divided, Rousseau was also alienated. So, too, it was Rousseau, more than anyone else in the eighteenth century, who made the most profound and tortured inquiry into the connections—the "chains"—that bind Men together in society, at the expense of their native independence. Though most scholars put Burke and Rousseau apart, the two men were, in fact, remarkably alike in their most deeply felt convictions, with each standing with one foot in an idealized past and the other foot in a troubling modernity to come.[11]

Perhaps the most famous line from Rousseau is the opening sentence, which I have already quoted, of the first chapter of *The Social Contract* (1762), where he announced that "Man is born free; and everywhere he is in chains." In *The Social Contract*, Rousseau set out to explore the conditions that would legitimate the chains, although he did so with a heavy and divided heart. His true allegiance was to the lonely individual, the solitary being, who stood, like Robinson Crusoe, free of all social connections. Still, Rousseau knew that Man had to enter society. It was in *Emile*, published in the same year as *The Social Contract*, that Rousseau plumbed the depths of "double men," that is, men like himself, filled with contradictions.[12] Although many of his ideas were adumbrated in his earlier "Discourses," we will concentrate here on his great works of 1762, and make only a few references to the earlier writings.[13]

I want first to note that, in *Emile*, whatever misgivings Rousseau had about social chains, he had few about the Great Chain of Being. He strongly inclined to a belief in fixed species, and declared that "the insurmountable barrier that nature set between the various species, so that they would not be confounded, shows its intentions with the utmost clarity. It was not satisfied with establishing order. It took certain measures so that nothing could disturb that order." And Rousseau followed suit: "Remain in the place which nature assigns to you in the chain of being," he expostulated. Fortunately, as he added, Man's place in the chain was the foremost, his species "incontestably in the first rank." Man, indeed, is "king of the earth."[14]

Oddly enough, in *The Social Contract*, Rousseau seems to have wavered on this issue of Man's fixity, and speculated in a kind of pre-Lamarckian manner on possible human development: "On this subject I could form none but vague and almost imaginary conjectures. Comparative anatomy has as yet made too little progress, and the observations of naturalists are too uncertain, to afford an adequate basis for solid reasoning. So that, without having recourse to the supernatural information given us on this head, or paying any attention to the changes which must have taken place in the internal, as well as the external, conformation of man, as he applied his limbs to new uses, and fed himself on new kinds of food, I shall suppose his conformation to have been at all times what it appears to us at this day."[15] Overall, then, Rousseau was his usual ambivalent self in this regard, as well as others.

In *Emile*, all Men, as a species, are kings, and thus equal; or so Rousseau appears to imply. Such, at least, is the case in a state of nature. Why, then, should Men want to leave such a state, and take on "chains" other than those of the chain of being? Rousseau, in fact, has mixed feelings, and is not sure they should.

Man's "natural" condition, according to Rousseau, can be deciphered only by studying Man outside of society. Only thus do we know what belongs to nature and what to nurture. But everywhere we see Man in society, and only there. Thus, we must perform a "thought-experiment"—Rousseau speaks of "conjecture"—and reconstruct, or build up from the beginning, Man as he is before or separate from society, as a matter of speculative history. This is the task Rousseau undertakes in all of his "Discourses"; in *Emile*, he seeks to do it by imagining an education according to nature.

Natural Man, according to Rousseau, is solitary Man; and Rousseau asserts that "A truly happy being is a solitary being." Then, indulging in one of his grandiose fantasies, he adds, "God alone enjoys an absolute happiness."[16] (The paradox is that Man, alone, cannot love anything, and how, as Rousseau remarks, can one love nothing and be happy?) If one is attached to society, one must inevitably hurt others, "for in the social state the good of one necessarily constitutes the harm of another." Thus, out of both philosophical conviction and a sense of guilt, Rousseau decrees an education for Emile that holds him aloof from society until his adolescence.

Emile's education is to be from nature, which never misleads us. Some of Rousseau's most savage prose is reserved for books, which he even considers consigning to the fire—this from a prolific author! (In his first major work, "A Discourse on the Moral Effects of the Arts and Sciences" (1750), Rousseau had made a devastating attack on the arts and sciences en masse.) Yet, because we must have books, Rousseau will allow one to his youthful pupil: it is, as I have already noted, *Robinson Crusoe*.

It is in discussing Defoe's novel that Rousseau indicates one of the main reasons why Man has not remained in his happy, isolated state. Earlier, I indicated that one usage of the term "connections" related to the connectiveness of nature, mirrored in Man's mind as knowledge. Rousseau, too, speaks of "the chain of knowledge." Such knowledge can be acquired by a single individual, a Crusoe, who, under the spur of his essential needs, can learn the practice of the natural arts. Such knowledge of connection among things, however, must soon give way to, or be joined by, a knowledge of the connections among Men, that is, society. As Rousseau puts it, ". . . the chain of knowledge forces you to show him [your pupil] the mutual dependence of men." Such dependence arises from Man's desires for luxuries. "So long as one knows only physical need, each man suffices unto himself. The introduction of the superfluous makes division and distribution of labor indispensable; although a man working alone earns only subsistence for one man, a hundred men working in harmony will earn enough to give subsistence to two hundred."[17] (We may add that what Rousseau calls the "superfluous," Marx will identify as "surplus value"; both graphically portray its evil consequences for Man.)

Besides superfluous needs, Rousseau offers other sources for the solitary's entrance into society. There seems to be an inherent quality in Man's very own nature, an ontological ground, so to speak, for his establishing connections. In the "Discourse on the Origin of Inequality" (1755), Rousseau puts it in terms of the two principles of self-preservation and of natural compassion for others. In *Emile*, he speaks of *amour de soi* (self-love) and *amour propre* (not easily translated; it is somewhere between vanity and self-esteem). Self-love regards only ourselves. But such self-regard leads us to love those—our mothers, our nurses—who preserve us. Thus a widening circle of attachments arises. *Amour propre* seems to be the Satanic side of self-love, for it makes comparisons and can never be satisfied (as *amour de soi* can be), "because this sentiment, preferring ourselves to others, also demands others to prefer us to themselves, which is impossible."[18] Man, then, is what Immanual Kant, as noted earlier in Chapter 1, was to call an "unsocial-social" animal, drawn to society by a loving part of his nature, as well as by his needs, and repelled from it by his hating, envious part.[19]

Sex is also a powerful magnet. "It is not good for man to be alone,"[20] Rousseau exclaims, when Emile reaches the time of adolescence, though earlier Rousseau has been singing the glories of solitude. And, indeed, much of the last two books (out of five) of *Emile* are devoted to a sentimentalizing, fantasizing, and highly

moralizing eroticism, telling us more about its author than its fictional adolescent. The point is, however, that Man cannot live alone,
for reasons of sex, wants (in contrast to sheer needs), love, and sheer
ontological cussedness (or, in more proper terms, his divided
nature).

Thus, Man must enter into a "connected" state. The chains draw
quickly about him. In existing society, the newborn infant is swad-
dled; as Rousseau puts it, hardly has the baby emerged from its
mother's womb, with freedom to move about, than it "is given new
bonds." "The first gifts" we give children, he goes on, "are
chains."[21] Swaddling, fortunately, is a convention that can be done
away with (and indeed, partly as a result of Rousseau's writing, it
was largely abandoned). Alas, the want and weakness of the first
condition of Man is a fact of nature, not nurture. The child is
dependent, and must shed tears to attract attention to its needs.
From these tears, Rousseau informs us, "is born man's first relation
to all that surrounds him; here is formed the first link in that long
chain of which the social order is formed."

In the nature of things, society denatures Man. It binds and
enslaves him. "So long as he keeps his human shape," Rousseau
says, "he is enchained by our institutions."[22] Even the arts and sciences merely "fling garlands of flowers over the chains which weigh
them [men] down. They stifle in men's breasts that sense of original
liberty, for which they seem to have been born. . . ."[23] Emile's entire
education is an effort to keep as close to his natal freedom as possible, to remain "natural" and thus free.

In debating these issues, Rousseau is torn between what is and
what should be. He agonizes and thrashes about over this fundamental issue, and in the process foreshadows much of what will
engage later social science. The "what is" causes Rousseau to offer
a penetrating description of social relations in his own culture and
others; the "what should be" moves him to want to change these
existing institutions. The two modes intersect frequently, and partly
account for Rousseau's paradoxical position, as I shall argue, as both
a breaker and a lamenter in regard to the matter of connections.

Rousseau's starting point is that Man is naturally good; evil
comes only from bad social institutions, from the unnatural connections established among Men. If Man could remain solitary, a savage, he would be both good and free. But he would not be virtuous,
or, indeed, moral, for virtue is only possible inside a social order.

The reasoning is very complicated. It involves Rousseau in the theodicy question, where he must justify the ways of God to Man. Not only Emile but Rousseau will have read *Robinson Crusoe* to advantage, and now finds himself forced to wrestle with his Father in heaven.

Rousseau starts with the postulate that, by definition, God is all good and all knowing. Then how can evil exist? To this perennial question, Rousseau offers mainly traditional answers: Man cannot know God's intentions; thus, what seems evil is not ultimately so. Man has free will; thus, he may choose good over evil, or what seems to be evil. What Rousseau then adds that is novel, or at least put in a novel way, is that evil emanates not from God, or even from original sin, but from social institutions. At this point, the revolutionary Rousseau makes his appearance with the message: change the institutions, and thus institute the reign of virtue on earth.

In the process of working out his new theodicy—and it was on the subject of religion as well as the arts and sciences that he differed so profoundly from his fellow *philosophes*—Rousseau both analyzes existing chains and indicates his preferred form of connections. His exposition, as we know, inspired many subsequent thinkers, even if they were moved only to argue against him, and it is for this reason as well as for his own worth that Rousseau is so essential to our discussion of the putative breakdown of connections.

Rousseau's analysis is most fully deployed in *Emile* and in the "Discourses," though never unmixed with his preferences. We have already glanced at the drives and motives for Man entering society: wants, love, sex. Rousseau goes further on the subject of wants, which he had described as leading to the division of labor and surplus value. He adds that "No society can exist without exchange." And exchange requires a medium of value—money—which is "only a term of comparison for the value of things of different kinds." It is in this sense, Rousseau concludes, that "money is the true bond of society."[24]

Carlyle, and Engels and Marx were later to speak of the cash nexus, and to excoriate the money tie. More dispassionately, Rousseau was saying that, in fact, money ties people together, for it is the medium of exchange, which in turn is the basis of all societies. In itself, money is merely a convenient invention to facilitate human intercourse. Rousseau, of course, was not unaware of its possible perversions: he warned that money has never "made anyone loved";[25] and in the inequality discourse he noted that "every man finds his profit in the misfortunes of his neighbour."[26] But he reserved his invective for evil society, not for the neutral medium that facilitates its exchanges.

The society that Rousseau despises is the false, artificial, hierarchical high society of eighteenth-century French culture. Above all, it is the society of the city, and of civilization. The Rousseau who at first aspired to be an accepted part of that glittering scene, but always felt uncomfortable and even boorish in its midst, turned savagely against what he now saw as its unnatural bonds. The rural-urban dichotomy that has loomed so large in later sociological treatises finds its most powerful and fervent early expression in the works of Rousseau.

Health and good morals, Rousseau tells us, reside only in the countryside, close to nature. Here Man is as near his original equality as he can be, and still be in a society. In the rural setting, Man can be self-sufficient, satisfying his simple wants with his own hands. With the rise of superfluous desires, equality disappears, as we have seen, property is introduced, and a hierarchical ordering of ranks emerges, whose locus becomes the luxury-soaked city. Rousseau's attack is broad. "Men," he says, " are made not to be crowded into anthills but to be dispersed over the earth which they should cultivate. The more they come together, the more they are corrupted. . . . Man is, of all the animals, the one who can least live in herds." "Cities," Rousseau declares, "are the abyss of the human species." In them, races degenerate, and "the young people, exhausted early, remain small, weak, and ill-formed."[27]

With prophetic insight, Rousseau warns his contemporaries that "We are approaching a state of crisis and the age of revolutions." The existing bonds of society will be broken. "You trust in the present order of society without thinking that this order is subject to inevitable revolutions," Rousseau declares. Then he shows how he is educating Emile to occupy any station or rank in society to which fortune may call him, even that of a carpenter. "What is more ridiculous," Rousseau asks, "than a great lord who has become destitute and brings the prejudices of his birth with him to his distress?"[28]

Such is the tenor of Rousseau's reflections on the future state of the individual. What about society itself? When the "what is" of existing society is overturned, the "what should be" aspect of the nature of Man's social relations emerges as the key issue. To this question, Rousseau turned his attention directly in *The Social Contract*, while also sketching its features in the last part of *Emile*. Clearly, the child educated there, as close to nature as possible, is to enter into connections and to become the ideal member of what is, nevertheless, a denaturing society.

The Social Contract has given rise, naturally, to extended commentary (as have all of Rousseau's works); I shall discuss here only a few of its ideas relevant to our subject of connections, simply to fill out the account. Rousseau begins his inquiry into how social chains can be made legitimate by dismissing all existing governments as based on a form of might rather than right. Such systems, he declares, may be termed "aggregations," but not "associations." The problem, therefore, is "to find a form of association which will defend and protect with the whole common force the person and goods of each associate, and in which each, while uniting himself with all, may still obey himself alone, and remain as free as before." The famous solution is a social contract, in which each individual— the Emiles of this world—gives up his natural rights and freedom to an association in which everyone has agreed to obey the general will, which now represents his better self. The general will is, in fact, a complicated idea, but basically it is the good of the society as a whole, however arrived at (and Rousseau agitated a good deal over its determination), to which the individual subordinates his private self-interest. In doing so, he takes on another kind of freedom and independence. In Rousseau's words, "whoever refuses to obey the general will shall be compelled to do so by the whole body. This means nothing less than that he will be forced to be free; for this is the condition which, by giving each citizen to his country, secures him against all personal dependence."[29]

Such forced freedom also entails morality; whereas freedom of an unsocial kind had existed in the state of nature, virtue only arises in the social state. As Rousseau declares, "The passage from the state of nature to the civil state produces a very remarkable change in man, by substituting justice for instinct in his conduct, and giving his actions the morality they had formerly lacked."[30]

Alas, along with virtue comes inequality in civil society; but Rousseau is at great pains to minimize the necessary loss of equality, by keeping the state small, restricting the amount of property allowed any individual, and keeping at bay corrupting cities (the state itself, however, is a city-state) and civilization. To prevent private self-interest from overwhelming the general will, he prohibits partial societies, for example, political parties. He opposes representative government, and insists on unanimity as the best approximation to the general will.

Nothing is to stand between the individual, now become a citizen, and the general will, now embodied in the state. Rousseau scathingly attacked existing Christianity, and especially Roman Catholicism, for seducing the citizen away from the state and dividing his loyalties. In *Emile*, Rousseau had written the long "Profession of Faith of a Savoyard Vicar," which extolled natural religion (the "Profession" caused *Emile* to be banned in Paris and burned in Geneva). He believed, by heart and reason, in God and the immortality of the soul. But these beliefs were to be held by individuals, who were not bound together in religious organizations. Only a civil religion, which sounds exactly like modern nationalism, is permitted, tying the individual directly to the state.

It is clear, even from this précis, that Rousseau was advocating the breaking of all existing connections, in order to forge one rigid chain, leading from the individual to the new citizen, or subject, of the general will. Since the general will was beholden only to itself, and could therefore change, Man was not even bound to a historical past. In this aspect, Rousseau was one of the great "breakers" of the eighteenth century. However, he was also one of the great lamenters over the breaking that he saw occurring around him, which is why I include him, rather, among the lamenters. He who both predicted and advocated a break with the past was nostalgic about Man's natural and bucolic origins, to which he wished to return. As much as Burke, Rousseau detested what he also called the "age of calculators,"[31] though he accepted money as the true bond of society. Extolling individualism, he set his natural "individual" against the corrosive individualism of modern, bourgeois civilization, while selling his Emiles into the chains of the state, and labeling it a new freedom.

Rousseau was a "double" man, even more contradictory in his selfhood and conception of society than was Burke. Between them, they staked out the great philosophical positions—conservatism and revolutionary radicalism—on the subject of connections. Both saw the cosmos as a chain of being. Both saw the rural life as Man's proper state in society. Then they diverged. Where Burke wished to conserve a hierarchically connected society, Rousseau fought to dissolve it in the solvent of social equality, and to establish a new order where the only connection that existed was between each individual and the state. The difference is profound, and the politics of the early ninteenth century revolved around it.

The legacy of Rousseau was as "double" as his personality: on one side, he was the great breaker of existing connections; on the other side, the great bewailer of the new civilization that was breaking the chains. In the end, Rousseau can be seen as yet another Jeremiah, lamenting over his own handiwork, a strange artisan of history.

William Wordsworth

William Wordsworth was not an artisan of history; he did not shape the political and social world as did Burke and Rousseau. Instead, the great poet lyricized over the world that was breaking up around him, and taught his generation the tones in which to lament and to reconnect a public realm in a private mode. In fact, for Romantics such as Wordsworth, there was no division between poetry and philosophy. As Thomas McFarland points out, ". . . to Romantic sensibilities poetry and philosophy tended to be the same activity."[32]

It is not that Wordsworth had isolated himself from the tumultuous events around him. As a young man, on a walking tour on the Continent, he came to France a year after the fall of the Bastille, and fell in love with the Revolution, which he saw as a radical break with the past. He hailed it as the creation of a new world and a new Man, and subsequently took up residence in Orleans in 1792 to observe matters at first hand. Returning to England, he wrote poems in favor of republicanism. The Reign of Terror, however, unsettled his revolutionary belief; and the English declaration of war on France threw him into emotional conflict. Gradually, and episodically, he lost faith in what he now saw as Godwinian illusions and utopian hopes. The history of his mature life is a history of growing conservatism.

Wordsworth now came to lament the breaking power of the Revolution and the convictions behind it (as well as to oppose the followers of Rousseau). In fact, Wordsworth was not so much opposed to the revolutionary break as such, as to its failure. He perceived that the old Adam was still with us. Man's salvation, Wordsworth came to believe, lay elsewhere than in the political world.

Wordsworth's Miltonian task was to offer a new version of *Paradise Lost*. In the process, he would re-establish connections in this world and with this world. The form in which he did this has been called "Natural Supernaturalism" by the critic M. H. Abrams.[33] The phrase itself was Carlyle's, and by it the latter meant the tendency of his time to naturalize the supernatural and to humanize the divine. It is fitting that Wordsworth, intended originally for the clergy, was instrumental in setting forth a secularized version of religion.

This outer history of Wordsworth's concern with public disconnection was matched by an inner history, with the two weaving in and out of one another. In his own childhood, he had early recognized his yearning for solitude and for a direct, unbroken communion with nature. At an early age he lost both his parents, and felt the break of the generations in his own heart. At Cambridge University, he felt different from others—"A feeling that I was not for that hour,/Nor for that place." In London, he felt himself "a transient visitor," shocked by its "perpetual whirl of trivial objects."[34] In France, he fell in love with a young woman, Annette Vallon, who bore him a daughter out of wedlock; events and Wordsworth conspired so that he ended up feeling he had deserted them (as in truth he had). It was a feeling echoed in some of his poems, in stories of family breakup, guilty seduction, and tales of wandering solitaries. The result of all these experiences was that Wordsworth felt an increasing sense of being disconnected as a conscious agent from his own actions, a kind of alienation.

His salvation came partly in the form of his sister Dorothy's love, and the friendship of Coleridge. Through the ties to them, he could be restored to himself. Thus strengthened, he could seek to re-establish a sense of unity and coherence in both the inner and outer worlds, and to construct a vision in which all things cohered.

There was a philosophical background, or justification, for Wordsworth's feelings in the German philosophical school of Jacobi and Schelling (and behind them, Kant), with their insistence on the distinction between "Understanding," or scientific knowledge of particulars, and "Reason," or the intuition of reality as Being, suffusing all particulars. Mediated through Coleridge, it is this philosophy that pulses through Wordsworth's intimation of nature as filled with a mysterious presence, a kind of World-Soul that rolls through all things, and binds them as one.[35]

I have already touched on the experience of political breakdown, and Wordsworth's mixed emotions of hope and disappointment. He was also aware of the other revolution—the industrial—taking place around him. For him, it was personified in the form of the city, and, like Rousseau before him, Wordsworth is one of the great singers of dichotomy, opposing nature to the city, and the solitary individual to the teeming multitudes.

We have already noticed Wordsworth's discontent in London. This feeling is the occasion of some of his greatest lines. It stands in back of his utterance, "The world is too much with us; late and soon,/Getting and spending, we lay waste our powers:/Little we see in Nature that is ours...."[36] It manifests itself in the poem "Composed upon Westminster Bridge," when Wordsworth eulogizes what is, in effect, a dead city, unpeopled:

> This City now doth, like a garment, wear
> The beauty of the morning; silent, bare,
> Ships, towers, domes, theatres, and temples lie
> Open unto the fields, and to the sky;
> All bright and glittering in the smokeless air.

Even when peopled, there is no true life, no sense of connectedness in Wordsworth's view of the city. Thus he tells us how

> ... Above all, one thought
> Baffled my understanding: how men lived
> Even next-door neighbours, as we say, yet still
> Strangers, not knowing each the other's name.[37]

No wonder Wordsworth tells us he was "a discontented sojourner," imprisoned in the "vast city," and eager to escape.

Some of Wordsworth's friends and contemporaries took a different view. Charles Lamb wrote to Wordsworth, "I don't much care if I never see a mountain in my life. I have passed all my days in London, until I have formed as many and intense local attachments as any of you mountaineers can have done with dead Nature." William Hazlitt wrote that Mr. Wordsworth "represents men in cities as so many wild beasts or evil spirits, shut up in cells of ignorance, without natural affections, and barricaded down in sensuality and selfishness," but Hazlitt, a city-dweller and a Republican, denied the truth of this description, and, in fact, declared the city-dweller a better citizen, more independent and community-minded than the solitary inhabitants of the countryside.[38] As we know, however,

Wordsworth's poetic genius tended to carry the day, and, at least symbolically, to throw over the city his dark and despondent coloring.

Wordsworth's most specific recognition of the growing industrialism was in his poem "On the Projected Kendall and Windemere Railway," written late in his life, in 1844. Here he sounds the note so common in other observers, such as Emerson and Thoreau. "Is there no nook of English ground secure/From rash assault?" he asks, and wonders, "how can this blight endure?" In a footnote, Wordsworth eulogized the "attachment" of a yeoman to his small inheritance, demonstrated by his refusal to fell a magnificent tree, even for a very profitable price.[39]

More broadly, Wordsworth opposed the entrepreneurial and capitalistic spirit behind the new industrialization, symbolized by the city and the railroad. He spoke of "how dire a thing/Is worshipped in that idol proudly named/'The Wealth of Nations.' . . ." For him, such wealth was only for "the wealthy Few," who "while they most ambitiously set forth/Extrinsic differences, the outward marks/Whereby society has parted man/From man, neglect the universal heart."[40] From such sentiments, Wordsworth turned and made haste "to regions . . . Whose shades have never felt the encroaching axe,/Or soil endured a transfer in the mart/Of dire rapacity." He has specifically in mind here, of course, the agricultural enclosures, which formed so vital a part of the Industrial Revolution and were changing the visual landscape of England as well as its soul.

Wordsworth is often thought to be anti-science, but that is too simple a judgment. In fact, in the Preface to the "Lyrical Ballads" he placed the Man of Science next to the Poet and declared both to be truth-seekers, and promised that when science made its findings palpable, the poet would lend his divine spirit to aid in the "transfiguration." Yet the emotions of his poetry undercut such statements. His general description of the scientific spirit was as a cold, disconnecting, and destructive one. Typical is his description of science as:

> Viewing all objects unremittingly
> In disconnection dead and spiritless;
> And still dividing, and dividing still,
> Breaks down all grandeur.[41]

Wordsworth saw, correctly, the limits of natural science and its potential narrowness and dehumanizing quality. What he did not emphasize as well—though in his better moments he knew it—is that science is as creative, imaginative, and, indeed, as visionary as poetry. Strange to say, he did capture that vision in his phrase "that other eye," as already noted, and especially in his magnificent lines on the statue of Newton, ". . . with his prism and silent face,/The marble index of a mind for ever/Voyaging through strange seas of thought, alone,"[42] but Wordsworth did not sufficiently recognize what he had caught in his image.

As with science, so with books: Wordsworth saw their positive side—he, himself, had taken nourishment from them—but the steady drumbeat, as with Crusoe and Rousseau, is that books come between the reader and the real world. "Up! up! my friend," Wordsworth tells us, "and quit your books."[43] The irony is that Wordsworth extols poetry, and thus books of poetry, as revealing that real world and bringing us in immediate touch with it. Of course, what he is really saying is that some books are arid and pedantic, and put us out of touch with nature as Wordsworth would like us to know it.

The fact is that Wordsworth could never make up his mind as to whether we possess a "meddling intellect," as he says in "The Tables Turned," or a "discerning intellect," as he describes it in the Preface to "The Excursion." What he did know was that he and his time were threatened by a sense of breakdown, of disconnection, whose manifestations were to be found in the snapping of generational ties, the fragmentation of political bonds, and the attenuation of social attachments, and were fostered by excessive rationalism, cold science, a selfish pursuit of wealth, and an alienating urban environment. From all these he fled.

He took as his mission the task of reconnecting Man to Man, Nature, and God. Poetry was the divine means, for the Poet alone "binds together by passion and knowledge the vast empire of human society, as it is spread over the whole earth, and over all time."[44] The Poet seeks his inspiration by first isolating himself in nature. In solitude, he can cultivate the powers of imagination and memory, and so reconstruct a connected universe. As Irene Tayler so well puts it, describing Wordsworth's poem, "The Cumberland Beggar," "the solitary beggar, roaming from door to door (connecting people to himself and to one another through the act of sharing) is in some ways an early model for Wordsworth's view of himself as a poet, living in solitude yet working to bind his readers into community."[45]

Only "connect/The landscape with the quiet of the sky," Wordsworth exhorts us in "Lines Composed a Few Miles above Tintern Abbey."[46] So, too, he joins land and sky in one arching image, when he begins his great autobiographical and philosophical poem, "The Prelude," with a "gentle breeze" that brings joy "From the green fields, and from yon azure sky";[47] the connection sets him free to wander through a world unified by his poetic imagination. It is this imagination, drawing upon "emotion recollected in tranquility," which relieves him of "the heavy and the weary weight/Of all this unintelligible world." Wordsworth's poetic reconnection serves the same purpose we had seen in Adam Smith: it makes the world again intelligible.

His most powerful invocation of the vision given to him is voiced in the Conclusion to "The Prelude." There, he tells us, he "beheld the emblem of a mind/That feeds upon infinity, that broods/Over the dark abyss." So inspired, he is fit to hold

> . . . converse with the spiritual world,
> And with the generations of mankind
> Spread over time, past, present, and to come,
> Age after age, till Time shall be no more.
> Such minds are truly from the Deity,
> For they are Powers; and hence the highest bliss
> That flesh can know is theirs—the consciousness
> Of Whom they are, habitually infused
> Through every image and through every thought,
> And all affections by communion raised
> From earth to heaven, from human to divine.[48]

Such are the Powers that Wordsworth envisioned as fusing Man, earth, and heaven. He had lost faith in political power as a connecting force—indeed, the French Revolution had shattered the ties that bind Men together—and had learned from the "Genius of Burke," as he tells us, to distrust "all systems built on abstract rights" and to affirm "the vital power of social ties/Endeared by Custom."[49] True, Wordsworth, loyal to his earlier affections, was aware that the Revolution was actually not the result of a false philosophy of popular government and equality, but rather of

> ... a terrific reservoir of guilt
> And ignorance filled up from age to age,
> That could no longer hold its loathsome charge,
> But burst and spread in deluge through the land.

Such awareness, however, did not bring consolation or heal the gap that had been opened up among Men, and between Men and Nature. Wordsworth's own being, and that of society as a whole, had suffered a possibly mortal fracture. It could be healed only by a turning inward, by Men in solitude—Wordsworth is still within the individualist tradition, as much as any thrusting Crusoe-like capitalist, though with a difference. Such Men, coming into touch with their true powers, will reform, not intellectually, but through direct fellow-feeling, Man's sense of wholeness and his coming together into a reborn spiritual community. Such a preachment in poetic form was Wordsworth's way of coming to terms with the trauma of what he perceived to be an almost total breakdown of traditional ties to God, Nature, and other Men.

4

The Lament:
Prophets and Novelists

Thomas Carlyle

In the lamentation over the perceived breakdown in connections occurring in the early nineteenth century, philosophers such as Burke and Rousseau write in impassioned prose, while a poet such as Wordsworth can be seen as writing a prose-like poetry; but whatever the chosen voice, the dominant note is of discontent, alienation, and fragmented existence. I am arguing that it is in their intellectual and artistic work that we see vividly displayed patterns of thinking and feeling that anticipate the problems and concerns of a future "science" of sociology.

With Thomas Carlyle (1795–1881), a generation or so after Wordsworth (1770–1850), we hear a similar song of lament, but the chords struck are in a very different key, and modulate in another direction. This is in large part because Carlyle is responding more directly to the massive transformation in the organizing principle of social enterprise, which he came to call "industrialism," and to a later phase of it, one in which textile factories and iron works had wrought much of their change in both the external landscape of England and the internal consciousness of its inhabitants. If anyone gave shape to the lamentation over the effects on connection occasioned by the Industrial Revolution, it was the dyspeptic Scotsman Carlyle.

Carlyle saw himself as a prophet, not a poet or a philosopher, whose searing glance not only penetrated the past and present but peered far-sightedly into the future. Dismissing on one side the

Wordsworths of this world he wrote his brother John "that for us in these days prophecy (well understood), not poetry, is the thing wanted. How can we *sing* and *paint* when we do not yet *believe* and *see?*"[1] On the other side, Carlyle also waved away the likes of Burke and Rousseau, or those he called "the modern guides of Nations, who . . . go under a great variety of names, Journalists, Political Economists, Politicians, Pamphleteers. . . ." As he put it, "Vain hope to make mankind happy by politics." If poetry was inessential, politics in the form of utilitarian schemes, reform bills, poor laws and other such attempted ameliorations was ineffective and even pernicious. In their place, Carlyle advises turning to "the ancient guides of Nations, Prophets, Priests."

We have already noted two features of his time and ours revealed to us by Carlyle's prophetic eye: the cash nexus, with which I began Chapter 2, and his notion of "Natural Supernaturalism." I also suggested earlier, when discussing Adam Smith's use of Wonder as the impulse underlying the desire for connecting phenomena in a scientific manner, that Carlyle would employ the term for another end. I want now to look a little more closely at these matters.

"Natural Supernaturalism" is Carlyle's revelatory phrase for describing the great transformation which he wished to bring about, in place of the political revolutions of his time. He recognizes as one of the major signs of the times that "there is a deep-lying struggle in the whole fabric of society; a boundless grinding collision of the New with the Old," of which the French Revolution was the most visible emblem.[2] Looking deep into the grinding collision, Carlyle sees that "the truth is, men have lost their belief in the Invisible, and believe, and hope, and work only in the Visible; or, to speak it in other words: this is not a Religious age." Instead, as Carlyle divines in his memorable lines, it is "the Mechanical Age. It is the Age of Machinery, in every outward and inward sense of that word."

Carlyle, a deeply religious unbeliever, accepted the demise of Religion in its traditional garb, and set out to rescue his age from its death-like mechanical nature by prophesying "Natural Supernaturalism." What is this new doctrine? In his journal entry for February 1, 1833, he writes:

That the Supernatural differs not from the Natural is a great Truth, which the last century (especially in France) has been engaged in demonstrating. The Philosophers went far wrong, however, in this, that instead of raising the natural to the supernatural, they strove to sink the supernatural to the natural. The gist of my whole way of thought is to do not the latter but the former.[3]

He was convinced that he ought not to fear that his "great message of the Natural *being* the Supernatural will wholly perish unuttered." In making the natural one with the supernatural, Carlyle saw himself repairing the torn fabric of society and re-establishing "the communion of man with man."

Having announced his theme in 1829, in "Signs of the Times," he proclaims it again loudly in 1833, in *Sartor Resartus*. There, Natural Supernaturalism and "Clothes Philosophy" go together, and are "exactly what all intellectual men are wanting."[4] The one links heaven and earth in a new revelation, and the other gnomically analyzes Custom and Illusions, that is, the fabric or clothes of culture, in order to transcend them and lift Man into a new social communion.[5] It is all very mystical.

Carlyle, however, brought his insight crashing down to earth in his riveting phrase, "cash payment has become the sole nexus." It is the phrase that Carlyle uses to describe the only relationship surviving for Man in the Mechanical Age. In his most despondent moments (in fact, he knew better), Carlyle felt that all connection was gone, that, as he wrote his brother John in 1831, "there is nowhere any tie remaining among men."[6] As he had written to John earlier, in 1830, wryly deploring his own lack of money, "Pity that poor fellows should hang so much on cash! But it is the general lot, and whether it be ten pounds or ten thousand that would relieve us, the case is all the same, and the tie that binds us equally mean."

It is out of this personal insight that Carlyle then went on to develop his metaphor of the "cash nexus," first, as I have noted, in 1839, in *Chartism*, and then even more powerfully in 1843, in *Past and Present*. In the hands of Engels and Marx, it became a piece of social analysis as well as a rallying cry against the capitalists. In either form, it symbolizes dramatically, in a concrete image, the sense of loss that suffused the early-nineteenth-century climate of opinion, and it does so in one terrible simplification.

Natural science, too, seeks simplification. As in Adam Smith's eulogy of Newton, the aim of science is to connect in the fancy the movements and effects already present in reality, and science does this by abstracting and simplifying until, ideally, it arrives at one unifying law. It starts from Wonder, and ends with its surcease. Carlyle will have none of this. Science, for him, does not assuage Wonder; it destroys it, and with it all sense of the divine. Putting his own views into the mouth of his hero, Professor Teufelsdröckh, Carlyle has him say,

> "Wonder . . . is the basis of Worship: the reign of wonder is perennial, indestructible in Man; only at certain stages (as the present), it is, for some short season, a reign in *partibus infidelium.*" That progress of Science, which is to destroy Wonder, and in its stead substitute Mensuration and Numeration, finds small favour with Teufelsdröckh, much as he otherwise venerates these two latter processes.

Continuing, Carlyle says,

> The man who cannot wonder, who does not habitually wonder (and worship), were he the President of innumerable Royal Societies, and carried the whole *Mécanique Celeste* and *Hegel's Philosophy*, and the epitome of all Laboratories and Observatories with their results in his single head—is but a Pair of Spectacles behind which there is no Eye.[7]

As Tony Tanner points out in his book, *The Reign of Wonder*, Carlyle has turned his wondering eye into a "definite mode of philosophic understanding to be set up against analysis. . . . For the universe has now changed from being the fine intricate mechanism of a divine watchmaker and become 'one vast Symbol of God.'"[8] In Carlyle's prophetic vision, Smith's "invisible chains" and "invisible hand" have become mere "Mensuration and Numeration" and "cash nexus." Both Carlyle and Smith are engaged in simplification, but to very different purposes. In *Past and Present*, Carlyle alludes to his fellow Scotsman's *Wealth of Nations* only to point out that while England may be full of wealth, its people are in poverty. Earlier, Carlyle admits, "in the time of Adam Smith, Laissez-faire was a reasonable cry";[9] it is so no longer. England now lies under enchantment, Carlyle goes on, in which wealth turns into its opposite; what we find is not a beneficent "invisible hand" leading a mythical economic Man to affluence, but real Men possessed by an "accursed invisible Nightmare."

Behind the "nightmare" stood the reality of an industrializing

society. Carlyle, in fact, is the person who coined the term "Industrialism" to describe the new society spinning and forging itself
around him in early-nineteenth-century England.[10] Unlike Wordsworth, who had some but only a little good to say of the new system, Carlyle was extremely ambivalent. He was also more knowledgeable; he had studied and taught mathematics, and for a while
he had contemplated being a civil engineer. He was aware of the
attractions as well as repulsions of industrial society. Carlyle, who
defined Man as a "tool-using animal" (thus echoing Benjamin
Franklin's earlier "tool-making animal" image), could cry out to his
contemporaries,

> . . . cannot the dullest hear Steam-engines clanking around him? Has
> he not seen the Scottish Brassmith's IDEA (and this but a mechanical
> one) travelling on fire-wings round the Cape, and across two
> Oceans; and stronger than any other Enchanter's Familiar, on all
> hands unweariedly fetching and carrying: at home, not only weav-
> ing Cloth; but rapidly enough overturning the whole old system of
> Society.[11]

And later, in *Past and Present*, his most nostalgic lament for a society
now past, Carlyle could still lyricize about how

> Certain Times do crystallise themselves in a magnificent manner;
> and others, perhaps, are like to do it in rather a shabby one!—But
> Richard Arkwright too will have his Monument, a thousand years
> hence: all Lancashire and Yorkshire, and how many other shires and
> countries, with their machineries and industries, for his monument!
> A true pyramid or "flame-mountain," flaming with steam fires and
> useful labour over wide continents, usefully towards the Stars, to a
> certain height;—how much grander than your foolish Cheops Pyr-
> amids or Sakhara clay ones! Let us withal be hopeful, be content, or
> patient.[12]

He could even recognize that industrial society was a new connecting force; in a powerful image, Carlyle speaks of how the stagecoach—he could have said the railroad engine—"came on made
highways, from far cities towards far cities; weaving them like a
monstrous shuttle into closer and closer union."
Yet this is the same Carlyle whom we have seen lamenting the
fall of his society into a mechanical state, where Man has become

mechanical "in head and heart as well as hand." It is the same Carlyle whose images of the universe bespeak a sense of terror and helplessness being visited on Man by the new powers: "To me," Carlyle groans, "the Universe was all void of Life, of Purpose, of Volition, even of Hostility: it was one huge, dead, immeasurable Steam-engine, rolling on, in its dead indifference, to grind me limb from limb. O, the vast, gloomy, solitary Golgotha, and Mill of Death!"[13]

The same tortured ambivalence manifests itself in Carlyle's feelings about the city. Of a rural, agricultural background, Carlyle was drawn in spite of himself, by ambition, to the city. As he wrote to his brother John in 1821, "Edinburgh, with all its drawbacks, is the only scene for me. In the country *I am like an alien*, a stranger and pilgrim from a far-distant land"[14] (emphasis mine). This was a most extraordinary admission, one that Carlyle was quick to reverse. It was the city, he came to insist, which was alienating. Speaking of London, he talks typically of "the din of this monstrous city"; of Edinburgh, in similar vein, he speaks of "the uproars and putrescences (material and spiritual) of the reeky town." Nevertheless, Carlyle was attracted to these "infernal" regions, as when describing Birmingham—this "Tubal Cain"—with its "Torrents of thick smoke, with ever and anon a burst of dingy flame . . . issuing from a thousand funnels . . . The clank of innumerable steam-engines, the rumblings of cars and vans . . . The rolling mills . . . their iron works where 150,000 men are smelting the metal." At the end, however, he cannot help but conclude that "the whole is not without its attractions, as well as repulsions, of which, when we meet, I will *preach* to you at large" (emphasis mine).

The imagery is religious; the feelings that of a divided soul. Carlyle's "Natural Supernaturalism" was not to be purchased by any easy form of exchange, but to be suffered for by one who was a prophet, rather than a profiteer. Carlyle's spiritual wrestling between the two worlds of the natural and the supernatural is perhaps best exemplified in *Past and Present*. Here he comes to grips with the old monastic world, unified by a shared religious belief, and the new industrial world, held together only by the cash nexus. The first is epitomized by the Abbey of St. Edmundsbury, and exemplified in the Abbot Samson; the second, by Manchester, and in the persons of Watts, Arkwrights, and Brindleys, engineers instead of saints.

Religion in the middle ages, Carlyle tells us, "is not yet a horrible restless doubt."[15] Nevertheless, Carlyle realizes that, in the modern age, in spite of all our lamentations, doubt cannot be laid to rest. We cannot return to an idyllic, that is, sentimental or rural, past, but must go forward to an uncertain future. It is a future of growing industrialism. What is needed, therefore, is a new religion, a bringing of the invisible into the visible world. And the gospel whose preaching will accomplish this prophetic task is the Gospel of Work. Not love, as such, but work will bring Men into communion again. It is a very Calvinist message, in new clothes.

Even before the Reformation, according to Carlyle, the good Abbot Samson, his hero of *Past and Present*, had perceived this truth. Though the idea of work was still wrapped for him in spiritual belief, he also saw that "it is *in* the world that a man, devout or other, has his life to lead, his work waiting to be done."[16] The full realization of Abbot Samson's perception, however, had to await the nineteenth century and the coming of what Carlyle calls "The Modern Worker." Carlyle the prophet saw what Wordsworth the poet could only deplore, that Man's true connection to other Men and even the invisible is through the power of work, and not only through the power of imagination. "The spoken Word, the written Poem," Carlyle admits, "is said to be an epitome of the man." "How much more," he then exclaims, "the done work." It is Man's industrial deeds that sing their own song. They do not need some clean-handed poet to give them immortality. "Thy Epic," Carlyle lyricizes in his fervent prose, "unsung in words, is written in huge characters on the face of this Planet,—sea-moles, cotton-trades, railways, fleets and cities, Indian Empires, Americas, New Hollands; legible throughout the Solar System!"

If work is noble—"All work, even cotton-spinning is noble"[17] (do we not hear echoes of the French and Industrial revolutions, rejected by Burke?)—and its products are legible and laudable, what has gone wrong? Carlyle's answer is that Man has lost sight of work's purpose and the worker's true ties to his followers, and thus created a hell instead of a heaven on earth. Striking out savagely at the sins of capitalism—its egoism, its false laws of economics, its cruel commercial crises, its lack of compassion—Carlyle is able to gather all his criticisms up into the striking image of the cash nexus. "Behold!" he thunders forth, "Supply-and-demand is not the one Law of Nature; Cash-payment is not the sole nexus of man with man,—how far from it! Deep, far deeper than Supply-and-demand, are Laws, Obligations sacred as Man's Life itself: these also, if you will continue to do work, you shall now learn and obey."

In *Chartism*, Carlyle had already seen that the cash nexus was not enough to hold a society together. "What constitutes the well-being of a man?" he asks. "Many things," he answers, "of which the wages he gets, and the bread he buys with them, are but one preliminary item."[18] Of course, a better sharing of wages is necessary; but it is not enough. A new bond between Men must be wrought—"man is not independent of his brother," Carlyle had written in his diary in 1829—a bond of understanding worked out in the deed, which would then transcend the material connection.

Carlyle's notion of the cash nexus, and his denunciation of the ills of capitalism, found ready welcome in both Engels and Marx. They, too, embraced his positive acceptance of the world of work and its industrial achievements. In their own Hegelian mode, they also moved toward a Natural Supernaturalism, wherein the gods come down to earth. Where they parted company with Carlyle was in the proposed remedy. Where they advocated and worked for revolution, Carlyle preached revelation. This is the great divide in the nineteenth century's response to the travails of industrialism in its capitalist form. Against the call for class warfare, Carlyle issued his appeal for class understanding:

> How inexpressibly useful were true insight into [the question of the working classes]; a genuine understanding by the upper classes of society what it is that the under classes intrinsically mean; a clear interpretation of the thought which at heart torments these wild inarticulate souls, struggling there, with inarticulate uproar, like dumb creatures in pain, unable to speak what is in them! Something they do mean; some true thing withal, in the centre of their confused hearts,—for they are hearts created by Heaven too: to the Heaven it is clear what thing; to us not clear. Would that it were! Perfect clearness on it were equivalent to remedy of it. For, as is well said, all battle is misunderstanding; did the parties know one another, the battle would cease. No man at bottom means injustice; it is always for some obscure distorted image of a right that he contends.[19]

In the end, then, Carlyle, the prophet, joins hands with Wordsworth, the poet. Both are saying that we must peer into the hearts of common Men, and join with them through fellow feeling. For

Wordsworth, it is the Cumberland Beggar who shows us the way;
for Carlyle, "He were an Oedipus . . . who could resolve us fully!"[20]
We have no eyes to see, he is saying, blinded as we are by our egoistic, worldly strivings; we must turn to the prophetic inward eye to
see the real world around us. Then, and then only, can we heal our
divided souls, and reunite Man with Man and the visible with the
invisible world.

A Defensive Distance

Carlyle the prophet, like Wordsworth the poet, before him, not only
symbolized and expressed the lamentation over a felt disconnect-
edness that seemed to envelope the first half of the nineteenth century, but also proclaimed a healing message. It was a message
preaching, among other things, the need for sympathetic understanding. As Russell Noyes notes in an interesting little book,
Wordsworth, "By using all the devices of language, meter, and dramatic modes available to him as a poet . . . hoped to convey passion
to readers not accustomed to sympathize with men in the lower levels of society whose manner and language are different from their
own."[21]

The genres Carlyle resorted to were varied: essays such as "Signs
of the Times," historical works such as *The French Revolution*, and
an unusual form of the novel in autobiographical form, *Sartor Resartus* (in 1827, Carlyle had actually tried his hand at an abortive novel,
Wooton Reinfred).[22] Although Carlyle cannot be said to have made
his mark as a novelist, yet he influenced, explicitly or implicitly,
almost all the English novelists after him, as they attempted to portray the divided society of industrial Britain, and, through a sympathetic recreation, to heal the gap between the classes.

The world they faced, an industrializing world, was one in which
extremes of wealth and poverty existed separately from one another,
disconnected in consciousness. As the novelists saw it, wealth and
poverty there had always been; but the poor man's hovel might be
found close by the noble's castle, and the nobleman was well aware
of his tenant's existence, and even knew his name. Those bonds
might be feudal, but they were bonds. In the new industrial cities
such as Manchester, the rich and poor were sharply separated not
only in consciousness but in geography: within the limits of a single

town, the two might coexist as if they were on different planets. As Engels pointed out, the city was *as if* planned (though it had in fact developed haphazardly) so as to insure that the rich would never have to *see* the poor, living among hidden cesspools, behind walls, in a distinct part of the city.

We can understand that a certain distancing was a not unexpected response to appalling conditions. The concepts of "numbing" and "blocking," which we mentioned earlier, are all too familiar to us today; we simply deny feelings that are unacceptable to us— unusual danger, such as a military threat, or painful impressions, such as dire poverty among our fellowmen. Such defenses often make us into "double" Men, where one part of our self commits evil, but is detached from our other self, which remains pure and guilt-free. Some of the nineteenth century's absorption with the "doppelgänger" would seem to flow from this deployment of self: for example, the employer, sustained by classical economics, sees himself as pursuing his "duty," which is then detached from its awful consequences by blocking them from awareness.

One way of indirectly breaking through such a defense was to anthropologize reality. One could look at the desperate poor as if they were an exotic tribe, or inhabitants of a foreign land. W. Cooke Taylor captured this perspective when he lamented that "Ardwick knows less about Ancoats than it does about China, and feels more interested in the conditions of New Zealand than of Little Ireland."[23] Similarly, Disraeli wrote of his heroine, Sybil, penetrating into unknown territory when she went into the poor quarter of London: "The houses, the population, the costume, the manner, the language, through which they whirled their way, were of a different state and nation to those with which the dwellers in the dainty quarters of this city are acquainted."[24] The imagery was of "explorations" of a different "nation," of a "savage" population, and of a separate "breed" of men (and women).

The goal of the lamenters was, through the power of sympathy, to connect the broken fragments of mankind within their own country, making native again—and the word native must be taken here in the two senses of near and far (meaning both "at home," or native to one, as well as "foreign," in the sense of "primitives")—what had been foreign. Thus, the novelists who abandoned the "silver fork" tradition, which was devoted to the chronicling of high society, embraced a new realism, in which they sought to bring to the attention of the middle and upper classes the real world of poor people and poverty surrounding them, and also to make them acknowledge the breakdown of connection in both sensibility and society.[25]

Some Novelists

As my prime examples, I shall take Elizabeth Gaskell (1810–65), Benjamin Disraeli (1804–81), and George Eliot (1819–80) as representative of many others. Another "industrial novelist," Charles Kingsley, whom I could have added to the list, apologized for the sordidness of some of his descriptions by telling his readers that they "ought to know what the men are like to whose labour, ay, lifeblood, they owe their luxuries."[26] Kingsley has a more pronounced "Chartist" tone to his novel, *Alton Locke,* but it is in the same genre as those of Gaskell, Disraeli, and Eliot in trying to understand the "have-nots," their lives and discontents, in a cash-nexus society, and to preach sympathy as the solution. (Carlyle's influence on Kingsley, incidentally, is directly displayed throughout the novel, with countless invocations of the prophet's name.)

In fact, with all its drawbacks and class-biased assumptions, the effort to arouse sympathetic understanding with regard to a social problem—working-class misery—by means of a novel genre rather than, say, Parliamentary Reports or statistics, is well grounded in human psychology. One portrait of a destitute worker, John Barton, the hero *manqué* of Gaskell's novel *Mary Barton* makes the subject come alive in its individualization, far more than any "mass" presentation (as any reader of a newspaper knows—hence "human interest" stories). Individualization, of course, is a (the?) prime way in which the novel—that product of bourgeois individualism—works.[27]

Elizabeth Gaskell

In any event, the two novels of Gaskell that we will consider from this perspective are *Mary Barton* and *North and South.* Elizabeth Gaskell was the wife of a Unitarian minister in Manchester, and experienced at first hand the disassociation of which she wrote. In *Mary Barton,* published in 1848, the same year as Marx's *Communist Man-*

ifesto, she focused on "the most deplorable and enduring evil that arose. . . . this feeling of alienation between the different classes of society."[28] At about the time she was writing, the workers, cut off as they were from the rest of society, formed their own combinations, that is, trade unions, even though the government pronounced many of their activities illegal. Feeling that the political authorities knew not of their misery, the workers, according to Gaskell, also turned to Chartism to make known their plight, only to be accused of rebellion. The result, predictably, was the setting of class against class.

Gaskell's appeal is for understanding on both sides, but in *Mary Barton*, mostly on the part of the upper middle class for the lower. Thus, she enters upon scenes of lower-class life, seeking to make her reader feel and see the common humanness of it all, to recognize and thus to sympathize with what are fellow humans, even of a different station in life. What she cannot abide is the factory owner who says, "I don't pretend to know the names of the men I employ; that I leave to the overlooker."[29] Such reduction of human relations to the cash nexus, in Gaskell's view, can lead only to disaffection and the breakdown of society.

Gaskell, however, is not a revolutionary. As a realist, for so she sees herself, she accepts the division of society, the division of labor and rewards, as a necessary feature of social existence.[30] It is the unnecessary emotional division of the different classes that she decries. To heal this division, she preaches a message of enlightened religion, not revolution. Thus, she concludes *Mary Barton* with the hope:

> that the truth might be recognized that the interests of one were the interests of all; and as such, required the consideration and deliberation of all; that hence it was most desirable to have educated workers, capable of judging, not mere machines of ignorant men; and to have them bound to their employers by the ties of respect and affection, not by mere money bargains alone; in short, to acknowledge the Spirit of Christ as the regulating law between both parties.[31]

By the time of *North and South*, in 1855, Gaskell had become as much concerned with explaining the industrial entrepreneurs to the workers and to the aristocrats as vice versa. The novel is a dialogue, as its title suggests, between the world of Manchester and that of Oxbridge. Mr. Thornton, the manufacturer, is set off against Mr.

Hale, who is taken to represent "the old worn grooves of what you call more aristocratic society down in the South."[32] It is the cash nexus versus the feudal connection. In between is Mr. Hale's daughter, Margaret.

In fact, the contention is friendly, as both men grope to understand the other, and Margaret to unite her feelings toward her potential lover and her father. Outside their debate, however, stand the workers, and it is Margaret who seeks to understand their human needs and to bring them to the attention of both the entrepreneur and the aristocrat (Mr. Hale, though not one, symbolizes the aristocratic culture). Such needs are real, and must be attended to, she tells them. But the laborers, on the other hand, are misled if they think their salvation is in militant unionism. Such militancy merely substitutes for the "tyranny of the masters" a tyranny of the Union. For Gaskell, it is a false reconnection. As her father, reflecting Margaret's views, expostulates with one of the workers, "Oh! your Union in itself would be beautiful, glorious,—it would be Christianity itself—if it were but for an end which affected the good of all, instead of that merely of one class as opposed to another."[33]

On another side, debating Thornton, Margaret and her father encounter the resort to Individualism rather than Unionism. Out of the depths of his own self-pride, Thornton truly believes that

> the masters would be trenching on the independence of their hands, in a way that I, for one, should not feel justified in doing, if we interfered too much with the life they lead out of the mills. Because they labour ten hours a-day for us, I do not see that we have any right to impose leading-strings upon them for the rest of their time. I value my own independence so highly that I can fancy no degradation greater than that of having another man perpetually directing and advising and lecturing me, or even planning too closely in any way about my actions.[34]

The answer given to him is in the form of a question: has he not been driven to a cold and lofty assertion of independence "because there has been none of the equality of friendship between the adviser and advised classes? Because every man has had to stand in an unchristian and isolated position, apart from and jealous of his brother-man: constantly afraid of his rights being trenched upon?" As in her earlier novel, *Mary Barton*, Gaskell brings all the parties together again through the healing message of Christian love. At the end of *North and South*, Thornton is brought to say that "My only wish is to have the opportunity of cultivating some intercourse with the hands beyond the mere 'cash nexus.'" Challenged as to how this can be done, he responds,

> I have arrived at the conviction that mere institutions, however wise, and however much thought may have been required to organize and arrange them, cannot attach class to class as they should be attached, unless the working out of such institutions bring the individuals of the different classes into actual personal contact.

Central to Gaskell's awareness is the reality of an existing "cash nexus" as the only tie holding industrial society together. For Gaskell, it is not enough. Without desiring to do away with the system it represents, she wishes to ameliorate the existing conditions. By means of her novels, she seeks to draw people together, masters and workers alike, by depicting the reality of their lives, hitherto hidden from one another. Knowing will bring sympathy. New bonds, of love, will bring a reborn communion of souls, if not of material circumstances. The novel, in Gaskell's hands, seeks to take on a power of reuniting society that elsewhere we have seen claimed for poetry and prophesy, as well as for politics and philosophy.

Benjamin Disraeli

With Benjamin Disraeli, we have the novel used directly for political purposes, by a writer who wished also to be a statesman, and ultimately succeeded in becoming Prime Minister of England. Disraeli was a strange being, a dandy who became the darling of the conservative establishment, a Christianized Jew who inadvertently helped bring into being the dividing force of racism (though it could also unify), and a snob who from his elevated position sympathized with the lower orders, reaching across the middle classes (while at the same time characterizing Manchester as a "new Athens"), to embrace the workers in a new alliance.

I first take as my text one of his novels, *Sybil* (1845). Its subtitle is "The Two Nations." When Egremont, the younger brother of an English earl, comments that "our Queen reigns over the greatest nation that ever existed," the stranger to whom he is speaking asks, "Which nation? for she reigns over two." Continuing, the stranger says,

> "Two nations; between whom there is no intercourse and no sympathy; who are as ignorant of each other's habits, thoughts, and feelings, as if they were dwellers in different zones, or inhabitants of different planets; who are formed by a different breeding, are fed by a different food, are ordered by different manners, and are not governed by the same laws."
> "You speak of—" said Egremont, hesitatingly.
> "THE RICH AND THE POOR."[35]

Disraeli, indeed, is not particularly consistent in his account of the two nations: at one point we are told that "Atween the poor man and the gentleman there never was no connection, and that's the wital mischief of this country"; at another that "we are divided between the conquerors and the conquered", that is, the Normans and the Anglo-Saxons; and at yet another point that it is "the interests of Capital and Labour" that are not "identical."[36] It doesn't matter; a novel, unlike a political tract, aims not at consistency but at lifelike depiction of different views. (In fact, Disraeli's knowledge of the actual working class, like that of Marx, was derived more from Parliamentary blue books than from personal experience.) What united all these viewpoints, however, was the sense that England was divided into fragments that no longer knew one another.

Disraeli's real anathema was the Whig capitalists, who ruled only by virtue of the cash nexus. In opposition, Disraeli harkened back to noblesse oblige, and exhorted a new aristocracy, Young England as he called it, to spring forward and grasp a modern form of stewardship. Although offering few details, Disraeli made clear that at a minimum what was needed, as he has one of his characters state, was a "correct conception of the relations which should subsist between the employer and the employed. He felt that between them there should be other ties than the payment and the receipt of wages." What is lacking in England, as the stranger tells us, "is the principle of association"; that is "the want of the age."[37]

What, in fact, *is* this principle of association? Disraeli is mysterious. At one point, he has one of his characters announce that

> It is not individual influence that can renovate society; it is some new principle that must reconstruct it. You lament the expiring idea of

Home. It would not be expiring, if it were worth retaining. The domestic principle has fulfilled its purpose. The irresistible law of progress demands that another should be developed. It will come; you may advance or retard, but you cannot prevent it. It will work out like the development of organic nature. In the present state of civilization, and with the scientific means of happiness at our command, the notion of home should be obsolete. Home is a barbarous idea; the method of a rude age; home is isolation; therefore antisocial. What we want is Community.[38]

In *Sybil*, Disraeli mainly hews to a call for aristocratic renewal, whereby an elite will link up with the rest of the nation in a new form of community or association. All that is needed is a new leader. And Disraeli calls forthrightly for a leader who, "to be successful, should embody in his system the necessities of his followers, express what every one feels, but no one has had the ability or the courage to pronounce."[39] It is clear that Disraeli has someone in mind: himself. The rest of his life was an effort to become such a leader, embodying the felt needs of his followers. The novel has become a form of politics, which recognizes the sense of division in society and seeks to end it by bringing Men together again into one nation, which will, in fact, be a single community based on the deepest unconscious longings for unity.

One unexpected form taken by that unconscious longing turns out to be racism. Disraeli speaks darkly, in *Sybil* and other works, of a new form of community, one bound together by an aristocratic race. His new aristocracy, however, is based on "quality," not heredity of the usual sort; paradoxically, that quality, embodied in what Disraeli sees as the "animal man" or possessor of a vital energy, is a racial one (which, of course, though he does not acknowledge this, is itself hereditary). In his clouded, if not confused, vision, Disraeli foresees rule by a chosen race, working through a kind of secret society, or what others might call an international conspiracy.[40] In fact, as Hannah Arendt has commented, Disraeli "almost automatically produced the entire set of theories about Jewish influence and organization that we usually find in the more vicious forms of antisemitism."[41]

We get the flavor of Disraeli's fantasies in *Coningsby* (1844), where he has Sidonia, a charismatic figure, speak of how "the Jewish mind exercises a vast influence on the affairs of Europe. I speak not of their laws, which you still obey; of their literature, with which your minds are saturated; but of the living Hebrew intellect. You never observe a great intellectual movement in Europe in which the Jews do not greatly participate. The first Jesuits were Jews; that mysterious Russian diplomacy which so alarms Western Europe is organised and principally carried on by Jews; that mighty revolution which is at this moment preparing in Germany, and which will be, in fact, a second and greater Reformation, and of which so little is as yet known in England, is entirely developing under the auspices of Jews. . . ."[42]

In writing in this manner, Disraeli hardly had in mind the way in which his personal fantasies could be cited or twisted by others into evidence of a "Jewish Conspiracy." He was calling, rather, for the construction, or reconstruction, of community on the basis of a new class of men, who were connected not by the cash nexus but by the bonds of elite race. Put more dramatically, to the revolutionary ideology of Equality he was opposing his ideology of Racism, or rule by an aristocracy of "blood" (paradoxically in the shape of inherited "brains").

In the next century, the effort to solve the problem of connection through a final solution, by appeal to the ties of blood, took monstrous form in the doctrines and actions of Nazism. Disraeli, of course, not only would have been a victim of Hitler's Germany but would have seen in it only a perverted version of his vision, and a rule by a rabble rather than by his true aristocracy. Thus, we must avoid anachronism, and realize that he was dealing with mid-nineteenth-century England and its problems of economic and social dislocation; his solution was racist only in these particular terms, as a reaction to the increasing dominance of the cash nexus. Still, it must be said that Disraeli's intuition did run ahead of his intention. And his leader expressing "what everyone feels" took on a sinister shape in the twentieth century, not foreseen by the novelist-politician.[43]

George Eliot

In general, our lamenters, as well as the sociologists with whom we shall soon deal, played down or neglected race as a basis for community; by and large the anxiety about the breakdown of connection and the yearning for community, leading as it did to a variety of hopes and proposed solutions, focused not on racism, though as we shall see further this did play a supporting role, but on the cash nexus. It is in this latter context that we shall begin to look at George Eliot, and first at her novel *Felix Holt* (1866).

Eliot was, in fact, influenced by Disraeli—and this in spite of her scoffing at his "idyllic masquerading" as to the relations of aristocrats and common people. Thus, she based Holt's "Address to Working Men" on one of Disraeli's speeches, and appears to have wanted one of her other novels, *Daniel Deronda*, to be noticed by him. Nevertheless, she reserved her most outspoken approval for Wordsworth and Carlyle. In the opening pages of *Felix Holt*, for example, she referred to Wordsworth's Wanderer in his poem "The Excursion." In an earlier writing, she confessed that she had discovered her "own feelings expressed" in Wordsworth's poetry "just as" she "could like them."[44]

George Eliot had been born Mary Anne Evans, in a family of conservative political inclinations and conventional religion; later, she was to go through a period of evangelical piety.[45] Her own life came to mirror the breaks occurring in society; like so many in her generation, she had to emancipate herself from her family and her early convictions, yet hold on to the past and associate it in some sort of unity with the present. As with Wordsworth, it was memory that provided the power of unification and the healing balm for the sense of disharmony.[46]

In addition to Wordsworth, Eliot drew sustenance from the ideas of Auguste Comte, the French positivist, and from the so-called higher critics in Germany. Indeed, her translation of David Friedrich Strauss's *Life of Jesus* signaled her own emancipation from traditional religious beliefs, influencing many of her contemporaries at the same time, as well as embodying her effort at a new linking of Man and God, through reason.

From these and other sources, she drew her awareness that society was a "tangled web," a matter of complex relations, which could come apart easily.[47] In *Felix Holt* she remarks that "society stands before us like that wonderful piece of life, the human body, with all its various parts depending on one another, and with a terrible liability to get wrong because of that delicate dependence."[48]

It is in this novel that Eliot most fully and consciously examines the organic relations of society and the threat posed to them by a mechanical and materialist conception of society's nature. Setting her book in the past, at the time of the first Reform Bill in 1832, she wishes to explore her own time, for she is writing just before the passage of the second parliamentary reform act in 1867 (where Disraeli had dished the Whigs by appealing directly to the common workers). In doing so, she is trying to associate, through memory, the past and present.

Her hero is Felix Holt, a radical, who sees clearly not only the callousness of capitalist relations but the falseness both of aristocratic connections (the subplot deals with this aspect of society) and the dangers of simplistic radical claims of association. As she has Holt say in an "Address to Working Men," written as an appendix, "No society ever stood long in the world without getting to be composed of different classes . . . it is all pretence to say that there is no such thing as Class Interest."[49]

Yet the clear recognition of society's divisions does not bring with it a call for their abolition. Like Gaskell, Eliot accepts what she believes to be a necessary social reality. She was very aware of the delicate nature of social connection and remarked, "One fears to pull the wrong thread, in the tangled scheme of things."[50] So, too, she feared that the people might become a mob; and her novel depicts exactly this happening during an election campaign. Eliot shared the bourgeois fear of the mass as potentially violent and drunken.[51] The need was for the right sort of leaders who, conscious of ordinary people's legitimate needs, would nevertheless prevent them from falling into excess. The contrast with Disraeli's leader is clear, as Holt tells the laborers that what they need is "a demagogue of a new sort; an honest one, if possible, who will tell the people they are blind and foolish, and neither flatter them nor fatten on them."[52]

What, more specifically, will such an honest demagogue tell the people? The answer is: patience and trust in an awakened sense of sympathy on the part of the upper classes. It is the same answer as we have seen given by Wordsworth, Carlyle, Gaskell, and Disraeli, although with many and important variations. Eliot, too, recognizes the reducing power of the cash nexus and the cold comfort of its apologists:

> The tendency created by the splendid conquests of modern generalisation to believe that all social questions are merged in economical science, and that the relations of men to their neighbours may be settled by algebraic equations . . . none of these . . . mistakes can co-exist with a real knowledge of the People.[53]

As she remarks in her greatest novel, *Middlemarch*, "There is no general doctrine which is not capable of eating out our morality if unchecked by the deep-seated habit of direct fellow-feeling with individual fellow-men." Or again, as she writes in a letter to a friend, "Agreement between intellects seems unattainable, and we turn to the truth of feeling as the only universal bond of union."

In *Daniel Deronda* (1876), she pursues this theme, in terms of a vastly more complex analysis. This book, in fact, has perplexed its critics since its appearance, for it seems to encompass two novels instead of one in its eight-hundred-plus pages. The first novel, so to speak, is the story of Gwendolin Harlech, an imperious, self-willed and self-absorbed creature. We seem at first to be in the presence of a Jane Austen character, who is faced with the possibility, if not need, of rising in society, especially by a "good" marriage. There is constant concern with rank—and the name of the man Gwendolin marries (to her great unhappiness, for he is a cold, indeed sadistic, husband), Grandcourt, is redolent of this absorption. There is also a nice symbolic touch to Gwendolin's "aiming" at a higher social prominence in her fine performance at the archery club, "the most select thing anywhere," and the achievement of an invitation to dine with the Arrowpoints, a family of high social rank.[54]

On a more subtle level, Gwendolin, I believe, is intended to symbolize the egoistic, self-interested character of a cash-nexus society. Daniel Deronda first meets her at a gambling casino, which he presents to us as a microcosm of the larger society when he says, " . . . there is something revolting to me in raking a heap of money together . . . when others are feeling the loss of it. . . . There are enough inevitable turns of fortune which force us to see that our gain is another's loss:—that is one of the ugly aspects of life." Eliot's own concern with the industrial transformation of life is itself manifested in her characteristic authorial remark about the countryside looking much as it did "in the days of our forefathers—where peace and permanence seemed to find a home away from the busy change that sent the railway train flying in the distance."[55]

These quotations merely give us hints of Eliot's larger purpose. In *Daniel Deronda*, Eliot's aim is to have us share in Gwendolin's moral growth, as, under Daniel's tutelage, she comes to recognize her problem as a want of sympathy, cutting her off from others. "Try to care about something in this vast world," Daniel admonishes her, "besides the gratification of small selfish desires. Try to care for what is best in thought and action—something that is good apart from the accidents of your own lot."[56] Eliot's aim, then, is larger than Jane Austen's, for the latter seems concerned with the formation of an individual heroine and not the reformation of society. Suzanne Graver captures what I have in mind when she writes, "As an artist, George Eliot attempted to enlarge the experience of her readers and to alter their perceptions, in part by creating characters who experienced such changes as those she would ideally have her readers undergo. . . ."[57]

Eliot, like Gaskell and Disraeli before her, is using in this part of her book the method of sympathetic understanding, aroused by a particular form of experiencing through the novel, to remedy the ills of individual and society alike. But in *Daniel Deronda* she is aware that sympathy may not be enough; that, in fact, it may inhibit indignation leading to action. She has Daniel suspect that "A too reflective and diffusive sympathy was in danger of paralysing in him that indignation against wrong and that selectness of fellowship which are the conditions of moral force. . . ."[58]

The danger is that the "observer" can become a mere spectator, disinterested as well as impartial. Thus, as a spectator, Deronda risks losing the ability to be an actor as well. Something else, then, besides sympathy is needed to heal society's wounds and its pervasive sense of egoism and lack of community.

That something else turns out to be religious bonding in a new form: racism, or racialism. This is the message of the second novel, so to speak, to be found in *Daniel Deronda*. Daniel connects the two parts when he preaches to Gwendolin that "The refuge you are needing from personal trouble is the higher, the religious life, which holds an enthusiasm for something more than our own appetites and vanities."[59] Here we are still in the presence of individual sympathy, as Gwendolin pursues it in the direction of her personal moral growth. But Daniel's *Bildungsroman* is different. He finds himself, his identity, by discovering that he is a Jew, and fusing himself with his people and their "national" aspirations.

In the "first" novel, before being taken in hand by Daniel, Gwendolin, in her early, self-indulgent phase, gives voice to an unthinking anti-Semitism when, having lost at gambling, she complains that "these Jew dealers are so unscrupulous in taking advantage of

Christians unfortunate at play." In this, she mirrors her author, for Eliot as a young woman had also shared in the prevailing anti-Semitism of her time ("almost all their history is utterly revolting. . . . Everything *specifically* Jewish is of a low grade," she had remarked). Eliot's "conversion" came slowly, partly from her own further reading of Jewish texts and especially from a friendship with a renowned Talmudic scholar, Emmanuel Deutsch, who shared with her his dream of a Jewish national home in Palestine.[60]

Whatever its source, Eliot found in Zionism, before its actual establishment, an inspired answer to the problem of how to reconnect society and reconstitute community. The message is preached in the "second novel" by Mordecai, a scholarly antithesis of the stereotypic cash-nexus Jew, whose body, consumed by tuberculosis, is burning away, but leaving a spirit that is pure and visionary. He cries out, "Revive the organic centre: let the unity of Israel which has made the growth and form of its religion be an outward reality. Looking towards a land and a polity, our dispersed people in all the ends of the earth may share the dignity of a national life which has a voice among the peoples of the East and the West—which will plant the wisdom and skill of our race so that it may be, as of old, a medium of transmission and understanding." He even defends his vision as rational when he pleads with his fellows to "see more and more of the hidden bonds that bind and consecrate change as a dependent growth—yea, consecrate it with kinship: the past becomes my parent. . . ." Daniel's problem, earlier, had been that he was unable to make himself "an organic part of social life, instead of roaming in it like a yearning disembodied spirit, stirred with a vague social passion, but without fixed local habitation to render fellowship real." Now ties of blood and history—"the sense of brotherhood with his own race"—become his personal solution to the sense of rootlessness and anomie.[61]

As with Gwendolin, however, Eliot intends more than an individual solution with Daniel. His rediscovered Jewishness is to serve as an inspiration for society in general. Jews are simply Mankind writ large. "Since Jews are men," Daniel explains, "their religious feelings must have much in common with those of other men—just as their poetry, though in one sense peculiar, has a great deal in common with the poetry of other nations." Religion, however, in its "Zionist" form, is a higher connecting power than poetry; and the

Hebrew will show us the way to a "divine Unity": "See then—the nation which has been scoffed at for its separateness, has given a binding theory to the human race."[62]

This is only a phase of Eliot's total work; but in it she has come to an extraordinary conclusion. Most of her other work tries to exhibit the power of sympathetic evocation of character and situation, to awaken the reader's sentiment of fellow feeling. Acknowledging the breakdown of connection, Eliot had been seeking to reknit society through the unifying force of literature. As Suzanne Graver puts it, "In essence, through her art she attempted to create new and vital substitutions for the face-to-face encounters of traditional community."[63] In *Daniel Deronda*, I am suggesting, she began to lose faith in the efficacy of artistic sympathy, and turned to a mystical blend of religion and racism.

Natural History

In order to really understand this development in Eliot, one must go back to her essay "The Natural History of German Life: Riehl." This was a review that she did for the *Westminster Review* in 1856, just as she was starting to write her novels. W. H. von Riehl was an early sociologist of sorts, whose work was to be valued by Tönnies, among others, and who had just published *Die Bürgerliche Gesellschaft* [Bourgeois Society] (1855) and *Land und Leute* [Land and People] (1856). It was these books that Eliot reviewed, and we are interested at first more in her remarks than in the books themselves.

She begins by asking what associations are called up by the word "railways," reminding us how little we actually know of the thing itself. It is a collective term, summing up complex facts. The same is true, she tells us, of the terms "people," "proletariat," and "peasantry." Her comment sets the tone of what follows: "How little the real characteristics of the working classes are known to those who are outside them, how little their natural history has been studied, is sufficiently disclosed by our Art as well as by our political and social theories." Her call for realistic social novels, which will awaken our moral sympathies, is by now familiar. As she remarks, "Appeals founded on generalisations and statistics require a sympathy ready-made, a moral sentiment already in activity; but a picture of human life such as a great artist can give, surprises even the trivial and the selfish into that attention to what is apart from themselves, which may be called the raw material of moral sentiment.'"[64]

What is new is summed up in the term "natural history," and she finds inspiration in Riehl. Riehl, it appears, goes beyond general terms, such as proletariat and peasant, and gives us a "true conception of the popular character . . . to guide our sympathies rightly" and to "check our theories and direct us in their application." He offers a "real knowledge of the People," which can save the novelist from a false attribution of her own feelings to her subjects. In short, he offers a kind of science of society; and we can see that this is what Eliot has in mind when she reiterates the Comtean series of the sciences, from mathematics to biology, and then, instead of sociology, speaks of natural history for normal and pathology for abnormal conditions, as the continuation of biology in society. "A wise social policy," she insists, "must be based not simply on abstract social science, but on the Natural History of social bodies."[65]

Riehl shows the way in the case of Germany, or so Eliot assures us. He depicts the actual physiques and physiognomies of the peasantry, according to race, district, and province (an anticipation of physical anthropology?). He emphasizes their mental character, marked as it is by their "reverence for traditional custom" and hardy nervous system. In contrast, the city-dweller is prey to nervous diseases "of which the peasant knows nothing." Riehl's cure is summarized by Eliot as follows: "And a return to the habits of peasant life is the best remedy for many moral as well as physical diseases induced by *perverted* civilization"[66] (emphasis mine).

Eliot was so taken with Riehl and the concept of natural history that she does not pause to consider the dangers inherent in his attitude. A large part of herself sympathized with the emotions underlying a glorification of the country and a denigration of the city. "If I allowed myself," she wrote a friend, "to have any longings beyond what is given, they would be for a nook quite in the country, far away from Palaces crystal [she obviously has in mind here the Crystal Palace Exhibition of 1851] or otherwise, with an orchard behind me full of old trees and rough grass, and hedgerow paths among the endless fields where you meet nobody." Alas, she continued, "In the meantime the business of life shuts us up within the environs of London and within sight of human advancement, which I should be so very glad to believe in without seeing."[67] In these statements,

Eliot is experiencing the division not only in society but in her own soul as well.

Natural history, as applied to flora and fauna, was quite the rage in mid-nineteenth-century England. On the eve of the Darwinian revolution, it was still the clergyman's pursuit and the amateur's hobby. "Collections" of sea shells, beetles, birds, and so forth were to be found everywhere, even in poor people's houses. Such collections joined the city to the country. On a more professional level, they represented the classifying stage of biological science, about to become evolutionary in nature. Eliot's husband (in all but legal name), George Henry Lewes, for example, was the author of *Seaside Studies*, a typical effort in the genre of natural history books.[68]

Earlier, viewing the cabinets of natural history in the Jardin des Plantes in Paris, Ralph Waldo Emerson had caught the vision Eliot was to have of the uses of Riehl's work, when he declared, "I will be a naturalist." By this he meant a naturalist of the soul, and his first public lectures on his return to America were on "The Use of Natural History," where he declared, "It is in my judgment the greatest office of natural science (and one which is as yet only begun to be discharged) to explain man to himself."[69]

Eliot, who had met Emerson in 1848 and declared him "the first *man* I have ever met," felt herself called upon to take up the same task of explaining Man as a subject of natural history. In her case, of course, it was Riehl who served as primary inspiration. Thus, a few years after reviewing the German scholar, she suggested in *Adam Bede* (1859) that her reader look at Hetty Sorrel, the pretty but vain and thoughtless young girl, "as if you were studying the psychology of a canary bird, and only watch the movements of this pretty round creature as she turns her head on one side. . . ." And Adam, who is in love with her, sees her as only a "kitten setting up its back, or a little bird with its feathers ruffled."[70]

These are relatively trivial examples (and even here Eliot was to realize that such "appearances" might mislead one as to the moral reality); what they represent is Eliot's romance, so to speak, with natural history as a form of, or an adjunct to, social science, aiding the artist's use of sympathy to reconnect Man to Man, as well as to society and the cosmos.[71]

What Eliot seems not to have recognized is the direction in which Riehl's ideas could lead. In fact, he was a major inspiration for German *Volk*ish thought, with its claim that a people rooted in nature,

land, and history was superior to citizens of a mechanical and materialistic civilization. Riehl took the medieval, customary community
as his ideal, and wished to restore its hierarchical arrangement of
natural estates. In his *Die Bürgerliche Gesellschaft*, he did allow for
the accommodation of the bourgeoisie within the *Volk*, by rooting it
in small towns; and his idea of building German workers' cooperative home-building societies (he had a good word also to say for
Robert Owen) undoubtedly appealed to Eliot. Yet, what did Eliot
make of Riehl's exclusion from his system of the proletariat, whom
he distinguished from the "genuine" working class, and who lived
in cities, without any landscape of its own? Or of Riehl's fear of the
journalist and of the intellectual, who incited people to rise against
the established order, and especially of the Jew, who, dominating
the big city, spread his restlessness throughout the country?[72]

Eliot appears not to have noted the ominous side of these features of Riehl's lamentations against modernity, nor to have had any
prophetic insight into how he would become an ideologist adopted
by the Nazis. Instead, she seems to have used Riehl's "natural history" as an inspiration for giving the Jews, in *Daniel Deronda*, exactly
the land and history—Palestine—whose lack Riehl had claimed
denatured them as members of the Germanic organic whole. For
Eliot, natural history, or, to put it bluntly, racism, was a benign form
of community, and indeed its deepest and most powerful
embodiment.

Most of Eliot's novels, by virtue of her attention to connections,
serve as a bridge to the development of early sociology, which we
shall deal with shortly. Her stress on the need for community was
to be taken up anew by practitioners of the new discipline, though
they saw the solution to that need eventually in terms of a science
that was neither natural history nor literary sympathy. Her attention
to racism as a form of community, however, would fall outside their
work, to be taken up by non-sociological thinkers such as Gobineau
and Houston Stewart Chamberlain—with dire consequences.[73]

In all of this, in regard to Eliot, there is a paradox. Though she
idealized Jews as a race in *Daniel Deronda*, they were to be the group
who suffered most from European racist ideology. Their fate was
intertwined with the great debate over connection, and the cash
nexus. They run like the proverbial red thread through the European
anxiety over the onset of modernity. When Alton Locke, the hero of
Charles Kingsley's novel of that name (1850), deplores the fall of the

tailoring trade into a cash-nexus relation, his friend and mentor, Crossthwaite, speaks of the villains as "Messrs. Aaron, Levi, and the rest of that class" and, in case his message is not clear, goes on to say, "We shall become the slaves, often the bodily prisoners, of Jews, middlemen, and sweaters, who draw their livelihood out of our starvation."[74] Two lesser-known (to us) novelists of the time, J. M. Rymer and G. W. Reynolds, sound the same theme, and speak of "greedy Jews" in their respective novels, *The White Slave: A Romance of the Nineteenth Century* (1844) and *The Slaves of England: No. 1, The Seamstress* (1850). In the latter, Reynolds speaks of "The establishment of Messrs. Aaron & Sons" and tells us how "while poor Virginia, one of the countless victims of that diabolical system, sleeps in the silent grave, the toils of the *White Slaves* whom she has left behind are still contributing to the colossal wealth accumulated within the walls of that Palace of Infamy."[75]

A Thread Reknitted

Such sentiments, of course, were commonplaces of mid-nineteenth-century English culture. We are concerned here with the way they enter into the theme of connection. In many ways, the role of the Jew becomes one of the main litmus tests of the perceived breakdown of society, presumably caused by the onslaught of modernity. We have seen how novelists such as Disraeli and Eliot tried to incorporate a treatment of the Jews, as either heroes or victims, into their reconstruction of a world disfigured by the cash nexus. We shall soon see how Engels, Marx, Tönnies, and Weber deal with the Jews in their sociologies.

Nevertheless, in following the thread of racism and the Jews as it winds through novels, we may appear to have diverged from the main path of our concern with connections. Though in fact this is not so, a return to the more central treatment of the cash-nexus theme as a matter of sympathetic need, and especially to Eliot, our point of temporary departure, is in order here.

Out of necessity, I have given only a slight sketch of her full achievement and little hint of the novelistic skill and sublety she brought to the writing of *Felix Holt*, as well as to *Daniel Deronda* and her other books. I have cited her mainly to show how the theme of reconnecting society by the bonds of imaginative sympathy finally plays itself out in the second half of the nineteenth century. The two novels of hers that we have discussed serve as a sort of literary coda. With them, we witness more or less the end of the persistent novelistic response to a society perceived as characterized by the cash nexus and desperately in need of some new, or revived, unifying principle.

That novelistic response, as I have tried to show mainly through the examples of Gaskell, Disraeli, and Eliot, is at one with the political, the prophetic, and the poetic, with the ruminations of Burke and Rousseau, Carlyle and Wordsworth. Allowing for the differences among them, important as they are, these writers establish a tradition of lament, which, in turn, colors all further efforts by contemporaries to understand and to deal with the perceived sense of a breakdown of connections in modern Western society.

5

Fictions and Facts

History and Reality

What was the reality behind the perceived sense of breakdown in connections? How can we come to know this putative reality? Until now, we have been dealing to a large extent with literary materials. In themselves, they constitute "facts"; they talk to the historian about a cultural reaction on the part of some, an articulate minority, to a "reality" occurring around them. Are they "factual" also, in the sense of accurately describing a part of the reality, although in fictional form? Or are they mainly contributions to a myth, in this case, of the "cash nexus," which then becomes the veil through which we perceive "reality"?

It is important to ask such questions now, as we are about to move from primarily literary thinkers to sociologists, with the solution to perceived problems shifting primarily from a reliance on sympathy to a reliance on social science. Are so-called fictions actually more reliable than, for example, statistics, in the sense that while figures do not lie, liars figure, that is, bring ideological blinders to their calculations? Or is it that the metaphors used in fiction are mere devices to mislead, representing feelings but not any other reality? Do fictions and statistics each disclose different realities, or the same reality seen from different vantage points?

In what follows, I will not attempt to answer such questions in the abstract, but rather to look selectively at the way in which they played themselves out in the period when the sense of breakdown in connections first became all-pervasive. Against that background,

I will then try to bring to bear the perspective of a historian, using the conflicting evidences as provided by that discipline, and to offer an assessment as to the reality of a "cash nexus" society in the late eighteenth and early nineteenth century, as well as subsequently.

Fictions and Metaphors

In 1854, Charles Dickens's novel *Hard Times* appeared serially in his periodical *Household Words,* and subsequently as a book. The title carried a double entendre: the times were hard—depressed—and they were so because of hard-hearted men, the entrepreneurs of the Industrial Revolution. Such men were interested only in so-called facts—as the book opens, Thomas Gradgrind, cotton operative and philanthropist, is lecturing the school children in Coketown to the effect that facts and calculations alone "are wanted in life." The enemy is imagination and human emotion.

Dickens's portraits of Gradgrind, Bounderby, Sparsit, and others are admittedly caricatures, carried to the point of genius. But did Dickens's caricatures point to the reality of industrial life, or seriously distort that reality? Was his fiction, in fact, a betrayal of the true facts, rather than a revelation of them? His contemporary, Harriet Martineau, author of the popular *Illustrations of Political Economy* (1832) and doughty defender of free enterprise, certainly thought so.[1] She would have none of his defense that he was writing fiction, which has its own rules; by publishing his novel in *Household Words,* an organ dedicated to popular instruction and social reform, he places himself, she claims, before the tribunal of truth. Especially is this the case with a subsequent article published there alleging unnecessary and inhuman industrial accidents. The original tale (i.e., *Hard Times*), Martineau declares, will do little mischief, for in "its characters, conversations, and incidents, [it] is so unlike life,—so unlike Lancashire or English life,—that it is deprived of its influence. Master and man are as unlike life in England, at present, as Ogre and Tom Thumb." Dickens's allegation that the mill owner's machinery "mangle or murder, every year, two thousand human creatures" is rather, she tells us, a mangling of the very facts of which Dickens makes such fun: the average number is actually twelve a year (out of a work force estimated in 1851 to total a little over half a million in the cotton trade as a whole). To the citing of these figures by Martineau and the mill owners, Dickens's retort was, "As for ourselves, we admit freely that it never did occur to us that it was possible to justify, by arithmetic, a thing unjustifiable by any code of morals, civilized or savage."[2]

The rest of Martineau's article carries on the thrust and parry of the argument in the same terms. Ironically, her conclusion accuses Dickens of the very lack of sympathy and empathy that he had been attacking in *Hard Times.* Dickens, she says, is "satisfied to represent the great class of manufacturers—unsurpassed for intelligence, public spirit, and beneficence—as the monsters he describes, without seeking knowledge of their actual state of mind and course of life."[3] Here, in this exchange, without going further into the details, we can see joined the critical issue of fictions and facts. We can now explore a bit the nature and meaning of each category, and its relation to our subject, connections.

Fiction, in the form of the novel especially, was certainly one of the ways in which nineteenth-century bourgeois Western society tried to know itself. Gaskell, Disraeli, and Eliot are the examples I have cited, but many others could be added to the list. These novelists sought to portray and comprehend the profound transformation that England and a few other countries were undergoing as they moved from being predominately agricultural to industrial nations, or, as the early sociologist Sir Henry Maine would have put it, from custom to contract. Even a novelist such as Jane Austen, who seems at first glance merely to be describing a placid, unchanging world of social connections, is really chronicling the shifts in domestic life and in the relations of the sexes that were crowding in upon that supposedly tight little world. As Igor Webb comments, "the novelist who creates a social world necessarily engages in a kind of politics, for he or she will necessarily dramatize relations of power, within the family, between the sexes, between classes."[4] In short, fiction tells of truths that otherwise might go unrecognized or unvalued: truths about human relations and their vicissitudes in the new commercial and industrial world.

So, too, with the use of metaphor. When a writer (in this case, William Cobbett) pens such phrases as "Lords of the Loom" and their "real slaves," or, as Dickens does, compares the monotonous up and down movements of the piston of a steam engine to "the head of an elephant in a state of melancholy madness," or, as Adam Smith does, describes man as a "commodity," he is not noting literal truths, but seeking by metaphors and analogies to establish a connection between two orders of facts. As the philosopher Max Black points out, "a memorable metaphor has the power to bring two separate domains into cognitive and emotional relations by using language directly appropriate to the one as a lens for seeing the other."[5]

Thus, Corbett seeks to connect the nineteenth-century cotton magnates with feudal lords and their serfs, challenging thereby the whole notion of progress; Dickens to link the mechanical beast of burden to its animal predecessor, now gone sadly mad; and Smith to view man as economic man of the marketplace, subject like any other "good" to the forces of supply and demand. These are not mere metaphors or fictions, but profound truths of a sort. They become fictions in the narrow sense only when taken to represent all of a reality: cotton magnates to be only feudalistic, steam engines only symbols of melancholy madness, and man only a commodity.

The cash nexus is a metaphor of this type, perhaps the most powerful in the nineteenth century, central to the connections theme, and instrumental in giving rise, as I will try to show, to the "science" of sociology. Dickens does not use the term "cash nexus" in *Hard Times*, but it is certainly what he has in mind in the scene where Gradgrind, frantic to protect his erring son, forgets himself so far as to appeal for help, emotionally, to his hard-hearted disciple, Bitzer. The latter, brought up on a steady curriculum of facts, pays him back with, "I am sure you know that the whole social system is a question of self-interest." As Dickens sums it up, "It was a fundamental principle of the Gradgrind philosophy that everything was to be paid for. Nobody was ever on any account to give anybody anything, or render anybody help without purchase. Gratitude was to be abolished, and the virtues springing from it were not to be. Every inch of existence of mankind, from birth to death, was to be a bargain across a counter."[6]

We are not surprised that Dickens, like Carlyle and Marx before him, despised the cash nexus (though, or perhaps because, he wrote for money), and was repelled by the idea of a society based solely on its principles; the interesting thing to note, however, is that Utilitarians and economists often embraced the same metaphor, only in positive terms. Men such as J. R. McCulloch were not so far removed from a fictional Gradgrind, and wished, it often seemed, to construct a world bound only by the cash nexus. Ironically, then, the classical economists and the lamenters were in a tacit collaboration to see the world as the other saw it, as connected only by cash. The only difference was that, in one case, they sought to bring such a society more fully into being, and in the other case, to at least limit, if not prevent, its realization.[7] At one point, Dickens had considered calling his novel "Black and White"; indeed, both sides, the economists and their critics, such as Dickens, Carlyle, and Marx (who, of course, was also an economist but of an unusual kind), embraced the great dualism to which the cash-nexus metaphor had led them. At this point, the illuminating metaphor becomes a fiction, unrecognized as such, for both parties.

Nexus itself means a bond or chain, that is, a connection, and Sir Henry Maine traces its origin for us in Roman law. It is rooted, he says, in the development of contract, which was called a "*nexum,* and the parties to the contract were said to be *nexi.*" It thus embodied "the notion that persons under a contractual engagement are connected together by a strong bond or chain. . . ." In Maine's view, the development of *nexum* is a liberating idea. Indeed, for a while, it was reserved only for Roman citizens, with foreigners prohibited from becoming party to a *nexum;* they stood outside the chain of communal and commercial connection.[8]

Maine saw the development of *nexum* as part of a larger movement: from custom to contract, and from family to individual. For him, it was a progressive development: ". . . the individual is steadily substituted for the Family, as the unit of which civil laws take account. The advance has been accomplished at varying rates of celerity. . . . But, whatever its pace, the change has not been subject to reactions or recall. . . . Nor is it difficult to see what is the tie between man and man which replaces by degrees those forms of reciprocity in rights and duties which have their origin in the Family. It is Contract."[9]

Even feudal society, supposedly the complete opposite of industrial society, was bound by contract, though not of a cash nature. As Maine explains at some length,

> true archaic communities are held together not by express rules, but by sentiment, or, we should perhaps say, by instinct; and new comers into the brotherhood are brought within the range of this instinct by falsely pretending to share in the blood-relationship from which it naturally springs. But the earliest feudal communities were neither bound together by mere sentiment nor recruited by a fiction. The tie

which united them was Contract, and they obtained new associates by contracting with them. The relation of the lord to the vassals had originally been settled by express engagement, and a person wishing to engraft himself on the brotherhood by *commendation* or *infeudation* came to a distinct understanding as to the conditions on which he was to be admitted. It is therefore the sphere occupied in them by Contract which principally distinguished the feudal institutions from the unadulterated usages of primitive races.[10]

For the English jurist, just as feudal contract is an advance over primitive bonds, so the commercial contract of industrial society is an advance over feudal ones. It is a further step in the freeing of the individual.

Of course, this last statement is debatable. As I remarked earlier, one man's connection is another man's chain. The warmth of family may be viewed as a fiction, and the freeing of an individual from its fetid embrace a great relief; or the freedom may be seen as leaving the individual deprived of family support, isolated and anomic. The movement from barter to money may be seen, to anticipate our study of the sociologists, as a lamentable shift from *Gemeinschaft*, as Tönnies views it, or as a liberation of the individual, as Simmel views it.

Whatever the value judgments passed on these positions, we can make here an evaluation of a different sort: just as Maine's polar opposites are too drastic and simplifying, so is any polar opposition between fictions and facts. So-called fictions may reveal realities and truths to us otherwise unnoted, and so-called facts may obscure or distort that reality and leave us with a larger falsehood.

Statistics

If we look for a moment at the rise in the importance of statistics, we may be further helped in our understanding of the problem. For Dickens, statistics was a subject over which fun was to be made. In his "Full Report of the First Meeting of the Mudfog Association" (1837), he lampooned the tribe of statisticians in the person of a Mr. Slug. Certainly, statistics was a faddish subject of the day, with societies and their statistical reports mushrooming. Statistics of births, deaths, and marriages, correctly calculated, became the basis of insurance associations and social welfare projections (since the seventeenth century, arithmeticians had been delighted to observe the alleged constant ratio of 26:25 between the births of boys and girls all over Europe). Education, health matters, crime, and suicide all were subject to statistical inquiry, as a basis for social analysis and reform. To collect the requisite data, government agencies were set up apace in the nineteenth century: the first modern census was taken in 1801 in Britain, and by 1837 the General Register Office was established to supervise an expanded census and to collect mortality records. Parliamentary commissions caused statistical inquiries to be made as the basis for poor-law reform and to guide efforts at improved sanitation.

Some statisticians were more ambitious than to serve merely as mathematical purveyors to practical state reforms. They aspired to establish a "social physics" that would be as scientific as, for example, celestial physics. The great French natural scientist Laplace had said at the end of the eighteenth century, "Let us apply to the political and moral sciences the method founded upon observation and upon calculus, the method which has served us so well in the natural sciences."[11] In the 1830s the Belgian statistician Adolphe Quételet attempted to imitate the natural sciences in his *"mécanique sociale,"* by postulating an "average man" who would play the same role in sociology as gravitation in physics; alas, although Quételet made substantial contributions to the statistical art, he actually made little to social science.

Nevertheless, though statistics may not have succeeded in becoming a science of sociology, à la Laplace's dictum, it played an increasingly important, though still relatively modest, role in guiding social policy. Whereas German *Statistik* in the seventeenth century was intended to serve the political power of the state, in England, characteristically, it was mainly put to civil, private uses. John Sinclair, a Scottish pastor, popularized the term in his *Statistical Account of Scotland,* and made it clear that "the idea I annex to the term, is an inquiry into the state of a country for the purpose of ascertaining the quantum of happiness enjoyed by its inhabitants, and the means of its future improvement."[12]

By the 1830s a statistical section was attached to the British Association for the Advancement of Science (with Charles Babbage, pioneer of the future computer, as one of its founding members), while in provincial Manchester a Statistical Society was established in

1833, building on the interests of members (most drawn from inter-locking families) of the original Manchester Literary and Philosoph-ical Society, founded in 1781. Such societies, and other more spe-cialized ones such as the Manchester and Salford Sanitary Association, were not above looking "statistically," that is, "objec-tively," at the dark side of industrial society. Tocqueville, visiting Manchester in the 1830s, imaginatively rang the changes on the metaphor of "Filthy Lucre" when he wrote that "from this foul drain the greatest stream of human industry flows out to fertilize the whole world. From this filthy sewer pure gold flows. Here humanity attains its most complete development and its most brutish; here civilization works its miracles, and civilized man is turned back almost into a savage."[13] What he did not note was that the Sanitary Association, by making its statistical inquiries into the number and condition of privies, was seeking, with ultimate success, to rescue industrial civilization from, so to speak, going down the drain.

With this brief orientation as to the development of statistics, we can now review the overall situation. Earlier, we saw how novelists such as Gaskell, Eliot, and Dickens thought that the solution to the evils of industrial society and its gathering class conflict was the arousal of sympathy and understanding on both sides (but mainly on the part of the literate middle class). The way to do this was through the powers of imaginative fiction. Such fiction was to give a more truthful portrayal than any array of fact. So stated, the advo-cates of sympathy and sensibility seem opposed, at all points, to the proponents of statistics.

Looked at more broadly, however, both sides shared much in common. Both came to understand that the malaise affecting their society had its impact on both the haves and have-nots—for exam-ple, poor sanitation could give rise to plagues that killed members of both groups—and that a solution was not further class conflict but some kind of new sympathy and social policy. The difference is that statisticians thought "hard facts" would be more persuasive than imaginative depictions of the breakdown of affective ties; that science, based on statistics, rather than sympathy, based on sensi-bility, was the remedy for social disease.

Thus, the effort at social science that we have traced, of which statistics had become one part (one thinks of Marx's use of govern-ment documents, or, later, of Durkheim's work on suicide), aimed at a useful knowledge which included but went beyond mere emotion. The danger, of course, is that instead of science the result may well be "scientism," in which false, or at least misleading, science allows one to place human distress at an "objective" and thus safe distance. The facts may then be used to obscure the human dimension, reducing Man to a number or abstraction. On the other side, of course, there is the danger that imaginative sympathy will overwhelm rational and balanced judgment, creating a world of myths and fictions that make for poor, though virtuous, guides to the realities of life. Might one be forgiven for asking whether what is actually needed is an informed estimate of the role and worth of both fictions and facts, and a desire to use them properly for the amelioration of Man's lot in life?

"Facts"

How much fiction and how much fact, in the conventional sense of these terms, is involved in what we call the cash nexus? There were certainly those who proclaimed in loud, ideological terms that the only proper relation between Men was work on one side and wages on the other. Undoubtedly there were a number of employers who actually behaved in this fashion; before his awakening, Thornton, in Gaskell's *North and South,* is a convincing fictional representation of some Men who existed in real life. Were such Men statistically numerous or insignificant? Whatever the answer, and one might try to approximate it in particular industries, they certainly loomed large in the eyes of the lamenters. Did such Men compel others, through the threat of competition, to adopt the cash-nexus approach, or at least give tacit allegiance to it? Or have a few prototypes given rise to a myth of such compelling power that it obscures the historical reality?

A great deal of historical work has been produced lately related to these questions. It may require us to alter our traditional views and opinions. In what follows, I undertake only a most brief and partial review. (In this case, moreover, the notes take on more than a usual importance, serving almost as an integral part of the text; they are left as notes, however, in order that we not lose sight of the main lines of the argument, and its relation to the theme of connections.)

One way to begin addressing these questions is to look at pre-industrial society in England, as Peter Laslett has done in *The World We Have Lost*. That world, which may, in fact, be mythical, or, at best, an "ideal type," was one in which work and family tended to be inseparable, whether in a rural or urban setting. It was a world of households. Although "nuclear" rather than "extended kinship" in nature (except for the nobility), it was patriarchal; near-absolute authority, whether of father or father-figure, gave scope for widespread oppression, but such oppression was stable and traditional, and at some point the son could look forward to becoming a father. (For the daughter, I might add, motherhood, entailing the exchange of husband for father, was not necessarily a betterment.)

It was, in Laslett's terms, a "one-class society." Class, for Laslett, means people bonded together in the exercise of collective power, political and economic. Those who have no power, in his definition, belong to no class. In this sense, then, though there were a large number of status groups, there was "only one body of persons capable of concerted action over the whole area of society, only one class in fact." In this one-class society, about 5 percent of the population owned the bulk of the wealth and wielded almost all the power (and, though Laslett does not stress this, we are talking by and large of males). At the other end of the scale, if the seventeenth-century chronicler Gregory King (an early statistician) can be trusted, at least one-half of the population lived in intermittent poverty, even according to the standards of the times, and "begging was universal."[14]

The one class was primarily landowning—noble, gentry, and yeoman—though urban merchants and professionals also belonged. It was a class permeated by social "connections," its society one based on patriarchal community. Was this class completely overturned and its world lost by the industrial revolution? Did a "middle class" come to power? Was the new society composed of "self-made Men," independent individuals who rampantly broke all the old connections and turned community into cash nexus? Or was this the myth, perpetuated by both friend and foe of the new Man?

Focusing upon mid-nineteenth-century Britain to begin with, the evidence suggests, first, that there were at least two middle classes, the larger and wealthier one based on commerce and in London, the other on manufacturing and in the north of England, typified by Manchester. Together with the landed elite, these "contested for the benefits of wealth, status and power, and evolved separate means of

social control."[15] The largest part of that wealth and power nevertheless remained with the landowners, at least until the end of the
century. While there were nineteenth-century manufacturers and
industrialists who were millionaires—though only one Manchester
manufacturer during the period from 1809 to 1914 made it into this
category—the typical successful manufacturer appears to have left
an estate in the range of £100,000. The Marxist historian John Foster
takes an income of £25,000 as the distinguishing feature of his
industrial elite (with Friedrich Engels just making the grade).[16]

Disproportionately, the wealthiest members of the middle class
were to be found in London, in commercial or financial activities,
not manufacturing. Thus, a distinction must be made between these
two middle-class groups. In terms of status characteristics, the city
merchants were closer to the landowners than to the manufacturers
and industrialists. For a generation or two, in the mid-nineteenth
century, many of the new manufacturers and industrialists sought
to secure a cultural domination opposite to that of the landowners
and city merchants, and to establish a new society on "Manchester,"
or "cash nexus," principles (if not practice). This desire appears to
have been undercut, however, to some extent by a grudging but real
aspiration to the status symbols of the landed class; grandsons of
"tough" mill owners—the Thorntons of Gaskell's novels—were
soon being sent to the best schools and to Oxford and Cambridge.
Thus, in the end, the industrialists made the same concessions, and
adopted to a large extent the same lifestyle, as the other "two" classes.[17] Further, as I shall try to show, many manufacturers soon faced
the problem that their own life situations, especially domestic, ran
counter to their proclaimed ideology.

The ideology stated that the capitalist could, and should, rise
through life strictly on his own, and should more or less stay that
way emotionally. The fact is that very few of the new industrialists
(though these few were of great symbolic importance) were completely self-made men. They tended to come from respectable families and, if not inheriting an ongoing business, were originally
endowed with at least modest means and were equipped to raise
capital from small farm holdings, or local ale houses, or similar
sources.[18]

Unlike their London commercial counterparts, however, the provincial manufacturers found themselves having to make money in
mass labor-intensive industries. Here, in the midst of wage labor

relations—in the new textile industries alone were to be found hundreds of thousands of "hands"—is where the cash nexus supposedly came to dominate, if anywhere. Here, too, presumably, all the old connections were broken, leaving only the one, unconscionable tie.[19]

The issue, it appears, is not one of either/or but of more or less. The "callous cash payment" may in fact have been a relatively atypical, though not unusual, relation—the work and wages syndrome was certainly central to the competitive business world—and more characteristic of early Manchester and vicinity than other places (London being the exception) and later times. The norm, surprisingly, at least for the larger firms, is often paternalistic, and it is in this context that the wage-work relation needs to be viewed.

There is one other context that must be considered in regard to this issue. It involves the need for a new work discipline in the burgeoning textile mills and other factories. Such discipline went against the natural rhythms both of life and of long-time custom. Workers had to be coerced by the threat of dismissal and enticed by wages luring them to greater consumption. As Sidney Pollard tells us, ". . . men [to whom we should now add women] who were non-accumulative, non-acquisitive, accustomed to work for subsistence, not for maximization of income, had to be made obedient to the cash stimulus. . . ." The need for impersonal work rules, interchangeable "hands," and control over children who were no longer able to be disciplined by the traditional parental whippings (a commonplace of the time) all pointed toward the cash relation. The problem facing the entrepreneurs and managers of the Industrial Revolution was to "socialize" their work force in a new way. "Like the generals of old," Pollard sums up, "they had to control numerous men, but without powers of compulsion: indeed, the absence of legal enforcement of unfree work was not only one of the marked characteristics of the new capitalism, but one of its most seminal ideas, underlying its ultimate power to create a more civilized society."[20] In this context, the cash nexus was as much the result of disciplinary needs as of market requirements.

The fact is that the industrial middle class was caught in a dilemma. Its members were fully aware that a cultural vacuum had been created by the capitalist Industrial Revolution; the new industrial proletariat had been uprooted from old values and institutions, and were drifting between two worlds, the rural and the urban.

W. Cooke Taylor, a protagonist of the new world, wrote in 1842: "As a stranger passes through the masses of human beings which have accumulated around the mills . . . he cannot contemplate these 'crowded hives' without feelings of anxiety and apprehension. . . . It is an aggregate of masses . . . the manufacturing population is not new in its formation alone: it is new in its habits of thought and action, which have been formed by the circumstances of its condition, with little instruction, and less guidance, from external sources. . . ."[21]

This was recognizably a dangerous situation. In the same year, Benjamin Love's *Handbook of Manchester* speaks of how "there seems among the operatives, generally, a want of independent feeling. Few elevate themselves, even when they might, from a state of even servile dependence." And Love draws the conclusion that "the moral condition of this class wants elevating."[22] Hence the middle-class effort to abolish bear baiting, cockfights, and other such brutalities, and to substitute more temperate and more "cultured" forms of relaxation for the masses. When Love speaks of "independent feeling," he means, of course, a freeing from the old in order to take on the new bourgeois values, that is, middle-class culture.

Reflective employers realized that cultural and community connection were at least as important as, or even more important than, economic coercion if they were to retain legitimate authority over their men and women. In pre-industrial times, harsh as they were, traditional authority figures—landowners and clergy—were invested with the aura of inherited virtue. The cash nexus gave no such accepted shine. A compromise between stark ideology and flawed actuality was needed, and was soon reached by many of the employers. As Hugh Mason of Ashton put it, in 1868: "He was not indifferent to the teachings of political economy, but he should be very sorry if the rigid and abstract rules of political economy alone prevailed in his workshops. It would be impossible for him to buy the labour of his workpeople, and for the workpeople to sell him that labour the same as an ordinary commodity over the counter of a shopkeeper. He felt a deep interest in the welfare of his workpeople. . . . The bond which united them was not the cold bond of buyer and seller."[23]

Much earlier in the Industrial Revolution, Robert Owen had practiced the new paternalism in his New Lanark factory. In 1816, addressing his workers, Owen spoke of his predecessor and father-in-law, David Dale, and reminded them that "His wishes and intentions towards you all were those of a father towards his children. You knew him and his worth; and his memory must be deeply engraven upon your hearts." Owen was to go even further in his "fatherly" concern. Convinced that "Any character, from the best to the worst, from the most ignorant to the most enlightened, may be given to any community, even to the world at large, by applying certain means; which are to a great extent at the command and under the controul [sic], or easily made so, of those who possess the government of nations," he set out to shape the character of his employees from childhood on.[24] Aided by the almost complete isolation of New Lanark in Scotland, he shaped a new world of kindergarten, school, and regulated work that became a model of its kind. Aware that industrialism required a new discipline, he pioneered methods that today we would call "scientific management"; but the velvet that covered the iron was paternalism. For Owen recognized that the factory was more than a factory; it was also a community.

Was Owen as exceptional as is thought? For example, Josiah Wedgwood, with his powerful paternalistic and autocratic urge to shape his work force as much as he did his chinaware, was hardly in a cash-nexus relation to his employees; intending to "make such *machines* of the *Men* as cannot err," he may have had a mechanical mind-set (reminiscent of James Mill with his training of his son, John) but hardly an uncaring one, for he sought the personal improvement, according to his own values, of his laborers.[25]

Was Owen, therefore, simply the most successful of a "fatherly" breed of entrepreneur? After all, he himself simply followed in the footsteps of his father-in-law. Owen's distinction, it appears, may reside more in the degree to which he carried his paternalism, and in the fact that he sought to extend it so far beyond the confines of the factory community, than in his total originality.

A good deal of the new evidence in fact suggests that he was not alone in his own day, and that it was not until the 1820s and '30s that competitive small capitalists entering the textile industry began significantly to undercut the view of the factory as community and to subvert the effort to maintain decent working conditions.[26]

In this connection, interestingly enough, Anthony Howe, dealing with the investment of profits by the cotton masters in areas other than textiles, such as mines, lands, and railroads, makes the point that such diversification allowed the large manufacturers to ride out industrial crises without cutting wages or manpower. He quotes a contemporary of the time (1849), A. B. Reach, to the effect that "The mills at Ashton are generally the property of large capitalists, who can afford, and often do afford, to employ their workpeople at full hours when a period of temporary slackness in trade obliges those masters whose command of capital is less at once to curtail their producing operations. In this respect, Ashton is the reverse of Oldham. In the latter town small capitalists abound. . . . These employers conduct their operations in the hand-to-mouth style. . . . They spin, moreover, generally speaking, the coarse and inferior kinds of thread, and the slightest check in the demand falls at once upon the workman. There is no shield of capital to stand between the humble producer and the immediate fluctuations of the market." Another contemporary, W. Cooke Taylor, whom we have quoted earlier, writes in his *Notes on a Tour in the Manufacturing Districts of Lancashire* (1842) that "Experience has everywhere shown that great capitalists are more equitable and merciful employers than persons of limited fortunes." If this is true, then we may be faced with the paradox that it is not capitalism but shortage of capital that gives rise to the strictly impersonal cash-nexus relation![27]

Another way of looking at this whole problem is to see the Industrial Revolution, and especially the cotton industry, as inaugurating the modern trade cycle and thus creating a new situation in which customary forms of regulating wages were undermined. It took some fifty years to work out a new balance. As Stedman Jones points out, the first prolonged modern industrial slump, from the mid-1790s to 1820, "expressed itself not by a rise in the price of grain, but by wage-cutting and unemployment. It thus threw into disarray traditional methods of social control, which could contain a harvest crisis but had no solution to industrial grievances once wages ceased to be customary." The second crisis, 1830–47, saw a decrease in the price of cotton textiles, but, according to John Foster, as Jones summarizes it, there was no corresponding fall in materials and machinery. Thus, the decline in profits was again staunched by wage-cutting and unemployment.

In Jones's own account, the "mill owners pressed forward with mechanization in an effort to halt the catastrophic decline in their rate of profit by reducing labour costs." In the face of these conditions, labor sought to respond, by unions and political agitation. In

Oldham, for example, "one sector of the town's capitalists came out in favour of the limitation of factory hours," in an effort to restabilize the industry and reduce conflict. Jones then comes to an interesting conclusion: ". . . railway-building is what, more than anything else, resolved the capitalist crisis of the 1830s and early 1840s. It lessened the impact of cyclical crisis, stimulated coal, iron, steel and machine production, and resolved the crisis of profitability. More than any other single factor, it assured the successful transition to a modern industrial economy."[28] On this reading we come to the same conclusion as earlier: the worst features of the cash nexus resulted from underdeveloped capitalism, rather than being a continuously expanding feature of its growth.

In any case, to return to the textile industry, one way to deflect the "unfair" and debasing competition was for some of the cotton masters themselves to enlist in the movement to get Parliament to limit the working day and child labor. Such action went hand in hand with their effort to "improve" the workers' moral condition as well: domestic missions, temperance societies, Societies for the Prevention of Cruelty to Animals, and so on. Some of the employers, therefore, saw themselves as "fathers" as well as "masters" to their "men." Perhaps Cobbett's metaphor of "Lords of the Loom" was not so far off the mark, though in a sense not intended by him.

The task was more difficult than in the past. In a "Memoir on Pauperism" (1835), Tocqueville tried to comprehend the new form that being poor was taking: "poverty," now seen as Man-made and therefore amenable to being Man-unmade (whereas "being poor" simply came from God, and was, implicitly, merely to be accepted). He noted an important difference between poor laws and charity. "Individual alms-giving established valuable ties between the rich and the poor," he declared. "This is not the case with legal charity. . . . Far from uniting the two rival nations, who have existed since the beginning of the world and who are called the rich and the poor, into a single people, it breaks the only link which could be established between them . . . [and] prepares them for combat."[29]

As Tocqueville intuited, the very effort of the manufacturers to ameliorate poverty through the application of supposedly scientific means, for example, the utilitarian "felicific calculus," or the use of statistical research, seemed cold and distant in comparison with the caring and personal charity of the pre-industrial upper class. The fact that the industrialists were changing willy-nilly the entire structure of society that seemingly made the poor inevitable was only dimly perceived by the victims and lamenters of the time.[30]

What the depersonalizing tendency of social science reform, however well intended, did do was to set itself at variance with the traditional paternalism of the industrialists, which, I am suggesting, was more widespread than hitherto believed.[31] "Cold" social science ran up against the actual life situations of the employers who were, in general, patriarchal family men, and made for a special tension between their oft-proclaimed cash-nexus ideology and the reality of their lives, both at home and in the factory. Employers, in short, were not blank tablets, but part of an overall culture. Their home life frequently carried over to their business life. As one scholar puts it, the "distinction between the public and private spheres offers a way into the complexities of liberal culture. Though the middle-class family functioned as an institution for the protection and transmission of property it was also a sphere in which relations were not structured by abstract labour and the mechanisms of the market; it was precisely the kind of society which the disciples of laissez-faire affected to despise: 'a hierarchy of personal dependence.'" The carriers of middle-class culture, therefore, "derived their models of social relationship not from the sphere of exchange but from this alternative sphere of the private and personal. No less than the family, the religious community stood in opposition to the public sphere as an 'emotional fortress'—the 'heart of a heartless world,' to quote Marx—a place transcending social class."[32] Needless to say, the conflict between the models of the marketplace and the patriarchal household gave rise to unusual stress. It would be cynical to dismiss paternalism, as well as the social reforms, as merely self-serving devices employed by the capitalists. They were also reflections of their most cherished values.

Both paternalism and social reform, then, contended in the minds and hearts of the industrialists with their allegiance to a cash-nexus ideology. Such a mix of motives, while not logically tidy, seems to represent the actual psychological complexity involved. The result, in nineteenth-century Britain for example, was a comparable mix in actual social relations, with less-than-independent "self-made" entrepreneurs sometimes instituting a cash-nexus regime and others sometimes creating and sustaining patriarchal factory communities. Such factory owners were often open to social reform measures, inspired by social science, and prepared to treat their workers as independent mechanics or as dependent operatives. Such seems to be the actual muddle of history.[33]

The irony of the culture of the factory in mid-nineteenth-century England appears to be that the cultivation by the employers of a sense of community, when it occurred, often led to a loss of independence by working men and women, which took the form of an acceptance of paternalism in family and factory, and thus led to dependence and deference.[34] One scholar makes the caustic remark that "the traditional English landowning class placed an ideological gloss on their monopoly of power within the locality through the concept of 'community.'"[35] There is no reason to assume that the landowners, like the later manufacturers, were not operating out of ideological and cultural values as well as out of self-interest; in both cases the concept of community could be and was used in the interests of stability and social control.

An impressive range of evidence on the whole subject is laid out by Patrick Joyce in his book *Work, Society and Politics: The Culture of the Factory in Late Victorian England*.[36] The evidence is often confused, diffuse, and dense; nevertheless, a general and fairly persuasive picture emerges. In the developing factory towns of the 1840s, what we often see is a local employer residing in the vicinity of his factory, who strongly involves his family in its management—bringing sons into the business, celebrating family weddings with the "hands" in attendance—who is often inspired by dissenting religion to make better Men of his employees through firm rules against drinking, whoring, and gaming (Anglican employers pursued the same ends through different means), and who exercises a strong paternal rule in the name of a common "family" interest which claims to knit up everyone's well-being, in the context of the factory.[37]

As for the workers, they were generally prepared to offer deference and obedience as long as the economic promises of paternalism were delivered. Labor unions were sources of community for workers, but they were not separate from the general culture in which the workers lived. Most workers were not radicals—Dickens's *Hard Times* gives evidence of this in fictional terms—while well over half of them, women, the forgotten "minority," were in fact excluded from union action itself. As members of a factory community, as well as of a union, Joyce argues, workers were generally prepared to play their role in a paternalistic exchange that constituted far more than a mere cash nexus.

Only at the end of the nineteenth century, it appears, with the decline of family firms and their replacement by modern corporations distant from the towns and centralized in their operations, does scientific management and decision-making come to replace the patriarchal mode. With this change, according to Joyce, class politics replaces status politics. It is only at this time that the cash nexus, in a special form, softened beyond recognition by social welfare schemes, union protections, and corporate benefits, finally and effectively displaces paternalism.

If an analysis such as Joyce's, supported and qualified in other ways, as I have suggested, is accepted, a number of tentative conclusions emerge. The first is that the cash nexus is more an ideological metaphor than a comprehensive description of mid-nineteenth-century industrial reality. The actuality was often that of a factory community, patriarchal in nature; and whose patriarchy was accepted by both employers and employed. Nevertheless, the cash-nexus metaphor, rooted in a significant, and highly disturbing, amount of reality, dominated the imaginations of men and women on both sides of the connections issue, breakers and lamenters alike. The second conclusion is that by the end of the century, the depersonalizing cash nexus, in the shape of the modern, national corporation, had in fact dispossessed the local, patriarchal factory—but this finally triumphant "connection" was no longer callous, but girt around with the "caring" bonds of a "scientific" approach to management and of a social welfare state. As a result, the cash-nexus metaphor lost its earlier pull on Men's emotions, although the theme of connections, and disconnections, surged on as powerfully as ever.[38]

It is still not clear from all the recent historical research what the exact timing is of the various shifts I have been describing, in what localities they occurred, to what extent they held sway, and so on. The tangled web of facts and fictions must still be sorted out more carefully. What is clear is that the "cash nexus" was a powerful metaphor, with some, and perhaps a good deal, of truth at its core, which caught up in one luminous phrase the sense people of all persuasions and positions in society had in the nineteenth century that connections were being broken in society as well as in the cosmos.

At this point, the metaphor took on a life of its own, and what applied with a certain amount of sad force to a few decades of early industrialism was generalized by some to apply to all industrial capitalism and made innate to its nature.

Without making any final judgment on the historians' arguments over paternalism, which we have been reviewing, we can conclude that what the trope does not catch is the complexity of what was happening: the persistence of old forms of connection, the emergence of new connections, constraining and liberating, and the range and variability of industrial capitalistic social relations.

II
THE BIRTH
OF SOCIOLOGY

6

Backgrounds and Bridges

On the March

The future lay largely with the forces of industrialism and, apparently, the cash nexus. (Or so it seemed; in reality, state enterprise in Western Europe challenged the free market.) Thus, the worst fears of the lamenters appeared to be coming true. I have been designating as lamenters those who, by and large, deplored the effects of the great transformations—embodied in the French and Industrial revolutions—which they saw as entailing the breakdown of a wide, if often vague, range of connections. As it appeared to them, in the place of a motley array of traditional connections something labeled cash-nexus society was coming into dominance. It symbolized for them more the fragmentation of society than a new version. Further, as I have argued, for the lamenters the preferred prescription for solving the problem of breakdown was sympathy, evoked primarily by literary means.

Another hoped-for solution, however, was coming increasingly to the fore: a new science of society. This new way of viewing the world, this new solution, will be the subject of Part II of this book. Its emergence marks a novel way of thinking about the self and others, and about how the two are connected. As one scholar remarks about the rise to cultural dominance of the social sciences, though, as the present work shows, drastically over-polarizing, it marks "a decisive boundary in cultural history, a division between two different constructions of social reality, two quite different modes of understanding man's nature, his relations in society, and his place in the cosmos."[1]

Intimations of the emergence of sociology can be found before the middle of the nineteenth century. I have already touched on the Scottish school, and one must add to them Enlightenment thinkers such as Montesquieu and Condorcet (as well as, perhaps, French Restoration writers such as Bonald and De Maistre).[2] Attention should also be given to developments in Germany, especially to the Hegelian school, less because it aimed at a science of society than because it set the stage, intellectually, for the work of Engels and Marx, who, I will argue in the next chapter, play an indispensable role in transforming the literary into the sociological mode of perception and presentation.

At about the same time as the efflorescence of the Young Hegelian movement, in the 1830s, the idiosyncratic figure of Tocqueville arises, who must be placed in the pantheon of the founders of modern sociology, as well as his compatriot, Comte, who began the task of systematizing the new science.[3] It was not, however, until the 1860s–'70s that a true professionalization of sociology emerged, with the intention of making it a specialized, academic discipline with clearly defined boundaries. I will try in this chapter to sketch some of Tocqueville's and Comte's achievements, and to touch on the Hegelian background, but my main aim is to supply a context for the detailed analysis to come of how some late-nineteenth and early-twentieth-century thinkers—in this case, Ferdinand Tönnies, Georg Simmel, Emile Durkheim, and Max Weber—sought to give scientific form, and thus solutions, to the felt issues of the breakdown of connections in a modern society.

In passing, I should note the absence on my part of any concerted attention to socialism. Aside from the fact that others have treated it adequately and often brilliantly, I have chosen to concentrate, rather, on the way that those whom I have been calling the lamenters helped create the climate of opinion, the world of felt sympathy, in which the socialist aspirations to change reality could take seed and flourish. On the other side, of course, we must note the way the various efforts, theoretical and practical, of socialists and laboring people to offer alternate forms of association to that of the cash nexus affected the dominant conception and softened and transformed its cold features.

The French Connection

As the reader will be aware, aside from Rousseau, I have restricted myself up to now to English figures, on the grounds that the industrialization of society first took place in England, and that the challenge of connection and disconnection embodied in the phrase "cash nexus" first manifested itself most profoundly there. It would seem only natural, consequently, to expect the development of theoretical sociology to occur there as well. It did not. Why this is so, a source of some puzzlement, and why we must therefore cross the Channel to pursue our story, is a subject I will address toward the end of this chapter.

But first, we need to give a little more background to the early stages of Continental sociology itself, by looking briefly at the development in France and Germany of some intellectual responses to the French and Industrial revolutions.

In France, the sensed break was a result primarily of the French Revolution, a political upheaval, and only secondarily of the Industrial Revolution (cf. Chapter 2 for the relation of the two kinds of revolution). Rousseau, however, as we have seen, stood at the portals of both transformations. After the revolutionary break, in France a movement of restoration took place, both in thought and in political life. Men such as the Vicomte de Bonald and Joseph de Maistre, mentioned earlier as worthy of attention by historians of sociology, took up the Burkean effort to establish a conservative political philosophy.[4] Charles X sought to turn back the clock of history, and Louis Philippe to hold its hands still, in the realm of political life itself.

It was Alexis de Tocqueville, however, who most acutely analyzed the breakdown of connection brought about by the American and French revolutions. He recognized that the force of equality, that is, of democracy, had been loosed on the world, by Providence as he saw it, and that there was no turning back.[5] The spirit of change had taken over not only individuals but the family and the whole of society. As he wrote,

> Among democratic peoples, new families continually rise from nothing while others fall, and nobody's position is quite stable. The woof of time is ever being broken and the track of past generations lost. Those who have gone before are easily forgotten, and no one gives

a thought to those who will follow. All a man's interests are limited to those near himself.

As each class catches up with the next and gets mixed with it, its members do not care about one another and treat one another as strangers. Aristocracy links everybody, from peasant to king, in one long chain. Democracy breaks the chain and frees each link. . . .

Thus, not only does democracy make men forget their ancestors, but also clouds their view of their descendants and isolates them from their contemporaries. Each man is forever thrown back on himself alone, and there is danger that he may be shut up in the solitude of his own heart.[6]

For Tocqueville, it was democracy—rather than, say, a Marxist economic determinism—that gives Men a "distaste for agriculture and directs them into trade and industry."[7] It even dissolves the patriarchal family into an equality between father and son. The resultant independence and individualism has a price attached to it, however: Men, constantly seeking to improve their condition and to "keep up with the Joneses," as we would put it today, are never satisfied. That, Tocqueville tells us, "is the reason for the strange melancholy," or, as he also refers to it, "madness," so frequently found haunting the abundance of America: the price for its breaking of connections.

While Tocqueville emphasized the political, he was hardly unaware of the sweeping economic changes about him. He had visited England, as well as America, in the 1830s, and his "Memoir on Pauperism," as we have noted in Chapter 5, called attention to the way individual alms-giving by the aristocracy established warm ties between rich and poor, whereas public relief—the middle-class reformers' solution—made only for a cold, impersonal nexus.

By the time of the Revolution of 1848, Tocqueville believed that even in his own country "the industrial revolution" had brought into existence a "whole new population of workmen."[8] The result of industrialism in France, predictably, just as elsewhere, was that "Society was cut in two. . . . There were no longer ties of sympathy linking these two great classes."

As we can see, Tocqueville's language is the familiar one of disconnections and sympathy; but his aspirations were more novel and indeed anticipatory. He wished to understand and thus to ameliorate the problems of his time by discovering a new science. As he put it, "A new political science [an alternative translation is "science of politics"] is needed for a world itself quite new."[9] We can recognize now that his science, in fact, is a tentative effort at sociology, that is, historical sociology. Thus, amidst all his specific descriptions, whether of America or of France, he was really asking, "What makes any society possible?," and his attempt to answer this generalized question was by a combination of novelistic depictions, historical observations, and broad philosophical speculations.

Auguste Comte, although not following in Tocqueville's footsteps, wished to go much further. In his positive philosophy, whose lineaments we will very briefly sketch here, he sought to establish a new vision of intellectual connection, of the way in which the scientific mind links phenomena in terms of law-like relations. The last of such sciences that was to come into existence was "sociology," and Comte, as we have noted, gave public expression to the word in the forty-seventh lecture of his *Positive Philosophy* (earlier, in a private letter of 1824 he had coined the term; in his later work *Positive Polity* he added the subtitle "Treatise on Sociology"). On the basis of this new knowledge, a reconnected society was to be constructed, in which an organic period would succeed the dissolving, corrosive critical period of the Revolution.

Comte, too, used history as the basis for his new science. But it was really the philosophy of history rather than a close study of either the past or contemporary events that he had in mind. More to the point, he was most interested in the history of science—we noted earlier both his training as a professional mathematician and his informed interest in biology—and saw in its development the model for society. He claimed that a close study of the sciences of astronomy, physics, chemistry, and physiology (or what we should call biology) shows that they all proceed through three stages: the theological, metaphysical, and positive. Sociology, the study of Man, must necessarily also develop in this manner.

In looking at society as a subject of positive science, Comte discerned alternating periods, organic and critical, in its development. In the former, certain fundamental principles are accepted by all members of society (as we shall see, this bears some resemblance to Tönnies's *Gemeinschaft*); in the latter, which Comte also calls the negative period, individual free inquiry dissolves the old harmonious order, thus bringing about a breakdown in both social and intellectual connectedness.

Moving from his description of historical stages and phases,

Comte went on to elaborate an analysis of society in terms of statics and dynamics. In the former, political-social systems can be studied relative to their existing level of civilization, that is, as functioning cultural wholes. In the latter, attention is on the changing levels of civilization.

Comte's overriding conviction was that Man and society, too, are under general laws, just as are the phenomena studied by the natural sciences. The solution to our problem of social breakdown—for so he judged the world of 1789 and its consequences—is to establish these social laws, a Positive Sociology, which will rescue us from the anarchy and disorganization visited upon us by the French revolution. For our purposes, it is important to note that it was Comte's vision of a scientific sociology, much more than any of the details of his own execution of it, that served as a powerful stimulant for those, such as Emile Durkheim, who followed after him.

His inspiration also served in regard to the Saint-Simonians; but here it took a strange turn. Comte had begun his professional life as secretary to the Duc de Saint-Simon, founder of the Saint-Simonian movement. That personal relationship, however, in a few years broke down in acrimony, leaving Positivism and Saint-Simonianism in an uneasy juxtaposition, with each tugging at the other. Thus, where Comte emphasized science, the Saint-Simonians came to center their attention on technology and the industrializing process. Thomas Carlyle, as we have seen, noted the connecting power of the stagecoach; the Saint-Simonians went much further and elevated the canal, the railroad, and the steamship to almost mythical forces, bringing men together physically and subsequently spiritually. Both Comte's and Carlyle's tone was one of lament over perceived breakdown; the Saint-Simonians, one of jubilant welcome and acceptance of the new connections. For them, both the French Revolution and the Industrial Revolution cohered; and they were ready to press on toward a unified world, led by what can be described as a group of elitist semi-socialists, that is, Saint-Simonian technicians and industrialists.

The German Connection

What of France's neighbor to the East, Germany? It had experienced some of the liberating power of the French Revolution, especially in the Rhineland. With the fall of Napoleon, however, a reaction set in, under Prussian dominance. Here too a conservative political philosophy, strongly influenced by Burke, flourished. As for industrialization, Germany lagged at least two to three decades behind England, and even behind France, though textile factories were fast expanding, for example, in Engels's home area of the Wuppertal.

The sense of breakdown and disconnection was felt most keenly and fought out most acutely in the realm of religion. In the nineteenth century, Germany became the home of the "Higher Criticism" (a replay, in many ways, of the seventeenth-century movement associated with Pierre Bayle and his treatment of biblical texts in the same critical spirit that Renaissance scholars had been bringing to the classics). Religion, it was argued, must be brought by both critical and philosophical methods into accord with the rationalism to be found in modern science. Thus, religion must be "saved." In fact, as this "salvation" of religion proceeded, for many students and others the corrosive acids of rationalism ate away at the fabric of belief and destroyed it entirely. Nietzsche's "God is dead" lay just ahead; its shattering dissociation of Man from God was painfully implicit (and sometimes even explicit) in the early nineteenth century.

As a result, philosophy, replacing religion with a secular interpretation, joined industrial and political developments in eroding a comforting sense of place in a secure, hierarchical, and divinely organized world. All three movements—philosophical, economic, and political—intertwined with one another in complex, multicausal fashion, naturally differing in emphasis in each country.

In Germany, the religious fight came first, centering on Hegel and then his disciples. Hegel had sought to preserve religion by substituting Reason for God, and thus to connect the new forces of revolution with the old forces of revelation. His followers, the Young Hegelians, went further, though at first unintentionally. Starting out with a critique of religion, they ended with a critique of politics that metamorphosed into a critique of all existing social order, then seen as disorder.[10]

We catch the flavor of the movement in David Friedrich Strauss's *Life of Jesus* (1835), translated by George Eliot in 1846. As Strauss sums up the shattering force of eighteenth-century rationalism and revolution,

> The boundless store of truth and life which for eighteen centuries has been the aliment of humanity, seems irretrievably dissipated;

> the most sublime levelled with the dust, God divested of his grace, man of his dignity, and the tie between heaven and earth broken.[11]

It is a lament whose tune is now familiar to us. Unlike the English philosophers, prophets, poets, and novelists, however, the Young Hegelians did not appeal so much to a kind of insipid form of Christian sympathy for the injured as to a scathing critique of revealed religion in which they tried to save its humanistic truths by a new form of Reason.

With Ludwig Feuerbach and his *Essence of Christianity* (1841), also translated by George Eliot, theology became transformed into anthropology, and God was now seen as the creation, not the creator, of Man. "In place of the illusory, fantastic, heavenly position of man which in actual life necessarily leads to the degradation of man, I substitute the tangible, actual, and consequently also the political and social position of mankind," Feuerbach announced.[12]

It remained only for Karl Marx to give material shape to Feuerbach's generalized Man, and to do so by analyzing what he regarded as the real political and social position of Mankind in the early- and mid-nineteenth-century world of industrialization. As we have seen, for Marx, following on Carlyle, it was a world held together only by the cash nexus. Marxism, in this light, becomes an attempt, resorting only in passing to lamentation, to accept the break and to go on to establish a new form of connection for Mankind. As Marx intoned (I am inverting his actual word order), "Workers of the World, Unite. [You have] nothing to lose but your chains."[13] Such was Marx's unifying slogan.

An Emerging Science

"Connections" is one way of conceiving of scientific explanation, as we noted earlier in considering Adam Smith. Order is brought out of chaos by a chain of ideas, whose links in the mind, it is asserted, mirror links in reality. The problem, as conceived by many in the nineteenth century, was to extend this way of thinking, although increasingly with the notion of web substituted for chain, to social as well as natural facts. Auguste Comte, as we have stressed, was most fervent, and pioneering in this desire, although he had predecessors such as Montesquieu and others. A few years later, as we shall see, Comte was to be joined by Marx and Engels; while they started from different premises, and aimed at different results, that is, revolutionary ones, they too eventually hoped for a new, "positive" science of Man and society.[14]

As a result of these beginnings and other developments, sociology, by the end of the nineteenth century, would come into existence as a full-fledged academic speciality, calling itself a science.[15] Thus, the "social question" and the "social condition" had become the foci of much scholarly attention, with concentration tending to shift to sociology and away from political science and economics (though sociology remained closely connected to both older inquiries). As a result, the great classical sociologists whom we shall be treating—Tönnies, Simmel, Durkheim, and Weber—concerned themselves mainly with social relations, considering economics (this is true even for Weber) and political science only as subsets of the relational forms.

What was the core concept of their sociology? It was the idea of "community."[16] What, they were asking, are the bonds that hold Men together and thus form a society? Such a question is not new, in the sense that thinkers in early Greece and China, to take two examples, asked and tried to answer it in general philosophical terms. It took on "sociological" form, however, in a culture where the scientific attitude became prevalent, where individualism became the dominant mode through which the unsocial-social nature of Man was confronted, and where that confrontation appeared to bring on the dissolution of community, with the result being a felt breakdown of connections, expressed in terms such as alienation and anomie.

If individualism was one pole of connection (or disconnection) for the sociologists whom I have named, socialism, only briefly mentioned earlier, was the other. Sociology is not socialism; but it is animated by the same impulses that are seen to lead to the latter.[17] If Simmel and Weber rejected socialism as a political solution, while Tönnies and Durkheim embraced it in varied forms, they all were aware of it as the shadow hanging over sociology. (Marx and Engels called socialism a "specter" and plotted how to give it actual form, as a new social fact.)

Like our earlier political philosophers, poets, prophets, and novelists, these sociologists were fascinated by their vision of Man as tied into a chain, or as they would call it, web of connections. Community, association, and society were the terms most frequently used, which defined the human condition of this unique unsocial-social creature. All of these observers recognized that for a brief moment—at the beginning of the Industrial Revolution—this vision had been narrowed by the classical economists into one all-encompassing though impoverished connection: the cash nexus. For the economists as well as many of their literary and sociological critics, the web appeared reduced to one strand: self-interest, expressed in monetary terms. In such a reduced view, all the other ties, religious, ethnic, even political, could be translated into one, an economic nexus, or, sociologically stated, a "class" nexus. It was the self-conceived task of most of the sociologists to rediscover the multi-stranded web, the fabric, of society, scientifically, and, for some of them, where possible, to reorder it into a warm, secure garment for the individual human being. In the event, this last aspiration appears to have been only very imperfectly realized.

In attempting this task, the sociologists tried to give scientific form to what had been a very ambiguous and sprawling cultural response, to offer a way of understanding and restoring the bonds of the good society by means of a formal knowledge, in contrast to the literary way of doing so. With such a historical origin, however, the question is raised of how free from supposedly extra-scientific impulses was their work in actuality? Or, to phrase the matter more specifically, in what ways did the literary inspirations lead to the effort at a scientific understanding of the social facts related to community?

An especially good bridge, I have suggested, between what can be called sensibility (in the sense I have indicated) and sociology is the life and work of George Eliot. Although, as we have already noted, she lamented that "Agreement between intellects seems unattainable," she strove manfully to attain it, turning forcefully to the ideas not only of Comte but of David Strauss, Ludwig Feuerbach, Herbert Spencer, W. H. von Riehl, and Sir Henry Maine—all key figures in the development of Marx and Engels, as well as of our other scientific sociologists. In her own work, then, Eliot was an intellectual, interested in constructing a social science or natural history, as much as she was a novelist, although in the last resort it was to *feeling* as the bond of union that she turned. In resuming our inquiry, but dealing with the sociologists, we will need to be aware that their scientific strivings are also rooted in the Eliot-like feelings, as well as thoughts, that have been discussed in the previous two chapters.

One other point: in dealing with sociologists, I must emphasize again that I will not be treating them "in the round." Our major concern is not with their position in the history of sociology per se, which would require us to give sustained attention to the influences shaping their work, to their debates with other sociologists, and to the socio-political setting in which these debates took place. While I do make a stab of sorts at some of these matters, I am concentrating on the way in which our figures relate to the connections theme historically, turning that theme in a "scientific," that is, sociological, direction.

This approach carries distinct drawbacks aside from limited coverage: I shall have to cite material familiar to some readers, simply to set the stage; and I shall sometimes then have to follow out the connections theme in the work of our sociologists in what may occasionally appear a tortuous manner. (My interpretations, incidentally, are based more on a close reading of the primary texts, similar to that required earlier in our treatment of the industrial novels, than it is on the secondary literature, although that has been constantly consulted.) In the end, however, I trust that I will have shed some new light on our sociologists' endeavors, as well as having shown, in a manner previously not observed, how they both use and contribute to the connections theme.

The Broken Bridge: English Sociology

Before embarking on this task, however, we face a preliminary problem. Why was the bridge constructed by Eliot, even if only a swaying, rope one, not particularly trodden by British thinkers? Why was the development of a theoretical sociology essentially a Continental task and not an English one? The answers to these questions, I hope, will show why I will be crossing the Channel in order to examine the rise of the new scientific sociology, after having first dealt with a literary response to the sense of broken connections in Eliot's homeland.

Our general guide in this matter will be Philip Abrams, whose *The Origins of British Sociology: 1834–1914* (1968) gives an informed and persuasive account (which I will try both to paraphrase and to embroider on).[18] It is Abrams's view that, while Positivism of a general and varied nature served as the overall background for work in social science in Britain, it was overlaid by three other bodies of thought: political economy, ameliorism, and social evolution.

The first two were rooted in pre-Comtean developments. As I interpret Abrams's argument, the school of classical political economy dominated. Its basic concept circled around the individual and his self-interest, which led him by an invisible hand to the general good. Thus, community of interest, if not community as such, was an automatic consequence. What is more, though there existed an intense form of individual conflict, that is, competition, the system as a whole was without conflict (for example, of class). Any substantive clash, on this account, in such a system of basic harmony could come only from ignorance or unreason. If these existed, however, it was thought that they could be dispelled by correct information in the form of "facts." Such facts, of course, referred to aggregate data about the circumstances and behavior of individuals. Thus, statistics was believed to be the form of any conceivable social science.

Now we can draw for ourselves a few conclusions from the above account. As we can see, the core concepts of classical political economy correspond very closely with the cash-nexus metaphor of society. Society in any larger conceptual sense is dissolved, and there is no room for further speculation or theory outside the economic framework (Adam Smith, as we have noted, knew better; after *The Wealth of Nations* he had in mind to write a comprehensive study of jurisprudence, but he never got to it). For example, while demography and the study of poverty could be inquired into "statistically," and legislation enacted in the light of the findings, poverty itself was not conceivable as a product of the social structure, but only of individual decisions. What was possible for this school of thought, therefore, was "empirical" but not "theoretical" sociology.

The second pre-Comtean stream of opinion is what Abrams calls "ameliorism." It takes its rise from traditional religious and moral sources and, at least initially, believes them to be sufficient guides to policy. Its characteristic expression is philanthropy. It too focuses on the individual, and sees his problem as one of morals or character: too much drinking, promiscuity, and so on. Statistics, however, in the eyes of this school, is cold and unfeeling. (Eventually, even many of the statisticians came around to this view, as when the members of the Statistical Society of Bristol in the 1830s acknowledged that "in a simple state of society, a man may know tolerably well what his duties to the poor are . . . but what shall be said of that artificial and complicated state of things when a nation manufactures for half the world—and when the consequence unavoidably is the enormous distance between the labourer and his virtual and subdivided employer?," and then turned in moral perplexity to what I have called "sympathy.")[19]

Believers in statistics and sympathy often joined hands, especially in the second part of the nineteenth century, where they found themselves comfortable companions in a new organization, the National Association for the Promotion of Social Science, founded in 1856. They were united in rejecting any conception of an overall social system; instead they supported the notion that the state was the proper custodial agent for dealing with possible social problems, for these could only arise inadvertently from the interactions of "free" individuals.

As we can judge from the above, the ground for the origins of a theoretical sociology, which conceptualizes society in analytic terms, was not fertile in Britain. In fact, Britain itself was the problem: its very traditions of political economy and philanthropy were unique to it in their twining strength. Where else (aside from America) had the tenets of political economy achieved such strength? What other country (again, aside from America), for example, had a custom of widespread philanthropy (as distinct from mere charity)? It is not by accident, therefore, that political economy largely pre-empted the sociological possibility, and that sympathy, instead of a new science, flourished in Great Britain.

Yet there were other seeds that could have sprouted, if the environment had been different. As Abrams points out, these were to be found in what he calls "social evolution."[20] Without going into extensive detail, we can note again the Positivist strain in British thought. Certainly, here were intimations of a theoretical sociology, emphasizing fundamental laws of social organization, and even of their compatibility with laws of evolution. The same Harriet Martineau who we saw arguing with Dickens in favor of "facts," that is, statistics, translated Comte's *Positive Philosophy* into English in 1853, but it was largely ignored at the time. It is Abrams's contention, however, that Comte's influence in England, hard to specify in any case, may have been most important for the reaction it stirred up.

Of greater appeal, it appears, were the ideas and work of two other men: Frederick Le Play and Francis Galton. Le Play, like Comte a Frenchman, shared the ameliorist concern of the British with concern for the individual, but argued that the individual had to be understood in an institutional context, especially that of the family. The modern family, shaken and almost destroyed by the Industrial Revolution, Le Play claimed, was no longer able to serve as a basis for moral education and for stable social relations. It needed to be reconstituted, and to do so one needed to study it empirically. Thus, Le Play pioneered in field studies that took the family as its unit of attention.

As can readily be seen, Le Play largely remained within an atheoretical social frame (though he did adumbrate a shadowy typology of pre-industrial and industrial societies), lamenting the breakdown of connections and seeking to reknit them in traditional ways. In his native France, he and his followers figured more as an obstacle than an inspiration to the development of an analytic sociology; fortunately, if one favors the effort at theory, in France there were scholars such as Durkheim who in the late nineteenth century broke through the restraints to forge a formal science of sociology.[21] In Britain, Le Play's followers, such as Patrick Geddes, supported his emphasis on family and regional studies, and sought to rebuild a common physical and moral environment inspired by a largely nontheoretical sociology.

Unlike Le Play, Francis Galton cannot fairly be considered even a proto-sociologist. Yet his "science" of eugenics fitted into a kind of sociology by seeming to offer an alternative way of dealing with social problems (and, parenthetically, paying attention to race, though not as an obvious bond of community), and thus to obviate the need for sociology itself. Like the statistics of which it made such abundant use, eugenics, too, stood against misguided compassion and thus, in effect, against both sympathy and sociology.

When, finally, in 1903 a British Sociological Society was established, it was the followers of Geddes, and thus Le Play, and of Galton, and thus statistics, who dominated. Their only real challenge came from Leonard Hobhouse, who became editor of the *Sociological Review* in 1907 and in the same year co-holder of the first chair in sociology, at the University of London. Hobhouse is the one British sociologist who might be said to approach the stature of the Continental figures whom we are choosing to study; but he falls far short of them in establishing the main contours of the new field of sociology. By remaining a social evolutionist, he plowed ahead in what was, in the light of coming classical sociological theory, the wrong direction.[22]

Herbert Spencer, whom we have not mentioned in this account until now, preceded him, and must be accounted perhaps the one truly great British sociologist.[23] Spencer was a social evolutionist *par excellence*, writing in the 1850s and onward, who conceived of society as an organism whose parts function in an interdependent way. For Spencer, change takes place through adaptation—specifically through "survival of the fittest," a phrase he coined and bequeathed to Darwin—and evolution moves from homogeneity to heterogeneity—or, in short, to increased division of labor both in species and in society.

Though Spencer did conceive of society as a total social system (and the sketch I am giving here is very inadequate to his achievement), his teleology, his adherence to economic individualism, and his anti-ameliorism, among other things, eventually caused his influence to wither. "Who now reads Spencer?" Crane Brinton asked, and Talcott Parsons repeated.[24] Hobhouse did read him and, in reaction, elevated evolution to an "evolution of mind," a growth of human self-consciousness. This allowed for both amelioristic altruism and an appeal to the data of evolutionary anthropology; thus, according to Abrams, it seemed propitious for the development of a science of sociology even in England. Alas, Hobhouse's work too was largely overwhelmed by the forces of political economy and non-scientific ameliorism that stood at the origins of British sociology and then aborted its birth until, as Abrams sees it, a new genesis was possible after World War II.

We have come a long way from Eliot's bridge. I have gone into a good deal of detail, however, in order to show why we are moving to Continental thinkers, even though the original and fundamental experience of, and then the response to, the cash-nexus society mainly originated in England. We must go back now to the mid-nineteenth century and to non-English traditions and contexts in order to see how the initial literary response to the presumed breakdown of connections developed, over time, into a forceful and formal science of society—sociology.

7

Revolutionary Sociology: Engels and Marx

Links

Our starting point in this endeavor is Marx and Engels. They must be accounted the founding fathers of the new discipline of sociology, along with Comte and Tocqueville. They, in fact, linked England and the Continent, joining German philosophical thought as well as French revolutionary tradition, to English industrial conditions, and then proclaiming an international movement. Their contributions to our comprehension of ideology, class, economic relations, alienation, and so forth are fundamental. So, too, is their myth-making role in regard to our connections theme. Most of their political impact, however, arises out of their being socialists, as well as sociologists, who sought to develop sociology as a means of revolution.

It is, therefore, as revolutionary sociologists that I shall treat of them. And, in doing so, I want to highlight the fact that it is their literary power, and thus their ability to evoke their readers' passions and indignation, as much as their theories per se, which stands at the heart of their influence. They, more than any other sociologist, follow upon the work of Eliot and the other literary lamenters, and overtly link the earlier sensibility with the new sociology. In fact, Engels and Marx can be viewed as tripartite in their nature: breakers, lamenters, and sociologists all in one.

In treating of them in this light, I will again not attempt anything approaching a full analysis of their work, but will pick out a few items relevant to our theme; and, even here, I will not select for my texts their canonical works. What is more, I will pay as much attention to Engels, as a separate figure, as I do to Marx. And lastly, as an additional caveat, the full relevance of their work to the cash nexus will be to a certain extent implicit as well as explicit and will require the subsequent chapters to be made more convincing.

Engels

Now, Engels has already been cited as Marx's source of the phrase "cash nexus" (itself borrowed from Carlyle). In fact, Friedrich Engels, two years younger than his collaborator, had, unlike Marx, first-hand acquaintance of a sort with masses of workers, became interested in economic questions before his friend, and publicly proclaimed himself a communist before the latter did. The son of a patriarchal, Pietist textile-mill owner, Engels grew up amidst the opening stages of the Industrial Revolution in Germany, in the Wuppertal valley. His fight with his father—a stern representative of the bourgeoisie—was never fully resolved, and Engels became an unusual sort of "double Man": by day, a capitalist, helping to run his father's firm in Manchester, and by night, so to speak, a communist supporting Karl Marx and the cause, using for that purpose the profits "expropriated" from the factory hands.[1]

In the beginning, then, Engels was the more advanced, in this case, radical, of the two young men, and led the way to communism. (A re-examination of Engels's role is badly needed; although in the end Marx clearly became the dominant partner, in the process he borrowed heavily—and not only financially—from Engels.)[2] What, however, did the youth of twenty or so years—we forget how young these young radicals were—mean by the term communism?

In an article written in 1844 and published the next year, "Description of Recently Founded Communist Colonies Still in Existence," Engels declared that communism simply meant "community of goods," and tried to dispel the objection that this was a utopian aspiration by pointing to its realization in—utopian communities! Writing about three American communities, the Harmonists, Shakers, and Rappists, Engels depicted a social life in which money was dispensed with, work was freely chosen, and yet an abundance of goods was produced (his evidence was all second-hand, from accounts in an Owenite periodical, *The New Moral World*). He noted that these "colonies" were all characterized by a religious bond, which he called "irrational," but announced that their success was in spite of this drawback, and would be greater when "free of religious nonsense."[3] Similarly, he noted that they prohibited the teaching of science, but did not conclude that they thereby removed one of the powerful forces in modern society that had been dissolving earlier communal living.

Engels was quickly to move beyond the simple definition of communism and the utopian ease of achieving it: "New Jerusalems" he derisively called the colonies a few years later. Meanwhile, however, he pursued his career as a communist by addressing his fellow Wuppertalians, almost all professionals or members of the bourgeoisie, in a number of exhortatory talks. In a speech in Elberfeld, in 1845, he concentrated on the evils of exisiting society rather than on the supposed achievements of utopian colonies. His argument was that the pursuit of self-interest, the struggle of individual with individual, resulting in "an unregulated economic system," was irrational (rather than merely immoral). In fact, he states, it is "an obvious, self-evident truth" that "we cannot do without our fellow-men, that our interests, if nothing else, bind us all to one another." His appeal, therefore, was to a re-organization of society on "more rational principles."[4]

What would these be? Basically, planning by a central authority, which would easily be informed about both production and consumption needs. Yet, there will be less administration under communism than under capitalism because there will be no crime, requiring police, no conflict, requiring standing armies, and so on. Other savings of a sort are provided by town planning, which eliminates individual waste of space, and communal cooking, which saves on time. This version of communism, which Engels still defines as common ownership ("*Gütergemeinschaft*"—we will note the persistent use of the term *Gemeinschaft* by Tönnies and others later), is, he tells us, not "rooted in pure fantasy," but easily translated into reality. It can be arrived at by three measures: general education of all children; a re-organization of the poor relief system; and a general, progressive tax on capital, which he describes as a "purely communist" principle. In an optimistic and conciliatory mood, Engels ends by announcing his vision of the future as a real one, attested to "by the course of development of all civilised nations" and "by common sense and, above all, by the human heart."[5]

A week later, in a second speech at Elberfeld, Engels added that the communist future was inevitable. "With the same certainty with which we can develop from given mathematical principles a new mathematical proposition, with the same certainty we can deduce from the existing economic relations and the principles of political economy the imminence of social revolution."[6] What is more, Engels declared, if the upper classes would cooperate, the overthrow need not be violent or bloody.

The Engels I have depicted so far is both slightly naïve and propagandistically conciliatory. He is still close to the "sensibility" approach to the human heart, but combines it with an exhortation to rationality and, at the end, a claim to science. The "occasional" pieces I have cited have not the weight of his later writings, but reveal a young Engels vaguely aware of the social question, of the wrongs of a society based solely on the bond of self-interest, and of the need to move toward a community of goods. It is out of this mixture of ill-defined thoughts and longings, nevertheless, that Engels moved toward a more sustained wrestling with the problem he came to understand by the phrase "cash nexus."

From November 1842 to August 1844, Engels had lived and worked in Manchester, England. On his return to Barmen, his hometown, he not only prepared to give the speeches quoted above but rewrote a series of articles concerning Manchester, which emerged in 1845 as *The Condition of the Working-Class in England in 1844*. Here, the Engels of history steps forth. It is a long, full account, derived, as Engels proudly states, from first-hand observation of the actual conditions of the workers. Marx never had such an experience; the concept of the proletariat emerged from his philosophical musings, not, as with Engels, from the actual environment of the textile factories (in fact, Engels actually encountered very few members of the proletariat). Until his own research for *Capital*, undertaken in the British Museum after 1850, Marx was dependent on Engels for his presumably empirical knowledge of workers and working conditions.

Manchester was the town, as we have seen, in which Elizabeth Gaskell lived and upon which she drew for the factory operatives in her novels. It was visited by Alexis de Tocqueville in 1835 and occasioned his remark that "the whole of English society is . . . somehow tied up with money. It fills all the gaps that one finds between men, but nothing will take its place." In 1838, Carlyle came and saw a scene "hideous" and yet "beautiful as magic dreams": with a "thousand mills" and "ten-thousand times ten-thousand spools and spindles all set humming . . . sublime as Niagara";[7] in that same year also came Disraeli, who saw it as a new "Athens"; and Dickens, who was appalled and saved his vitriol for eventual release in his 1854 novel *Hard Times*.

Manchester, then, was both the shock town and the exhibition palace of the onrushing Industrial Revolution. To Engels, it represented the future of all mankind—unless something were done about it. Before industrialization, as Engels informs us, there had existed an "idyllic simplicity and intimacy," a contented society cushioned in a "patriarchal relation." Engels admits that he takes this picture, whole cloth, from Peter Gaskell's *The Manufacturing Population of England* (1833), to which he also owes the history of the development of the proletariat contained in his introduction.[8] Engels's procedure here is similar to his acceptance of the idyllic accounts of the American communist colonies. In this case, however, Engels sees a flaw in what he calls this "cosily romantic" existence: the pre-industrial workers "never thought"; in truth, "they were not human beings; they were merely toiling machines in the service of the few aristocrats." The Industrial Revolution merely carries their condition to its logical end, "making the workers machines pure and simple."[9]

In Engels's account, the pre-industrial idyllic but unthinking existence is broken by the invention of actual machines, especially by the spinning jenny. The other causal factor is cut-throat competition. Together, these forces produce not only textiles, for example, but a new class of beings, the proletariat. The latter, constantly increasing in number, stand opposed to the capitalists, who persist "in ignoring [their] poverty."[10] It is this ignorance on the part of the bourgeoisie that Engels initially sets himself to rectify by his book.

His basic method is to combine first-hand observation and description with moral strictures. Although elsewhere he dismissed "all the multi-volumed novels" (recommending only Carlyle's *Past and Present*) as not worth reading, he actually aims in this early work at the same cultivation of sensibility recommended by Elizabeth Gaskell in her 1848 novel, *Mary Barton*, as a partial remedy for the appalling division of men. Thus Engels approvingly quotes Peter Gaskell to the effect that "till the Bishop of London called the attention of the public to the state of Bethnal Green, about as little was known at the West-end of the town of this most destitute parish as the wilds of Australia or the islands of the South Seas." And, even more revealing, he comes to grips with his subject, the breakdown of connections, in a powerful passage that reminds us of nothing so much as some lines of Wordsworth:

> "The hundreds of thousands of all classes and ranks crowding past each other, are they not all human beings with the same qualities and powers, and with the same interest in being happy? And have they not, in the end, to seek happiness in the same way, by the same means? And still they crowd by one another as though they had nothing in common, nothing to do with one another, and their only agreement is the tacit one, that each keep to his own side of the pavement, so as not to delay the opposing streams of the crowd, while it occurs to no man to honour another with so much as a glance. The brutal indifference, the unfeeling isolation of each in his private interest, becomes the more repellent and offensive, the more these individuals are crowded together, within a limited space."[11]

Society, Engels declares, "is already in a state of visible dissolution." Without analyzing what exactly he means by society, Engels has a clear idea of it. Indeed, he reifies it when he speaks of it as committing "murder," just as an individual might do, when it condemns hundreds of proletarians to an early death. In fact, Engels then reduces society to one of its elements when he goes on to say, in a note added possibly under the influence of Marx,

> When as here and elsewhere I speak of society as a responsible whole, having rights and duties, I mean, of course, the ruling owner of society, the class which at present holds social and political control, and bears, therefore, the responsibility for the condition of those to whom it grants no share in such control. This ruling class in England, as in all other civilised countries, is the bourgeoisie.[12]

In *The Condition*, Engels is still ambivalent about the bourgeoisie. Part of his appeal is to their good nature; another part recognizes that they are either too enfeebled or too malevolent to take effective action.[13] In the end, Engels recognizes that the proletariat will have to emancipate itself. It will have been the bourgeoisie, however, who will have both created it and given it its strength.

The bourgeoisie has itself destroyed "the last remnant of the patriarchal relation between working-men and employers." It has reduced that relation to the infamous "cash payment," and here Engels quotes the "half German Englishman" Carlyle, as we have already seen. Society, therefore, is broken into two warring parties that have nothing in common; Engels rephrases Peter Gaskell's quotation, and comments that "the bourgeoisie has more in common with every other nation of the earth than with the workers in whose midst it lives. The workers speak other dialects, have other thoughts and ideals. . . ."[14]

What of these workers, what are the ties that bind them? On Engels's account, they have no religious belief, no national pride or what he calls "prejudice," and no longer even a common family life. Their only tie to the bourgeoisie, if it can be called that, is the cash one. What ties them (or should) to one another, however, is class hatred (the "only moral incentive by which the worker can be brought nearer the goal" of revolution).[15] It is the great cities that bring the workers together and make them feel as a class (this, it should be noted, is a new assertion, even if with mixed feelings, of urban superiority in the perennial city-country debate). It is the bourgeoisie, however, with its estranging cash payment, that turns the proletariat, a newly created Frankenstein's monster, into a revolutionary mass.

This is as far as Engels goes at this stage of his life and work. In dealing with it, I have tried to give some sense of the origin and context of Engels's reading of Carlyle and his cash-nexus vision. It remains to add one other piece to that context, touching on the neglected issue of racism alluded to earlier. It concerns the fact that some people saw the cash nexus as a Jewish plot. In the same paragraph in which he quotes the "Cash Payment" statement, Engels notes that the bourgeoisie's only bliss is in making money, and then refers to them as "bartering Jews," who are imbued with the "huckstering spirit."[16] Engels seems to have shared the easy social anti-Semitism of his times—his later life is filled with crude racial remarks of various kinds—but his friend Karl Marx's similar comments in "On the Jewish Question," of 1843–44, suggests a collegial sentiment, with one man—which first?—inspiring the other. In any case, for both of them, as well as for many others, such remarks mix religion and racism in a "critical" spirit (for critique, not inquiry, is the German approach, as evinced in the many titles with that word).

All these ties, religious as well as cash-based ones, will be done away by the one class, the proletariat, whose only ties are to one another as workers. In his penultimate paragraph, Engels takes up again the inspiration of Carlyle, and announces that *"Prophecy* [italics mine, to remind us of its use by the Scotsman] is nowhere so easy as in England. . . . the revolution must come; it is already too late to bring about a peaceful solution. . . ."[17]

At this point, Engels stands before us as at most a transitional figure to social science. His tone is more that of a descriptive novelist and prophet than of a sociologist. I have not mentioned earlier his abundant use of statistics; but these are brought in to bolster his moral indignation rather than to serve as a basis for analysis. He has spoken of the "mathematical certainty" of social revolution; but this attests more to a kind of Hobbesian inspiration than a truly nineteenth-century scientific conviction. The fact is that, with all his precedence over Marx in various matters, Engels, as he himself admitted, had to submit to his friend for a true effort at theoretical understanding of the society both forming and dissolving around him. It is to the genius of Marx that we must turn for an interpretation of cash-nexus society that can properly be called sociological as well as socialist.[18]

Marx

What Engels added to commentators such as Gaskell and Carlyle was an emphasis on the proletariat and a call to revolution. What Marx added was theory, which, though not mathematical, aspired to provide the analytical certainty of how and why the proletarian revolution had to come about. Where Engels had never finished gymnasium studies, Marx had proceeded to a doctorate in philosophy; though both had fallen under the spell of Hegel, it was Marx who truly ingested his teachings in profound and professional form, wrestling mightily with them. It was, therefore, the Hegelian philosophy, when stood on its head and suitably combined with concern about a cash-nexus society, which eventuated for Marx and Engels in a sociology as well as a socialism.

Again, my treatment of Marx will be highly selective, oriented to the theme of "connections." And, as with Engels, I will stress the early writings (rather than the great, canonical masterpieces, such as *Capital*). As Anthony Giddens remarks, writing on *The Economic and Philosophic Manuscripts* of 1844 (unpublished while Marx was alive), ". . . these fragmentary notes contain the germ of virtually all of the important ideas which Marx developed with greater precision in later writings" (I would want to add to the *Manuscripts* the book *The German Ideology* of 1846, also unpublished in Marx's lifetime).[19] By concentrating on more youthful writings, therefore, I can make my points in a relatively brief, synoptic treatment of Marx.

Karl Marx, as is well known, was a brilliant and ambitious young man, destined by his father for a career in law. Once at university, the young Karl turned to philosophy, and especially Hegelian philosophy. This last inspiration is complicated but, as already noted, essential. In early-nineteenth-century Germany, Hegel appeared to stand, by his content, for confirmation of the existing church and state, and by his method, for its transcendence. Above all, as we noted earlier, he represented the secularization of religion, that is, the replacement of revelation by Reason, and of God by the Idea. His disciples who stood to the left, the so-called Young Hegelians, pushed on from a reasoned, or critical, treatment of religion to a similar treatment of the state. Marx was among those who pushed on.

The Young Hegelians and associated critics such as Bruno Bauer (Marx's original mentor), David Strauss, and Ludwig Feuerbach are significant, of course, in their own right; here I only note their importance for Karl Marx, and single out two items of consequence.[20] First, their concern, and Marx's, was with the state of Germany, in which they saw something rotten. It is easy to forget, because Marxism became an international movement, how nationalistic the young Marx and Engels were; and as with so many other Young Germans, how both ashamed and arrogant they were about their motherland.[21] In his 1844 "Contribution to the Critique of Hegel's *Philosophy of Right:* Introduction," Marx lamented the fact that his nation was behind the British in practical, industrial terms, and the French in political; only in philosophical terms were the Germans ahead of the others. As Marx said, "We are the philosophical contemporaries of the present day without being its historical contemporaries."[22]

We shall see in a moment what his solution was, but before that the other item: Second, the Young Hegelian concern was initially and primarily with religion, whose ties had to be dramatically severed; as Marx wrote, ". . . the criticism of religion is the premise of all criticism," for once one realized that "Man makes religion; religion does not make man," then all of man's other "makings"—his entire social, political, and economic world—could also be brought back into his conscious control.[23] Or so Marx, if not the other Hegelians, said.

With these two points in mind, we can see how Marx wrestled with the problem of Germany's backwardness. In the beginning of his public activity, around 1841–42, he had been a liberal democrat, who hoped to reform Germany in a constitutional direction. He had little or no concern with the "social question" as such.[24] Then, partly under the influence of Engels, whose article "Critique of Political Economy" he helped publish, and admired, and also influenced by events such as the Silesian weavers' uprising in 1844, he became conscious, though not knowledgeable, about the subject.

In his "Critique" of Hegel, Marx glimpsed the essence of his German problem, if not of the social one: in Germany, the bourgeoisie were not, and probably would never be, manly and powerful enough to pull off a French-type revolution. Then how could Germany be brought into the forefront of actual progress? Was a jump possible? Marx had been groping in other writings toward a social analysis that said No; here, his revolutionary aspirations carried the day, and he proclaimed that the German bourgeoisie would bring into existence, unwittingly, a new class, the proletariat, which, as a class with *"radical chains,"* would dissolve the existing order—"emancipate themselves and become *men"* is Marx's exhortatory prediction—and destroy all partial connections that stood in the way, not only of a German but of a "total redemption of humanity."[25]

The language of the youthful Marx is still religious; it would become more and more the language of social analysis as he moved from the German problem per se to that of modern, capitalist society at large. The key to his entire analysis is the cash-nexus trope. His logic is as follows. If the bourgeoisie of Germany could not emancipate themselves and their country, they could, however, press on with industrialization. Industrialization would necessarily create the proletariat. Because of the bourgeoisie's egoistic life—the callous pursuit of profits—that proletariat would be an enemy, alienated in manifold ways. Q.E.D.: the cash nexus is a necessary step toward communism.

While developing these ideas in his "Critique" of Hegel, Marx was also writing at about the same time his essay "On the Jewish Question." I shall not deal here with what personal issues unconsciously he might have been solving; but, consciously, he tried to come to terms with the "egoistic life" he saw permeating modern existence as embodied in the spirit of the Jew.[26] Civil society, he proclaims, is the "sphere of egoism and of the *bellum omnium contra omnes*. It is no longer the essence of *community*, but the essence of *differentiation*. . . . man is *separated* from the *community*, from himself and from other men." This is a lament we have heard before. Accordingly, man, even in a politically emancipated society such as that of post-1789 France, is still removed from what Marx, following Feuerbach, refers to as his "species-being." On the contrary, Marx points out, "species-life itself—society—appears as a system which is external to the individual and as a limitation of his original independence. The only bond between men is natural necessity, need and private interest, the preservation of their property and their egoistic persons."[27]

What is extraordinary is that Marx then diverts his argument into an *ad hominem* identification of egoistic Man with the Jew. "What is the profane basis of Judaism? *Practical* need, *self-interest*. What is the worldly cult of the Jew? *Huckstering*. What is his worldly god? *Money*." (We have already noted this same identification in Engels.) The Jew, for Marx, stands totally outside of "community." He only follows individual self-interest and has no tie to others but money; as a man of money, he has no nationality other than that of the international financier, whose invisible liquidity gives him "universal domination" (which Marx, paradoxically, claims is also manifested in the form of Christianity).[28] From this crude personification of the cash-nexus man as Jew (arbitrarily hauled in here by Marx; which thus accounts for its seemingly arbitrary inclusion here by me), Marx moves on to the bourgeoisie *per se*; and, *mirabile dictu*, to a profound and penetrating analysis of what is involved in species-being and society.

According to Marx, what makes Man different from the other animals—and constitutes his species-being—is exactly his existence in a human society. It is society that shapes Man, gives him his particular faculties, needs, and goals, and makes him "human." The "isolated individual" of Locke or Rousseau in Marx's view is a fiction, for Man is necessarily born into an ongoing society whose "circumstances" he cannot choose freely but must accept and work within, even if to change them. As Marx asserts forcefully, however, "What is to be avoided above all is the re-establishing of 'Society' as an abstraction vis-à-vis the individual. The individual is the *social being*. His life, even if it may not appear in the direct form of a *communal* life carried out together with others—is therefore an expression and confirmation of *social life*." The "un-social" part of Man's being, in fact, has meaning only in a "social" setting. "Human essence is no abstraction inherent in each single individual," Marx declares in the sixth of his "Theses on Feuerbach." "In its reality it is the ensemble of the social relations."[29]

Starting from this general conception of society and the individual, Marx broke through to his materialist interpretation of history between 1844 and 1846. Its classic expression is in *The Economic and Philosophic Manuscripts* and *The German Ideology*, but there is a nice, concise statement available in a letter of 1846 to P. V. Annenkov. "What is society, whatever its form may be?" Marx asks himself. "The product of men's reciprocal action," he answers, in what is his shortest definition of "society." As he then goes on, and it is worth quoting at length:

> Are men free to choose this or that form of society? By no means. Assume a particular state of development in the productive faculties of man and you will get a particular form of commerce and consumption. Assume particular stages of development in production, commerce and consumption and you will have a corresponding social constitution, a corresponding organisation of the family, of orders or of classes, in a word, a corresponding civil society. Assume a particular civil society and you will get particular political conditions which are only the official expression of civil society.[30]

The key element in Men's "reciprocal action" for Marx is "material productivity," which in turn "produces . . . social relations." This is the famous materialist interpretation of history; I will not go into more description other than to say that Marx, in various of his works, of which the *Grundrisse*, written 1857–58 but unpublished until the twentieth century, is the most prominent and impressive, tried to give empirical, historical detail to his perception of the continuously changing yet "holistic" and related nature of society, in which material production figures as the centerpiece. In any event, material production serves as the underlying structure on which is then produced the ideas and categories, historical and transitory, that express in superstructural form the particular existing social relations.[31] It is this society and culture that Man inherits and which defines his species-being.

Where in all of this is Marx's particular concern with the cash nexus and what he perceived as breakdown of connection in his own epoch? The argument that I shall make necessarily involves a number of somewhat steep steps. Translating the Hegelian dialectic into material form, Marx announced that the productive forces already acquired by Men might—he was always tempted to say "would"—no longer be in accord with the social relations in which they had arisen. They become fetters. In such a situation they must be broken if progress is to be made.

How, and by what force, is this transcendence to be accomplished? It is at this point that "class" becomes so prominent a part of Marx's theory. In fact, Marx never really offers a full and formal analysis of what he means by class; to quote Giddens again, "It is an irony which has frequently been noted that the manuscripts which Marx left at his death should have broken off at the point at which he was entering upon a systematic analysis of the concept of class."[32] Implicitly, however, the notion of class as involving a grouping of individuals related in special fashion to the means of production runs through all Marx's works, from the famous "history . . . is the history of class struggles" of *The Communist Manifesto* to his last manuscript on *Capital*. Such a relation can be either objective, as perceived by an outside analyst, or subjective, as consciously experienced by the members of the class, or, of course, both. It is the famous problem of class consciousness. In either case, however, class must inevitably imply for Marx class conflict on the objective level.

For Marx, the bourgeoisie were simplifying the class struggle by eliminating all other types of stratification, and pushing more and more individuals into the proletariat. Or so Marx insisted. The fact is that Marx was more interested in a real social revolution than in an academic social analysis, and thus more interested in the proletariat as a monolithic unity than in any subtle differentiations.

Previously, in the eighteenth century, the customary language of social stratification was in terms of ranks, orders, estates, and so forth. For example, Adam Smith entitled his famous remarks in 1776 on the division of labor, "On the causes of improvement in the productive powers of labour, and of the order according to which its produce is naturally distributed among the different ranks of the people."[33] In 1789, it was still the three estates that were summoned to the Estates-General, which then turned into a National Assembly. Class is a newly emerging economic category, rather than a status designation.

So, too, the very concept and term "society" as we noted earlier (Chapter 1) is itself a late development: according to Marc Bloch, it was first consciously used in the modern sense by the Comte de Boulainvilliers in 1727 to describe "feudal society" as a whole, encompassing but distinct from a feudal regime.[34] Indeed, it is only with the passing of one form of society, the feudal, that Men become conscious of "society" as being conceptually separate from the individual and subject to change. The change in this case, as we know, was to "industrial society," the neologism coined by Thomas Carlyle. Moreover, only when there is a sense of "individualism," of the person as separate from society, can a true conception of society itself emerge. And only when there is an awareness of society as a problematic, changing entity can the sense of self flourish into individualism. Individualism and society, as noted earlier, are linked terms.

It is against this background that we can understand Marx's ideas about the two terms, and his capture of the term "class." He himself acknowledged predecessors in Guizot and Thierry, and we have already mentioned Disraeli's awareness of "two nations" as well as a similar awareness on the part of various other novelists. What Marx did, following Engels's efforts, was to tie "class" ineluctably to the "proletariat," who would abolish it. Marx captured the emerging sociological analysis and placed it in the service of his socialism, that is, communism.

The detailed means by which he accomplished this task is to be found in his mature economic writings, such as "Wage Labour and Capital" (1849) and *Capital* (1st volume, 1867). There, for better or for worse, Marx generally accepts the theories of classical economics as describing the real situation of capitalism, but makes two additions: 1) he points out that the "laws" of classical economics are not universal but merely applicable to capitalist conditions; and 2) he draws out the consequences of the labor theory of value to its surplus value conclusion. In grand and thunderous prose, bolstered by statistics, formulae, and parliamentary reports, Marx proves to his own satisfaction that the interests of the bourgeoisie and the proletariat are necessarily antagonistic, and must grow more so. This is the case even when the workers' wages appear to increase; as Marx remarks in "Wage Labour and Capital," "The material position of the worker has improved, but at the cost of his social position. The social gulf that divides him from the capitalist has widened."[35] In *Capital*, Marx hammers home this conviction in explosive fashion; the reader is buried under an avalanche of detail as well as theory. Even if, individually, Marx's various theories—labor theory of value, surplus value, increasing immiserization of workers, and so on—can be criticized, the reader is left with a powerful documentary account—a narrative more than an economic treatise—of how finally human relations have been plunged into the icy waters of the market relation, leaving only the cash nexus.

Long before the economic documentation, Marx had seen the necessary solution: communism. In the unpublished 1844 *Manuscripts*, he had already announced that communism is "the complete return of man to himself as a *social* (i.e., human) being—a return become conscious, and accomplished within the entire wealth of previous development" (i.e., including capitalist development). It is, further, the true resolution of the strife "between freedom and necessity, between the individual and the species. Communism is the riddle of history solved, and it knows itself to be this solution."[36]

In sum, the age-old split of Man into an unsocial-social creature could and would be healed. In insisting that the individual was, in essence, a social being, Marx also claimed to be preserving his individualism. In fact, Marx claimed that only in communist society could true individualism flourish.

There was a certain inconsistency—or, more favorably put, development—in Marx's formulation of his views. In the *Economic and Philosophic Manuscripts*, he says that money, instead of making for true individuality, destroys it. "In the light of this characteristic alone, money is thus the general overturning of *individualities* which turns them into their contrary and adds contradictory attributes to their attributes. Money, then, appears as this *overturning* power both against the individual and against the bonds of society. . . . "[37] In later writings, however, he stresses the positive effect of money on the rise of individualism, though it remains a selfish passion. Man, according to Marx now, starts out as a wholly communal being, and only through the process of history develops into an individualized being. It is increasing division of labor and market relations that brings this development about. As Marx puts it in the

Grundrisse, Man "originally appears as a *generic-being, a tribal being, a herd animal* . . . . Exchange itself is a major agent of this individualisation."[38] Thus, individualization is also part of the "entire wealth of previous development."

In *The German Ideology*, Marx had noted that "Only in community [has each] individual the means of cultivating his gifts in all directions; only in the community, therefore, is personal freedom possible." Thus, before developed communism, community could be only a matter of class, and the individual only a member of a particular, partial class. It was "always a community to which these individuals belonged only as average individuals, only insofar as they lived within the conditions of existence of their class—a relationship in which they participated not as individuals but as members of a class."[39] Class, then, was the middle term holding apart the desired unification of the individual and society. As Marx proclaims in *The Communist Manifesto*, "In place of the old bourgeois society, with its classes and class antagonisms, we shall have an association, in which the free development of each is the condition for the free development of all."[40]

Association will have replaced society, and individual relations, class relations. In the end, then, the theory that Marx brought to Engels gave, in the form of historical sociology, what could be seen as a scientific certainty: that socialism, that is, communism, would prevail; and, paradoxically, would do away with the sociology (if not society itself) that predicted this outcome.

I hasten to add that I have barely touched on the wealth of sociological theory that Marx elaborated in the course of his dialectical progression to the position I am asserting for him (and whose wealth can be detached from that final position; for example, class analysis and its attendant theory of ideology can persist even if Marx himself envisioned class and ideology as disappearing).

Two contributions by Marx to any future sociology are of special importance. The first is his emphasis on economic factors, his famous economic determinism, which, shorn of its exaggerations, is an essential corrective to previous one-sided stresses on political or intellectual factors. The second is his conception of theory and praxis, which allows him to escape the trap of Positivism (while, paradoxically, he approaches its edge with his economic determinism). Marx is surely right that the task of sociology is to comprehend the way individual wills interact with one another and with existing social structures, thereby preserving, destroying, and/or creating new structures and new individuals.

These and his other insights, and those of Engels, too, I have been claiming, were grounded in a concern with the cash-nexus form of the connections problem, which was central to both their thought and experience. Starting, as I have sought to emphasize, from a specific early-nineteenth-century and German situation, and a literary orientation, Marx and Engels quickly connected that situation to a universal concern—Man's unsocial sociability—developing in the process a generalizing and historical sociology which, in the end, promised a "total redemption of humanity," and thus its own obsolesence and expendability.

8

Academic Sociology: Ferdinand Tönnies

Into the Academy

Engels and Marx were "revolutionary sociologists" who never held academic positions. In their case, praxis was at least as important as theory. As I have tried to show, both the praxis and theory were closely aligned with their concerns about the cash-nexus society, resulting from the breakdown of connections. The Continental sociologists who followed after Engels and Marx were generally more interested in "pure" theory as such (though, in fact, such theory could and did play a major political role, as ideology, even when not so intended; and often the theory itself was deliberately aimed at solving social problems). Pursuing mainly theory, though with an underlying practical motive, these aspiring professional sociologists found their most congenial setting to be in the academic quadrangles and not on the barricades.

Getting into the universities, however, required a battle of its own, as we shall see. Trying to become a professor was part of the price required to become more professional. Another price, so to speak, was developing a dry, technical vocabulary, and generally eschewing the verbal flourishes of writers such as Engels and Marx. One result, alas, is that when reading a professional sociologist, such as Ferdinand Tönnies, one's eyes may tend to become glazed. Another consequence is that, sociology having become more specialized, my remaining chapters (except for the last) will tend also to be more specialized in treatment, though not in intent.

Nevertheless, perserverance is worthwhile. Following on Engels and Marx, the professional sociologists have structured the way we look at our societies. They have given us the categories and vocabulary by which to understand the connections that prevail, or might prevail, or should prevail, in the modern period. Whether as scientific concept or myth—an issue to be dealt with in our last chapter—their results powerfully affect our modern effort to understand the unsocial-social nature of ourselves.

Transition

Before we enter into the often arid stretches of professional sociological prose, however, I want to stress again its literary origins, and thus its source in the connections problem; and this means re-emphasizing the link provided by Engels and Marx. As we have seen, the literary qualities of their work, and especially that of Marx, are essential elements in its success. The stylistic touch is most dramatically present in *The Communist Manifesto*, but it crops up in even the most abstruse philosophic and economic treatises. It is, in fact, inseparable from Marx's effort at "scientific" persuasion, and is as powerful, emotionally, as the more strictly literary efforts of the poets and novelists who, before or along with him, had been lamenting the increasingly quantitative and monetarized cast of life.

Marx himself was aware that the sociological "science" implicitly partook of the very literary traits that it was condemning, as well as suggested a reality that was partly intractable to revolutionary fervor. Having occasion in 1863 to go back over Engels's *Condition*, Marx wrote to his friend:

> Rereading your book has made me regretfully aware of our increasing age. How freshly and passionately, with what bold anticipations, and without learned and systematic, scholarly doubts, is the thing still dealt with here! And the very illusion that the result will leap into the daylight of history tomorrow or the day after gives the whole thing a warmth and vivacious humor—compared with which the later "gray in gray" makes a damned unpleasant contrast.[1]

The "gray in gray" refers to Hegel's owl of Minerva, with its resignation to events transpired rather than prophesied. It also reminds us that the industrial, bourgeois, scientific world was seen by literary artists as dull and colorless—one need only read Dickens here—with the rainbow of imagination, as Keats might have put it, unwoven by the very factories that were weaving the new textiles.[2]

In what is an otherwise persuasive and compendious treatment of the concept of community (and related themes in sociology), Robert Nisbet errs when he declares, "The rediscovery of community is unquestionably the most distinctive development in nineteenth-century social thought, a development that extends well beyond sociological theory to such areas as philosophy, history, and theology to become indeed one of the major themes of imaginative writing in the century."[3] It is philosophy, prophecy, poetry, and creative literature, in my view, which inspires sociology, as much as or more than the other way around (George Eliot perhaps may be an example of the latter case). Sociology takes deeply felt concerns and tries to objectify them and give them scientific form. One does not necessarily reduce the "science" of sociology by seeking to understand the passional roots, which indeed comprise part of the social facts one is attempting to order and classify.

If Marx and Engels represent an intermediary stage between the literary and sociological visions, no one would accuse Ferdinand Tönnies, in his major work, *Gemeinschaft und Gesellschaft* (translated into English as *Community and Society*, or, in its British version, *Community and Association*), of allowing any literary qualities to slip in and soften his difficult, abstract prose. Yet in reading him, we must still be aware of his evocative use of language. It frequently places a covert meaning on his overt statements. Pejorative words such as "ruthless," "cold," and so forth, applied to *Gesellschaft*, with nothing comparable to *Gemeinschaft*, suggest a judgment that undercuts the claim to "impartiality." Tönnies himself grudgingly admitted this when he wrote later in life that

> On more than one occasion it has been said that I appeared to be taking sides for *Gemeinschaft* and against *Gesellschaft*, although I have been at pains to make plain the need "to consider such phenomena with the same neutral objectivity as the natural scientist exhibits in the study of the life cycle of plants and animals" (preface to the first edition). I must, however, concede that neither did I take every possible precaution to guard against that appearance, nor every possible step to secure my exposition against such an impression.[4]

In fact, I shall take as my text *Gemeinschaft und Gesellschaft* as it "appeared" to most readers, that is, as a lamentation as well as an impartial effort at sociology, and I will largely ignore at this point the corpus of Tönnies's work that could modify that impression (though I will offer enough on that score, I hope, to do justice to Tönnies). A writer, alas, is often condemned by the stereotype of his work, especially if he has set up a powerful typology, as Tönnies did. Toward the end of his life, Tönnies wrote perceptively, ". . . in a writer whose work extends over several decades there will occur contradictory statements. In such a case, the later statement must be considered the more mature and definitive one, provided that it is not invalidated by senile decay."[5] Tönnies was never senile, but writings do take on a life of their own and remain rigidly behind, even when their author has moved on. Such was the case with Tönnies's most famous work, *Gemeinschaft und Gesellschaft.*

Settings

I have spoken of the passional roots of sociology as a fact that must be accorded due recognition by the emerging science itself. One of the other social facts that must also be taken into account is the institutional and socio-political setting in which sociology arose. Put very briefly, sociology became an academic subject somewhere between the 1880s and the 1920s. In different countries—France, Germany, England, America—it underwent different tribulations, but in all it faced opposition from entrenched disciplines and bureaucracies; as I treat our individual sociologists, I shall touch upon some of their personal experiences in this regard. In spite of such opposition, however, sociological societies and journals were established, and sociological positions in the universities were opened up: for example, in France a *Revue Internationale de Sociologie* was founded in 1893, an *Année sociologique* in 1898, and a sociological position at the University of Bordeaux in 1900; in Germany, the *Archiv Für Sozialwissenschaften und Sozialpolitik* in 1904, and a German Society for Sociology in 1909; in England, a Sociological Society in 1903, and a *Sociological Review* (short-lived) in 1907; and in America, an *American Journal of Sociology* in 1895. In each country, also, its pedagogic structure seriously affected the form sociology took.

So, too, the socio-political setting behind the emergence of "scientific" sociology differed for each nation. In France, for example, the clash between religious and secular forces in the late nineteenth century, and especially the Dreyfus Affair, helped to shape the institutional form taken by sociology, and its intellectual perspectives as well. In Germany, the politics of Bismarck and the social democrats, the modernist dilemma of the mandarins (as Fritz Ringer puts it), and the late development of industrialism all played their role. Yet, once again, the central concern was with the challenges of modern, industrial society and its effect on community and individualism.

Our focus here is not directly on these socio-political forces, other than to acknowledge them and to underscore their importance for a different kind of inquiry into the origins of sociology, and to have them in mind as we treat of our individual sociologists in regard to our theme of connections and the cash nexus.[6]

Within this self-imposed limit, however, to better understand our first thinker, Ferdinand Tönnies, a further word on the specific German situation might be useful (in addition to our brief comments in the previous chapter). The most important facts in this regard are that late-eighteenth- and early-nineteenth-century Germany had not experienced an industrial revolution similar to England's—it had to wait at least another half-century—and that, unlike France, it had not undergone a 1789-type revolution—though sporadic attempts were made, including the ill-fated Revolution of 1848 and its abortive attempt at a national constitution. What is more, Germany, unlike England and France, was not even a unified nation until 1870.

Thus, some of the key features that we had earlier identified as giving rise to the increased Western awareness of breakdown in connections were not present, at first hand, in early-nineteenth-century Germany. They were, therefore, "experienced" only intellectually, at a remove, and at best in a commercial not industrial form. Moreover, because of the legacy of particularism, stemming from the historical role of the Holy Roman Empire, the numerous states, principalities, territories, and towns of Germany posed peculiar problems of development. All these combined factors of "backwardness" provoked a special sort of frustration among some of Germany's most critical thinkers, such as Engels and Marx.

Especially peculiar was the development of "communities," lying in size between the big cities and the surrounding countryside, and characterized by one scholar as "Hometowns."[7] When Germany's population increased in the early nineteenth century, it spilled mainly into these towns, ranging in population from about 15,000 to as little as 750. There were around four thousand of these towns, and they included about one-fourth of the German population (agrarian dwellers accounted for much of the rest, with cities about 7 percent). They created, or preserved, a *Gemeinschaft* sort of society in Germany, just when it was dwindling away in the more developed societies. In these communities, membership involved both political and economic rights—*Bürgerrecht*—controlled by the guilds and town councils, whose members watched over social and moral behavior, decided whether one could marry or enter a trade (the first being commonly the prerequisite for the second), and jealously excluded all undesirables—defined as strangers, outsiders, and, more colorfully, "ground rabbits."

This was the "individualized countryside" described by "natural historians" such as Riehl, embodying and defending the values of *Gemeinschaft*, and separating themselves defiantly from both the alien cities and the boorish countryside, in both of which settings men were seen as living "isolated" from one another. We are thus faced with a situation in Germany in which "community" is not seen as rooted in a rural setting; quite the contrary, for the idyllic picture of the agricultural village promoted elsewhere is here rejected. In nineteenth-century Germany, community generally meant small town. Its members lived within the town (often actually surrounded by walls), in what I would like to call "nets" rather than webs of relations, for the nets gave security but also a hampered, trussed-up feeling.

Threats to the cozy hometown life and values came from outside. The states, with their mobile civil servants, wished to stimulate economic growth and to promote the more rational and centralizing values of Roman law versus custom. The largest state, Prussia, showed the way in its own domains, in 1799–1805, by first liberating the peasant, and then, taking that as a model, pressing outside the agrarian area for a loosening of guild restrictions. The coming of Napoleon and his forces accelerated the process, and German civil servants showed themselves eager to adopt the Napoleonic frame: to establish occupational freedom, to aggregate communities into more rational administrative districts, and to extend *Bürger* rights to all taxpayers.

With the fall of Napoleon, the communities fought back nationalist reaction to Napoleon, of course, is a vastly compli subject; we are interested here only in the way the forces of "modernization," to use our present-day term, struggled against the forces of "custom," with both trying to identify themselves with true German nationalism. After the debacle of 1848, the struggle was won by the centralizing, modernizing forces embodied in Prussia, the North German Confederation of 1866, and the German Empire of 1870, thereby establishing late-nineteenth-century Wilhelmine Germany. The members of the communities became a class—*Kleinbürgers*—their guilds abolished and their walls breeched. Their values, however, persisted as a powerful force in the new Germany, whose actual economic development—by the 1860s, Germany had entered on its own industrial take-off period (to use W. W. Rostow's term)— appeared to be at a far remove from them.[8]

Tönnies himself, born in Schleswig-Holstein, the son of a well-to-do peasant, had a native attachment to the land (which suggests a certain essential ambiguity in his relation to community values as actually present in early-nineteenth-century Germany). Although he embraced an intellectual and urban life (living in the city of Kiel), Tönnies nevertheless retained his old loyalties. As he wrote in 1882, after a visit to the country house of the poet Theodore Storm, "I have really enjoyed the rural life. It is the only truth." Again, in 1884, he wrote of how he lived in the country "in serene and fine contemplation which one can never know in the sea of population; where the presence and press of man overstrains the imagination." He rejoiced in his "loneliness," although he admitted the need for the friend to whom he was writing. At another time, he confessed to the way "the whole sadness [*tristia*] of modern life" painfully gripped him.[9] We seem to hear the voices of Rousseau and Wordsworth.

So, too, Tönnies's dislike of modernity seems partly rooted in his antipathy to Prussian rule over his homeland, after the War of 1866. As one scholar puts it, Tönnies witnessed "the influence of rationalism on the old rural culture of his native province, Schleswig-Holstein, as it had to submit to the inroads of mechanization and commercialization."[10] And he resented it. That such early experiences, and others like them, colored Tönnies's perspective is highly plausible, and sheds light on his feelings.

The sketch given above may help to supply a useful context for our reading of Tönnies's *Gemeinschaft und Gesellschaft*. In its contours, we may see Tönnies as fundamentally opposing the bureaucratic tendencies of Wilhelmine Germany, but also in part trying to reconcile the values of the German nineteenth-century community experience with another set of values, socialist ones, as well as coming to terms with "modernism" and the industrial society springing up around him in real and not just literary terms. And we may see him especially as an intellectual, trying to transform the metaphor of a cash-nexus society into a full-fledged science of society, that is, sociology, in the light of his "German" traditions.

Gemeinschaft and *Gesellschaft*

In turning to Tönnies, we see a man who, like Marx before him, and Simmel and Durkheim after him, began his intellectual career as a philosopher. His early work was on Thomas Hobbes, some of whose manuscripts he discovered, and about whom, at age twenty-five, he wrote a short book, *Notes on the Philosophy of Hobbes* (1879–81), which he submitted as a thesis when he began to lecture at the University of Kiel. Hobbes in fact had a tremendous effect on Tönnies, demonstrating how one could take a scientific attitude to society. Hobbes had also postulated, approvingly, a society founded on contract, a society of the *Gesellschaft* type.

Hobbes, writing at the time of the English Civil War, started from the idea of political obligation.[11] Instead of deriving it from a mythical or religious sanction, however, he based it on a self-interested calculus made by each citizen: the individual is concerned only with his own self-preservation. What is more, Hobbes's individual is basically anti-social, and thus in a state of war with every other individual. He has no ties or loyalties to a larger community, such as government, aside from its ability to protect him. Thus, attacking myths, Hobbes had created yet another myth: that of the purely self-interested Man.

Yet, Hobbes really gave new existence to community, or what he called the commonwealth, by making it a self-interested rational construction of Man. In his middle age, Hobbes had chanced upon a copy of Euclid and become enamoured of the geometrical method, which in *Leviathan* he pronounced "the only science that it hath pleased God hitherto to bestow on mankind."[12] Fortunately, Hobbes came to believe, the same method could be applied to civil philosophy. Having declared that "the science of every subject is derived from a precognition of the causes, generation, and construction of the same; and consequently where the causes are known, there is place for demonstration. . . . Geometry therefore is demonstrable, for the lines and figures from which we reason are drawn and described by ourselves," he triumphantly concluded that "civil philosophy is demonstrable, because we make the commonwealth ourselves."[13]

Thus Hobbes glimpsed a fundamental fact, though simplistically so, for he saw it only as a purely conscious making: that Man makes society. This perception served as a powerful incentive to the constitution-creating aspirations of the Enlightenment and, along with Hobbes's espousal of the competitive, self-interested Man of nascent capitalism, laid much of the philosophical foundations for modern market society.

It appears that Tönnies moved quickly beyond Hobbes, however (I will have more to say about this later), and suffered a change in *Weltanschauung*, going from a positive regard for modernity to an anti-modern position. Between 1880 and 1887 he spent his time dedicatedly working out the ideas that emerged as *Gemeinschaft und Gesellschaft*. In this effort, Marx, for one, took primacy over Hobbes. Indeed, practically a third of Tönnies's famous book is a rather uninspired and pedantic exposition of the ideas of *Capital*, as underlying the characteristics of *Gesellschaft*. Though Tönnies changed his opinions, and sometimes sharply, about Marx, there can be no question of the latter's major influence on *Gemeinschaft und Gesellschaft*. In the preface to the first edition, Tönnies remarked of Marx (along with Sir Henry Maine and Otto Gierke) that he was "the most remarkable and most profound philosopher . . . whose views on economics were most important to me."[14] In a later addition, discussing the marginal utility theory of value, Tönnies made it clear that "Today, as ever, I stand for the maxim that only labor creates new values," that is, the labor theory of value.[15] Much later in life, Tönnies devoted a full study to Marx, which was sympathetic but critical. As he then admitted, he had not seen "how much the passion and confusion of Marx's youth was left in his [Marx's] own thinking." One result was that, "Despite his many significant accomplishments, his life leaves one with the impression of tragedy." In the end, "the greatest weakness of Marx's system of thought is the disregard of moral power. . . . [he] refuses to appeal to the moral consciousness of the laborer, much less to that of the capitalist, in order to improve or even to abolish . . . conditions.[16]

This was the "later" Tönnies, closer in spirit to a reforming Gaskell or George Eliot than to the revolutionary Marx. But at the time of *Gemeinschaft und Gesellschaft,* he was what I shall call a "sentimental" communist, affected not only by Marx's economics but by his entire *Weltanschauung* toward capitalism. The youthful Tönnies in 1881 could thus write, "If I were independent of family consideration, I would go with an open flag into the camp of the pure Communists."[17] It was a temporary enthusiasm. The more general influence of Marx remained, however, to permeate *Gemeinschaft und Gesellschaft.*

It is not only the Marxist parts, so to speak, of the book that make for difficult reading. As a whole it is dry, abstruse, scholastic—written in "unique, difficult, old German diction"[18] is how one scholar describes it—without any relieving oases. Why, then, its popularity and lasting effect? The fact is that, on its first appearance, in 1887, it attracted few readers; only in its 1902 edition did it gain attention, and a call for six more editions, as well as translations. Some gust of opinion in the pre-1914 culture took it up, and perhaps the sense of subsequent decline in the West kept its fame aloft.

Still, a more fundamental explanation is needed; and I believe it lies in the fact that Tönnies was the first to give substantial and sustained sociological form to an alternative to the cash-nexus Man of the classical economists. The general idea was certainly in the air—status vs. contract (and Tönnies admitted his debt to Sir Henry Maine), rural vs. urban, custom vs. change—but what Tönnies did was to add a psychological dimension to the emerging sociological one.[19] Hobbes had hinted at the *Gesellschaft* type of character; Marx and Engels had dreamed of a future *Gemeinschaft* being. Neither had really explored the nature of human wills as they entered into social relations. Tönnies claimed to do exactly this. The classical economists had established the type of what their twentieth-century successors would call "rational, maximizing man." Tönnies accepted this abstraction as appropriate for *Gesellschaft;* in turn he elaborated an equally simplifying abstraction of a natural, unified *Gemeinschaft* Man. Wills, then, were locked in struggle for modern Man's soul.

The book itself starts with a "General Statement of the Main Concepts" which in large part also comprises a summary of Marx's economics. It is in this section that the dichotomy between *Gemeinschaft* and *Gesellschaft* is firmly established. *Gemeinschaft* "starts from the assumption of perfect unity of human wills as an original or natural condition." What does this mean? In such a society, Tönnies tells us, all its members have no identity separate from the whole. They are united, without further thought, to one another by birth. The three pillars of *Gemeinschaft* are "blood, place (land), and mind, or kinship." The prototype is the family, and the prototypical form of authority is the paternal. The father rules, but for the good of all. Even servants, for they may exist in this society, are encompassed in the all-pervasive bond of love. There exists "an instinctive and naïve tenderness of the strong for the weak."[20] In such a "household" society, monetary exchange is not possible. Nobody is in conflict with another. In more developed form, the family can become or help comprise a tribe, town guild, and so on, but the same qualities must prevail.

Real understanding of *Gemeinschaft*, however, awaits Tönnies's depiction of its opposite, *Gesellschaft*. Here the accents of Marx are heavy. Where production in *Gemeinschaft* is for use, in *Gesellschaft* it is for exchange; in the former we may have barter, in the latter all value is monetarized. Here we also encounter Hobbes's war of all against all; such competition means that "everybody is by himself and isolated, and there exists a condition of tension against all others."[21] It is a "cash nexus" society par excellence. While Tönnies attempts to offer us an impartial description, or analysis, his use of terms such as "artifical," "negation," and "lust," as we remarked earlier, gives another gloss to his text.

Overall, Tönnies describes *Gemeinschaft* as "organic," and its opposite as "mechanical." The former is "real" and "the lasting and genuine form of living together"; the latter is "imaginary" and "a mechanical aggregate and artifact."[22] What Tönnies means is that a people bound by ties of blood, land, and kinship are part of a whole, which he calls organic. *Gesellschaft* members are connected, if at all, only through the division of labor, which in turn entails monetary exchange and individualism. This means that the resultant isolated individuals are linked only mechanically. (As we shall see, Durkheim was later to reverse the meaning of the terms organic and mechanical, a cause of some subsequent confusion.)

Part II is entitled "Natural Will *(Wesenwille)* and Rational Will *(Kürwille)*." Here Tönnies offers the psychological basis to his sociology. As he remarked in a 1911 Addition, "The association of ideas is analogous to the association of people. The associations of thought which form the natural will correspond with the Gemeinschaft, those which indicate rational will correspond to Gesellschaft." Then he adds, "Without knowledge and recognition of this psychological contrast, a sociological understanding of the concepts described here is impossible."[23]

If Tönnies's economics come from Marx, his psychology originates in Hobbes. Tönnies quotes the latter extensively, and declares he is "right in describing 'a general inclination of all mankind, a perpetual and restless desire of power after power. . . .'" Such desire, moreover, Tönnies asserts, is "well-nigh identical with the desire for money."[24] The aim of power, whatever its form, is to give the holder pleasure. And this search for pleasure, we are told, is perpetual and unceasing. Hobbes's psychological Man, therefore, with his "will" to power, turns out to be the same as Marx's economic Man.

How, then, can there be any alternative to the rationally willed *Gesellschaft?* Tönnies's argument is as follows. All life and volition, he admits, are self-assertive; the self tends to negate other selves. However, such self-assertion can best realize its own interest by being either friendly or hostile. In Tönnies's words: "By nature, every human being is good and friendly toward his friends and those he considers such . . . but he is wicked and hostile toward his enemies. . . . Our abstract or artifical human being is neither the one nor the other in his relations with other people."[25] In the family, however, it is clear that we obtain more pleasure by acting in a benevolent, friendly manner. Altruism "pays off," so to speak. The will behind such altruistic assertion is natural, rooted in our sympathies of blood, land, and kinship. It is the willed world of *Gemeinschaft.*

Opposed to it is the willed world of *Gesellschaft:* rational, false, and unnatural. The rational will, in such a society, has triumphed over the natural, and reduced pleasure from a qualitative to a quantitative good. Its psychological Man is a "calculating person," a description that reminds us of Edmund Burke's comment; according to Tönnies, such a person is "a climber" and "everything he does is intended to be profitable"; he is untrustworthy, for "the lie becomes a characteristic element of Gesellschaft"; and he is "without home, a traveler . . . flippant and double-tongued, adroit, adaptable, and one who always keeps his eye on the end or purpose he plans to attain."[26] *Gesellschaft* Man, in short, is rootless, a "stranger" (to use the term Simmel will make famous, but with a different evaluation).

Between *Gemeinschaft* and *Gesellschaft* Man there can be only conflict. In fact, the conflict is really between woman and man, for Tönnies goes off in a rather strange direction (though one whose signs are followed by many of his contemporaries, in all countries, who share his views on the sexes). It is men, he says, who favor the intellect and crowd into cities; it is women who are emotional and rooted in the land. As he puts it in what he calls an "old truth," "women are usually led by feelings, men more by intellect. Men are more clever. They alone are capable of calculation. . . ."[27]

This dichotomy is then metamorphosed for Tönnies, without any logical connection in the text, into the conflict of the proletariat versus capitalist. It is a strange alchemy, but its elements are as follows. Tönnies is actually asking whether the time of *Gemeinschaft* is over and done with. Has woman, too, succumbed to that which is "foreign and terrible to her original inborn nature"? His answer is vague and rather mystical, for he answers that

> the possibility of overcoming this individualism and arriving at a reconstruction of Gemeinschaft exists. The analogy of the fate of women with the fate of the proletariat has been recognized and out-lined long ago. Their growing group consciousness, like that of the isolate thinker, can develop and rise to a moral-humane consciousness.[28]

Here, Tönnies ends his discussion of will, and passes on to the third part of his book, "The Sociological Basis of Natural Law." As we shall see, he has not dropped his question but only deferred it. In this section, he tries to draw together his economic and psychological observations into a sociology. Some of what he says is repetition, but, in discussing the united, organic nature of *Gemeinschaft*, he does open up a Rousseauian possibility when he remarks that the whole "may be conceived as being in a chosen group of leading minds or even in one single individual who embodies in himself the will and being of the rest of the community."[29] More important, he also sketches, in abstract terms, a kind of historical development, from human relations centered around custom and mores, a homeland, ceremonies, and so forth, to a commonwealth, or *polis*, dominated by a warrior nobility, to associations of special interest groups (of which the State is merely one), all based on contracts. The validity of these contracts is enforced by the State which, however, Tönnies also views as a *Gesellschaft*, that is, a "general association . . . established for the purpose of protecting the freedom and prosperity of its subjects."[30] At this point, both state socialism, which does not eliminate the fundamental social class structure, and international capitalism are possible. In a rather startling statement, Tönnies comments that "In this context it must be pointed out that the most modern and Gesellschaft-like state, the United States of America, can or will least of all claim a truly national character."[31]

At this point, Tönnies is more or less finished with the elaboration of this phase of his sociology. In a short "Conclusions and Outlook," however, he reverts to the problem of the future. It lies with the "class struggle." "City life and Gesellschaft doom the common people to decay and death," Tönnies declares. Only a revolution can rescue the masses who "become conscious of this social position . . . [and] proceed from class consciousness to class struggle." The outcome is hazy (as is the passage):

> This class struggle may destroy society and the state which it is its purpose to reform. The entire culture has been transformed into a civilization of state and Gesellschaft, and this transformation means the doom of culture itself if none of its scattered seeds remain alive and again bring forth the essence and idea of Gemeinschaft, thus secretly fostering a new culture amidst the decaying one.[32]

In fact, Tönnies earlier had given us a secret hope. In his third part, he had stated, in passing, that

> the primordial memory of a right of Gemeinschaft that "is born with us" has persisted in the folk soul, slumbering like the wheat-grain in a mummy, but capable of new growth. For if understood as the idea of justice, natural law is an eternal and inalienable possession of mankind.[33]

The ultimate struggle, then, is not really between classes, as suggested by Marx and Engels, or even between natural and rational wills, but between the "primordial" and the "mechanical." Such is the final message of Tönnies's sociology.

Context

I have said "final message." It is really only the last word of *Gemeinschaft und Gesellschaft*, not of Tönnies's entire work, for I have been focusing on this book with little concern for his overall contribution. Thus, a certain distortion of his life work has resulted. It is time, briefly, to render him a little more of his due and, then, in this context to summarize his overall contribution.

In the 1887 book, Tönnies was offering both a philosophy of history and a typology. The philosophy of history sees a development from *Gemeinschaft* to *Gesellschaft*; as Tönnies remarks, "Gemeinschaft is old; Gesellschaft is new as a name as well as a phenomenon."[34] On the basis of the historical development, Tönnies then establishes his ideal types, or so he claims. The problem is that the two are constantly conflated. Tönnies does not actually look at the phenomenon of modern society *itself*, but only as its being a representation of *Gesellschaft*, an abstraction he imposes upon it. Similarly with *Gemeinschaft*, where he sets up an ideal construct that corresponds in only chance fashion with any actually existing "primitive" society.

In principle, ideal types are a valuable heuristic device in sociology—we shall keep coming across them in what follows; in this particular case, one may ask whether they distort rather than illuminate the reality of modern society. Instead of describing and analyzing contemporary social facts, *do the types become social facts themselves, that is, part of the sensibility and the ideology of certain members of that society, drawing deeply on a tradition of lamentation such as I have depicted earlier?*

What makes Tönnies more complex in this regard than earlier lamenters, is that, as we have seen, he started from Hobbes, the prototypic exponent of modern contractual society, and went on to become a sociologist. Here we find the critical insight that inspired him, about which earlier I had promised to say more. What Hobbes had glimpsed was that Man did indeed construct society—the commonwealth—just as he constructed figures in geometry. As with geometry, such a construction could be "scientifically" understood. It was, in fact, according to Hobbes, deductive, the product of Man's mind.

Hobbes wrote before the great Neapolitan Giambattista Vico, whose obscure work, *The New Science* (1725), only slowly made its way into the consciousness of modern Man. It is worthwhile taking a short detour to look at Vico's thinking because, in his new science, Vico ostensibly rejected the Cartesian model embraced by Hobbes, but reached the same conclusion by other, more humanistic, means. Why, Vico asked, should Man be able to understand natural science, whose objects had been created by God, and therefore was at one remove from Man, and not comprehend social science, whose objects had been created directly by Man, and was thus more intimately accessible to him? Indeed, as Vico announced, we can have greater certainty about the matters of mind and therefore, society, than of nature.

Tönnies seems never to have been aware of Vico (though Marx was, and cites him importantly in *Capital*).[35] Instead, Tönnies followed the line leading from Hobbes, while going beyond him; it is this Ariadne's thread that led to the profound insight at the basis of sociology: that society does not exist separately from individuals, but is the totality of their social relations which, in turn, are a reflection of mind. Only in this sense can we talk of "society" as something conceptually separate from individuals, that is, as a whole greater than the parts, which takes on life seemingly of its own, and then gives life to the individuals who compose it.

Tönnies was one of the first to glimpse this characteristic of social facts and to set to work professionally to spell out and analyze the nature of these social relations. It was, in fact, under the influence of developments in anthropological studies at the end of the nineteenth century which gave a different picture from Hobbes of the so-called state of nature, that Tönnies moved forward (and here we encounter the sole attempt by the author of *Gemeinschaft und Gesellschaft* at an empirical underpinning of the ideal type, and that quite limited). In the Belgian writer Emile de Laveleye's work on primitive property, especially, Tönnies found inspiration for the view that village and house communities were the early form of society, united by *Gemeinschaft* bonds rather than being in a state of a war of all against all.

If de Laveleye confirmed Tönnies's view of a real *Gemeinschaft* past, Carlyle could support Tönnies's condemnation of the social and economic trends of present life. As he wrote his best friend, Paulsen (to whom, in fact, he dedicated *Gemeinschaft und Gesellschaft*), he found *Past and Present* a "gripping and provocative sermon" (Engels, we remember, was also powerfully affected by the book). Tönnies was similarly impressed by what it had to say of the strengths of the believing Middle Ages and of the weaknesses of the rationalizing and individualistic modern period. As his friend Paulsen remarked appreciatively upon reading Froude's biography of Carlyle, "Perhaps there is no man to whose way of looking at things [*Anschauungsweise*] you [Tönnies] stand closer than C[arlyle]."[36]

Paulsen, as Tönnies replied to his friend, was only partly correct. Others also stood close to him, especially Marx (as we have already noted). When Marx remarked that "It may be said that the whole economic history of Gesellschaft, i.e., of the modern nations, is in essence summarized in the change in the relationship between town and country," another piece of the puzzle fell into place for Tönnies.[37] The result was his own unique synthesis—and sociology.

After *Gemeinschaft und Gesellschaft*, Tönnies labored long and hard, and changed greatly, if ambivalently. His writings on Hobbes and Spinoza, on Hegel, Marx, and Comte, on Spencer and Durkheim, on the development of sociology in Germany, on the rise of scientific method, on the methodology of the social sciences, as well as on empirical problems such as public opinion, suicide, and so forth, are both lucid and thoughtful. They mark an important contribution to the establishment of sociology as a professional field of study.[38]

Yet it is *Gemeinschaft und Gesellschaft* that serves as Tönnies's major legacy to his chosen field, and beyond that to the general literature on modern society.[39] With that work, Tönnies had obviously struck a responsive chord in the mythic mind of his time, metamorphosing the earlier cash-nexus metaphor into a typology and a drama of a Manichean-like divided social creation and a double Man; the chord still vibrates loudly in our time. Never mind that in some primitive societies fathers destroy their infants with little cause, as Darwin noted with the Fuegian savages; or that some religious communities war savagely with one another; or that, in modern society, there are many other forms of association than the monetary ones. The stereotypes of *Gemeinschaft und Gesellschaft* loom over our modern consciousness as if they were huge Stonehenge figures. Only in later work did Tönnies seek to look more closely at the sociological gods he had set up, and even then the old primordial longings kept tugging at him. It was the price he, and we, pay for his revelation that society is a matter of human wills that express themselves in social relations—a revelation which then became the subject matter of a study we have come to call sociology. Once this new science was envisioned, other scholars could then look more closely than did the author of *Gemeinschaft und Gesellschaft* at the actual, complicated nature of the wills and the relations involved.

9

Academic Sociology: Georg Simmel

A Life

Ferdinand Tönnies and his fellow German sociologist, Georg Simmel seem almost to be polar ideal types, at least in terms of their origins and their two major books, *Gemeinschaft und Gesellschaft* and *Philosophie des Geldes (Philosophy of Money)*. Where Tönnies came from a peasant, provincial background, Simmel was born in Berlin in 1858, of a family engaged in business, and he studied and lived in the metropolis almost all his life. Where Tönnies breathed the air of religious pietism, and briefly held anti-Semitic prejudices (shaken off vigorously toward the end of his life), Simmel was born of Jewish parents (although his father converted to Catholicism and his mother to Protestantism), was baptized into the Protestant faith, and quickly fell away from it and from all religion. Although both Tönnies and Simmel were denied major university posts, and were shunted to the periphery of the academic establishment partly because of their involvement with the new and undefined discipline of sociology, their versions of sociology differed sharply: where Tönnies praised *Gemeinschaft*, Simmel prized *Gesellschaft*.[1]

For Simmel, one of the archetypal figures involved in *Gesellschaft* relations is what he revealingly calls the "stranger"; and one senses the autobiographical note to the abstract sociological thought. The concept includes not only the intellectually marginal figure but, even more centrally, the merchant, or trader, moving in an out of groups where all others economic positions are already occupied. He has mobility, and according to Simmel, his mobility, moving as he

179

does on the margin of two or more cultures, gives him greater objectivity. Objectivity, in turn, means increased intellectuality. And all of these traits together make for a form of freedom. Such traits are clearly approved of by Simmel, in spite of his comment that "it is our task not to complain or to condone but only to understand." In any case, seen as a type, not as an individual, the final encomium reserved for the "stranger" is that he connects us to the rest of humanity.[2]

Shades of the cash nexus! And what a difference from Tönnies! It is as if all the value signs had been reversed. Calculation and rationality are good, not bad. The cash nexus, so to speak, has been vindicated. Quietly, and without direct argument, Simmel has taken the lamenting cries and turned them into cheers. His work is, in this sense, a *tour de force*. What is more, Simmel boldly accepts the stereotypic charges made against the Jews, as Shylocks, and converts these moneychangers into freedom-bringing strangers.

Beneath all the rational, scientific, sociological arguments, various nasty fights were going on. One of them, as I am suggesting, involves the Jewish "thread" that we have observed running through the so-called industrial novels. Now it manifests itself in relation to sociology: the latent accusation (sometimes even overt) is that sociologists are often Jews, and that the "scientific" study of society—sociology—is a tainted science. Jews, so the argument goes, are uprooting and overturning proper society by the insiduous teachings of sociology.[3] Thus, the Jew is both creator of cash-nexus society—the Messrs. Aarons of the sweatshops—and propagator of its false "values," that is, the Simmels in the universities.

When Simmel, for example, was being considered for appointment as a full professor, he was freqently opposed on the grounds that he was "negative" and "critical." These were not so much sociological, Comtean judgments, but code words. We catch the flavor in a letter written in response to a request for evaluation by the Cultural Ministry, when Simmel was being considered for a chair of philosophy at Heidelberg. The evaluator, named Dietrich Schaefer, calls attention to the consequence of Simmel's appointment, that it would allow "even broader space than it already occupies among the faculty to the world view and philosophy of life which Simmel represents, and which, after all, are only too obviously different from our German Christian-classical education." He describes Simmel's ideas as tending to "undermine and negate more than they lay foundations and build up, during an era which is inclined to set all pillars asway." At the end, the charge is made on academic grounds.

> It is my view, however, that sociology has yet to earn its position as a scholarly discipline [*Wissenschaft*]. It is, in my opinion, a most perilous error to put "society" in the place of state and church as the decisive [*maszgebend*, literally, *yardstick-providing*] organ of human coexistence.[4]

By now it should be clear that the sides taken on the issue of "connections" and the sociology that claims to study them are themselves to be examined on political as well as sociological grounds. Echoes of such disagreements necessarily persist into sociology itself, as in Tönnies's professional evaluation of Simmel's work. Tönnies admired Simmel as the first to give the title "Soziologie" to a major work in the German language, and as a scholar of "profound erudition" and a "multiplicity of charming observations, brilliant insights, and blinding dialectics." According to Tönnies, however, Simmel's problem is that he is completely absorbed with forms of human interaction such as superordination and subordination, and

> never fully attains the recognition that the most proper objects of sociological inquiry are the social structures [*Gebilde*] which arise out of the thoughts of men themselves, out of their subjects. To distinguish sharply all mental objects [*Gedankendinge*], such as alliances and leagues, clubs and cooperative societies, parishes and states, churches and orders, from the "groups" and "circles" which are externally recognizable—that, in my opinion, is the precondition for the solution of the specifically sociological problem.[5]

The Jew-baiter, Schaefer, had been suspicious about Simmel's study of "society" undermining Church and State; the charge is defused by Tönnies, although a slight echo remains, by his lifting the argument into a legitimate one about the nature of sociology itself: church and state for him are more important subjects for study than mere forms—clearly a different perspective from that of Simmel.[6]

It is on these great issues of connections, cash nexus, community, and the nature of community that Tönnies and Simmel and sociologists of the time take their most important stands. In 1903 Simmel wrote an essay, "The Metropolis and Mental Life." He notes that, originally, primitive man carried on a conflict with nature for his existence, producing culture and society as a result. In modern times, the conflict has shifted in two regards: locus and form. As Simmel remarks, "The decisive fact here is that in the life of a city, struggle with nature for the means of life is transformed into a conflict with human beings and the gain which is fought for is granted, not by nature, but by man." Specifically, he has in mind the way in which, by division of labor and specialization, the human species is able to expand the number of niches it can occupy. Such a development involves, as we have seen, intellectual growth, and Simmel approves. Thereby, he declares, "The essentially intellectualistic character of the mental life of the metropolis becomes intelligible as over against that of the small town which rests more on feelings and emotional relationships."[7]

Early on, Simmel had become involved with the Stefan George circle, with its anti-philistine poets and artists (an extramarital intimacy with a woman poet in the circle, with whom Simmel had an illegitimate child, lent a special quality to the involvement). It may have had some effect on Simmel's feelings about modernity, for the George circle has been described by one scholar as an "antirationalistic protest against urbanization, rationalism and materialism."[8]

Whatever the anti-modern effect of the George circle, the steady characteristic of Simmel's life and work was surely that of a cool, calculating evaluator of the pros and cons of the cash-nexus society, with the balance coming down on the pro side. At the end, he recognized his own persistent marginality, and judged it good. As he remarked wryly,

> I know that I shall die without spiritual heirs (and this is good). The estate I leave is like cash distributed among many heirs, each of whom puts his share to use in some trade that is compatible with *his* nature but which can no longer be recognized as coming from that estate.[9]

How like Simmel to use the form of the cash-nexus trope to make his connection with the generations to come after him! A "stranger," wandering in the new world of sociology, he had brought "home" riches from his intellectual tradings that could be bequeathed to humanity, as well as to European society at the end of the nineteenth century.[10]

Money

The Philosophy of Money was published in 1900, but had its origin in an 1889 paper, "The Psychology of Money," prepared by Simmel for a history seminar. Like almost all of Simmel's writings, only more so, it resembles a Bach fugue, returning on itself, with variations. What is presented in one place is taken up again in another, although in a new key. There are no footnotes, and almost no references to other works (Marx is the notable exception); what we are exposed to is the seemingly free play of a subtle, highly erudite mind.[11] We are not presented with a single, structured argument, logically pursuing its end, but a kind of continuous revolving of thought, in which layers are peeled away from a core idea and then rewound around it.

Such a style, of course, makes it difficult to present Simmel's ideas in summary form; we face the comparison between a butterfly leisurely folding and unfolding its wings over a flower, and the same creature stuck in a cabinet drawer with a pin. In contrast to Tönnies, Simmel needs to be read at first-hand in order really to comprehend his ideas. In lieu of this reading we need to remember that at the heart of Simmel's philosophy is a belief in the variform nature of truth, and the consequent need for attention to ambivalences, ambiguities, variations, and balances. There is a gain of sorts as well: because he repeats his ideas in so many different guises, the repetition itself serves as a sorting device for noting which ideas are most critical for Simmel.

The notion of exchange is one of his major starting points. It is exchange as an abstraction, a universal definition of human interaction, irrespective of particular contents, that Simmel has initally in mind. As he remarks, "It should be recognized that most relationships between people can be interpreted as forms of exchange." Exchange as such aims "to increase the sum of value; each party offers to the other more than he possessed before."[12] Thus, exchange is productive in itself. Though Simmel is not yet talking of economic exchange, it is clear that he is implicitly challenging the view of many economists, such as the Physiocrats or Marxists, that trade is nonproductive.

In the quote above, Simmel uses the term "value." This also is a major concept for him. He offers a long disquisition on the subject, discussing the fact that value is a quality not of objects themselves but of our judgment upon them. It is a Kantian and Nietzsche-like philosophical discussion, in which the emphasis is on Man as a value-creating being. Simmel believes neither in natural laws à la Tönnies nor in absolute rights, but only in relations between Men to which values are attached, and he ranges in his discussion of values from aesthetics to economics.

It is in this larger context that he then continues his fugue-like ruminations on the particular form of exchange that we recognize as economic. Needless to say, most professional economists look with either disdain or incomprehension at what passes for economic analysis in Simmel; what he is doing, of course, is calling into question their most fundamental psychological and methodological assumptions.

Exchange, Simmel had said, adds value (which is in the eye or stomach of the beholder). The ideal form of exchange is love. Another form is intellectual. Here the exchanges are mutually enriching. In Simmel's words,

> In all those emotional relationships where happiness lies not only in what one receives but just as much in what one gives, where each is mutually and equally enriched by the others, there develops a value the enjoyment of which is not bought by any deprivation on the part of an opposite party. Similarly, the communication of intellectual matters does not mean that something has to be taken from one person so that another can enjoy it.[13]

Economics, while it also adds value, does have other notable features absent in love or intellectual exchange. For one thing, it requires sacrifice of some already existing good. Even Robinson Crusoe, according to Simmel, would have to calculate and evaluate, for "the totally isolated economic man, who neither buys nor sells, would still have to evaluate his products and means of production— would therefore have to construct a concept of value independent of all exchange."[14] For another, economics requires a restraint of direct subjective desire. Nevertheless, like all the other kinds of exchange, it involves mutuality, that is, interaction and mutual benefit. Thus, the very notion of barter means each exchanging something he has for something he prefers.

The quintessential expression of value in economic exchange is found not in barter, however, but in money. Simmel is lyrical about the virtues of money. It is "the incarnation and purest expression" of the concept of economic value. It is a great symbolic construction, an unparalled invention of the human mind. As Simmel tells us,

> One of the greatest advances made by mankind—the discovery of a new world out of the material of the old—is to establish a proportion between two quantities, not by direct comparison, but in terms of the fact that each of them relates to a third quantity and that these two relations are either equal or unequal.[15]

Thus, all goods, no matter how incompatible, can be related to money, and thus to one another. It is money that allows for the connections that make up our modern world, that remains after consumption and thus serves as capital for renewed production, and that makes our world go round, as if it were the gravitational force holding it in orbit.

Money also allows for the creation of a "community" of merchants, ever expanding. Money's depersonalized nature allows for the development of the most extensive community, based on the largest number of persons. The basis of such a community is trust—trust in the value of money. Money in itself, of course, has no value. Only if we all believe in what I would describe as a kind of submission to the monetary "general will" (Simmel might have said that "In God We Trust" really means "In Each Other We Trust") does money fulfill its desired functions.

For Simmel, "society" does not really exist before exchange. It is created by exchange. In Simmel's words:

> The exchange of the products of labour, or of any other possessions, is obviously one of the purest and most primitive forms of human socialization; not in the sense that "society" already existed and then brought about acts of exchange but, on the contrary, that exchange is one of the functions that creates an inner bond between men—a society, in place of a mere collection of individuals.[16]

The latent message is clear: for those who would do away with money and exchange, Simmel is saying that they will also be doing away with any society other than perhaps the simplest.

Money, in short, is the prime symbol and creator of our complex, interrelated society, merely reaching its ultimate flowering in capitalism. As itself a symbolic construction, money assumes a certain intellectuality in mankind, enabling one to perceive a logical connection between goods-money-goods. "It is possible," Simmel explains, "to exchange the most valuable things against a printed form only when the chain of purposes is very extensive and reliable and provides us with a guarantee that what is immediately valueless will help us to acquire other values." And this, in turn, is possible "only with a growing intellectuality of individuals and with the continued organization of the group."[17] Here, then, we have another example of the fact that increased connections in the mind, a perceived "chain of purposes"—whether expressed in scientific or in "ordinary" language—is seen as the prerequisite for increased connections in society; and vice versa.

Simmel, unlike the lamenters, is prepared to accept positively both money and modernity. Earlier thought, he comments, had been unable to reconcile itself to change, to accept the mobility and interchangeability of all things. Modern science, however, has introduced another world-view, and Simmel welcomes it. Though Simmel does not specifically cite him, Comte in his positivism had given up the search for metaphysical absolutes and announced that all scientific laws were mere descriptions of relations; and Darwin and Herbert Spencer had established the "coming and going of all terrestrial forms of physics and mental life."[18] The new world-view is necessarily relativistic. Truth, for example, is a relative concept. But to say this is equivalent not to skepticism for Simmel but rather to what I would describe as a Gödel-like understanding of the universe, where no postulate or assumption is itself immune to logical dissolution. In such a universe, there are no absolutes, but only subjective-objective interplays, or exchanges.

Money, it might be said, moves through the world for Simmel as a kind of Hegelian world-historical hero. It tramples down many an innocent flower, but paves the way for the modern world of science, intellect, freedom, and widened community. Simmel is well aware of the negative aspects of money. He realizes that it takes on a life of its own, can be destabilized in value, and can lead to inflations and financial crises. He fully understands how its depersonalizing nature could eventuate in a kind of faceless society. (I might add that money in its most abstract form, credit, forgoes even the presidential and monarchical faces on its notes and coins that can help to symbolize a community.) He recognizes fully how it changes from a means into an end, becomes a new form of concentrated, unrepresentative power, and can lead to various forms of prostitution, sexual and social.

In spite of such drawbacks, however, Simmel sees money as basically a liberating force. It dissolves rigid social structures and allows space for déclassés, whether Quakers or Jews, and thus promotes at one and the same time both greater individuality and equality. Ironically it frees the laborer, too, as a person, though it does so first by turning him into a "commodity"; sociologically speaking, however, he is subordinate not as a person in, say, a feudal system, but only during the hours of work in which he is a commodity in the labor market. Even in the arena of marriage, what starts as marriage by purchase in primitive society becomes marriage by individual choice in late bourgeois society.

Such views of Simmel clearly bring him, even if not overtly, into conflict with Marx. It is worth pursuing their other differences, for such a comparison highlights the different value placed by our sociological versions of breakers and lamenters on the modern cash nexus, and the civilization that stands behind it.

Marx, as we know, had written three volumes, of about seven hundred pages each, comprising *Capital*. (Two of the volumes were published posthumously; *Theories of Surplus Value*, also published posthumously, has sometimes been described as volume four of *Capital*.) Simmel's *Philosophy of Money* consists of one volume of about five to six hundred pages. Capital, for him, is only one shape taken by the abstraction "money" which is, in turn, only one embodiment of the universal interaction of exchange. Marx would have snorted and accused Simmel of bleaching away the present excrescences of capitalism by immersing it in a timeless, ideal type; he would have dismissed him for not dealing with capital as a productive force, to be analyzed in classical economic terms. Simmel's response would have been a mere shrug of the shoulders, and a gentle reminder that he was trying to understand the nature of money and the most basic social assumptions underlying the theories of economists.

For Marx, money is the "common whore"; for Simmel it is a sign of "growing spiritualization," representing the essence of mental activity, which is "to bring unity out of diversity."[19] In Simmel's eyes Marx's theory of value, and especially his labor theory of value, is philosophically naïve and economically simplistic and wrong; consequently, the theory of surplus value also falls to the ground. To say that the laborer creates all the value in production and should, therefore, to all intents and purposes, receive it all is, Simmel informs us, to ignore or misunderstand the factors that enter into production. The concept, for example, of a locomotive on which the laborer works, and the quality of the labor involved in conceiving the engine on the part of the genius, who builds on the achievements of others but is uniquely endowed, is given by Simmel in illustration of his point.[20] (And Simmel will not accept the Marxist view that the above is all dealt with satisfactorily by the notion of "socially necessary labor time," which supposedly equalizes all labor.) Simmel, of course, could have appealed to marginal utility theory, but he prefers to deal with the subject on a larger, more philosophical ground than that occupied by the economists who followed after Marx.

Where Marx sees in the growth of institutions a matter of alienation, Simmel sees necessary reification. Such institutions (e.g., state, law, customs) Simmel views as higher forms of human interaction, attesting to the growing size and complexity of the group and symbolic of Man's greater mental progress. Defining a tool as an instrument for an end, Simmel describes a social institution as a tool allowing the individual to achieve a purpose beyond his own means.[21] And the purest example of such a tool is—money! Marx, in *Capital*, had defined Man as a "tool-making animal." Can not one hear his gasp if he were to read Simmel's casual and ironic comment that "Money is perhaps the clearest expression and demonstration of the fact that man is a 'tool-making' animal, which, however, is itself connected with the fact that man is a 'purposive' animal"?[22]

Just as coolly, Simmel takes Marx's indignation at the idea of Man as a commodity in the capitalist market, and holds it up to the light of historical sociology. Before capitalism, he points out, slaves were sold as commodities, and, even more telling, *Wergelt* in primitive societies was also a way of treating Man as a commodity. It is not that Simmel necessarily approves of the present, capitalist form of expressing what he calls "The Money Equivalent of Personal Values." It is simply that he seeks to analyze it as a "given" in human interactions and to understand its various embodiments rather than, as he would see it, to wrap himself in moral righteousness.

What Marx saw as "fetters," that is, bourgeois institutions holding back further change, Simmel sees as "forms," fostering genuine progress. He believes that socialism cannot do away with the forms, only modify them. And such modification would have their own share of flaws. As Simmel sees it, there are in any society two basic types of personality, one guided more by freedom and the other by equality. In his last comprehensive statement, *Fundamental Problems of Sociology (Individual and Society)* [*Grundfragen der Soziologie (Individuum und Gesellschaft)*] (1917), he remarks of the proletariat that "only because the class, whose interests are represented by socialism, would feel equality as freedom (at least during the initial period of socialist equalization), can socialism overlook the antagonism between the two ideals."[23] For Simmel, one of the inevitable basic forms in sociation is superordination and subordination (others are "competition, division of labor, formation of parties, representation, inner solidarity coupled with exclusiveness toward the outside," and so forth). These are not simply capitalistic devices; they are inevitable forms of human interaction. Spelling this out, Simmel adds that "It follows that the group as a whole needs a leader—that there are bound to be many subordinates and only few superordinates."[24] Simmel was fully aware that one Man's connection was another Man's chain; one might prefer the chains of socialism but they still would be chains.

Obviously, Marx and Simmel were deeply different in their reactions to the problem of the cash nexus. To Marx, Simmel's views would have seemed cold and callous; for Simmel's part, while acknowledging the cold and "heartless" features of modern society, he also saw the good features and realized the drawbacks to socialism; for him, Marx was one-sided and philosophically shallow. Yet such differences must not blind us to a certain fundamental view held in common by the two. It involves sociology, not socialism. We must remember that Marx too had dismissed the notion of society as an abstraction, separate from the interactions of Men. Society, he had said, is "the product of men's reciprocal action," and the individual, in turn, exists only as a member of that society. Simmel would admit that Marx had achieved a most sophisticated understanding of the subject matter of sociology. The two also agreed that capitalist development was a magnificent productive achievement, a triumph of material development leading to greater individualization; and, as Marx noted, "Exchange itself is a major agent of this individualisation."[25]

The agreement breaks down over the spiritual not the material achievement embodied in capitalist society. Simmel did not believe that the modernist achievements—science, rationality, liberty, freedom, and so forth—could be detached from their materialist, that is, "cash," connections and simply carried over into a "cashless" society. Philosophy, for him, addressed the "totality of being";[26] things hung together (as Marx, too, recognized in another context), and the task of sociology was to explore these connections. In the Preface to *The Philosophy of Money*, Simmel writes that he is attempting "to construct a new story beneath historical materialism." As he goes on,

> such that the explanatory value of the incorporation of economic life into the causes of intellectual culture is preserved, while these economic forms themselves are recognized as the result of more profound valuations and currents of psychological or even metaphysical pre-conditions. For the practice of cognition this must develop in infinite reciprocity. Every interpretation of an ideal structure by means of an economic structure must lead to the demand that the latter in turn be understood from more ideal depths, while for these depths themselves the general economic base has to be sought, and so on indefinitely.[27]

He is saying that economic determinacy will not suffice. Sociology, as a science, unlike socialism, must deal with multi-causal relations, with corresponding processes, in which the complexity of actual, empirical data is comprehended by universal concepts, or "forms." It was to the study of these forms, and thus of society, that Simmel devoted his work in a philosophy-become-sociology.

Antinomies and Forms

A study of sociological thought as such has not been my aim here any more than it was with Tönnies, and, for this reason if no other, I have given only a partial view of Simmel's work. It will be well, however, for a fuller understanding of his place in the connections discussion, to give a little more of his formal sociology and especially to look at his very Kantian position on the unsocial-social nature of man. In *The Philosophy of Money*, the influence of Kant is implicit and often explicit throughout, and shapes almost all that Simmel has to say on value and cognition. In one explicit passage, analyzing the "structure of our reason," Simmel reminds us that

> Ever since Kant we know that all experience, except for mere sense impressions, requires definite forms, inherent in the mind, by which the given is shaped into cognition. This *a priori*, which is brought by us to experience, must therefore be absolutely valid for all cognition and immune to any changes or to any possibility of correction by accidental sense experience.

It is this assumption that gives credence to Simmel's conception of universally valid forms. "But the certainty that there are such norms," he remarks, "is not matched by an equal certainty as to what these norms are."[28] Exactly here, however, is where Simmel has set himself his task: to establish the nature of these norms, that is, social forms. Kant, in analyzing the structure of our reason, elaborated his famous doctrine of the antinomies. The mind, he contended, is so constructed that it cannot solve certain problems, for example, the coexistence of freedom and determinism, the noumenal and phenomenal worlds. Nor, for example, can we possibly answer the question of whether God has always existed or is the first cause, for our minds are so constituted as to ask, "What came before the first cause?," for nothing can be uncaused, as well as to ask, "How can God exist eternally?," for we cannot really imagine infinity.

Simmel's thought is equally antinomial. He restricts his treatment of antinomies, however, to social not metaphysical problems. "The development of each human fate," he tells us in *The Philosophy of Money*, "can be represented as an uninterrupted alternation between bondage and release, obligation and freedom."[29] Money exchange brings both increased independence and dependence; increased impersonality in economics and increased self-consciousness and thus personality; greater subordination to machines but also greater equality; and participation in a larger community while shattering the ties of existing ones.

In the sociological world the greatest antinomy of all, for both Kant and Simmel, is that between man's unsocial and social nature. In *The Idea for a Universal History from a Cosmopolitan Point of View* (1784), Kant had written that the means which nature uses to achieve its end with Man is "the antagonism of men in society." By calling this characteristic "unsocial sociability," Kant had in mind Rousseau's formulations; but Kant wished to extrapolate them to history. Will nature succeed in the task of making Man perfect? The problem is complicated, for Kant recognized that "One cannot fashion something absolutely straight from wood which is as crooked as that of which man is made." Nevertheless, Kant was optimistic. Nature, having imposed this task on Man, will not allow him to fail. Employing a teleological model, Kant assures us, though with some trepidation, that nature's plan must be realized, and, in spite of his unsocial sociability, Man will progress to the full perfection of his capacities.[30]

Simmel retained Kant's unsocial-social antinomy, but without the optimism; in this he was truer to Kant's real insight than the mentor himself. In his 1892 book, *Die Probleme der Geschichtsphilosophie* (*The Problems of the Philosophy of History*, revised in 1905 and again in 1907), Simmel credited Kant with having freed Man from nature by his conception of natural science as a construct of mind, that is, we impose our "laws" on nature, rather than vice versa. The philosopher's task now was to do the same for history, and then for society. "Man," Simmel declared, "as something known, is made by nature and history; but man, as knower, makes nature and history."[31] Man is even more of a "knower" in the social world, Simmel asserts in a modern version of Vico, for that world exists, so to speak, only in Man's own mind, as "forms" of interaction. As Simmel announces in a later article, "How is Society Possible?" (1908),

> there is a decisive difference between the unity of a society and the unity of nature. It is this: In the Kantian view (which we follow here), the unity of nature emerges in the observing subject exclusively; it is produced exclusively by him in the sense materials, and on the basis of sense materials, which are in themselves heterogeneous. By contrast the unity of society needs no observer. It is directly realized by its own elements because these elements are themselves conscious and synthesizing units.

It is worth finishing Simmel's observation.

> Kant's axiom, that connection, since it is the exclusive product of the subject, cannot inhere in things themselves, does not apply here. For societal connection immediately occurs in the "things," that is, the

individuals. As a synthesis, it, too, of course, remains something purely psychological. It has no parallels with spatial things and their interaction. Societal unification needs no factors outside its own component elements, the individuals.[32]

These individuals, however, as we have seen, are unsocial-socials. Simmel draws the inevitable conclusion,

A society is, therefore, a structure which consists of beings who stand inside and outside of it at the same time. This fact forms the basis for one of the most important sociological phenomena, namely, that between a society and its component individuals a relation may exist as if between two parties.

In short, "The individual can never stay within a unit which he does not at the same time stay outside of, that he is not incorporated into any order without also confronting it." Simmel's conclusion might have made Kant (and certainly Hegel) wince: ". . . to be one with God is conditioned in its very significance by being other than God."[33]

A form of alienation, to use the term associated with Rousseau, Marx, and many other nineteenth-century lamenters, is thus for Simmel the inevitable human condition. Man does not exist outside of society; and in society, which is in his mind, his individuality is opposed to his social role. He is in conflict with himself, as well as, in his social role, with others. Thus Simmel's treatment of the unsocial-social problem goes well beyond the commonplace egoism-altruism dichotomy. As Simmel puts it, ". . . it seems to me, the basic struggle between society and individual inheres in the general form of individual life. It does not derive from any single, 'anti-social,' individual interest."[34]

Simmel has often been accused of neglecting the role of conflict in society. In comparison with Marx, of course, this is true. Or rather it is that Simmel sought to analyze conflict, as one of his sub-headings puts it, as "an Integrative Force in the Group."[35] In Simmel's view, there is bound to be not only competition but mutual repulsions and hostilities. Such forces, along with the attractive, make for a form of connection, linking the members of the group engaged in opposition, that is, providing internal unity for them. It was this awareness that kept Simmel from being a utopian of any kind. He believed that the effort to eliminate all harmony or disharmony, all attraction or repulsion, all love or hate, would dissolve the glue holding together any social formation. It was in this spirit that he comments that "the progress resulting from the relative increase of socialist measures does not justify the conclusion that their complete implementation would represent further progress." Then, characteristically even-handed, he adds, "It is the same with periods of increasing individualism."[36]

Yet, it is clear where his sympathies lay. It was the cash nexus, not socialism, that had brought about the mental acuity, the intellectuality, that allowed a man such as Simmel to roam freely, in his mind, as well as (ideally) in society, and to cogitate about both the mental and social connections in terms of a science called sociology. Science, not sensibility, was Simmel's primary inspiration and guide.[37] One of the prime findings of such a science was that Man was necessarily and eternally an unsocial-social creature. Socialism might seek to change the "condition" of Man, but it could not change his fundamental divided nature. Sociology, on the other hand, for Simmel, could study the "forms" in which the unsocial-social creature, Man, might express himself, whatever the particular combination of individual and socialist elements. And that, realistically, was all that it could do.

10

Academic Sociology:
Emile Durkheim

Forward

With Tönnies and Simmel, we have seen the connections problem, especially in its cash-nexus version, given what must count as its earliest significant elaboration in the form of modern sociology. The two men stand at the beginning of the professionalization of the "science," and they give classic conceptualization to the polar terms of "community and society," placing opposite valuations on the two types.

In turning to Emile Durkheim and Max Weber, we also have classic expressions of modern sociological positions, what might be called the positivist and Verstehen positions, but with the difference from Tönnies and Simmel that they are issued, so to speak, *ex cathedra*; both Durkheim and Weber held university chairs, and came to speak with a kind of canonical authority.

Moveover, they both appear to have moved further away from the literary origins that I have been stressing as present at the birth of modern sociology. Although all four men were born within a decade or so of one another, Durkheim and Weber seem to be in another world, so to speak, from Tönnies and Simmel in this regard. Yet my argument, as will be readily apparent from what follows, is that Durkheim and Weber, too, were also starting from the connections problem, and constantly had it in mind, even while distancing themselves further from its terms—especially Weber—as they sought to elaborate a formal and autonomous sociology.

Influences and Outcomes

Emile Durkheim was born in Lorraine, France, in 1858, the son and grandson of rabbis, and was originally destined for the rabbinate. On his mother's side, the family was in trade—beer and horses. Fairly early on, however, after a bout with mysticism inspired by a Catholic schoolmistress, the young Emile turned against a religious vocation as such, to pursue his studies at the local College and then at the prestigious École Normale Supérieure. Here he also broke, painfully, with his Judaism and dedicated himself to academic studies, especially philosophy.[1] Nevertheless, we can see from these brief allusions to his early life how a kind of mysticism might persist in Durkheim's thought; as his friend Georges Davy recalled, "This convinced rationalist always kept . . . a sort of fundamental religiosity . . . when, with the impassioned ardor of a prophet, he expounded his doctrine."[2]

Another major influence on Durkheim were the political circumstances of mid- and especially late nineteenth-century France.[3] One could argue that Durkheim's concern with stability arose to a large extent from the sense of frequent changes in politics and the defeat of France by Germany in 1870 as well as from more philosophical and economic origins. Certainly, affairs such as the Boulanger and the Dreyfus—the latter apparently helping to awaken Durkheim's religious as well as political interests—made him acutely aware of the republic's fragility and the need to preserve it.

At the École itself, philosophy was much connected with political discussions—Jean Jaurès, the future leader of the socialists, was Durkheim's close friend—and these undoubtedly made their mark also on the young scholar. Among the teachers who strongly affected him, although mainly by their writings, were Charles Bernard Renouvier, a neo-Kantian philosopher, and Fustel de Coulanges, a classical historian (to whom, in fact, Durkheim dedicated his Latin thesis, on Montesquieu). Fustel de Coulanges's effect on Durkheim was in the direction of a more historical sociology, for he himself was trying to revitalize classical studies by a comparative study of family organization, rituals, and myths.

In the background, looming over all the others, was the influence of Tocqueville and Comte. All of these influences combined—the political, philosophical, and historical—would enter into Durkheim's future work as a sociologist, a professional specialization, however, which did not formally exist in the French university structure at the time, and was, effectively, only to be created by Durkheim himself.[4]

Upon graduation, Durkheim taught philosophy at various provincial lycées from 1881 to 1887, interrupted by a year, 1885–86, in Germany, where he went to study philosophy and to acquire a knowledge of collective psychology and a taste for "collective life."[5] Earlier, having read Comte, he had decided that his doctoral thesis would be on "the relations between the individual and society," though he still conceived of it as a philosopher would. Now, however, he began to glimpse his true calling, sociology. In a number of reviews of German social thinkers, he made evident his new interests. Writing in 1885 about Albert Schaeffle's *Bau und Leben des Socialen Körpers*, Durkheim noted that the German thinker had stressed that animal organisms are governed "mechanically," whereas society is bound together by "the tie of ideas";[6] this, suitably reworked, was to become a seminal idea in Durkheim's own work on the relations of the individual and society, reversing Tönnies's organic and mechanical classification.

The visit to Germany also made Durkheim realize that "sociology," which, as he remarked, "is French by origin [he was thinking of Montesquieu, Tocqueville, and Comte], is becoming more and more a German science."[7] Durkheim, patriotically, decided to reverse this trend. Meanwhile, he returned to France and his teaching, receiving in 1887 an appointment to the Faculty of Letters at Bordeaux, where he remained for the next fifteen years, lecturing on subjects ranging from pedagogy to the family, suicide, religion, and social science, while also writing a number of books, of which *The Division of Labor in Society* (1893) is the most famous. In his first year at Bordeaux, he also married, enjoying, with two children, a happy family existence thereafter, or at least until World War I when his son was killed.

The year 1902 is an especially noteworthy one in Durkheim's life and work. In that year he not only published another book, *Suicide*, but helped to found *L'Année sociologique*, a review journal that both formalized sociology as a discipline in France and became the vehicle for a Durkheimian "school" of thought.[8] Georg Simmel was the only non-Frenchman on the board of *L'Année* for the first volume. He also published in it a programmatic paper, advocating his formal approach to sociology. Durkheim forcefully opposed this approach, and no further paper of Simmel's was ever published in *L'Année* again, nor did he remain on the board for the next issue.[9]

In this same year, 1902, Durkheim was also called to a post at the Sorbonne, again, however, in education, which was converted to one in "Education and Sociology" only over a decade later. Like a latter-day Rousseau moving from *Emile* (at Bordeaux, Durkheim had given four lectures on *Emile*) to the *Social Contract*, Durkheim, having been appointed a professor of pedagogy, slowly converted it to sociology. Here he remained, publishing his epochal *The Elementary Forms of Religious Life* (1912), among other writings. He was then caught up in the turmoil of World War I, and died in 1917.

Durkheim's life serves as an illustration of the vicissitudes of sociology as a new scholarly discipline. We see sociology, as we did with Tönnies and Simmel, emerging from philosophy (thus imitating the journey of the natural sciences from philosophy to specialized disciplines such as physics and chemistry). Unlike Tönnies and Simmel, however, even with all the difficulties of converting his academic posts to sociology rather than pedagogy, Durkheim did enjoy professional success and recognition: he eventually held a major chair, in his chosen field, at the most prestigious university in France, the Sorbonne. Moreover, he had founded a respected (though controversial) professional journal, and he had disciples and a "school" of sociology to leave behind him. In the person of Durkheim, in France, the sensibility we have been studying in terms of an earlier breakdown in connections and the lamentations to which it gave rise finally flowered, now in perennial form, as an "established science," sociology.[10]

Debates

Dealing with Durkheim necessarily involves some heavy going, and the reader is hereby warned. The effort is nevertheless worth making. Durkheim grappled with the core problem of connection in society: what are the bonds that held and can hold Man together? In his first major work, *Division of Labor*, he analyzed and thus implicitly justified, as I shall argue, modern society with its extensive division of labor.[11] The cash nexus, therefore, did not mean simply a breakdown of old connections (though Durkheim deplored the excesses of economic individualism), but the construction of new ones. In his last great work, *The Elementary Forms of Religious Life*, Durkheim took quite a different tack. He focused on the religious ties that bind, and at this point we can see more clearly than before that all along he had been viewing economics, in its "individualistic" guise, that is, characterized by the division of labor and the cash nexus, as a new form of "religion." Yet by his shift of attention to and his approval of the "primitive" roots of religion, Durkheim altered the whole tone of his discussion, and appeared to call into question his commitment to modernism. In the last resort, then, part of the difficulty in reading Durkheim resides in his ambiguities and ambivalences, and these, in turn, reflect the complexity as well as critical importance of our connections subject. As we continue to follow the movement from sensibility to science, Durkheim is an essential but Hamlet-like guide.

Before entering on a detailed examination of some of Durkheim's texts, however, we need to clear the way by acknowledging a number of scholarly problems which, if our aim were primarily a history of sociology, would have to be addressed at length. There is first the question whether Durkheim remained consistent in his ideas or changed fundamentally at some point. I have touched on this issue in the paragraph above, but we need to address it further and in the context of the debate that often takes the form of an assertion that Durkheim shifted from being a positivist to being an idealist.[12]

I take the following position: Durkheim, in spite of his desperate efforts at intellectual rigor and clarity, and his general brilliance, was frequently also muddled and inconsistent in his thought. However, I believe that he remained a positivist (though frankly I believe the whole debate as to his supposed shift is misframed when stated this way—a tempest in a philosophical teapot), but did change his emphasis as to what constituted the correct bonds holding society together; that is, he moved his focus from individualism to religion more traditionally conceived. Still, he persisted in the fundamental conviction that both individualism and traditional religion were forms of the *conscience collective*, meaning a body of beliefs and sentiments held in common and embodied in institutions (incidentally, in French, *conscience* means both consciousness and normative conscience). To put it provocatively, if George Eliot moved from the problem of connections in its individualistic, cash-nexus form to its racial-religious form in one book, *Daniel Deronda*, Durkheim did it via two books, *Division* and *Elementary Forms*, each at one end of the time spectrum of his writings.

A second question is whether Durkheim was a conservative or a radical, a liberal or a socialist. Or was he something else? Again, the matter is cloudy. In fact, the case can be made that Durkheim embodied all of these elements in his own person. His values were in many ways conservative, reflecting the influence of Comte. But as one scholar puts it so well, "The intellectual feat of Durkheim was to attempt to disengage certain general, if not universal, values such as community and the need for social discipline from reactionary historical longings and to reconcile these values with specifically modern needs. . . ."[13]

Similarly, Durkheim was in no way a Marxist: he apparently studied Marx while in Germany, and was somewhat familiar with *Capital*, but was not impressed by the overall schema. In general, Durkheim paid little overt attention to Marx and Marxism, although in 1897 he reviewed a work by Antonio Labriola, a Marxist, his one extended discussion of the subject. Yet if not a Marxist, Durkheim was a socialist, of sorts, mostly in the tradition of the Saint-Simonians; and, indeed, in 1895–96 he gave lectures at Bordeaux subsequently published as *Socialism and Saint-Simon*, whose title indicates its focus. By socialism Durkheim meant "every doctrine which demands the connection of all economic functions, or of certain among them, which are at the present time diffuse, to the directing and conscious centers of society"; nevertheless, he remained uncommitted to socialism as a movement.[14]

In these early lectures, Durkheim was at some pains to differentiate socialism, an ideology, from sociology, a science. Thus he viewed socialism as akin to sympathy, remarking that "Socialism is not a science, a sociology in minature—it is a cry of grief, sometimes of anger, uttered by men who feel most keenly our collective *malaise*."[15] In his later thinking, if one were to summarize Durkheim's view of a correct socialism, one might be tempted to say that it was the putting into effect of the findings of a science of sociology.

I suggest that one of the better ways of viewing Durkheim, for our purposes, is, in part, as a "revolutionary sociologist," and thus akin to Engels and Marx, but as one whose "revolution" was an attempted fulfillment of the promise of 1789, that is, an attempt to redeem an old, not to realize a new, revolution. Guilds, for example, in Durkheim's view, were properly abolished in the French Revolution, but a vacuum was left between the State and the individual which needed to be filled by a new intervening connection, that of corporations (as we shall see). The revolutionary rhetoric was of liberty, equality, and fraternity; the subsequent bourgeois reality was far distant from their realization. Thus, of our four sociologists, only Durkheim was responding to the breakdown of connections originating as much in the French as in the Industrial Revolution.

There are many other such debates concerning Durkheim. Did he ignore conflict, or allow for it in his sociology? Was he hostile to psychology, or had he included it in his definition of his new field? Was he historical or ahistorical in his thinking? These are all important and interesting questions; but they are not the ones that engage us here, where we are centrally concerned with the way in which Durkheim figures in the connections problem and in the shift from literary lamentation to the effort at a science of society, seen as responding to the sense of a world where everything had dissolved into a cash-nexus relation.

The Division of Labor

Thus, leaving aside all sorts of major issues in Durkheimian scholarship, we shall concentrate on just two of his seminal works, *The Division of Labor in Society* and *The Elementary Forms of Religious Life*. First, the *Division of Labor* (actually, the original title is *De la division du travail social*, which should be translated as "The Division of Social Labor"): Durkheim's starting point here was the simple Comtean assertion that social facts are as much subject to law, or scientific explanation, as natural facts (this first rule of method was subsequently developed by Durkheim in his *Rules of Sociological Method* (1895)). By "social" Durkheim often meant "moral," in the sense of the spiritual solidarity that bound the individual and society together, the declared theme of his doctoral dissertation. That dissertation became *The Division of Labor in Society*, where Durkheim announces in the Preface that he will be treating "the facts of the moral life according to the method of the positive sciences." His approach will be neither deductive nor, like Herbert Spencer, scientific in the sense of borrowing propositions from other positive sciences, for example, biology, and then claiming the resulting moral life, or ethics, as scientific. Instead, Durkheim announces, "We do not wish to extract ethics from science, but to establish the science of ethics, which is quite different. Moral facts are phenomena like others; they consist of rules of action recognizable by certain distinctive characteristics. It must, then, be possible to observe them, describe them, classify them, and look for the laws explaining them."[16]

One consequence of Durkheim's method, then, is an implicit claim to what I shall call value-free inquiry. Although intensely concerned with the moral crisis of his time, Durkheim saw its solution in terms of a scientific sociology, in which "we seek to determine what is or has been, not what ought to be." Thus, as he concluded, "the antithesis between science and ethics, that formidable argument with which the mystics of all times have wished to cloud human reason, disappears."[17]

It can be argued that "value-free" is the wrong language to use with Durkheim. In his analysis of a division of labor society he speaks, as we shall see, about anomie and about social health and normality. Thus his language is that of pathology, where something is wrong in the body social and needs to be cured. "Is" in this case is surely not what "ought" to be, and the idea that something is "wrong" suggests that the researcher has in mind for comparison some state that is "right."

In my view this is yet one more example of Durkheim's sometimes misleading way of philosophizing. It should not, I am arguing, obscure his basic and persistent commitment to the Positivist tenet that science, dealing with what is, is therefore at the same time dealing with what ought to be. True, Durkheim was confusing his sociology of morals, where understanding cannot really condemn any practice, with ethics, which seeks to establish the philosophical right. The result is that Durkheim's functionalism—all social practices serve a legitimate purpose—implicitly conflicts with his "revolutionary" aspirations and, when in the ascendency, lands him in an avowedly value-free position. And all this in spite of the fact that Durkheim's language in the end betrays him as being just as judgmental as Tönnies about "abnormal" conditions![18]

In any event, applying his conception of social science to the "fact" of the division of labor, Durkheim produced another consequence: the replacement, basically, of economics by sociology, which he envisioned as a much broader study. In the first half of the nineteenth century, classical economics can be said to have replaced politics in the schemes and theories of a number of thinkers. Robert Owen and the Saint-Simonians, for example, as well as Marx and Engels, clearly shifted primacy from politics to economics, indeed effectively eliminating any role for political activity in the process. Now, in the second half of the century, Durkheim took this trend one step forward by replacing economics with the larger science of sociology.

In an early series of lectures, published as "Course in Sociology: Opening Lecture," Durkheim credited economics with leading the way. It had been the first to proclaim that social laws are as necessary and possible as are physical laws. As Durkheim says, "Extend this principle to all social facts and sociology is established."[19]

Now, in the *Division of Labor*, he turned rather unfilially upon the parent science. He made his challenge directly on the ground centrally claimed by the economists: the division of labor. This, after all, was the subject of the opening chapter in Adam Smith's *Wealth of Nations*; it is the *bête noire* of Karl Marx, who wishes to do away with it; and it is the presumed prime cause of the breakdown in connections, leaving as the sole remaining tie between Men the infamous cash nexus. As Durkheim points out, however, "the division of labor is not peculiar to the economic world."[20] It manifests itself in specialized political, administrative, and judicial functions, in the breakdown of philosophy into specialized, scientific disciplines, and especially in the biological world as a general law governing the functions of the organism. It is much too important, therefore, to be left to the economists. Thus, Durkheim claims the inquiry into the division of labor for his new science of sociology.

Such an inquiry takes Durkheim to the major problem confronting modern Man, the nature of connection and community, or, as he puts it in one of his lectures, "What are the bonds which unite men one with another?"[21] If he could answer this question correctly, Durkheim also felt that he would be answering the question, "What are the bonds which *should* unite man one with another?" or as he himself puts it, "Is the division of labor, at the same time that it is a law of nature, also a moral rule of human conduct?" It is a rhetorical question for Durkheim, for, as we have seen, "is" and "should be" are implicitly the same for him in his close embrace at this point of positivistic science.

Tönnies, as we know from our earlier discussion, gave a very different answer. In analyzing *Gemeinschaft* and *Gesellschaft*, he made it very clear that he thought the latter, that is, cash-nexus society, characterized as it is by division of labor, is unnatural and mechanical, not a social fact to be accepted but an abnormal growth to be eliminated. In 1889, Durkheim prepared for his work on the division of labor by reviewing Tönnies's classic book. Accepting the German scholar's contention that *Gemeinschaft* was the earliest form of social solidarity, Durkheim rejected Tönnies's conclusion that it was therefore the only natural and acceptable form. I quote at length: "Now, I hold that the life of the great social agglomerations is just as natural as that of small aggregates. It is neither less organic nor less internal. Apart from purely individual movements, there is in our contemporary societies a genuinely collective activity which is just as natural as that of the less extended societies of earlier times. It is certainly distinct; it constitutes a different type. But between these two species of a single genus, however diverse they may be, there is no difference of kind. To prove this would need a book. . . ."[22]

The book, of course, becomes *The Division of Labor in Society*, whose author obviously has Tönnies in mind (though this is not made explicit in the text itself). For Talcott Parsons, however, the book "is to be understood mainly as a polemic against the utilitarian conception of modern industry."[23] I believe this a one-sided interpretation, for the *Division of Labor* is at least as much against the *Gemeinschaft* critique of modern industrial society as it is against, say, Spencerian economic individualism. What Durkheim is doing is seeking his own synthetic understanding.

In the course of the book, Durkheim makes a number of powerful statements, which can be summarized as follows (the actual text is by no means as clear-cut, and for other purposes one would want to follow the author's own mental progressions). His starting assumption is that there is no state of nature, as predicated by Rousseau and others, from which individuals emerge by joining together to form a society. Rather, individuals take their very being from society, and cannot exist separately from it.

In its earliest shape, this unbreakable link between Man and society takes the form of what Durkheim calls "mechanical solidarity," that is, Tönnies's *Gemeinschaft* (which he, of course, had called "organic"). Here men are bound to one another by a collective sentiment based on mental contagion—Durkheim appeals to the work of Le Bon and other crowd psychologists—and not by personal interest. Their solidarity is born of "resemblances," and, indeed, each individual is replaceable by every other individual—there is no unique individuality. Such a society brings Men together by means of "mechanical causes and impulsive forces, such as affinity of blood, attachment to the same soil, ancestral worship, community of habits, etc."[24] We easily recognize in this list the traits of Tönnies's *Gemeinschaft*; today we would characterize them as "primordial ties."

Over time, such a society can and does evolve to a more differential one, whose fundamental trait is the division of labor. Society, therefore, is not formed from the division of labor but produces it historically. Durkheim's revolutionary assertion, so to speak, is that the division of labor and its attendant phenomena does not represent the breakdown of society and community, but is merely a new form of social solidarity, and one that is as binding as the preceding, mechanical, one.

For his new form of solidarity, Durkheim proposes the adjective "organic." "This solidarity," he explains, "resembles that which we observe among the higher animals. Each organ, in effect, has its special physiognomy, its autonomy. And, moreover, the unity of the organism is as great as the individuation of the parts is more marked. Because of this analogy, we propose to call the solidarity which is due to the division of labor, organic." The paradox is that the increased interdependence of society is matched by the increased independence of the individual. Individuality flourishes in a way impossible in mechanical society. In Durkheim's terms, "the activity of each is as much more personal as it is more specialized."[25]

Tocqueville, in *Democracy in America*, as we noted, had wrestled with differences, if any, between egoism and individualism (a term which he made central to modern discussion).[26] Defining egoism as unrestricted love of self, he saw individualism as an enlightened form of such self-love, where self-interests led to rational consideration of others' interests as well. Gloomily, however, Tocqueville concluded that individualism, too, would collapse into egoism.

Durkheim was more optimistic. He believed, as Anthony Giddens so well puts it, that "the sentiment of the supreme worth of the human individual is thus a product of society, and it is this which decisively separates it from egoism. The 'cult of the individual' is based, not upon egosim, but upon the extension of quite contrary sentiments of sympathy for human suffering and the desire for social justice."[27] What is more, where Tocqueville saw the march of Providence leading inexorably to increased equality, Durkheim saw scientific confirmation of the trend toward both increased individualism and justice.

What had produced and what would ensure the continued progress of the division of labor? The starting point seems to be the difference between man and woman, which serves as the basis for the sexual division of labor, which in turn serves as the source of conjugal solidarity. Families are the original form of society. Grouped together, without further elaboration of form, they comprise a horde. This can become a clan, and linked clans become what Durkheim calls "segmental societies."[28]

Such is an ideal-type history of the development of society. But Durkheim is not really interested in such conjectural history; he concerns himself mainly with the reasons for segmental society turning into modern organic society.[29] The main factors he lists are increased population, the growth of cities, and the spread of communication. Such developments in the direction of greater volume and density make the struggle for existence more acute. At this point, again, Durkheim takes what is really a revolutionary turn, in contrast with the lamenters. Where they see the struggle for existence—competition, as they would put it—as a mounting evil, Durkheim takes an explicitly Darwinian, and sometimes even Lamarckian, point of view (although opposing social Darwinism, as a quite different position). Thus he argues that the struggle for existence leads to different niches for individuals, to greater division of labor, consequently permitting more people to stay alive and society as a whole to expand and prosper. As Durkheim explains, "In the same city different occupations can coexist without being obliged mutually to destroy one another, for they pursue different objects."[30] Unexpectedly, we have found the answer to Hobbes's war of all against all, the starting point as we recall for Tönnies's speculations on society. As Raymond Aron summarizes the issue, ". . . social differentiation is, so to speak, the peaceful solution to the struggle for survival. Instead of some being eliminated so that others may survive, as in the animal kingdom, social differentiation enables a greater number of individuals to survive by differentiation. Each man ceases to be in competition with all, each man is only in competition with a few of his fellows, each man is in a position to occupy his place, to play his role."[31]

Durkheim was not blind to the deficit side of increased social differentiation. He speaks of *anomie*, best described as a situation in which a controlling normative structure is disorganized, leaving the individual feeling disoriented and his actions meaningless. Durkheim recognizes that self-destruction is one index of *anomie*, and later devoted his book *Suicide* to an empirical and theoretical exploration of its role in modern life. He was aware, too, of crime as a measure of general social unhappiness. Industrial crises also figured in Durkheim's account of the price paid for its relative affluence by contemporary society. However, where for a Marxist such disorders in society were seen as normal outcomes of social fragmentation, for Durkheim they were "Abnormal Forms." They could not be totally eliminated, for Durkheim accepted the necessity of conflict in society, but they could be ameliorated. In any case, one did not condemn modern organized society for its abnormalities.

What form might amelioration or reform take? In the Preface to his second edition (1902), Durkheim expounded an idea that he admitted to be "undeveloped" in the first edition: "the role that occupational groups are destined to play in the contemporary social order."[32] Put simply, the idea is corporatism. Neither the economy at large—what might be called civil society—nor the State can do away with the evil of *anomie*; thus, occupational groups, which he identifies with corporatism, which are necessary more for moral than economic reasons, must form and move to dominance. Durkheim is aware that this is a recommendation as well as an analysis, but in a sketchy version of a philosophy of history he tells us that society has been moving from ties based on consanguinity to territory and now to occupation. Thus, he saves his commitment to the inseparability of "what is" and "what should be."

Many critics find Durkheim's corporatism the least persuasive part of his work, with perilous implications, which I shall explore later. In any case, his espousal of corporatism is not intrinsic to his basic analysis in *The Division of Labor*. What is impressive is his fundamental analysis of social solidarity in general. In this part of his work it is true he is highly derivative, borrowing heavily from a whole host of both German and French thinkers who were occupied, as I have tried to suggest, with the problem of connections and community.[33] Nevertheless, after all the derivations are acknowledged, one is left with an original synthesis, and thus analysis, on Durkheim's part.

What Durkheim has done is to lift the concept of connections, as I have outlined it earlier, to a new level of abstraction and generality. He talks not of "sensibility" or the "cash nexus" but of "solidarity" and the "division of labor." He seeks to establish a science of these matters: sociology. The roots of Durkheim's sociology in the felt experience of the recent industrial revolutionary past are less exposed than, for example, in Engels and Marx, in Tönnies, or even in Simmel. Yet all of these thinkers-cum-scientists are leaves on the same tree of knowledge.

Durkheim's extraordinary achievement is his analysis of the way in which increased individualism and increased social dependency go together. In this, he moves beyond Simmel's impressionistic treatment and offers us a more formalistic, functional-structural analysis of the paradox. As Durkheim puts it in a review written in 1904 for *L'Année sociologique*, the division of labor is "the sole process which enables the necessities of social cohesion to be reconciled with the principle of individuation."[34] However he might seek to be neutral, Durkheim implicitly assumes individualism to be a good thing, as long as it is not at the expense of others. So, too, is increased differentiation, or division of labor. He does not make it clear, however, whether these are good things in themselves or as means to an end. The most plausible reading suggests that he values them as means to an end we might call modernity, in contrast with the primitivism he implicitly looks down on in mechanized society. (By *Elementary Forms*, he appears to have changed his attitude to primitive society; logically, of course, all societies should always have been equally valid in Durkheim's eyes, but again his language betrays his conflicting values.)

Durkheim recognizes the fundamental unsocial-social nature of Man. "There are in each of us," he says, "two consciences: one which is common to our group in its entirety, which, consequently, is not ourself, but society living and acting within us; the other, on the contrary, represents that in us which is personal and distinct, that which makes us an individual."[35] While this divided state might sometimes give rise to *anomie*, it did not have to eventuate in alienation. Quite the contrary: only in society, and a divided society at that, that is, one marked by the division of labor, can the individual return to himself, for the paradox is that he is only himself *in* society, and conscious of himself as self in a society beyond the primitive, "mechanized" stage. Divided society becomes the solution, therefore, to divided Man, its own creation.

Elementary Religion

In discussing organic solidarity in *The Division of Labor,* Durkheim notes that religion was occupying a smaller and smaller portion of modern social life—an observation made, as we have observed earlier, by lamenters such as Carlyle—but he notes as well that the individual is becoming the "object of a sort of religion." Durkheim confesses, however, that "We do not actually possess any scientific notion of what religion is. To obtain this, we would have to treat the problem by the same comparative method that we have applied to the question of crime, and that is an effort which has not yet been made."[36] These words were published in 1893. A year or so later, Durkheim was lecturing on religion at Bordeaux. At that point, in 1895, he claims to have "achieved a clear view of the essential role played by religion in social life." Durkheim writes of a "revelation"—he says that "that course of 1895 marked a dividing line in the development of my thought."[37] He now reviewed all his previous researches from this perspective, and plunged into a study of religious history and ethnography, some of which first manifested itself in his treatment of suicide. The full result, however, came seventeen years later, with the publication of *The Elementary Forms of the Religious Life.*

The time was propitious. Ethnography, or, more widely stated, anthropology, had been attracting increasingly professional devotees since the 1870s; like sociology, it was slowly becoming an acceptable academic discipline. Tylor's *Primitive Culture* was published in 1871, and Frazier's *Golden Bough* in 1890. Almost all anthropology, it must be added, was at the time "armchair anthropology," that is, written up on the basis of reports by travelers, missionaries, and the like, rather than by trained observers working in the field. Only with Bronislaw Malinowski, around 1917, did field work become the required method for anthropologists. Durkheim, working via "armchair anthropology" and, indeed, often by a secondary reading of such accounts, was in the anthropological tradition of his time. It is important to remember this, inasmuch as later scholars have pretty well discredited the "facts" Durkheim claimed to be using.[38]

A romance with the primitive was also part of the culture of the times. For example, a Musée d'Ethnographie du Trocadero (now called the Musée de l'Homme) had been opened in Paris in 1882. Viewing the collection in 1906–7, Picasso discovered primitive art;

it was, in fact, while in the process of painting "Les Demoiselles d'Avignon" that he visited the Trocadero, and experienced a revelation—"exorcism" is how he referred to it—in a confrontation with the tribal objects exhibited there. His revelation, incorporated in his paintings, began a revolution in the way Westerners regarded primitive art, as well as the primitives who produced it.[39] In the field of music, we need only think of Igor Stravinsky's *Le Sacre du Printemps* (1913) for a comparable example. This is the context, then, in which Durkheim claimed to have crossed a dividing line in his thought.

In seeking to understand the result, I shall again offer a summary, without trying to follow Durkheim's own outline in the text. A word on Durkheim's method of writing, on his style, however, is in order. His characteristic style of presentation is to discuss alternate explanations to his own, as found in other writers, to show their shortcomings, and, by a kind of negative proof, to establish the validity of his own positively stated explanation. Thus, in *The Elementary Forms*, we are taken through an extended criticism of animism and naturism, of Edward Burnett Tylor and Max Müller, in order to arrive at the correct view on the origins of religion. The erudition is impressive, if often wearying; the critique, Talmudic and philosophical.

Durkheim takes as his basic assumption that religion is reasonable, and that there is no real discontinuity between the primitive and the civilized, or scientific, mind. Unlike the *philosophes*, who also claimed to study religion "scientifically" but saw in it mere delusions and superstitions to be eliminated by reason, but, rather, like Vico, who recognized that religion merely uses a different language, myth, to express its rational meaning, Durkheim declares religion both rational and comprehensible. It is rational, not an "illusion," because it is made by Man, and it is comprehensible because, like any social or moral fact, it falls under the domain of positive science.

Durkheim's great "revelation" is that all religions, though different, serve the same function in society. That function is to bind Men together. Hence, at this point in his thinking primitive society becomes as "good" as modern society. Religious belief and rites serve as the basis of community. As Durkheim remarks, specifically of the function of cults, "By the mere fact that their apparent function is to strengthen the bonds attaching the believer to his god, they at the same time really strengthen the bonds attaching the individual to the society of which he is a member, since the god is only a figurative expression of the society."[40] What exactly Durkheim means by this, I shall make clearer as we go along. Here we need to note, however, that whatever his "revelation," Durkheim is pursuing the same inquiry that has animated him from the time of his dissertation—the relation of the individual to society—which comprises the *leitmotif* of his sociology. What needs emphasis is that he has dramatically shifted his focus, though not his positivist approach: in *The Division of Labor* he was previously analyzing the bonds—differentiation and individualism—that united "organic" society; now he is concentrating on the bonds—primordial religious feelings—that unite "mechanized" society. He is going back to his and society's roots.

The most elementary form of religion, Durkheim found, was totemism, as practiced by the Australian bushmen. Durkheim relies most heavily on two observers, Spencer and Gillen, who worked around the turn of the century, though he compares their work with others. His analysis, in essence, is that the totem, usually in the form of an animal or vegetable, sets up a universe of things that are forbidden to the clan members: they may not eat of the flesh of the totemic animal, marry within the clan, and so on. The details are not important, though Durkheim goes into long and exhaustive discussion of them. What is critical is that in the belief system a domain of the sacred is set up, demarcated from that of the profane (apparently, Fustel de Coulanges was the source of this idea for Durkheim). As Durkheim puts it, "All known religious beliefs, whether simple or complex, present one common characteristic: they presuppose a classification of all the things, real and ideal, of which men think, into two classes or opposed groups, generally designated by two distinct terms which are translated well enough by the words *profane* and *sacred*. This division of the world into two domains, the one containing all that is sacred, the other all that is profane, is the distinctive trait of religious thought."[41]

The real significance of the sacred for Durkheim is that for those who share in its belief a bond is established, uniting them in a community and separating them from others. Such community, and communion, it should be noted, is in Men's minds. It is made manifest in rites and given explanatory power in terms of myths (which are, therefore, not the source of religious feelings). The totem itself is merely a symbol, in which Men personify themselves; and this is the same with more developed gods. In worshipping these symbols, Men worship themselves, that is, their being in society. Reinforced by communion, orgies, and so on, it is this self-worship, at first unconscious and then in modern society conscious, that constitutes the society. Erroneous as Durkheim's primitive ethnography may be, and sweeping as are some of his speculations, his overall presentation is powerful and partly persuasive.[42]

His similarities and differences with the Young Hegelians and Karl Marx are worth noting. They too had maintained that gods are created in Man's image, and not vice versa. And Marx, especially, had argued that religion mirrors the social structure. His conclusion was that, once the veil of illusion is ripped off, religion will disappear—Man will destroy the false gods whom he has set above himself. Durkheim too saw religion as, in part, a mirror of the social structure. But at this point he diverged sharply from his German predecessor and moved to a formal sociology of religion. Unlike Marx, Durkheim plunged into the then-existing empirical and historical material on the subject. On this basis, he claimed not only that Man created religion in terms of his social structure, but that that very social structure was formed and continued to exist solely in terms of that religious belief. Society and the gods exist, so to speak, only in Men's minds, and must coexist. In Durkheim's words, "If the idea of society were extinguished in individual minds and the beliefs, traditions and aspirations of the group were no longer felt and shared by the individuals, society would die. We can say of it what we just said of the divinity: it is real only in so far as it has a place in the human consciousness. . . ."[43]

What is more, this collective consciousness takes on a life of its own. It is not simply an epiphenomenal superstructure. With an eye directly on Marx, Durkheim declares:

> . . . it is necessary to avoid seeing in this theory of religion a simple restatement of historical materialism: that would be misunderstanding our thought to an extreme degree. In showing that religion is something essentially social, we do not mean to say that it confines itself to translating into another language the material forms of society and its immediate vital necessities. It is true that we take it as evident that social life depends upon its material foundation and bears its mark, just as the mental life of an individual depends upon his nervous system and in fact his whole organism. But collective consciousness is something more than a mere epiphenomenon of its

morphological basis, just as individual consciousness is something more than a simple efflorescence of the nervous system. In order that the former may appear, a synthesis *sui generis* of particular consciousness is required. Now this synthesis has the effect of disengaging a whole world of sentiments, ideas and images which, once born, obey laws all their own.[44]

These laws are, in essence, the laws of sociology. Such laws, according to Durkheim, tell us of the necessary relations of individuals to society—*any* society, including a Marxist or a socialist one.

If, however, religious feeling is essential to all societies, how can Durkheim reconcile this "law" with his own earlier statement that religion is declining in his time? The answer had already been given in the earlier book, *The Division of Labor*. God is dead, but Man has become the object of his own worship. The new form of religion is individualism, and the new totem, so to speak, holding society together, is the division of labor. Individualism, Durkheim declares, is "itself a social product, like all moralities and all religions. The individual receives from society even the moral beliefs which deify him."[45] In short, religion is not a set of transcendental beliefs but a form of social glue, and any form will do, in principle.[46]

Having said this, or implied it, Durkheim was nevertheless aware that his was a time of moral crisis, "a stage of transition and moral mediocrity." Like Matthew Arnold before him, he declared that "the old gods are growing old or already dead, and others are not yet born." A fully accepted though regulated individualism was one solution; corporatism, as we have seen, was for Durkheim even better. He was sanguine that "A day will come when our societies will know again those hours of creative effervescence, in the course of which new ideas arise and new formulae are found which serve for a while as a guide to humanity. . . ."[47] How shocked Durkheim would have been to recognize only a few short years after his death and the end of World War I that his call for renewed community, for "hours of creative effervescence," might take the form of Fascist marches (in the name, incidentally, of corporatism) and Nazi rallies. Yet that is what happened, as Durkheim's nephew and disciple, Marcel Mauss, ruefully confessed in a private letter:

One thing that, fundamentally, we never foresaw was how many large modern societies, that have more or less emerged from the Middle Ages in other respects, could be hypnotized like Australians are by their dances, and set in motion like a children's roundabout. This return to the primitive had not been the object of our thoughts. We contented ourselves with several allusions to crowd situations, while it was a question of something quite different. We also contented ourselves with proving that it was in the collective mind [*dans l'esprit collectif*] that the individual could find the basis and sustenance for his liberty, his independence, his personality and his criticism [*critique*]. Basically, we never allowed for the extraordinary new possibilities. . . ."[48]

Alas, the dreams of sociology had turned into the nightmares of history.

Religion as Knowledge

Under this shadow, let us return to Durkheim's sociology of religion. In believing that what he called religious feeling was eternal—else there could be no society—Durkheim also came to believe that religion could be and had been transformed into science. I shall call this set of ideas Durkheim's sociology of knowledge, that is, a kind of sociological epistemology. It is a highly suggestive piece of speculation. His thesis is that all of Man's mentality—his categories, logic, concepts, language, etc.—comes from his experience in society and mirrors the social organization he has constructed there. Thus, the idea of class, or classification, is modeled upon the social organization, for example, the clans. Because Men are themselves organized, they can organize other things. Because society is hierarchical, we can see nature in terms of hierarchy. "It is society which classifies being into superiors and into inferiors, into commanding masters and obeying servants . . . [and] it is in their image that the powers of the physical world have been conceived."[49]

In an earlier chapter, I spoke of Adam Smith's "connecting" view of science, that is, the way in which science connects phenomena in our mind, thus mirroring the connections in the outside world. Durkheim appears to have a similar view, although with a different perspective attached to it. As he declares, ". . . the essential thing was not to leave the mind enslaved to visible appearances, but to teach it to dominate them and to connect what the senses separated; for from the moment when men have an idea that there are internal connections between things, science and philosophy become possible. Religion opened up the way for them." Our scientific logic, he concludes, was born of primitive logic: "between the logic of religious thought and that of scientific thought there is no abyss."[50]

The encouraging conclusion for Durkheim is that science, rather than being the enemy of religion, is its heir; and that science in the form of sociology demonstrates the need for religious feeling, broadly interpreted, as a prerequisite for the existence of community. Burke (and Comte) had said that there can be no society without some form of religion; Durkheim goes beyond this to say that science and individualism are to be viewed as modern forms of religious feeling. It is a startling reconciliation, a conservative-revolutionary reunion, sometimes labeled "civic religion."

Is Anything Left Out?

In 1898, having tentatively traced our perception of the world, our ethical conceptions, and our structure of society back to "religious beliefs which are their primordial forms," Durkheim paused and asked "whether economic organization is an exception and derives from another source."[51] We see his first provisional handling of the problem in the Preface to the second volume of *L'Année sociologique* just quoted, when he goes on to say that "Religion holds within itself, from the very beginning, but in a muddled sort of way, all the elements that have given rise to the various manifestations of collective life by a process of separating, redefining, and combining in a thousand different ways. It is from myths and legends that science and poetry have arisen; it is from religious ornateness and cult ceremonies that the plastic arts have arrived on the scene; law and morality have arisen from ritual observances. . . . At the very most we may ask ourselves if economic organization provides an exception and comes from a different source; although we do not think so, we grant that the question may be set aside."[52]

In *The Elementary Forms*, he came back to the issue, and added,

> Only one form of social activity has not yet been expressly attached to religion: that is economic activity. Sometimes processes that are derived from magic have, by that fact alone, an origin that is indirectly religious. Also, economic value is a sort of power or efficacy, and we know the religious origins of the idea of power. Also, richness can confer *mana*; therefore it has it. Hence it is seen that the ideas of economic value and of religious value are not without con-

nection. But the question of the nature of these connections has not yet been studied.[53]

This is slightly puzzling. Not only had Durkheim himself written on the division of labor (although admittedly not from an economic point of view), which he now had connected to society in a religious manner, but Max Weber had written *The Protestant Ethic and the Spirit of Capitalism* in 1904. Durkheim simply ignores the latter's work, as well as his own earlier ruminations.

Thus, though he offers us reconciliation, he does not appear to offer us resolution. Man is still the unsocial-social being, though now with a new gloss. "Man is double," Durkheim acknowledges in *The Elementary Forms*, though he is at one with his society, conceptually. In practice, Durkheim recognizes that "We cannot give ourselves up entirely to our own egoism at once." We must, in fact, lead "two existences at the same time." All previous explanations of this fact, he tells us, have been in religious terms: "The only explanation which has ever been given of this singular necessity is the hypothesis of the Fall, with all the difficulties which it implies. . . ."[54] Now, in place of the religious explanation, Durkheim is offering us a new Genesis of divided Man: the science of sociology. For a few, brief years the new revelation seems to have held doubt at bay. By 1914, however, Durkheim wrote,

> We must . . . do violence to certain of our strongest inclinations. Therefore, since the role of the social being in our single selves will grow ever more important as history moves ahead, it is wholly improbable that there will ever be an era in which man is required to resist himself to a lesser degree, an era in which he can live a life that is easier and less full of tension. To the contrary, all evidence compels us to expect our effort in the struggle between the two beings within us to increase with the growth of civilization.[55]

In the end, then, the optimism and confidence of *The Division of Labor*, where the challenge of a cash-nexus society appears to have been met head on, seems to have foundered on the unresolved problem of Man's double nature: his economic activity and his religious community, his unsocial being and his social being. And this in spite of Durkheim's heroic efforts to solve the problem through a science that could even embrace religion.

11

Academic Sociology: Max Weber

The Final Turn

In turning to Max Weber as the last of our sociologists, we reach the end of our journey. With this great thinker, we come to a moment of major significance: a transformation of the entire "cash nexus" focus, as I have tried to outline it, into a new, kaleidoscopic shape.[1] Effectively, Weber took "actions," rather than "bonds," "connections," or "relations," as his primary unit of analysis, and dissolved the cash-nexus problem into a general sociology, inquiring into the nature of *all* social action of which the economic is only one aspect.

In a sense, as I have been arguing, Tönnies, Simmel, and especially Durkheim had all been going in the same direction. Their work, however, was more closely tied to the central social question of their time—the primacy of the cash nexus—than was Weber's. It is not that that same inspiration, as I shall emphasize, is not to be found in Weber; it is that he relegated it to a less important role, playing it down in his attempt to understand the emergence in the history of human social action of Western, rational capitalism as a unique development. And, in the total complexity of Weber's monumental general sociology, even Western rational capitalism is, in principle at least, merely one example of how economics, religion, and a host of other factors conjoin into particular historical figurations, which themselves can be rationally understood.

217

French and German Science

In order to see this transformation in some detail, we can profit from a few initial observations, comparing Weber and Durkheim directly, before proceeding to an analysis of Weber's achievement by itself. As noted, Emile Durkheim had written a book on economic activity and another on religious activity; in the end, however, he left them unrelated, making only a few puzzling allusions to the need for further inquiry on the possibly "exceptional" nature of economics. He appears to have taken no notice of Weber's *The Protestant Ethic and the Spirit of Capitalism.* Yet in that work, published in 1904, Weber implicitly, if not explicitly, rose to the challenge presented by his French sociological counterpart.

Thus it is curious that, at a time when sociology was first laying claims to being a discipline of a universal, scientific character, its two greatest figures, Durkheim and Weber, almost completely ignored one another's work and went their separate ways. We seem to have, rather than one science, a French and a German science. Though some modern scholars argue for a convergence in Durkheim and Weber's work, I would put it differently: what links them are common areas of concern, rather than common findings.[2]

I want to highlight two of the areas where both labored on the same concern, but with very different results. One is that both Durkheim and Weber were engaged in the study of religion. But for Durkheim, it was primitive religion—the elementary forms—that engaged his attention, in what I have called the "romance" of his era. Weber, on the other hand, mentioned totemism only in passing, and was concerned almost exclusively with the great religions of the modern world—Judaism, Christianity, Islamism, Buddhism. Moreover, Durkheim moved from his elementary forms to speculations about their service as epistemological forerunners of our scientific conceptions, rather than about their relations to economics. Weber, in contrast, saw science as separable from religion and wished to understand "scientifically" the relation of religious activity and ethics to other forms of social action, especially the economic.

A useful way to view Weber's work in this area is to see it as the fulfillment of the earlier German development, wherein Hegel and the Young Hegelians had engaged in a vigorous and far-reaching critique of religion, especially Christianity. In the hands of Karl Marx, as we have noted, this critique appeared to lead naturally to a critique of economics. It was Weber's genius to link the two concerns in a new synthesis, scientifically fashioned. In doing so, he developed, in place of *critique*, a *sociology* of religion.

The second major area where Durkheim and Weber diverge, again reflecting their national cultures, pertains to the central methodological issue at the heart of social science: the "what is" and "what should be" problem. Durkheim, as I have argued, tended to do away with the problem by announcing that there was little difference between them; the existent and the normative are, ideally, one and the same. This is the Positivist position, derived from his predecessor, Auguste Comte. Weber resolutely took a different stance, announcing that a scientific sociology must concern itself solely with the "what is," recognizing that it can say nothing about "what should be" except that values themselves are held by different groups over time and comprise part of the phenomena of "what is."

This is the famous "value-free" position of Weber. He was firmly convinced that science could not prove or disprove any particular value. Values come from sources other than reason. There can be no cumulative "progress" in values as such, no important new discoveries (as there are, for example, in scientific knowledge). Moreover, values are always plural and in conflict with one another. As Weber confessed about himself, "Anyone who lives in the 'world' (in the Christian sense) can experience nothing else than the struggle between a number of set values each of which, if viewed separately, appears to be binding. He must choose which of these gods he wants to and ought to serve, and *when* he will serve one or the other. But then he will always find himself in conflict with one or more of the other gods of this world. . . ." What was true for Weber should be true for any sociologist. The result is that the sociologist must study the values of his historical subjects, complicated as they are, and not impose his own values on these subjects.[3] This methodological rock on which Weber stood had enormous consequences for his subsequent intellectual constructions, as when he sought to understand various social phenomena, and especially "charisma," whether possessed by a Hitler or a Gandhi (my examples), in a value-free fashion.

The key word is "understanding." Against Positivism and its imposition of scientific laws on the facts, Weber followed the principle of "Verstehen," best described as the effort to understand "the *subjective* meaning, the meaning intended by the actor himself as an ultimate, concrete, empirically graspable reality, not some thought structure that is speculatively superimposed upon reality."[4]

Numerous books and articles have been written about Weber's "understanding" principle and his value-free position; I do not wish here to continue that discussion, but only to touch on the subject sufficiently to make clear its role in Weber's thought as it bears on our subject of connections.[5] By "understanding," Weber does not mean mere "empathy" or "intuition," though I assume that these enter into it. He means instead a science of social action—to be described in more detail later—that takes as its data the subjective meanings of the subject being studied, by an "objective" scholar, in the sense of his not imposing his values (though these will guide him to his subject) on the study of the data. Here there is an interesting comparison, and, to some extent, a contrast, that can be made with a Gaskell or Eliot-type "sympathy."

The result of Weber's methodological convictions, as well as his interest in fusing the concerns of religion and economics, to name only two of his subjects, is an enormously complex edifice of scholarship and thought. He himself was a complex personality, and though he tried to remove himself from his work in the name of objectivity, nevertheless, as we shall see, it remains a foundation of that multiplicity and complexity of thought. While Weber wrote in a legal, logical, and forceful manner, we ought not to confuse clearness with simplicity. I have spoken of Simmel's fugue-like style; everything in Weber also runs forward and backward, but in an overtly systematic fashion quite different from what we find in Simmel.

A Life-Work

The complexity of Weber's life, and its intimate relation to his work, justifies fairly extended attention. Unlike our other sociologists, Max Weber came from an Establishment background. His father, born into a family of linen merchants and textile manufacturers, became a jurist, municipal magistrate, member of the Prussian House of Deputies, and eventually a member of the Reichstag. On the mother's side, we meet civil servants and wealthy patricians; she herself was a deeply Calvinistic as well as cultured woman. Between the vigorous, practical, unbelieving father and the prudish, idealistic, pietistic mother a great deal of tension existed, and young Max was deeply divided as well as inspired; the marks were left on both his psyche and his work.

Intellectually, the family provided a most cosmopolitan setting. As a youth Weber was exposed to famous and gifted politicians and intellectuals, and a similar setting prevailed when he went to study at Heidelberg University. Here he concentrated on economics and legal history, as well as on the study of theology and philosophy; he was clearly bright beyond his years, and the story is told that when examined by the great historian, Theodore Mommsen, the latter was so impressed that he announced, "There is no one to whom I would rather say, 'Son, here is my spear; it is getting too heavy for my arm.'"[6]

Weber wrote his doctoral dissertation on the history of trading companies during the Middle Ages, learning Spanish and Italian in order to do so (earlier, he had learned Hebrew in order to read the Old Testament). He then went on to write a second treatise on "The History of Agrarian Institutions," over which the famous encounter with Mommsen took place. Here we see Weber's economic interests, reflecting that side of his family inheritance—one thinks, too, of Engels and his textile family background—as well as demonstrating the breadth of his interests, which extended from trade to agriculture.

Upon completion of his treatise, Weber undertook an inquiry into the conditions of East Elbian land workers for the *Verein für Sozialpolitik*. It is an important preview of his later work: Weber showed how a status group, the Junkers, accepted capitalistic values and commercialized their farms, hiring Polish laborers and losing Germans who would not give up their traditional holdings in exchange for wage contracts. His analysis is of "unintended consequences," whereby the Junkers, ardent nationalists and anti-capitalists, betray both of these positions.

In this work, Weber came to grips with much of what was to occupy him in the rest of his scholarly career. As Wolfgang J. Mommsen remarks, "It was at this time that capitalism became the young scholar's chief obsession." One lesson Weber learned was that maximization of production could obviously have undesirable national and cultural effects: as a "value" it might stand in opposition to other "values."

More important for our purposes, Weber became highly sensitized to the breakdown of connections problem. As he stated about this time in a speech to the Protestant Social Congress, "Above all there takes place a phenomenon of incomparable significance: the replacement of personal relationships of dominance by the impersonal dominance of class. . . . The personal relationship of responsibility goes; the impersonal 'dominance of capitalism' takes its place." Weber then continued his analysis of what I have called cash-nexus society in class terms. "And above all this has natural psychological consequences. . . . The resignation of the subordinate masses disappears, and as personal relationships are replaced by the dominance of class, so personal hatred is replaced with natural inevitability by the phenomenon of 'objective hatred'—the hatred of one class for another."[7] It was a subject he pursued in his address, "Capitalism and Rural Society in Germany," at the St. Louis Universal Exposition in 1905.[8]

Before this, in 1894, the year after he married Marianne Schnitger, Weber was appointed a full professor of economics at Freiberg University. He was all of thirty years old (one thinks of Tönnies's and Simmel's years of waiting). Two years later, he moved on to a professorship at the more distinguished university, Heidelberg. His career seemed secure and more than promising. In 1897, however, his father died, and a year later Weber began to exhibit extreme nervous symptoms—the connecting details are spelled out in Mitzman's *The Iron Cage*—culminating in a breakdown that lasted for five years, with subsequent minor recurrences. He could not read, write, or lecture. Finally in 1902 he began to resume his usual activities—he read Simmel's *Philosophy of Money* (and later his *Schopenhauer and Nietzsche*)—and in 1904 became a coeditor, with Werner Sombart and Edgar Jaffe, of the *Archiv für Sozialwissenschaft und Sozialpolitik*. This last was to give him the kind of journal, comparable to Durkheim's *L'Année sociologique*, that could serve as a vehicle for putting into place a Weberian school of sociology; Weber himself published the first part of his *Protestant Ethic* in the *Archiv*, calling it in a letter to Heinrich Rickert an "essay on cultural history."[9]

In 1904 came the trip to the United States for the St. Louis Exhibition, marking Weber's first successful return to the lectern. In America, like Tocqueville before him, he saw democracy in the making, only with new features, to be described in his future work. On his return to Germany, Weber plunged into renewed activity, reading voraciously, learning Russian (in order to follow the 1905 Revolution, on which he wrote two important essays), helping to establish a German sociological society, and taking on the editorship of a series of sociological handbooks. As his own contribution, Weber began to write what subsequently emerged as his most magisterial work, *Economy and Society* (*Wirtschaft und Gesellschaft*; this title is not Weber's own, but the one given to it on the book's posthumous publication in 1926).

On the more personal side, around 1910 Weber fell in love with Else Jaffe, a former pupil married to a friend of his, and his wife Marianne's best friend. The details are all very confused, but what is clear is that Weber was discovering, perhaps for the first time (it is believed that his marriage was never consummated), the erotic side of life. His discovery took place at the same time as acquaintance with the poet Stefan George and his free-thinking circle, replete with Freudian overtones and overtures.[10] The love affair with Else was probably also unconsummated, but Weber may have had a physical relationship with a pianist a few years later, to be followed at the end of his life with a renewed relation (including the sexual) to Else Jaffe.

Such details would be left private and unmentioned here except that Weber's life experiences powerfully affected his sociological work. It made him more aware of emotionalism, and helped prepare the way for his deeper understanding of charisma. It helps explain why, in the dry prose of *Economy and Society*, we encounter such a passage as: "For sexual love, along with the 'true' or economic interest, and the social drives toward power and prestige, is among the most fundamental and universal components of the actual course of interpersonal behavior."[11] It broadened his sense of how emotional motives as well as "rational" ones could enter into economic and political life. Thus, the world-view of Weber, unlike Marx's, includes persisting emotions and drives that can lead to conflict.

Power and prestige, not love, were the motives that erupted in World War I. Weber was an ardent nationalist (defining the nation as a community of sentiments, rooted in objective factors), who prided himself on his hard-headed realism—this, too, relates to his complex personality—and also even on his capacity for "brutality" of view. At first, like so many others on both sides, he welcomed the war as a "great and wonderful" event.[12] War, he felt, would integrate Germany as a community, and Germans, of course, would fight in a civilized and honorable fashion. Weber tried to serve in the army but was given a bureaucratic post. It must immediately be added, as we shall see further, that Weber was also individualistic and liberal. As the war went on, the balance tipped more and more to that side of his views, and he became increasingly critical of the government and the military leadership.

With the end of the war, Weber found himself involved politically, as well as intellectually, in the effort to reconstruct a German government. Opposed to the radicals, he also became opposed to the monarchists. There was little time personally to affect Germany's future, however, for his life was shortly to end. In 1919, he accepted a position at Munich University, where he delivered lectures that were eventually to be published as his *General Economic History*. Then, in 1920, he died.

A Protestant Ethos

The complexity of Weber's life, the often hidden underground springs, helps us to understand the complexity of his work. It alerts us to the ways in which his politics and sociology are related, and how he sought to synthesize his national and liberal commitments.[13] It helps explain why this most rational of men, engaged in a study of the increasing spread of rationality in the modern world, could also comprehend, increasingly, the role of irrationality in history, and yet try to subjugate it to a rational explanation in his sociological science.

Given his psychological difficulties, and the relatively short span of his life, Weber's productivity was enormous. Yet, he is known to general readers, if known at all, for one book, *The Protestant Ethic and the Spirit of Capitalism*. In that book, he defined capitalism, "the most fateful force in our modern life," and analyzed its relationship to religious and social forces.[14] The end result for our purposes, as we shall see, was to free cash-nexus society from its alien and parochial attributions, classifying it among other forms of social action, to be viewed neutrally.

In part, Weber was able to do this because, while agreeing with Marx that economic factors were of great importance, he argued that other factors were of equal significance, that historical developments emerged from a multiplicity of forces, interrelating in both unique and general fashion with one another. Thus, in the case of capitalism, rational technique and law were as critical as rational economic behavior, and both were dependent on Men's dispositions to behave in a certain fashion. In turn, such dispositions were largely based on "magical and religious forces, and the ethical ideas of duty based upon them" which in the past have "always been among the most formative influences on conduct."

Capitalism, according to Weber, is not unique in its pursuit of gain or of money; pirates and kings, landowners and Roman merchants have been just as avaricious. Western capitalism alone, however, pursues profit in a steady, calculating, rational manner. It alone systematically defers gratification in order to accumulate capital, which it then rationally employs in the pursuit of further profit. Although there have always been moneymakers, Weber claims, only in the West did a money economy develop, marked by free labor, rational bookkeeping, exact calculation, and an advanced degree of rationality of capitalistic acquisition. And, as had Adam Smith, Weber endows rational capitalism with an ethical significance; bourgeois capitalism, he argues, was a pursuit of morality as well as money.

How did this achievement come about? Weber discusses the role of technology, science, law, and administration, among other factors, with an emphasis on the rational character of each, while stressing the interrelationship of one with another (parts of each, he informs us, can be found in a rational form elsewhere than in the West). In this book, however, his major interest is in the role of religion, and especially the Protestant religion.

He starts from an observed fact: that the occupational statistics of any country with a mixed Catholic-Protestant population show a pronounced correlation of Protestantism with capital and capitalist enterprise. Weber's argument is that Protestantism has an affinity with the "Spirit of Capitalism," in the sense not of causally determining it but of fostering the attitudes necessary for its development. In one crucial area, Calvinism prepared the way, by a religious change, for the cash-nexus ethos in the economic field: as Weber writes of the Puritan, "The sharp condemnation . . . of all dependence on personal relations to other men was bound unperceived to direct his energy into the field of objective (impersonal) activity."[15] Once established, capitalism no longer requires its original religious support and becomes self-sustaining through competition. Like modern Western science, it has taken on a self-generating power.

The details of Weber's famous argument are subtle—and controversial.[16] His overall thesis is that not only Protestantism but one particular form of Protestantism, Calvinism, historically conditioned the emergence of capitalism in the West. Within Calvinism, moreover, one particular feature—the notion of the "calling"—was crucial. Emerging from Calvin's doctrine of predestination—one was saved or damned from birth, irrespective of one's good "works"— the notion of the calling required Men nevertheless to labor in the world as if called to one's situation by God. Paradoxically, then, a doctrine that told Men that nothing they might do could affect their salvation nevertheless spurred them to activity rather than passivity. Such activity was to be not asceticism in a monastery but worldly asceticism, that is, the "Fulfillment of the obligations imposed upon the individual by his position in the world."[17] Working in this manner, the individual glorified God and, pursuing an irrational drive, his calling, helped to create rational capitalism: such are the unintended consequences of history.

As for the calling, Puritans such as Richard Baxter joined it to the idea of specialization and the division of labor. Weber always supports his assertions with historical evidence, and he uses his sources to good effect in this case. He links Baxter to Benjamin Franklin, quoting him as well, and concludes that "Limitation to specialized work, with a renunciation of the Faustian universality of man which it involved, is a condition of any valuable work in the modern world; hence deeds and renunciation inevitably condition each other today."[18] For what used to be praised as a "Renaissance Man," Weber has harsh words; such a Man in the age of developed, specialized capitalism has become a "dilettante," a mere member of the literati.

Yet Weber also recognizes, by the end of his book, that specialized work in a calling has congealed into a rational, mechanistic, irresistibly conditioned economic order. As he remarks, "In Baxter's view the care for external goods should only lie on the shoulders of the 'saint like a light cloak, which can be thrown aside at any moment.'" Then, in what is probably his most famous sentence, Weber adds ominously, "But fate decreed that the cloak should become an iron cage."[19]

The iron cage is a metaphor to be more extensively examined later. In its way, it is far more somber and threatening than Marx's vision of capitalism as a bloodthirsty vampire or Tönnies's description of "ruthless" *Gesellschaft*. Yet it would be a serious distortion of Weber's views to convey the impression here that the iron cage represents Weber's final word on capitalistic society. His thought is both too complicated and too "scientific" for such a sweeping generalization. We shall need to situate his metaphor in the larger corpus of his work before coming to a more conclusive judgment.

The Protestant and the Jew

Before doing that, however, there is one other point in connection with *The Protestant Ethic* that needs attention. It is the way in which Weber in this book has shifted attention from the role of the Jews in the rise of capitalism to that of the Protestants. He downplays the roles of the Jews mainly by implication, mentioning them only a few times in the text and, in a more important way, in the footnotes; but in neither case to any great degree or significance. It is only by reading his further comments in *Economy and Society*, and then returning to *The Protestant Ethic* that we can recognize what Weber is up to in this regard. In *Economy and Society*, he deals with the issue explicitly, even if briefly; thus, while acknowledging his friend Werner Sombart's thesis that the Jews played a "conspicuous role in the evolution of the modern capitalistic system," Weber diplomatically adds, "however, this thesis of Sombart's book needs to be made more precise." What Weber then does is to argue that the Jews played very little role in the organization of industrial production and the factory system, or in the development of the rational activities "characteristic of modern Occidental capitalism." The Jews were, essentially, not a "class" of capitalists, but a "status" group, a "pariah" people. Indeed, their major connection to capitalism is through the "kinship of Puritanism to Judaism," for the Puritans saw themselves as the heirs of the Old as well as the New Testament.[20]

We need only recall Marx and Engels's animadversions on the Jews as the "hucksters" responsible for the modern world of capitalistic industrialism and its evils to realize the significance of what Weber is doing so quietly. By detaching capitalism from the Jews, in

favor of Protestant Christianity, Weber frees capitalism from the
sense of its being "alien"; for in the underground of the Christian
spirit the Jew has always been seen as foreign to the dominant, settled community. And by doing this, Weber has also freed capitalism
from the charge of alienation imposed on it, in so far as it is psycho-
logically felt as an "alien" imposition. (Simmel, of course, with his
emphasis on the "stranger" had unintentionally strengthened the
possible sense of alienation.) With this done, capitalism, and its off-
shoot, industrialism, even as an iron cage, could then be analyzed,
in principle, in a comprehensive, objective sociological manner.

Economy and Society

Weber's most monumental work is his *Economy and Society*, which
runs over 1400 pages in its English version. In it, we see both the
polyhistor and the sociologist at work; the master of the historical
detail and the projector of sociological categories and concepts. Its
title, imposed as we noted by others, does indicate its main focus,
though the table of contents gives a much broader perspective,
including such topics as: a conceptual exposition, in which Weber
defines his basic terms and sets up his basic categories; an overview
of "The Economy and the Arena of Normative and De Facto Powers"; a sociology of religion; and a sociology of law. Each of these
headings, in turn, contains a wealth of subtopics: under the sociology of law, for example, Weber considers not only law but political
communities, domination and legitimacy, bureaucracy, charisma,
and the city. In this book, if anywhere, we have the full, intercon-
nected exposition of Weber's sociology.[21]

In seeking to extract only those parts that bear most heavily on
our theme of connections, we face a task more difficult than with
our other sociologists, for each part of Weber's analysis depends
strongly on the other parts, and ought not readily to be isolated from
them. The way he seeks to integrate sociological generalizations and
typologies with historical explanations is especially important.[22]
With this caution in mind, however, I shall single out a number of
relevant matters. Because of Weber's complex way of contributing
to the subject, their link to our overall theme may not be apparent
immediately, and patience, again, is necessary.

Weber and Marx

Of great importance is Weber's relation to Marx and the materialist interpretation of history, which we touched on briefly before. Major controversies reign in this area: Did Weber take Marx seriously? Had he read his major works? Did Weber confuse Marx and Marxism, that is, late-nineteenth-century German Marxist intepretations of Marx? Did Weber reject or complete Marx's economic interpretation of history?

Weber obviously had read carefully *The Communist Manifesto*, which he referred to as a "prophetic document" and "a work of scholarship of the highest order" (though he rejected its critical theses).[23] He just as obviously could not have read much of the present-day corpus of Marx's writings, for many of the items in it had not yet been published in his day: *The Economic and Philosophic Manuscripts, The German Ideology, Grundrisse,* and so on. Weber, therefore, shared in the perspective held by many of his contemporaries on Marx, which scholars today describe as late-nineteenth–early-twentieth-century Marxism. When, in 1918, Weber lectured on "Socialism" to the Austrian officers in Vienna, he had in mind the Marxist movement of his time, as well as Marx's own published writings.[24]

Yet I would argue that Weber had a relatively good picture of Marx's materialist interpretation of history—and, from his early writings on East Elbian land workers on up to the works of 1920, was positively influenced by it. Nevertheless, while acknowledging the theory's partial truth, he ended by seeing it in its dogmatic form as both gross and simple-minded, more propaganda than true sociology. Weber's web of community is broader and more responsive to tugs from its various strands. For example, he gives at least equal play to political power, and at one point goes so far as to say that "In the last analysis, the processes of economic development are struggles for power." He calls our attention to the way war and migration, not themselves economic processes, have nevertheless been responsible "for radical changes in the economic system." Earlier, we have seen that Weber includes sexual love among the fundamental components of interpersonal behavior. Nor does Weber ignore the role of cognitive and intellectual motivations, or, as he puts it, "more particularly the metaphysical needs of the human mind as it is driven to reflect on ethical and religious questions, driven not by material need but by an inner compulsion to understand the world as a meaningful cosmos and to take up a position toward it."[25]

As recent literature has emphasized, Weber can serve as a corrective to the "scientific" Marx, that is, the Marx unmodified by the more humanistic, Hegelian writings that remained unpublished during his lifetime, and thus peripheral at the time to Marxism. Thus, one scholar writes that "It is therefore no exaggeration to say that Weber's transformation of economic historical dogmatism into an economic interpretation of history realized Marx's original aim, which he himself failed to achieve." More sweepingly, another scholar declares that "Weber demonstrates, through a series of crucial historical experiments, that economic motivation derives as much from value traditions as from external demands. In doing so he lays the groundwork for the truly multidimensional understanding of social life that Durkheim and Marx never achieved."[26]

The Web

As we noted earlier, human activity is envisioned by Weber as multi-causal, or, rather, as a set of corresponding and interrelated processes. Each of these processes, however, can be conceptualized as more or less autonomous. So viewed, however, each phenomenon and development must then be related to all other social phenomena, in an over-arching sociological interpretation. The web has succeeded to the chain. Thus, for example, the "laws" of administration relate in part to the kind of political domination under which they function, as well as to the kind of economic activity which they may serve. Weber's eye is always on the balance of forces and the changing tension between them; as he characteristically remarks on the roots of Occidental culture, it "must be sought in the tension and peculiar balance, on the one hand, between office charisma and monasticism, and on the other between the contractual character of the feudal state and the autonomous, bureaucratic hierarchy."[27]

It is the interplay of ideas, interests, and values that makes for history. Using a wonderful image, Weber discusses their general relationship: "Not ideas, but material and ideal interests, directly govern men's conduct. Yet very frequently the 'world images' that have been created by 'ideas' have, like switchmen, determined the tracks along which action has been pushed by the dynamic of interest."[28] Thus, where Marx had tended to see ideas as more or less the reflection or expression of interests, as ideological scaffolding erected on the basic foundation of material concerns, Weber preferred to conceptualize them in terms of "elective affinity." Ideas, as he shows in repeated detail, originate separately from interest groups; they come from individuals seeking metaphysical answers, for example. An interest group then "elects" to use the idea, and for a while it presumably serves its purposes. Although Weber does not say so explicitly, the idea can still lead a life according to its own "laws" and thus be available as a source of inspiration for other groups. So viewed, ideas become as important as interests, with their relations open-ended and "electable" in a form foreign to the materialist interpretation of history.

For Weber, unlike Marx, there is no final science. The task of sociology is to achieve the conceptually clearest, most empirically well-grounded, and most "objective," that is, value-free, understanding of social action. At the beginning of *Economy and Society*, Weber gives a definition of sociology that tersely sums up much of what Tönnies and Simmel had been trying to establish. It is "a science concerning itself with the interpretive understanding of social action and thereby with a causal explanation of its course and consequences. We shall speak of 'action' insofar as the acting individual attaches a subjective meaning to his behavior—be it overt or covert, omission or acquiescence. Action is 'social' insofar as its subjective meaning takes account of the behavior of others and is thereby oriented in its course." As for meaning, it may be of two kinds. The first is that held by a particular actor, or group of actors. The second is an ideal, or pure, type of meaning, that is, a subjective meaning, hypothetically attributed in its most rational form to the particular actor by the "objective" sociologist. Yet, Weber hastens to add, "In no case does it refer to an objectively 'correct' meaning or one which is 'true' in some metaphysical sense. It is this which distinguishes the empirical sciences of action, such as sociology and history, from the dogmatic disciplines in that area, such as jurisprudence, logic, ethics, and esthetics, which seek to ascertain the 'true' and 'valid' meanings associated with the objects of their investigation."[29]

Starting from such a methodological assumption and definition,

Weber establishes categories of sociological interpretation of enormous range and power. Any summary is well beyond the intent of this chapter, but among his key contributions one would have to reckon with his analysis of domination and legitimacy into the three types of legal, traditional, and charismatic, as well as his analysis of stratification and power in terms of the categories of class, status, and party. (It is in the course of this latter analysis, incidentally, that he remarks, "In our terminology, 'classes' are not communities; they merely represent possible, and frequent, bases for social action.")[30]

Realism

From the wealth of this work, I wish to stand back and treat only three aspects: realism, bureaucracy, and individualism. The first relates to what at least Weber would have viewed as realism. As David Beetham remarks, "The political virtue most frequently emphasized by Weber was thus that of 'Sachlichkeit'—matter of factness, realism."[31] It must be made clear, however, that realism is not necessarily equivalent to *Realpolitik* (and, indeed, Weber sometimes made fun of the so-called "realism" of some of the contemporary political parties). "Anyone," Weber declared, "who wants to pursue an earthly policy must be free of illusions and be acquainted with the fundamental fact of the eternal struggle of men with one another."[32] Often, Weber saw that struggle in Darwinian terms, as when he remarks apropos of his attempt to define basic sociological terms, "Selection is inevitable . . . even on the utopian assumption that all competition were completely eliminated, conditions would still lead to a latent process of selection, biological or social, which would favor the types best adapted to the conditions. . . ." Such Darwinian sentiments, of course, were practically clichés at the time Weber was writing.

So, too, was his nationalism, which we noted earlier. Weber saw Germany as one among a number of nations competing for power. He accepted the idea that power ultimately meant violence. Indeed, he defines state power as the control of legitimate violence and coercion. In his speech "Politics as a Vocation" he declares, ". . . politics for us means striving to share power or striving to influence the distribution of power, either among states or among groups within a state."[33] Weber accepted and approved of Germany's imperialistic drives. When he argued for increased democracy in Germany, it was as much out of a belief that that was the only way to strengthen the post-World War I state, and to allow it to play an effective part in world history, as it was out of a true commitment to democracy as an ideal.

Now, whatever our own evaluation of Weber's nationalism, it is important to recognize its contribution to his sociology. Derived as it was from his political activity as much as from his historical scholarship, it nevertheless encouraged Weber to treat the nation-state, if not nationalism itself, as a fundamental feature of modern social action. Thus, national feeling, as a connection that both includes and excludes others, which was largely neglected, at least in their sociology, by others of our thinkers—Marx and Engels, Tönnies, and Simmel all come readily to mind—figures fully both in Weber's historical accounts and in the categories of his political analysis, for example, domination and legitimacy.

Conflict, then, in Weber's schema is inevitable. It manifests itself both in nation form and in capitalism. "Capital accounting," he declares, "presupposes the battle of man with man." Continuing in such Hobbesian terms, he thinks it worthwhile to repeat that "the battle of man against man on the market is an essential condition for the existence of rational money-accounting. . . ."[34] As he readily admits, such conflict is motivated by self-interest. As a realist, Weber accepts such conditions.

He will not accept, however, that self-interest characterizes only capitalism. "In an economic system organized on a socialist basis, there would be no fundamental difference in this respect."[35] Capitalism, therefore, is only one form for expressing individual self-interest. Individuals in *any* economic system will pursue their ideal and/or material interests. And individuals in *any* political system will pursue these same ends through what Weber calls parties, varying according to the structure of domination, but eternally with us. Weber the realist therefore sees any form of community, of human connections, as necessarily characterized by conflict in both the economic and political spheres. Implicitly, he sets himself against the lamenters' view of capitalism, industrialism, and sometimes the nation-state, all three of which they viewed as unique and novel forms of alienation and perverted or broken connection.

Bureaucracy

For Weber, it is not cash-nexus capitalism as such that is cause for lamentation and foreboding. That response is provoked by another historical development, related to capitalism but not restricted to it: the second of the three aspects I wish to consider, bureaucracy. Where Marx saw the coming of the proletariat, Weber felt he was witnessing the arrival of administration as the dominant feature of modern society. As Weber remarked, "It is the dictatorship of the official, not that of the worker, which, for the present at least, is on the advance."[36]

With his usual multi-causal perspective, Weber is aware that bureaucracy had existed before modern capitalism—for example, in China and Egypt—and had been promoted by non-capitalistic needs, such as those required for the creation of standing armies, for increased police protection, for the provision of social welfare, and so on. He recognizes that bureaucracy's existence is also strongly related to the development of democracy. Whatever its sources, however, once in place in modern society it takes on a seemingly cancerous life of its own. "The future belongs to bureaucratization," Weber announces, adding in a pessimistic moment that it is "escape-proof."[37]

It was a future that filled him with trepidation. Borrowing a phrase from Friedrich Schiller, Weber speaks of "the disenchantment of the world," meaning the displacement of magical and religious ways by technological and scientific ways of seeing and being. Earlier, we noted how Schiller had lamented the fragmentation of the modern world and its increasingly mechanized character (Chapter 2); in a similar vein, Weber constantly refers to the bureaucracy as a machine. In a speech of 1909 reported by Marianne Weber, he speaks about how "No machinery in the world works as precisely as this human machine (the bureaucracy)." In *Economy and Society*, he expands on this notion, and declares that "An inanimate machine is mind objectified. . . . Objectified intelligence is also that animated machine, the bureaucratic organization, with its specialization of trained skills, its division of bondage which men will perhaps be forced to inhabit some day, as powerless as the fellahs of ancient Egypt." Such a bureaucracy, Weber fears, might reinforce the state of bondage "by fettering every individual to his job."[38]

In this mood, Weber might almost be fitted into the camp of the early-nineteenth-century lamenters such as Keats and Wordsworth, bewailing the increased rationalization of the world. It is only on close inspection that we realize that Weber's "lament" is actually for the loss of the seventeenth-century bourgeois capitalistic pursuit of the worldly "calling," and not for the loss of some mystical communitarianism. Weber accepts capitalism, but he wishes for an heroic, expansive capitalism, before its ossification into bureaucracy.

Marx had spoken of capitalism as "fettering" the full development of the means of production; Weber's usage points us in a different direction. Carlyle, Marx, and others had spoken of capitalism as depersonalizing all relations, reducing all connections to the one cash nexus. Weber, instead, sees bureaucracy as the depersonalizing agent—"it does not establish a relationship to a person . . . but rather is devoted to *impersonal* and *functional* purposes"—and he opposes to it the capitalist entrepreneur who "is the only type who has been able to maintain at least relative immunity from subjugation to the control of rational bureaucratic knowledge."[39] The implication is that non-capitalistic systems, and especially socialism, are even more mechanical and depersonalizing than the cash-nexus society; capitalism itself, though powerfully promoting bureaucracy, also produces entrepreneurs who are especially positioned to escape its constraints.

Individualism

Aside from all of us becoming capitalistic entrepreneurs (an unlikely outcome), is there any other hope for escaping from the iron cage of bureaucracy? "The question," as Weber puts it in his 1909 speech, "is what we have as a counterpoise to this machinery so as to keep a remnant of humanity free from this parceling out of the soul, from this exclusive rule of bureaucratic ideals of life. . . ."[40] His attempts to answer this question bring me to the third aspect of Weber's thought that I wish to consider as especially germane to our grand theme of connections. It involves his views on individualism, and takes the form of another anguished question: "How can one possibly save any remnants of individualist freedom in any sense?"

One might overlook Weber's commitment to individualism because of his strong national feelings and his "realistic" support of state power. This would be an error. Individualism is, scientifically, at the heart of Weber's value-free sociology; once established there, it can take on historical and personal dimensions. Thus, we will be dealing with individualism in Weber in two forms: one is method-ological individualism, and the other is historical individualism, that is, the unique Western development whose most evident shape is economic independence. In his methodology, Weber insists on the individual as the starting point for all understanding of social action; he does not accept the state, church, or any other reified concept as existing in its own right, apart from individuals. "Even a socialistic economy," he points out, "would have to be understood sociologi-cally in exactly the same kind of 'individualistic' terms; that is, in terms of the action of individuals. . . ." The important empirical sociological question, he continues, is "What motives determine and lead the individual members and participants in this socialistic com-munity to behave in such a way that the community came into being in the first place and that it continues to exist?"[41]

Weber is fully aware that, though all community, all social action, is comprised of the relationships of individuals (as defined by him, for example, in *Economy and Society*), "individualism," and its accompanying freedom, itself was a recent and indeed unique Western development. Much of his work is devoted to specifying the historical conditions for this development: the presence of ratio-nal law, the rise of the medieval city and the "bourgeoisie," the emergence of "estates" under a feudal monarchy, and so forth. A critical force, of course, had been Calvinism, which tied religion to economics and economics to these other developments in the form of market independence. In rather wordy fashion, and we have already noted his analysis in an earlier context, Weber shows how Calvinism, as opposed to almsgiving and charity, relieves market transactions of any ethical needs, and thus frees the individual from any personal judgment on the nature of the exchange: in short, pre-pares the way, in our terms, for the "cash nexus." His conclusion is that "the growing impersonality of the economy on the basis of association in the market place follows its own rules."[42]

It is this same impersonal market force, however, that also shat-ters the feudal status system, a development which itself forms one of the historical conditions for the unique rise of individualism in the West. In Weber's multi-causal scheme, any causal agent is itself subject to development and changes over time: thus, the status order of feudalism first serves to facilitate the rise of economic individualism, and then, in another sphere, hinders its free development. "The notion of honor peculiar to status absolutely abhors that which is essential to the market: hard bargaining." In turn, the capitalistic market (and its processes) "knows nothing of honor," and in unintended fashion dissolves the existing status order. In fact, it is destructive of all traditional social groupings. "The market," as Weber tells us, "is a relationship which transcends the boundaries of neighborhood, kinship, group, or tribe."[43]

These are terms familiar to us from our previous study of breakdown in connections. What is new is that Weber then goes on to link the rise of economic individualism to the growing threat of an inescapable bureaucracy. As a value-free sociologist, he must simply describe and analyze this linkage. As a concerned political actor and exponent of individualism in the broadest sense, he cannot help but be distressed. On his own analysis, Western individualism as such is a unique historical product and a major contributor to modern bureaucracy; it is hardly likely, therefore, to be the cure.

The Call of Charisma

At this point, Weber turns, or so I construe his thinking, to an unlikely possible solution: charisma. In analyzing political legitimacy, Weber had delineated three types: the legal, based on rational rules; the traditional, based on custom and heredity; and the charismatic, based on the personal qualities of the leader. Much discussion of charismatic legitimacy has stayed within the basically political framework that Weber gave to his concept. It is worthwhile, however, to explore its relation to the iron cage and to individualism.

Charisma, Weber reminds us, must be approached like any other social phenomenon, in a value-free manner. Instancing the Mormons, he remarks characteristically, "If we were to evaluate this revelation, we would perhaps be forced to call it a rank swindle. However, sociology is not concerned with such value judgments."[44] We might think that, rationally, all charisma is open to the charge of being a "rank swindle"; sociologically, however, charisma has other meanings.

According to Weber, charisma may play an important role as the force that originates and then holds together the earliest organized communities, and does so in a communistic form. In Weber's precise, definitional terms, "An organized group subject to charismatic authority will be called a charismatic relationship [*Vergemeinschaftung*]." He adds, "Disciples or followers tend to live primarily in a communistic relationship with their leader. . . ."[45] We appear to have Tönnies's *Gemeinschaft*, to which Weber has added the concept of charisma.

In the nature of things, according to Weber, a charismatic community cannot last. Based as it is on the personal qualities of the charismatic leader, its legitimacy fades with his death. The successor problem emerges, interests assert themselves, and in a short time charismatic domination must become routinized, that is, changed into the traditional or perhaps legal type.

Much of Weber's *Economy and Society* is devoted to studying the specifically historical fashion in which the modern Western state and society have developed out of such charismatic beginnings. The result, as we have seen, is the traditional nation-state, capitalistic society, and then the iron cage, which threatens to imprison the individual in its purely rational embrace. It is at this point that Weber (it seems to me) turns back to charisma for the possibility of an escape from the "escape-proof" bureaucratic society.

Charisma, by its essence, "is specifically foreign to economic considerations," Weber points out. Even when rationalized into religious institutions—a church, for example—it "has its own dynamics, which economic conditions merely channel. . . ."[46] Thus it not only stands autonomous from the materialist interpretation of history but, potentially, exists as a force free from the otherwise inevitable trend toward bureaucracy, whether capitalistic or socialistic.

There is a curious passage in Weber's discussion of charisma. "Wherever it [pure charisma] appears," he declares, "it constitutes a 'call' in the most emphatic sense of the word. . . ."[47] I cannot help but think of Weber's treatment of the "calling" in Calvinism, and his own personal attraction—almost a compulsion—to the pursuit of a calling, his own scholarly work.[48] That attraction to a call appears to carry over to his feelings about charisma. It was reinforced, I believe, by his own erotic awakening around 1910, and his involvement with the George circle. Indeed, in mentioning the "circle of Stefan George," he specifically refers to it as an "artistic type of charismatic discipleship."[49] Such personal experience, I contend, opened Weber up to the possibilities for individual fulfillment latent in charismatic action.

It also allowed him, in a rational and value-free—and decidedly paradoxical—manner to understand the explosive power in charisma. In his view, it was this type of domination that stood at the beginning of political creation, and, according to Weber, it is this type that still has the power to blow apart the iron cage. "In this purely empirical and value-free sense charisma is indeed the specifically creative new force in history," he announced. It is "the great force," especially in traditionalist periods, he adds.[50]

Weber deals with the revolutionary power of charisma by calling for and expecting its emergence more significantly in politics than in religion. Like the capitalistic entrepreneur shaking off the iron constraints in economics, the great political leader must break free of bureaucratic "duty" and assert his personal, individual qualities and beliefs.

The paradox of Weber, the value-free sociologist, as an active politician in 1917–18, calling for the renewed coming of charisma, is matched by another paradox: the charismatic leader, when he emerged in Germany, was Adolf Hitler, and his attack on the iron cage was certainly not in the service of individual freedom. Weber misjudged the forces actually latent in his advocacy of charisma as a revolutionary force, just as Durkheim had done with corporatism.[51] In declaring, however, that the future would be "an age, which, inevitably, would still remain capitalistic for a long time," at least in the West, Weber seems to have been more prescient in his prediction;[52] and it is, in the last analysis, as the great, classical sociologist of capitalism, and thus of a putative cash-nexus society, that Weber still looms over us.

An Ending

With Weber, we end our consideration of the sociologists. Their central concern, I have been arguing, has been with community, with the bonds that connect Men to one another in society. They took the wide-ranging sentiments and ruminations of our earlier breakers and lamenters—about the connections of Man to God, to Nature and to Society—and narrowed them more or less to one type of tie, that of Man to Man. Further, they took the specific concern of their predecessors with the social question, formulated as the "cash nexus" problem, and tried to transform it into a scientific sociology.

That effort came to its most developed and most formal exposition in Weber's work. He analyzed capitalism in the large, as a historical and sociological form, transcending the self-interest and cash-nexus terms so often employed in regard to it. He investigated (and in the process went well beyond the feelings and experiences of a Gaskell or an Eliot) the relations between religion and economics in general, and especially their relations in regard to Western capitalism. By removing capitalism from its Jewish "taint," as I have suggested, he partly neutralized the subject, allowing it to be treated in a more value-free manner than hitherto. (Again, the paradox is that the charismatic leader Hitler, brushing aside Weber's scholarship, persisted in blaming the Jews for capitalism as well as for communism, and both for the evils of society.)

In doing all of this, it must also be noted that Weber ignored the perception worried about by earlier thinkers, and nowhere spoke of the unsocial-social, or double, nature of Man. He took it for granted, and got on with his analysis. The voice of neither the breakers nor the lamenters is explicitly present in the objective sociology of Weber.

Nevertheless, although this statement is correct we must then add that in the undertones of Weber's works, we hear their echoes. One scholar rightly characterized Weber's persistent query as, "How, given the conditions of the 'destined' increasing 'bureaucratisation,' of the scientific 'disenchantment,' of the world, are human freedom, responsible actions and meaningful existence possible?"[53] Whereas Carlyle used the term "mechanical," Weber spoke of "rationalisation"; they were both asking the fundamental question of what the experience of capitalistic industrialism, with its attendant phenomena, signifies for our human condition.

III

SOME CONCLUSIONS

12

Conclusions and Evaluations

Sensibility into Sociology

We have come a long way, from nineteenth-century connections, through the cash nexus, to modern sociology. Are there any lasting ideas that emerge from our encounter with the breakdown of connections—whether as "fiction" or as "fact," as myth or as history—and the resultant development of a new social science? Ideas that may give us a truer, or at least more profound, understanding of our unsocial-social nature, and of the nature of society itself? Any theories and concepts that can claim some sort of "scientific" validity beyond that reached by common sense and observation? Is there any real difference, say, in terms of conceptualization and rigor of analysis, between, on the one hand, Rousseau, Wordsworth, and Carlyle with their lamentations, and, on the other hand, Simmel, Durkheim, and Weber with their efforts at social science? In fact, do the literary inspirations of the lamenters bring us closer to the reality of their world, and ours, than do the analytic methods of the social scientists? And, finally, what value shall we attach to these theories, and, as important, what evaluations shall we ourselves make concerning the problem of connections?

For most of our lamenters—the philosophers, poets, prophets, and novelists—deploring as they did the snapping of the ties, science itself was one of the causes rather than cures of the social ills around them. Burke bewailed the age of calculators and economists, Rousseau decried the effect of scientific progress on the state of morals, Wordsworth poeticized about the murdering and dissecting character of science, and Carlyle sighed over the displacement of the supernatural by the natural; and this they did though with ambivalent and divided hearts and minds. Of our industrial novelists, Gaskell and Disraeli have almost nothing to say about science, though their concern with the effect of technology on their society is at least implicit in all of their writing, and only Eliot can be seen as both caught up in the movement of science, natural and social, and eager to participate in its advance.

All of them, however, as we have seen, observed keenly some of the new social reality developing around them. To their eyes, much of society was coming apart. Traditional ties between Man and Man, Man and Nature, Man and God were snapping or frayed to the danger point. They saw, or thought they saw, dangerous dichotomies between head and heart, mind and feeling, mirrored in a division of Man and Man, haves and have-nots. Industry and science, hailed by the breakers who were helping to promote them as a great progressive transformation of Man and society, were denounced by our lamenters, though often ambivalently, as the destroyers of community and of Man's body and soul.

The solution for the lamenters was to appeal primarily to the emotions of the newly emerging middle class itself, and to do so through the agency of literature. Poetry, philosophy, prophecy, and fiction were all employed as instruments to arouse sympathy; once the reading public knew the "facts" of disconnection, their fellow-feeling would cause them to ameliorate the situation. I have called the lamenters' approach that of sensibility. It stands apart from socialism, or the resort to revolutionary social change, on one side, and from science, on the other.[1]

"Scientific" understanding of the "facts" of connection and disconnection most prominently manifested itself in the development of a discipline of sociology, and I have, as a result, counterbalanced sociology to sensibility. The figure who best links the two approaches, I have argued, is George Eliot. It is she, in her novels, who sought to explore the resources both of intellect and of feeling, and their power to fuse and thereby bring Men together in real society. It is Eliot who also sought to take the first precarious steps to a "natural history" that would prefigure the coming of a sociology going beyond the Comtean.

Perhaps her major achievement was to help shift the metaphor by which Men gave, and give, a linguistic ordering to their experience of the theme of connection. Instead of a "chain," she spoke of a "web." Chain was the omnipresent image of late-eighteenth–early-nineteenth-century society as it attempted to comprehend the nature of connection. A chain, as we have noted in Chapter 1, invokes the notion of a linear linking, a hierarchical ordering, a unilateral causal relation, which either has to be rigidly maintained or painfully broken. It speaks either of secure restraint or oppressive servitude, depending on one's attitude and place in the chain. Web, on the other hand, is many-stranded, and represents an awareness of constant pulls and tugs, emanating from many directions, of many possible lines that hold one to others. It is an organic metaphor (whereas chain is largely mechanical), and it speaks of living adjustments and of growth. It evokes the idea of connection as possessing an ecological nature.

The intellectual power behind the metaphor of web was, of course, Charles Darwin. Yet it was George Eliot who domesticated the image for society and was the linking figure to Ferdinand Tönnies and thus the other sociologists treated in this book. Only with Max Weber (who was following on Marx's anticipatory work, in spite of the generally monist emphasis to be found there), I argue, do we reach something like the same vision in sociology as in literature, with Weber's multi-causal analysis matching Eliot's literary web of affinities.

With the shift from Eliot to Weber, from the literary lamenters to the sociologists as our context, we can now return to the question asked at the beginning of this chapter: What, if anything, are the ideas and theories of lasting, perhaps "scientific," value that emerge from the metamorphosis of sensibility into sociology?

Achievements

In what follows I shall try to highlight some of the achievements of our sociologists, described earlier in more detail. A caution is necessary. Their concepts, the very terms they use, are embedded in a theoretical framework that gives them their full meaning. In lifting these ideas and terms from their framework, we risk both doing an injustice to their authors and misapplying the ideas and terms themselves; this is an especial danger into which a historian may fall.[2]

What is more natural, however, than an attempt to apply our

sociologists' theories and concepts to our own analysis of connections and the cash nexus? In part, of course, the subject itself is
already framed in "class" division, in "community" metaphors, and
so on, by the actors themselves, and in explicit as well as implicit
terms. What is more, our own present description and analysis has
also been shaped and colored by the conceptual approach of the
sociologists, as part of the cultural climate in which we live and
breathe.

Would an attempt to make explicit at every point the use of a
sociological concept be of benefit, as a way of testing the concept as
well as more clearly illuminating the historical materials? I shall
advert to this possibility again a little later, but merely say here that
such an attempt runs the risk of subjecting the historical materials
too much to the conceptual cookie cutter; and, in any case, it would
be a task different from the one I have undertaken here, calling for
another book. Instead, let us try to sift out the most salient ideas
from our sociologists, thereby indicating, however loosely, the new
perspective that they have bequeathed to us. It is by means of their
paradigms that we, today, discern and construe our relations to one
another and to our past, if not to Nature and God.

Friedrich Engels and Karl Marx

At the beginning, Engels and Marx are the great names. They most
vividly carried over the sensibility approach into socialism (the goal
of their efforts), and then into sociology, the means by which they
aspired to know how to achieve a socialist society (in Marx's sociology, knowledge is, dialectically, both a means of knowing the
world and a mode of changing it). We see this transition occurring
first in Engels's *Condition of the Working Class*, where whole passages
can be exchanged with those we find in Carlyle and Gaskell. Even
more important is the spirit of sympathy, suggesting as it does that
we will feel our way to the correct solution once we sense what is
happening, which reminds us of our literary lamenters.

What is different in Engels from the other literary lamenters is
his sharpening of a romantic anti-capitalist feeling into a root and
branch attack on industrial capitalism in the name of a socialist revolution. The carrier of that revolution was to be a new class, the
proletariat, which Engels saw as increasingly arranged against and

estranged from the bourgeoisie by the cash nexus. That term and concept, as we have seen, he specifically borrowed from Carlyle.

Engels's *Condition* was proclaimed to be an empirical study. Aside from the idea that machines such as the jenny create both a competitive, industrial society and a proletariat, with conflict between them inevitable, there is little of sociological theory per se in his work.

The theory came mainly from Marx. Most of our other sociologists drew their original inspiration from Comte or Kant; Marx went back to Hegel. In turning him on his head, Marx incorporated Hegel's idealistic dialectic into sociology in a materialistic form. Engels's class of proletariats and their struggle in nineteenth-century England becomes a universal and extended class conflict over the whole reach of history: "History . . . is the history of class struggles." Henceforth, class emerges as a fundamental form in which to conceive social stratification (overriding or eliminating for Marx all other forms). It also becomes the form in which the economic conditions of production (reified into a general concept, and no longer restricted to the condition of England) will manifest themselves and become the force driving history and humanity forward, through conflict.

So, too, the materialist interpretation of history, with its emphasis on economics and technology, summarized the work of many other thinkers; henceforth, it would carry a Marxist imprint. As its attendants, Marx also formulated concepts of ideology, class consciousness, and the sociology of knowledge. In his earlier work, he had emphasized the concept of alienation; in his later work he studied the economic concepts of surplus value and immiserization of the proletariat. His overall framework, in terms of sociology itself, was the recognition of the individual as a social being, with neither the individual nor society existing as an abstraction in isolation but each defining the other.[3]

Such are some of Marx's major contributions to sociology. In fact, Marx began his effort at a revolutionary sociology as a solution, specifically German in its nature, to the problem of modernism. Quickly, he moved from the German problem to the world-wide dimensions of industrialism. In his earlier phase, he had wrestled with a part of the problem in terms of "egoism," which he identified with Jewish "huckstering"; as he broadened his perspective, he spoke directly of the cash nexus and the bourgeoisie as the source of disconnection and misery. The solution, he believed, had to be a revolutionary one; and Marx sought constantly to combine theory and praxis, sociology and socialism, in one overarching synthesis. In the end, if Marx's thought was to be successful, sociology would have to wither away as an independent subject, becoming incorporated in the dictatorship of the proletariat and the community of communism. Marxism, then, which in many ways can be seen as the beginning of sociology, can also be seen, in theory, as marking its end.

As we know, Marxism has not been successful, at least yet, in accomplishing this last ending. It has, instead, profoundly influenced the development and continued existence of sociology. Marx, denied a professorship of philosophy, never had a chance, as did Durkheim, to convert his philosophy into a new academic discipline, sociology. This achievement was pushed along, however, by some of his disciples.

Ferdinand Tönnies

Though strictly speaking not a disciple of Marx, one of those who was strongly and positively influenced by him was Ferdinand Tönnies. Tönnies, starting in philosophy, slowly worked his way to a teaching position in sociology. As an academic sociologist, his style reflected his position: not for him the dramatic, vivid writing of Marx, or even of Engels, seeking to influence their readers by the pull of sensibility. Rather, he employed the formal, even pedantic, prose of a scholar speaking to other scholars: the beginnings of sociological jargon can here be discerned (Marx, of course, in his more philosophical writings can also be accused of obscurity and jargon).

In *Gemeinschaft und Gesellschaft*, Tönnies took cash-nexus Man and made him into the rational-willed individual of society, setting him off from the natural-willed member of community. These polar concepts of Man and his social forms were reified into ideal types— a conceptualization in sociological thinking to be taken up and developed further by Max Weber (the relation to reality of Tönnies's reifications can and should be questioned by the critical reader). In addition, Tönnies, implicitly if not explicitly, attached intense feelings—values—to his ideal types. He is one with the earlier lamenters in content if not in style: the organic is greatly preferred to the mechanical, the natural to the rational will, the countryside to the city, and so on.

Above all, however, Tönnies's contribution to sociology lies in his conceptualization of society itself. Inspired by Hobbes, he realized that society is constructed by Men, who have no existence separate from their "will" (which has produced both *Gemeinschaft* and, more recently, *Gesellschaft*). Again we are in the presence of a reification: society is the totality of Men's social relations. The task of sociology, for Tönnies, is to study and analyze the structures that result from Men relating, one to another.

Georg Simmel

Georg Simmel sought to carry the task forward with a different stress: on social forms rather than structures. All structures, he contended, whether of churches, armies, states, and so on, are necessarily characterized by relations such as super- and subordination, competition, specialization, inner solidarity, and outer exclusiveness. Such relational forms are to be found in so-called *Gemeinschaft* as well as *Gesellschaft*; it is a matter of degree. And they will be found in socialism as well as capitalism, for they are inherent in all types of society.

Central to Simmel's conceptualization of society is the notion of exchange. It creates society by creating bonds between Men. It is necessarily productive, for each party enters into the relationship in order to gain. Its purest forms are intellectual or sexual, but its most prevalent manifestation is economic, with money as the great symbol of communion. The cash nexus for Simmel is an admirable achievement in abstraction, that is, intellectuality, and, while open to possible abuse, in its better state is a vehicle for Man's ever-expanding community.

As part of his analysis of exchange in its many forms, Simmel also took up the subject of value, seeking to carry it beyond the merely economic. Here his inspiration was Immanuel Kant. Following Kant, too, Simmel accepted the unsocial-social nature of Man as ontologically given and not, as with Marx, something to be overcome by means of the dialectic. Man, then, is not alienated by the institutions of economy, state, and law that he forms, but rather is given his actual social being by them. Simmel, like Tönnies a long time in achieving academic respectability as a sociologist, nevertheless helped move other practitioners in his chosen field to a willingness to accept modern industrial society, and then to an aspiration to comprehend it as one among many forms of social relations.

Emile Durkheim

Emile Durkheim, who first achieved true academic acceptance for the new discipline, shared with Simmel a relatively optimistic view of modern society. In his first great book, *The Division of Labor,* he expanded the analysis of this form of human relatedness from the purely economic to the social. He recognized it as a relatively new form of solidarity, but argued that it binds Men as much in *Gesellschaft* as other more primordial ties do in *Gemeinschaft.* Reversing Tönnies's classification and valuation, Durkheim lauded the division of labor as supplying "organic" ties versus the primordial "mechanical" ones. In the former, individualism has its place, and increases with the proliferation of dependence; in the latter, the members of the society are interchangeable, alike parts.

Further, where Marx spoke of alienation, Durkheim talked of *anomie,* but saw it as an abnormality of modern society, not as its characteristic. As an abnormality, in any of its forms such as crime or suicide, it could be scientifically analyzed and politically ameliorated.

Lastly, Durkheim turned his attention to religion, which he saw as similar to the division of labor in being a source of social community. His is a functional analysis, where religion is not judged for its truth value but for its power to constitute society. It does this by supplying mythical classifications—the products of human minds—which mirror and are also mirrored in social classifications. Drawing on ethnography, and especially accounts of totemism, Durkheim postulated a division of the world into sacred and profane domains. These and other social classifications constitute society, for they order Men's relations to one another as well as to nature. Thus, where materialism for Marx gives rise to Men's social conceptions, religious ideas and practices help give rise for Durkheim to Men's material relations.

Max Weber

Max Weber also focused on religion as part of his overall effort, but went much further than Durkheim toward developing a true sociology of religion. In this sector of his work, Weber tried to understand the contemporary form of the great world religions rather than their primitive beginnings, and to analyze the way they interacted with their political, economic, and social environment. Perhaps because his background was in historical studies more than in philosophy, Weber was concerned with the actual, detailed way in which societies, but especially modern society, had come into being. The details he explored, however, were not particularly in the form of historical events, but were ideas, institutions, forms, and structures, that is, sociological developments.

In seeking to understand modern, capitalist society, Weber was aware that it was part of an increasingly "rational" world. He defined capitalism, in fact, as the rational, consistent pursuit of profit by individuals. As is well known, in *The Protestant Ethic and the Spirit of Capitalism*, Weber examined the relations of economics and religion, in the form of capitalism and Calvinism, and concluded that there was an "elective affinity" between that particular pair. Once in place, capitalism could then proceed under other, non-Calvinist terms. In this work, too, incidentally, Weber shifted the emphasis from capitalism as a product of Jewish "hucksterism" to a stress on its links to Christianity and especially Protestantism. By so doing, he largely did away with capitalism's hitherto "alien" image.

At the end of industrial capitalism's development Weber saw not communism and the free proletariat but bureaucracy, whether in a capitalist or socialist guise. Such a society would be an "iron cage." The only way to break the bars—the new version of chains?—would be through a revival of charisma, a term Weber used to describe "irrational" authority and legitimacy. Charisma, appealing as it does to powerful individual and emotional forces, alone has the potential to destroy the iron cage and restore Men to a more individualistic form of social relations. While the concept of charismatic authority is a brilliant contribution by Weber to sociological analysis, one must question his usage of it in the particular case above.

Weber's analysis overall was always multi-causal. He rejected Marx's materialist interpretation of history as too monist and simplistic. The economic was merely one form of social action, interacting with many others. Ideas, for example, have an equal role in historical development, and can have an independent, inner logic of their own. Thus, Weber found room in his sociology for nationalism and *Realpolitik*, for continuing religious strife, and for persisting self-interest in all social systems. Parties, statuses, and classes, and the aspirations for power embodied in them, are not unique to capitalism, he argued, but will be found in socialism and in all other possible forms of advanced social community as well.

In the end, then, Weber transformed the cash-nexus concern, which stood at the center of the connections problem, into a general analysis of all social action. The economic, in this conceptualization, is merely one form, one way, in which society manifests itself. Community, if not a many-stranded web, as with George Eliot, is a multi-causal system of human relations.

According to Weber, one seeks to understand this web or system in its historical manifestations and in its own terms, that is, by means of a value-free approach which he called the method of understanding *(verstehen)*. In Weber's schema, we should not impose or impute our own values, other than that of scientific understanding, on different forms of connection. Because these latter are formed out of what goes on in Men's minds—with mentality thereby being the basis of society—we must enter into these minds as best we can. In sum, with his sociological concepts and this methodology, Weber tried to encapsulate the sympathy approach and then to establish a "science" of society, rooted in the concern for connection and disconnection felt by early-nineteenth-century observers, but freed from their limited and time-bound perspectives.

Validity

Such is the array, then, of ideas, concepts, and theories to be found in our sociologists. They set the terms of any present discourse on the nature of society and its connections. *Gemeinschaft* and *Gesellschaft*, alienation and *anomie*, class and status, communism and bureaucracy, ideology and charisma, superordination and subordination, exchange and division of labor, organic and mechanical, sacred and profane—these are the modern words and concepts by which we try to deal with the issues of individualism and community, with Man's double nature. Even if we were to shed the formal theories behind them, the words themselves have become the common coins of our intellectual exchange.

Can these words, ideas, concepts, or theories claim any sort of "scientific" validity? In terms of the positivist aspirations that lie in back of them, in general, I think not. Verification, repeatability, predictability—the standard terms used in natural science—find little secure place in sociology.

If, however, by "science" we mean greater systematic understanding of a phenomenon, then I believe that the combined work of Engels and Marx, Tönnies, Simmel, Durkheim, Weber, and others like them has made a definite contribution to the "science" of society. Their work, I would argue, helps us to organize our understanding of society as a peculiarly human creation, and this is a relatively new way of structuring such understanding. Further, their ideas allow us to bring intellectual classification into what otherwise seems a chaos of social experience, and to frame that experience in ways that accord with our desire for rational ordering of empirical data, that is, with our need for "scientific" (as opposed to religious or literary) understanding.

Evaluations

I am thus claiming that the classical sociologists whom we have been considering did make important contributions to a science of society, but the paradox we come to in the end, I also claim, is that some of these same sociologists and their disciples also created powerful myths, inspired in part by the literary lamenters (who, to complicate the paradox further, saw a part of reality overlooked, for example, by economists).

In my view, two such myths in particular have been perpetuated. I believe that a number of sociologists, including Marx and Tönnies, misread reality to a substantial degree, and that we will do so too if we put on their spectacles. The first great myth, still frequently triumphant (and this in spite of the work of Simmel, Durkheim, and Weber), is that modern society is the scene of a breakdown in connections, rather than a transmutation in their form. The other great myth (in this case, one not completely shared by Marx) is that the earlier connections were somehow "better."

Certainly, a sense of waning connection *does* characterize our present-day societies. Such a sense stems from a number of real factors. The most basic and persistent over time is what I shall call our "evolutionary nostalgia." As an evolutionary creature, it is only natural that the human being has a deep nostalgic feeling for the countryside and a rural background, and behind that an even more primordial longing for a hunting past and its peculiar forms of isolation and freedom. These serve as the emotional wellsprings of our discomfort with urban, industrial life, and our sense of painful change—identified, during the last two centuries, as broken connections.

Such basic emotions then joined with the actual experiences of dislocation and fragmentation to be found in industrializing societies. The most fundamental feature in this regard is probably that provoked by the novel system of discipline and the new sense of time, most prominently present in the factory but permeating the whole system of interactions and communications between humans, for example, being on the job "on time," working at a pace set by machinery, meeting railroad and airline time tables, listening to radio and TV "hourly" reports, and so on. Such discipline runs counter to our natural rhythms, given in the woods and the countryside by the rising and setting of the sun.[4] The "jar" to our nervous system reverberates with the cosmic jarring occasioned by the substitution of "eternal" electric night for the moon's monthly light, whereby society becomes an around-the-clock phenomenon.[5]

In addition to such fundamental factors there are all of the worst features of industrial society itself, often most extreme in its early capitalistic form: erratic employment, exploitive working conditions, overcrowded and unsanitary urban surroundings, and so on, much of which has been summed up in the phrase "cash nexus."

The true issue, as I have tried to describe it above, has often been obscured, however, because many of the lamenters and early sociologists, and thinkers inspired by them, have too often equated cash nexus with immiserization. Such an equation, even when it corresponds with the facts, misses the essential point. The real issue is not immiserization, a temporary phenomenon, but the shift from agricultural or even commercial relations to industrial ones.

Even under the most benign conditions, however, change of any degree, and certainly the massive change of mechanization, will be for most people a daunting experience. A sense of disconnection is hardly unnatural. What has made it so acute has been the very success of the industrial revolution, and its accompanying increases in individualism and affluence. Individualism, with its expansive self, makes us more conscious of both what is happening to us and to what we might aspire. Affluence both gives rise to heightened expectations and makes us aware of the new people who have succeeded to the roles of those who formerly held power and position by virtue of inherited and traditional right. Hence, an enlarged sense of discontent and disconnection arises.

With all this said, however, there is another side to the matter. It is that the human animal also appears to chase after change. If this is so, we must conclude, even if reluctantly, that Man is impelled by his nature, and certainly by his history, to transform his connections. The record seems to show that there is a human drive to seize control of the evolutionary process itself and to create the very environment which then exerts further survival pressures. Especially through technology and science, Man apparently seeks to construct a completely "artificial," that is, Man-made, surround in which to lead his life. In this regard, once again Man shows his "doubleness," torn between his desire to mold himself to a larger "Nature" and to remold that Nature in a mechanical image.*

Much of recent historical writing has consisted of the attempt to tell the story of, as I shall call it, this "evolutionary schizophrenia," a condition that has taken on much expanded dimensions recently in terms of industrialism, and to understand and evaluate it. In this attempt, a gap frequently has been opened between reality, as best it can be established, and some of our intellectual and emotional needs as represented in myth. Thus, a mythical past, whole and connected, is contrasted with a supposedly disconnected present, and "community" glorified, without much examination of its nature. Earlier horrors, such as primitives subjected by their societies to excruciatingly painful rites and tortures, or medieval apprentices tyrannized by their masters, are thus overlooked or played down

---

*This is a theme that I am currently pursuing in a book in progress with the working title "Man, Animals, and Machines." For a preview of some of what is involved, see my paper, "The Evolutionary Machine," presented at the Stanford Humanities Center Conference on Humans, Animals, Machines (April 23–25, 1987), and to be published in *Boundaries of Humanity* (Berkeley, forthcoming), James J. Sheehan and Morton Sosna, eds.

(where, incidentally, are the "Parliamentary Blue Books" documenting such abuses, to set besides the nineteenth-century inquiries into factory work?).

A Triptych

Perhaps I can best get at these issues of perspective and normative judgment by noting first that the sense of community is often seen by observers as a widening circle of connection, going from family to tribe, to province, to nation, and, perhaps, eventually to all Mankind. In turn, economic development is perceived as going from hunting and gathering to agriculture, and, most recently, to industrialization. In this perspective, I want to sketch three vignettes. They are deliberately intended to be stereotypic, partially mythical, creations (just as the perspective itself is also schematic).

The first is of a girl in the Kikuyu tribe, Central Kenya. We can find her portrait in the Natural History Museum in Nairobi. Around her neck are hung heavy metal necklaces, from her ears dangle chains, intercoiled and connecting, while other parts of her body carry other ornaments. Whatever their aesthetic element, these ornaments also indicate the girl's status: that she is a virgin, that she has had a clitoredectomy, that she is married, and so on. This young woman, like everyone in her tribe, has a "place," and she and everyone else knows exactly what it is. There is no room for *anomie*, alienation, or impersonal relations. She is enveloped in "community," although the places she may enter are sharply delineated.

On the other hand, the price of her security is that there is no escape. At the proper age, she will be circumcised, in a painful rite, her husband will be chosen for her, and she will have little choice but to be his wife and raise his children (although she will have the possibility of divorce, and perhaps to be a shaman). She may live in a society constantly at war (as is ours), exposed to numerous parasitical diseases, afflicting both the tribe's cattle and herself, and often on the edge of want. In this "primitive" existence, she will probably live a relatively short life, within a securely defined community, but circumscribed by very strict rules and taboos.[6]

Our second vignette is of a feudal serf, say, in France of the fourteenth century. He is part of a settled village, secure, by contract, in his right to till certain fields. He can expect protection on the part of his lord in return for services. His religion comforts him in this life, and promises him eternal life (if he is saved) in the next. Having inherited the use of his land from his father, he can expect to pass it down to his son, and his son's son, *ad infinitum*. In the same way that he cannot alienate his land, so he is virtually unalienable from his small community, to which he is connected by numerous ties.

On the other hand, he is vulnerable to bad harvests, to soldiers trampling over his lands, to extortions from grasping lords. He must pay tithes, work on his master's land and roads, and possibly give him part of his crop. The religion that consoles him also terrifies him with its ominous depiction of damnation. He may be prey to some great plague, such as the Black Death. He cannot leave his land, and he cannot marry without his lord's permission. The price of his security is rule by custom in which he has little say and by authorities whom he may not question.

Our last vignette is of a textile worker, say, in nineteenth-century Manchester, England. He or she (and the bisexual usage points to an important development) works in a factory, under a strict, new discipline of time, and may lose his/her job in times of commercial crises. His/her housing may well be crowded and unsanitary (it is different from the Kikuyu and feudal huts, but whether better or worse is not clear; their housing, for example, is in the countryside, and as inhabitants they cannot be dispossessed). If he/she has a job, however, his/her income will be higher, and the food he/she eats better than his/her rural counterparts. He/she is part of a society in rapid change, and is alleged to feel alienated and cut off from his/her fellow Men—though he (in this aspect, not she) may belong to a labor union, and feel part of a factory community. According to the lamenters of his/her epoch, his/her only form of connection is the "cash nexus."

On the other hand, money considerations aside (an important aside), he/she is free to move around and to seek jobs freely. Part of that movement may be upward, in terms of mobility, if he/she has the requisite ambition, abilities—and luck. He/she may marry as fancy strikes, if the woman or man will have him/her. (In practice, of course, cross-class marriage rarely occurs.) He/she can look forward to children surviving in greater numbers, and to himself/herself having a higher life expectancy than previously. He may become part of political life, as in the Chartist Movement, although at first to little effect. His/her life, in various vague ways, is more "individualistic," and perhaps therefore more fragmented, than that of his/her ancestors.

Now, I have drawn these portraits with a broad brush, less concerned with their "actuality"—for historians, sociologists, and anthropologists can and will argue over their representativeness and accuracy—than to set up a suggestive triptych. In each of my three sketches, I have depicted a member of the society who occupies one of its lower ranks. In judging these matters, one ought always to take a Rawlsean "original position," that is, one which imagines that all individuals have to decide on the ideal societal structure without knowing what their specific place in society would be.[7] If we were to be a Kikuyu male chieftain, we might make one judgment; so, too, as a feudal lord or a cotton magnate; and these would probably be quite different from the one made if we knew we were to be a Kikuyu female, a feudal serf, or a factory "hand."

What these three vignettes are intended to illustrate is that on a spectrum that measures community, alienation, security, individualism, and so forth, each particular time, and each particular society in that period, will naturally exhibit a different profile. All the elements will be present in some form in each society, and in each position in that society, but in vastly different balances. And how an individual judges his/her own and society's condition will very much depend on his/her historical sense as well as vantage point in society.

A New Perspective

Throughout this book I have been trying to enlarge our historical sense. In studying changing perspectives toward self and society and their "connectedness," I have tried to look back, not so much at individual countries, although this is what I have done specifically—England, France, Germany—but at a "Western" experience, highly generalized from the particulars. England, for example, in the late eighteenth century was distinctively characterized by relatively open aristocratic and parliamentary institutions; France by a centralized, absolutist regime, which then underwent revolution; and Germany by divided and communal authorities along with a unique civil service. All of them, however, faced the common phenomenon of the connections problem, and, with all their differences, reacted in a "connected" way, sharing common features and drawing upon one another's intellectual resources.

We can also look at the present, and the future (though I have not done so in any detail in this work), and see how in society after society a struggle over old and new connections similar to the one we have described has been taking place. In Pakistan, to take one example, as one writer explains, "the fabric of the society [is] being pulled out of shape by the tugs and tensions between the coming new and the going old. . . . people . . . wanted to have it both ways: to have the miracles of the new world but not give up the faith and the customs of the old. Without consulting the masses, I thought there did seem to be a Pakistani consensus on commitment to both currents, modernization and Islam—contradictions or not."

Or another example: in Russia, as a recent news story tells us, quoting a leading Soviet demographer, "the Soviet Union is in the grip of a demographic and social revolution that is breaking up families, lowering the birthrate and contributing to alcoholism, juvenile delinquency and crime." As the story continues, "the problems stem from an extensive urban-rural shift of nearly two million people a year that some sociologists say is transforming the country's social structure as none of the wars or internal conflicts of this century have changed it."[8] One can substitute the names Iran, Kenya, India, China, or Mexico: the individual details are vastly, and importantly, different, but the overall trend, or at least problem, is the same.

Today we deal with this general problem mainly in terms of development economics (or sometimes in terms of "modernization" theory, which usually embraces the sharp dichotomies that I have been deploring and, when it does, is thus unacceptable). One of my hopes, consequently, is that the concept of connections can supply a useful context and an enriched conceptualization for present-day development theory.

The Question of Community

Let me expand on this notion a bit further. For example, in dealing with development and its problems, a central issue is frequently the notion of community. A glance at any major library reveals shelves and shelves of books devoted to that subject, vague as it may be.[9] I am arguing, however, that, important as the notion of community is, it should be viewed as merely one part of a larger concept, connections, which, rooted as it is in history, allows us more readily to embrace and to comprehend the changing condition of Man.

Community is an essentially static notion, and an excessively normative one at that; or as one definition of community puts it, "community is both empirically descriptive of a social structure and normatively toned. It refers both to the unit of a society as it is and to the aspects of the unit that are valued if they exist, desired in their absence."[10] To give another, more enlarged, definition, as Robert Nisbet reports, "Community is founded on man conceived in his wholeness rather than in one or another of the roles, taken separately, that he may hold in a social order. It draws its psychological strength from levels of motivation deeper than those of mere volition or interest. . . ."[11] Useful as these definitions of community are, and important as the ties embodied in the concept are, I am arguing that the possibilities for distortion embedded in this way of perceiving matters are disconcerting.

The fact is that, as Durkheim and others realized, *any* actual community is "unnatural," in the sense that it is created by Men and is not a "natural" or "organic" product.* This fact is latent in the very concept of society worked out by all the classical sociologists, including Tönnies. To think otherwise is to run the risk of denying responsibility for what is institutionalized in a community—for example, the exclusion by nineteenth-century German home towns of so-called "undesirables." The fact is that particular communities and corporations in the past have pursued their own self-interest in the name of an abstract concept, community, which allowed them to deny their own ruling self-interest and to attribute such a sordid notion only to *Gesellschaft*.

We need, in the light of historical data, to realize that power in a society can come from the ability to establish the categories of social analysis, as we talk about subjects ranging from guns (and gun control) to money. How meaning is attached to various cultural phenomena is of immense significance. "Hegemony" has become a

---

*By saying this, I do not mean that community itself, in the abstract, is unnatural; for Man is an animal that does not live alone. In fact, social bonding is probably a genetic trait. The *forms* of social bonding, however, are "unnatural" in the sense indicated above.

popular way among some scholars of expressing what David Hume had earlier referred to as the reign of public opinion. What is today variously called "discourse analysis" or "hermeneutics" can be a sharpened way of coming to understand the manifestations of social power as it expresses itself in texts. As these notions suggest, a debate over terms and categories such as "community" is hardly a mere ivory-tower affair.

Thus, an emphasis upon the pure classical sociological concept of community may be a way of pretending that custom can reign outside of time, untouched by change; such a concept can be employed to ensure that nothing will change, or, conversely, be used to inspire a utopian movement. In contrast, history, written in terms of connections, points to the actuality of changing experience. In fact, much of what one actually sees in history consists of successive waves of community structures, with breakdown and fission succeeded by construction and fusion, often in the very same locale.[12]

The Argument

Overall, therefore, my claim is that though the concept of community is a useful, and even necessary, one, a broader perspective is both desirable and possible. By conceiving the issue as one of connections, I am claiming, we include the communitarian concern, but see it as part of a greater whole. In this whole, related notions of self, society, individualism, sympathy, altruism, sincerity, egoism, isolation, alienation, and the like also take their rightful place.

These notions have been central for modern Man, as he has wrestled with problems of a rapidly changing society. It is in their terms that, frightened by a sense of breakdown in connections, modern Man has sought to understand his position. Comfort can and has come from the "scientific" conceptualizations of sociology, especially as they reveal the complexity of our "double nature," caught between self and society. What history adds to sociology is a broadened understanding of this ever-present human condition, as Men experience the vicissitudes of changed circumstances.

The shift from chain to web, as the dominant image related to connections, I have argued, symbolizes our changed situation. The image of a chain, whatever its security, often means a kind of servile dependency (and even serfdom or slavery itself). Web connotes a many-faceted relationship to others, in which individuals play many roles, and can seek, creatively, to define themselves.

Liberation from "secure" chains, and thus a fixed self, did entail in the eighteenth and nineteenth centuries (and still does) a metaphysical *angst* for numerous individuals. It also awakened a great deal of social as well as religious anxiety in many quarters. So, too, many observers (for example, Wordsworth) were distressed at the chain's destruction because they thought the result was a snapping of ties to nature.

On the other hand, it appears that many men, as well as women and children, have found, or are finding, a position of greater dignity and freedom in the social web than was afforded them in the chained world. One can also argue that the notion of web has brought with it an enriching and widening perspective of ecological relatedness. And for some, there is a deep secular awe, rather than *angst*, in belonging to a universe in which Man must create his own values, as well as his own society.

There was, and is, an affinity between the breaking of chains and what is partly summed up in the term "individualism." Individualism, correctly delimited, I believe, is one of the great glories of modern society. It is unquestionably a difficult position to maintain: loneliness, *anomie*, a sense of fragmentation—these are real threats. It can turn into self-absorbed selfishness, and, as Tocqueville warned, it can degenerate into egoism.

Individualism, too, like community, can degenerate into a myth, and fictions about it become difficult to distinguish from facts. At its best, however, coupled as it must be to a sense of connection with other men and women, individualism can allow for the fullest flowering of each person along with a maximum contribution to society. Indeed, it can be the basis of types of connections not to be found in earlier arrangements, and only possible in an individualistic society.*

---

*Let me argue further that lamenters, by focusing only on the breakdown of old connections and refusing to support new associations that might embody some of their most cherished values, leave the field, in fact, to the breakers, who often badly need the balancing virtues of the lamenters.

Taking Sides

By now, it must be clear that I, for one, rejoice in the expansion of the self (whose dark side, admittedly, is the "empty self" that may result from what others lament as the breakdown of connections). I have tried, however, not to let a personal view such as this unduly color my attempt to describe and to define the connections problem, and to establish the dimensions of the unsocial-social nature of the human condition. Thus, I like to believe that a reader might reject my personal evaluation, given much emphasis in this chapter; yet, as a scholarly enterprise, judge my overall account on its own merits.

My main focus, to repeat, while informed by contemporary concerns, has been not on a present sense of fragmentation but rather on its source in the unusual concern over connection and disconnection that arose over two centuries ago, when Western Man entered into industrial society.

I have tried to deal, specifically, with the literary and sociological attempts to comprehend what was happening in the modern era, summed up for many by the metaphor "cash nexus." Throughout, my interest has been both in what people thought was happening and in what, as best we can tell, actually was happening. As the reader probably realizes, however, having now arrived at the end of this book, I am convinced that the two "happenings" are part of one unified story, with what goes on in the mind ineluctably connected to what goes on in society, and vice versa.

Appendix

Among those who have written importantly on one or more strands of the connection theme are the following. In *From the Closed World to the Infinite Universe* (New York, 1958), Alexandre Koyré seeks to describe the shift indicated in his title. As he summarizes what happened, "This scientific and philosophical revolution . . . can be described roughly as bringing forth the destruction of the Cosmos, that is, the disappearance . . . of the conception of the world as a finite, closed, and hierarchically ordered whole . . . and its replacement by an indefinite and even infinite universe which is bound together by the identity of its fundamental components and laws, and in which all these components are placed on the same level of being. This, in turn, implies the discarding by scientific thought of all considerations based upon value-concepts, such as perfection, harmony, meaning and aim, and finally the utter devalorization of being, the divorce of the world of value and the world of facts" (4). The other book to be read in this connection is Arthur Lovejoy, *The Great Chain of Being* (Cambridge, Mass., 1936) (see my comments in Chapter 2).

On the sensed breakdown of connection between Man and God, see J. Hillis Miller, *The Disappearance of God: Five Nineteenth-Century Writers* (Cambridge, Mass., 1963). The part that concerns us is the introduction rather than the chapters on the specific authors, De Quincy, Robert Browning, Emily Brontë, Matthew Arnold, and Gerard Manley Hopkins. In Miller's view, "the nineteenth and twentieth centuries seem to many writers a time when God is no more present and not yet again present, and can only be experienced negatively, as a terrifying absence. In this time of the no longer and the not yet, man is 'Wandering between two worlds, one dead,/The other powerless to be born.' His situation is essentially one of disconnection: disconnection between man and nature, between man and man, even between man and himself. Only if God would return or if we could somehow reach him might our broken world be unified again" (2). He then adds, "Life in the city, the breakup of medieval symbolism, the imprisoning of man in his consciousness, the appearance of the historical sense—all ways in which man experiences disappearance of God" (12).

Thomas McFarland, *Romanticism and the Forms of Ruin: Wordsworth, Coleridge, and Modalities of Fragmentation* (Princeton, N.J., 1981), is an important book which deals with the break, primarily between Man and Man and Man and Nature, as experienced by the Romantics. McFarland writes about the Romantics' need for "reticulation," which he defines as "a universal concern, the need to harmonize, to tie things together" and argues that "It is, indeed, possible that the whole thrust to unity so characteristic of Romanticism, as opposed to the classifying instinct of the eighteenth century, should be primarily seen . . . as an intensification of the reticulative need" (5). His book is a learned disquisition on "the pervasive longing of the Romantics for an absent reality," and he stresses their "prevailing sense of incompleteness, fragmentation, and ruin" (11).

Suzanne Graver, *George Eliot and Community* (Berkeley, Calif., 1984), has anticipated one part of my work in her penetrating analysis of the relation of George Eliot's ideas to those of the German sociologist Ferdinand Tönnies. I must confess that coming upon her book after having myself independently conceived the broad outlines of this present book, with its central theme of the movement from sensibility to sociology and its orientation around the cash-nexus trope, I felt greatly relieved at having encountered a fellow spirit, who had written about community before me, in a similar vein. See, too, John Killham, "The Idea of Community in the English Novel," *Nineteenth-Century Fiction* 31 (1977), 379–96.

Raymond Williams, *The Country and the City* (New York, 1973), is a tour de force, elegantly and passionately written, dealing with an absolutely critical element of the connections theme. He traces attitudes to the country and the city from antiquity to the present, infusing the topic with his own personal experience, but keeping his subjectivism under control, and, indeed, using it as a refined instrument to probe his subject. As he shows so well, "plus ça change, plus ça reste," that is, the laments were the same two thousand years ago as they are today, even though circumstances have changed drastically.

Werner Stark, *The Social Bond: An Investigation into the Bases of Law-abidingness* (New York, 1976 and 1978), 2 vols., is an interesting and impressive effort to assess a wide range of empirical studies devoted to aspects of Man's unsocial-social nature. Among other topics in Volume I, he deals with the social bond in regard to animal nature, isolated Man, and primal society, with reflections at the end on sociobiology. Stark's thesis is that the social order "rests on the reduction and control of animal propensities, not on their free unfolding" (viii). Thus, Man is a self-contradictory creature whose egocentric and sociocentric tendencies are rooted in nature, but whose expressions are determined by culture. In his Preface, Stark says he envisages a total of six volumes in order to deal fully with his subject.

Habits of the Heart: Individualism and Commitment in American Life, by Robert Bellah et al. (Berkeley, 1985), is the work of five authors, concerned with the possibility that an over-extended individualism will undermine the conditions of its existence. They stress the "empty self" of many twentieth-century Americans and their need to reconnect with others. The authors' solution is a call for renewed community of various sorts—their treatment of this subject often takes on a kind of pietistic tone—and for a common language of sociability. Their method of analysis is through the use of interviews (they admit that these are limited to "white, middle class Americans"), which adds much human interest to their account, and reflections on history and sociology. This book (incidentally, a popular success) is clearly and importantly related to our central concern with connections. Well written, informed, and openly committed to one point of view, it serves as an excellent illustration of the vitality of the connections theme.

Marshall Berman, *All That Is Solid Melts into Air: The Experience of Modernity* (New York, 1982), is a brilliantly written book whose topic overlaps our connections theme in many places. Berman ranges widely over literary and historical sources and offers interesting treatments of such figures as Marx, Baudelaire, and Dostoevsky, as well as of subjects such as the Crystal Palace. One small quibble: in the *Manifesto*, Marx writes, "Alles Ständische und Stehende verdampft, alles Heilige wird entweiht, und die Menschen sind endlich gezwungen . . . " (Karl Marx, *Die Frühschriften, herausgegeben von Siegfried Landshut* (Stuttgart, 1971), 529). Although the first part is widely translated as "All that is solid melts into air," "Ständische" itself refers to the "estates of the realm," which were so central to German social and political life, and which were being shaken. Marx therefore was saying that the bourgeoisie were dissolving the old hierarchical ordering of society, and he was saying this practically in the same breath as he was claiming that they were leaving "no other nexus between man and man than callous 'cash payment.'" Because of the weight Berman puts on the "All that is solid . . . " phrase, it is surprising that he does not note the full original statement by Marx. (I owe the inspiration for this observation to my friend, Wolf Schäfer.)

Notes

Introduction

1. Bruce Mazlish, *James and John Stuart Mill: Father and Son in the Nineteenth Century* (New York: 1975), 24, 427.

2. See the new introduction in the paperback edition of *Mill* (New Brunswick, N.J.: 1988) for a fuller exposition of these points.

1. A Beginning

1. Norman Brown, *Life against Death* (New York, n.d., orig. pub. 1959), adds a psychoanalytic polarity to this list when he writes ". . . the two levels of culture which sociology has distinguished under various labels—primitive and civilized, Gemeinschaft and Gesellschaft, folk and urban—can be distinguished psychoanalytically. Primitive is that level of culture in which the rhythm of what Freud calls the primary process—the rhythm of dreams and childhood play—is predominant. Civilized is that level of culture which effectively represses the rhythm of primary process in favor of rationality and the reality-principle" (37).

2. Cf. Marshall Berman, *All That Is Solid Melts into Air: The Experience of Modernity* (New York, 1982). See further my comment in the Appendix.

3. See Chapter 2 for the actual citations by Carlyle and Marx.

4. Quoted in Michael McKeon, *The Origins of the English Novel, 1600–1740* (Baltimore, 1987), 204. In addition to being an excellent treatment of its main subject, this book gives a solid exposition of the emerging commercial world of the seventeenth century in England.

5. Cf. Lionel Trilling, *Sincerity and Authenticity* (Cambridge, Mass., 1974) for a discussion of the newness of the concept "society," dating the concept to the sixteenth century. Marc Bloch, *Feudal Society*, tr. L. A. Manyon (Chi-

cago, 1961), xvii–xviii, argues for a much later date, 1727, and the Comte de Boulainvilliers, for significant use of the new terminology. David Frisby and Derek Sayer, *Society* (Chichester, England, 1986), gives a good historical sketch of the concept in their first chapter.

6. For the reader interested in pursuing this particular thread, see for example, William Letwin, *The Origins of Scientific Economics* (London, 1963), and Joyce Oldham Appleby, *Economic Thought and Ideology in Seventeenth-Century England* (Princeton, N.J., 1978). One can see Appleby's applicability to the connections theme when she says, "The advent of the market, and the reorganization of social life through it, made men reconsider the terms of their lives. Like the simultaneous effort to reimagine the mechanical relationships of the physical universe, the process of conceiving the market economy became an intellectual influence of paramount importance to the developments it investigated. The imaginative reconstruction of economic relations by seventeenth-century thinkers created new truths, suggested possible activities, imposed moral lessons, and contributed analogies to the other areas of social thinking" (22).

7. J.G.A. Pocock, *The Machiavellian Moment: Florentine Political Thought and the Atlantic Republican Tradition* (Princeton, N.J., 1975), and *Virtue, Commerce, and History: Essays on Political Thought and History, Chiefly in the Eighteenth Century* (Cambridge, England, 1985). An earlier and shorter version of Pocock's basic argument can be found in his *Politics, Language and Time: Essays on Political Thought and History* (New York, 1971), Chapters 3 and 4. On the general subject, see also Zera S. Fink, *The Classical Republicans: An Essay on the Recovery of a Pattern of Thought in Seventeenth-Century England* (Evanston, Ill., 1945), and Caroline Robbins, *The Eighteenth-Century Commonwealth Man* (Cambridge, Mass., 1959). For an implicit but incisive critique of Pocock's interpretation of Machiavelli, see Mark Hulliung, *Citizen Machiavelli* (Princeton, N.J., 1983). An attack on Pocock's thesis, as well as its extension to America, can be found in John Patrick Diggins, *The Lost Soul of American Politics: Virtue, Self-Interest, and the Foundations of Liberalism* (New York, 1984). Of related interest, though not involved in the specific debate, is Albert O. Hirschman, *The Passions and the Interests: Political Arguments for Capitalism before Its Triumph* (Princeton, N.J., 1977).

8. The quotation is from Adam Ferguson, *An Essay on the History of Civil Society* (1767), ed. Duncan Forbes (Edinburgh, 1966), xxxi. The standard book on the subject, though one senses a need for a fresh view, building on her work, is Gladys Bryson, *Man and Society: The Scottish Inquiry of the Eighteenth Century* (Princeton, N.J., 1945). *The Scottish Moralists: On Human Nature and Society*, ed. with an introduction by Louis Schneider (Chicago, 1967), includes excerpts from some of these early "sociologists" on various topics.

9. Pocock, *Politics, Language and Time*, 146.

10. For a full-scale argument to this effect, see Martin J. Wiener, *English*

Culture and the Decline of the Industrial Spirit, 1850–1980 (Cambridge, England, 1981).

11. Cf. Thomas L. Haskell, *The Emergence of Professional Social Science: The American Social Science Association and the Nineteenth-Century Crisis of Authority* (Bloomington, Ill., 1977), 1. As this book was going to press, I became aware of the existence of Wolf Lepenies, *Between Literature and Science: The Rise of Sociology*, tr. R. J. Hollingdale (Cambridge, England, 1988), whose title suggests a similar interest.

12. Before the novel, there was the theatre as a popular literary form. In his brilliantly argued book, *Worlds Apart: The Market and the Theatre in Anglo-American Thought, 1550–1750* (Cambridge, England, 1986), Jean-Christophe Agnew has explored the relation of the theatre to the emerging market economy from the sixteenth to the eighteenth centuries. Drawing upon a variety of disciplines he shows how the theatre, which was originally set up physically at the fair grounds, came to mirror and inspire a sense of changed and changeable forms of human relations in terms of the cash nexus. Monied exchange called into question settled statuses and values, raising doubts as to the nature of the self as well as of established society itself. Self became as speculative as the market transactions in which the self operates. And the dramatic representation, with its quickly shifting persona, served as a theatre of the real world as well as of the proscenium.

The theatre, one might add, was a *public* arena in which the competitive market could find its true nature and in which its economic actors might attempt to discover their authentic selves. What if authenticity, however, turned out to be a chimera? In that case, insincerity and display, rather than sympathy, it appears, could become the central motives of a mercantile stage. And at this point, the advocates of sympathy would turn readily to the novel, *private* and *sincere* in its nature. For an important treatment of the problem of sincerity, see Trilling, *Sincerity and Authenticity*.

13. David Marshall, *The Figure of Theatre: Shaftesbury, Defoe, Adam Smith, and George Eliot* (New York, 1986), 217. This is a fine treatment of the theme of sympathy, although its focus is on spectacle and the theatrical consequences of the subject.

14. Adam Smith, *The Theory of Moral Sentiments*, eds. D. D. Raphael and A. L. Macfie (Indianapolis, 1982), 9 and 24. See, also, Thomas Douglas Campbell, *Adam Smith's Science of Morals* (London, 1971).

15. Laurence Dickey, "Historicizing the 'Adam Smith Problem': Conceptual, Historiographical, and Textual Issues," *Journal of Modern History* 58, No. 3, Sept. 1986.

16. *The Theory of Moral Sentiments*, 21–22.

17. Richard F. Teichgraeber III, *"Free Trade" and Moral Philosophy: Rethinking the Sources of Adam Smith's Wealth of Nations* (Durham, N.C., 1986), 4. Focusing on Francis Hutcheson and David Hume as major influ-

ences on Smith's thought, this book studies his economic doctrine against a background of broad developments in early modern European thought, especially moral philosophy. In general, in recent years a great deal of new and important literature on Smith has appeared. Among others, see *Wealth and Virtue: Political Economy in the Scottish Enlightenment*, eds. Istvan Hont and Michael Ignatieff (Cambridge, England, 1983); see also the footnotes to Dickey, "Historicizing the 'Adam Smith Problem,'" for other important works.

18. Mary Shelley, *Frankenstein or, The Modern Prometheus*, ed. James Rieger (Chicago, 1982), 143.

19. Charlotte Brontë, *Shirley* (Harmondsworth, England, 1985), 115. Although I do not deal with it separately in what follows, the entire book is worth reading for its treatment of sympathy and our other themes. Also, in this connection, one might read Elizabeth Gaskell's *Life of Charlotte Brontë* (n.p., 1857).

20. Cf. David Potter, "American Women and American Character," in *History and American Society*, ed. Don E. Fehrenbacher (New York, 1973), where he wisely counsels us that in making any general statement about mankind we ask whether it also applies to women.

21. Brontë, *Shirley*, 82 and 363.

22. George Eliot, *Daniel Deronda* (Harmondsworth, England, 1967), 694.

23. *The Subjection of Women* (1864) was the title of John Stuart Mill's great philosophical treatment of the subject, where the basic ideas of what is now called the women's liberation movement are first explored. For my own treatment of some of these issues, see my *James and John Stuart Mill: Father and Son in the Nineteenth Century* (New York, 1976; ppr., New Brunswick, N.J., 1988), passim.

24. Brontë, *Shirley*, 116.

25. Ibid., 377. This quotation is an interesting anticipation of the thesis advanced by Thomas L. Haskell in his important and suggestive two-part article, "Capitalism and the Origins of the Humanitarian Sensibility," *American Historical Review* 90, Nos. 2 and 3 (April and June 1985).

26. Ronald Dworkin, "Report from Hell," *New York Review of Books*, July 17, 1986, p. 16.

27. Alfred Marshall, *Principles of Economics*, 8th Ed. (Philadelphia, 1982; 1st Ed. London, 1890), 38. For a discussion of the two possibilities latent in Marshall, one, the development of neo-classical economics, which neglects sympathy, and the other, of social economics, which includes it, see Neva Goodwin, *Social Economics: The Third Way* (Macmillan, England, forthcoming).

28. For a useful exposition of Comte's ideas along these lines, see *The Early Essays of Auguste Comte*, introd. by Ronald Fletcher (n.p., 1974).

29. I am indebted to G. S. Rousseau for recalling my attention to Haller, and making me see him in this connection. Another effort to give a "scientific" explanation for the differential propensities for sympathy was to

root the latter in phrenology, and locate it in the organ of comparison (see Brontë, *Shirley*, 76).

30. Social phenomena, as Comte remarked, "must be considered and cultivated as an entirely distinct science [from individual physiology], by reason of the progressive influence of generations upon each other. This influence, which in social physics is the preponderating consideration, cannot be rightly studied from the physiological point of view." Comte's conclusion was that the laws of one level of facts could not be explained by the laws of another (*The Early Essays of August Comte*, 21). For consideration of Comte's work as rooted more in biology than in mathematics, see the important article, "La Philosophie biologique d'Auguste Comte et son influence en France au XIXe siècle," by Georges Canguilhem in his *Etudes d'histoire et de philosophies des sciences* (Paris, 1983).

31. Reinhold Bendix, "Tradition and Modernity Reconsidered," *Comparative Studies in Society and History* IX (1966–67), 294.

32. Smith and the other Scottish economists and early sociologists, of course, were writing in the context of the general Enlightenment; but it is sometimes overlooked that the Man of self-interest is also the Man of the *philosophes*. Laplace, the great French physicist, had announced that, given knowledge of the location and motion of every particle in the universe he could predict every future state; in short, he would have perfect knowledge. No less is assumed by the economists for their rational self-interested Man. With each Man presumed to have perfect knowledge, his self-interested actions would insure both his individual well-being and that of society as well.

33. We are impelled to remember Sigmund Freud's query to Albert Einstein as to whether, in the end, "does not every science come . . . to a kind of mythology?" (*The Standard Edition of the Complete Psychological Works of Sigmund Freud*, ed. James Strachey (London, 1964), Vol. XXII, 211).

34. David Beetham, *Max Weber and the Theory of Modern Politics* (Cambridge, England, 1985 (1974)), 275.

35. The classic work is Arthur Lovejoy, *The Great Chain of Being* (Cambridge, Mass., 1953). For futher details, see Chapter 2.

36. Cf. William H. McNeill, *Mythistory and Other Essays* (Chicago, 1986).

37. In *Stone Age Economics* (New York, 1972), the anthropologist Marshall Sahlins outlines a picture in which it is early hunting-and-gathering Man who leads the affluent life. Thus, what can be called the prelapsarian myth may in fact have a grounding in reality. Yet even Sahlins goes on to show the inevitable way in which such a society moves from a purely domestic economy to primitive exchange; with further evolution more or less unavoidable.

38. See Neil McKendrick, John Brewer, and J. H. Plumb, *The Birth of a Consumer Society: The Commercialization of Eighteenth-Century England* (London, 1982), 30–31. This is a very important book for understanding a neglected aspect of the Industrial Revolution.

2. The Break

1. Thomas Carlyle, *Selected Writings*, ed. Alan Shelston (Harmonds-worth, England, 1980), 195 and next quote on 199.

2. Thomas Carlyle, *Sartor Resartus Heroes Past and Present* (London, 1910), 29, 58, 126, 146, 160, 161, and 162. Oddly enough, though the phrase "cash nexus" caught on, Carlyle himself seems never to have used it in that form, though he is certainly its source. His habitual phrasing is "cash payment," which then serves as the "nexus."

3. *Karl Marx and Frederick Engels: Collected Works* (New York, 1975–), 3, 457 and 461. (Hereafter referred to as MECW.)

4. Carlyle, *Selected Writings*, 199, and MECW, 4, 309, 329, and 426. But see Chapter 7 for an elaboration of Engels's views on the price paid by the workers for their "cosily romantic" situation. Incidentally, the word "idyllic" is often used today as synonomous with "edenic." In the nineteenth century, it almost always meant, as the OED reminds us, "full of natural simple charm or picturesqueness."

5. It is also possible that Engels actually wrote the passage on the cash nexus, and that Marx, as was his wont, simply incorporated it in his own version of the "Manifesto." My friend Arthur Mitzman suggests that Jules Michelet may have also influenced Marx in this regard. In *Le Peuple* (1846), Michelet, comparing his imaginary trip through the different strata of French society to the ascent of a mountain, having reached the bourgeois top writes, "J'atteins la région des neiges. La végétation morale disparaît peu a peu. . . . C'est comme un monde saisi en une nuit d'un froid subit d'égo-ïsme et de peur . . . c'est l'égoïsme pur du calculateur sans patrie; plus d'hommes, mais des chiffres. . . . Vrai glacier abandonné de la nature. . . . Qu'on me permette de descendre, le froid est trop grand ici pour moi, je ne respire plus." As Mitzman points out, Engels was in Paris in January 1846, when *Le Peuple* appeared, and Marx in Brussels, where Michelet's books were about as available as in Paris. I suspect, however, that Marx and Michelet were simply responding to the same imagery in the air; for direct influence, Engels was the sufficient source for Marx.

6. "The Spirit of the Age," in *Essays on Politics and Culture* by John Stuart Mill, ed. Gertrude Himmelfarb (Garden City, N.Y., 1963), 2.

7. *Troilus and Cressida*, Act I, Scene III. This is echoed in the seventeenth century, when John Bulwer observes that "All other creatures keep their ranks, their places and natures in the world, only man himself disorders all, and that by displacing himself, by losing his place" (quoted in Jean-Christophe Agnew, *Worlds Apart* (Cambridge, England, 1986), 96).

8. Arthur O. Lovejoy, *The Great Chain of Being* (Cambridge, Mass., 1953), 182.

9. These quotes are from *ibid.*, 232. Those that follow are from 8, 60, 80, and 81. See also pp. 253 and 326.

10. For an argument that Newton's science served as an ideology behind

which Latitudinarian religious and political interests could advance, see Margaret C. Jacob, *The Newtonians and the English Revolution: 1689–1720* (Ithaca, N.Y., 1976). Jacob's remark that "The ordered, providentially guided, mathematically regulated universe of Newton gave a model for a stable and prosperous polity, ruled by the self-interest of men. That was what Newton's universe meant to his friends and popularizers . . . " (18), suggests the way a universe of "self-interest," and all that follows from that conception, was being substituted for the Great Chain of Being's hierarchical community.

11. Adam Smith, *Essays on Philosophical Subjects* (Indianapolis, 1982), 38. The next quote is from p. 39.

12. *Ibid.*, 45–46, and 48. One major source of Smith's view of nature as a cosmic harmony is Stoic philosophy. Thus, in *The Theory of Moral Sentiments* (Indianapolis, 1982), he quotes Marcus Aurelius on the universe as "one immense and connected system . . . the whole machine of the world" (289).

13. Smith, *Essays on Philosophical Subjects*, 104. The next quote is from p. 66.

14. *Ibid.*, 44. Cf., for example, the second paragraph of the very first chapter of *The Wealth of Nations*, where Smith says, "The effects of the division of labor . . . will be more easily understood by considering in what manner it operates in some particular manufactures. It is commonly supposed to be carried furthest in some very very trifling ones . . . those employed in every different branch of the work can often be collected into the same workhouse, and placed at once under the view of the spectator. . . . In those great manufactures, on the contrary, which are destined to supply the great wants of the great body of the people, every different branch of the work employs so great a number of workmen that it is impossible to collect them all into the same workhouse. We can seldom see more, at one time, than those employed in one single branch. Though in such manufactures, therefore, the work may really be divided into a much greater number of parts than in those of a more trifling nature, the division is not nearly so obvious, and has accordingly been much less observed." Smith then proceeds to give the example of the division of labor in pin manufacturing.

15. "Our meddling intellect" is from "The Tables Turned," in *The Poetical Works of Wordsworth*, ed. Thomas Hutchinson (New York, 1933), 481. The long quote is from *Poetical Works*, ed. de Selincourt (Oxford, 1947–54), Vol. 1, pp. 12–13n. See also Wordsworth's lovely lines on Newton's prism face, Chapter 3 of our present book.

16. Cf. Thomas S. Kuhn, "Energy Conservation as an Example of Simultaneous Discovery," in *Critical Problems in the History of Science*, ed. Marshall Clagett (Madison, Wis., 1959), especially pp. 492–93.

17. Richard W. Burkhardt, Jr., *The Spirit of System: Lamarck and Evolutionary Biology* (Cambridge, Mass., 1977), 22–23.

18. See Madeleine Barthélemy-Madaule, *Lamarck: Ou le mythe du pré-*

curseur (Cambridge, Mass., 1982; orig. pub. Paris, 1979), 74. This is an important, though difficult, book, which argues that we must view Lamarck in his own right, and not as a precursor to Darwin. So viewed, Lamarck is an eighteenth-century man of the Enlightenment, to be evaluated in terms of the "cultural effects of the French Revolution" (21), as well as a pioneer of transformism. Of special interest to our theme is her comment about Lamarck's classification by series that "On the one hand, it allows him to become aware of the transformist idea; on the other, insofar as it is linear and continuous, it stands in a certain sense in the tradition of the earlier 'scales' or 'chains.' The concept therefore implies both a conceptualizing direction and an ideological survival" (58). Peter J. Bowler attempts to define and to place Lamarck in the framework of evolutionary theory in various of his books, *The Eclipse of Darwinism* (Baltimore, Md., 1983), *Evolution: The History of an Idea* (Berkeley, 1984), and *Theories of Human Evolution* (Baltimore, Md., 1986).

19. Burkhardt, *The Spirit of System*, 121.

20. *Ibid.*, 143.

21. Charles Darwin, *The Origin of Species* (London, 1951), xxii.

22. Burkhardt, *The Spirit of System*, 214.

23. See Robert E. Schofield, *The Lunar Society of Birmingham* (London, 1963).

24. Quoted in F. D. Klingender, *Art and the Industrial Revolution*, ed. Arthur Elton (New York, 1970), 40. See this work in general for interesting passages on Erasmus Darwin. For more standard treatments, see Desmond King-Hele, *Erasmus Darwin* (London, 1963), and Donald M. Hassler, *Erasmus Darwin* (New York, 1973). This last is an excellent study, emphasizing Darwin as a writer. Incidentally, he quotes Darwin as saying, ". . . the excessive study of novels is universally an ill employment at any time of life; not only because such readers are liable to acquire a romantic taste; and to return from the flowery scenes of fiction to the common duties of life with a degree of regret; but because the highwrought scenes of elegant distress display'd in novels have been found to blunt the feelings of such readers toward real objects of misery . . ." (79). As we shall see, the "industrial novelists," whom we shall be considering in Chapter 3, were writing partly with criticisms such as Erasmus Darwin's in mind, aware that they must counter the charge of novels serving as a distraction from real life.

25. Charles Darwin, *The Voyage of the Beagle* (London, 1960), 165 and 363.

26. Darwin, *Origin*, 554.

27. For a nice treatment of this matter, see Stephen Jay Gould, "Darwin's Middle Road," in *The Panda's Thumb* (New York, 1980), 65–66.

28. Darwin, *Origin*, 560; see also 551.

29. *Ibid.*, 548.

30. Darwin, *Voyage*, 229.

31. Cf. Ian Watt, *The Rise of the Novel* (London, 1957), and Lionel Trilling, *Sincerity and Authenticity* (Cambridge, Mass., 1974), for the roots of individualism in the seventeenth century.

I am treating individualism here in its broadest sense; more particularly, one can speak of possessive, utilitarian, expressive, and other forms of individualism. For a full discussion of the origins and meanings of individualism, see Steven Lukes, *Individualism* (Oxford, 1973). See, too, Nancy Rosenblum, *Another Liberalism: Romanticism and the Reconstruction of Liberal Thought* (Cambridge, Mass., 1987), especially 20–21. This book, which came late to hand, is implicitly a most interesting treatment of some of the themes we are considering.

For a provocative argument that individualism existed much earlier than most scholars claim, in fact, in the middle ages, see Alan Macfarlane, *The Origins of English Individualism* (New York, 1979), but also consult Stephen D. White and Richard T. Vann, "The Invention of English individualism: Alan Macfarlane and the Modernization of Pre-modern England," *Social History* 8, No. 3 (Oct. 1983), for an informed critique. *Reconstructing Individualism: Autonomy, Individuality, and the Self in Western Thought,* eds. Thomas C. Heller, Morton Sosna, and David Wellbery (Standford, 1986), attempts what its title suggests, but explicitly so only in the last essay, by Niklas Luhmann.

In *Discipline and Punish: The Birth of the Prison,* tr. Alan Sheridan (New York, 1979), Michel Foucault presents a very different perspective, a structuralist one, on the origins of individualism. He sees it as arising out of a "carceral" system, in which "Discipline 'makes' individuals" (170); or, as he further puts it, "The individual is no doubt the fictitious atom of an 'ideological' representation of society; but he is also a reality fabricated by this specific technology of power that I have called 'discipline'" (194). Certainly, Foucault's work is brilliant, and highly "individualistic," although its approach is not that of most students of individualism.

It would be of great interest to attempt a "structuralist" interpretation of our connections theme; to employ a systematic attention to what has come to be called "discourse analysis." For example, one might attempt to show how death rituals have changed: where an eighteenth-century person used to die in the midst of his family and in an atmosphere of religious consolation, today he meets his death in an impersonal hospital, his major "ties" being to the scientific apparatuses surrounding him. As Richard A. Etlin points out in his book, *The Architecture of Death: The Transformation of the Cemetery in Eighteenth-Century Paris* (Cambridge, Mass., 1984), even the cemeteries, once located next to the parish church, in the middle of the capital, were now moved to the outskirts of the city; thus, the relations between the living and the dead, both physically and symbolically, were broken. One could go on in this vein. However interesting the structuralist approach might be, it is not the one that I am generally employing here (although, without being overt about it, I hope that I have not been unaware of its possibilities).

32. Note that somewhat later, with Rousseau and others, solitude and isolation become a fulfillment rather than a threat. See Chapter 3. Perhaps we can also see in this reversal of attitudes a form of defense against the threat? (It is probably relevant that the shift to a view of solitude as something to be cherished coincides with the increased growth of cities.) W. H. Auden, *The Enchafèd Flood* (New York, 1967; original lectures in 1949), deals with the romantic iconography of the sea and the desert, and is idiosyncratically suggestive on the theme of solitude and isolation, especially in the third lecture. Harry Levin, *The Power of Darkness* (New York, 1958), in the course of treating of Hawthorne, Poe, and Melville, also has insights on solitude in the American context. Other such books could be cited, but a satisfactory overall treatment is still lacking. In fact, a whole book on the history of attitudes toward solitude and isolation could profitably be written.

33. Jean-Jacques Rousseau, *Emile, or On Education*, tr. Allan Bloom (New York, 1979), 184. Cf. Watt, *The Rise of the Novel*, 86.

34. Daniel Defoe, *Robinson Crusoe* (New York, 1961), 94.

35. *Ibid.*, 91 and 267.

36. Cf. Trilling, *Sincerity and Authenticity*, 24. Even though written in poetic form, Wordsworth's Prelude is, in fact, also an autobiography. See Chapter 3. There is, of course, an extensive literature on autobiography and its emergence as a modern Western genre.

37. The chapter titles are, in fact, not Defoe's, but later additions; nevertheless, they are true to the content.

38. Karl Marx, *Capital*, 2 vols., tr. Eden and Cedar Paul (London, 1951), I, 50–51. Marx's reading of the novel, my friend Arthur Mitzman suggests, would fit with an emphasis on its complex working-through of the conflict between traditional religious prohibitions of, and Weber-like inspirations to, capitalist economic activity.

39. Defoe, *Robinson Crusoe*, 205 and 236.

40. Watt, *The Rise of the Novel*, 92. Cf. my earlier remarks on the novel, Chapter 1, for the compatibility of this genre with the bourgeoisie.

41. Harold Perkin, "The Social Causes of the Industrial Revolution," in *Transactions of the Royal Historical Society*, 5th Series, Vol. 18 (London, 1968), 133.

42. See Bruce Mazlish, *James and John Stuart Mill: Father and Son in the Nineteenth Century* (New York, 1975), 67–74.

43. *Ibid.*, 68 for source of quote (emphasis added).

44. Adam Smith, *An Inquiry into the Nature and Causes of the Wealth of Nations*, eds. R. H. Campbell and A. S. Skinner (Indianapolis, 1981), 98.

45. Adam Ferguson, *An Essay on the History of Civil Society*, 1767 edition, ed. Duncan Forbes (Edinburgh, 1966), 19. At about the same time, Oliver Goldsmith, in "The Traveler" (1764), was expressing more or less the same idea in poetic form: "The independence Britons prize too high,/ Keeps man

from man, and breaks the social tie. . . . As nature's ties decay/ As duty, love, and honour fail to sway,/ Fictious bonds, the bonds of wealth and law,/ Still gather strength, and force unwilling awe." (Quoted in Watts, *The Rise of the Novel*, 64).

46. Quoted in H. J. Perkin, *The Age of the Railway* (London, 1970), 156–57. Scott's paragraph dates from 1820, and he may well have had Robert Owen's New Lanark in mind for his first example.

47. Friedrich Schiller, *Aesthetic Letters*, the Sixth, quoted in M. H. Abrams, *Natural Supernaturalism* (New York, 1977), 211.

48. Thomas Carlyle, *Past and Present*, in *The Works of Thomas Carlyle* (Centenary Edition) (London, 1896–99), X, 257, 186, 272–74, quoted in Abrams, *Natural Supernaturalism*, 311. See, however, our Chapter 3 for the distinction made by Wordsworth, another lamenter, between isolation as alienation, and isolation as solitude, to be welcomed.

49. Excellent books on the Industrial Revolution are Phyllis Deane, *The First Industrial Revolution* (Cambridge, England, 1965), David S. Landes, *The Unbound Prometheus* (Cambridge, England, 1969), E. J. Hobsbawn, *Industry and Empire* (New York, 1968), and T. S. Ashton, *The Industrial Revolution: 1760–1830* (London, 1948), which, though outdated, is still a useful short account.

50. Quoted in Edwin G. Burrows and Michael Wallace, *The American Revolution: The Ideology and Psychology of National Liberation* (Perspectives in American History) (Cambridge, Mass., 1972), Vol. VI. 1972), 287.

51. George Washington in *Speeches and Documents in American History*, ed. Robert Birley (London, 1951), Vol. I, 220, 222, 223.

52. All quotes are from William H. Sewell, Jr., *Work and Revolution in France* (Cambridge, England, 1980), 73, 75, and 76. For a statement similar to the last one quoted, cf. Charles I, in Michael McKeon, *The Origins of the English Novel, 1600–1740* (Baltimore, 1987), Ch. 5, p. 180. Incidentally, Parlement in France must be distinguished from Parliament in England; in France, the Parlement was a law court.

53. Wordsworth, XXVIII, "French Revolution," in *The Poetical Works of Wordsworth*, ed. Thomas Hutchinson (New York, 1933), 208.

54. Quoted in Sewell, *Work and Revolution in France*, 85. The quote that follows from Sièyes is on p. 80.

55. See William McNeill, *The Human Condition* (Princeton, N.J., 1980), 22, on the power of wars—as well as infectious diseases—to break down societies and the ties that bind them.

56. Perhaps a comparison with Robinson Crusoe's sudden turn to being an "absolute lord and lawgiver," once he had broken his own earlier dependencies, is in order here. On another side, one might consider Napoleon as the egoist who inspired individuals such as Carlyle to new ideas about the modern hero, charismatic in his powers. Such a consideration might then lead to thoughts about Carlyle's American admirer, Ralph Waldo Emerson, and his atomistic conception of the "I" ("eye") with nothing between it and

the cosmos. Some commentators accuse Emerson and the Transcendentalists of a failure "to appreciate the organic and necessary intermediate forms of community that go by the name of institutions" (I owe this last reminder to an exchange with Saul Touster). Along the same lines, Quentin Anderson speaks, in regard to Emerson and the Transcendentalists, of "The Imperial Self," in his book of the same name (New York, 1971).

Inasmuch as I would consider Carlyle (whom I treat in the next chapter) and Emerson as basically lamenters, these comments illustrate the complexity of reactions involved in the connections theme; for both Carlyle and Emerson in their transcending egoism also soar above the ordinary bonds connecting Men.

3. The Lament: Philosophers and a Poet

1. That term is first given public currency by Auguste Comte in the fourth volume of *Cours de philosophie positive* (1830–42), 47th lesson—though Alexis de Tocqueville, writing in the 1830s and 1840s, is often also considered a founder of the new field—but the fact is that sociology as a formal discipline does not really take shape until after the mid-19th century.

2. *The Writings and Speeches of Edmund Burke*, 12 vols. (Boston, n.d.), Vol. IV, 101. For Burke's connection with the argument about civic humanism, which in turn is related to the "ancient constitution" (see Chapter 1), see J.G.A. Pocock, "Burke and the Ancient Constitution: A Problem in the History of Ideas," in Pocock, *Politics, Language and Time* (New York, 1971).

3. Edmund Burke, *Reflections on the French Revolution*, ed. Thomas H. D. Mahoney (New York, 1955), 109. For the frequent use of filial images in this period, see Edwin G. Burrows and Michael Wallace, *The American Revolution*, passim.

4. Burke, *Reflections*, 110.

5. *Ibid.*, 88. Cf. Carlyle's "Mechanical Age" (Chapter 4) as well as Tönnies's "mechanical" usage (Chapter 8). Thomas Robert Malthus echoes Burke's distrust of "mechanical philosophy," and its effects on social connections, when he compares the scientific effort to force the growth of a flower to the point of bursting its calyx with the "forcing" of human development in terms of the French Revolution. As he remarks, "But an experiment with the human race is not like an experiment upon inanimate objects. The bursting of a flower may be a trifle. Another will soon succeed it. But the bursting of the bonds of society is such a separation of parts as cannot take place without giving the most acute pains to thousands: and a long time may elapse, and much misery may be endured, before the wound grows up again" (*Population: The First Essay* (Ann Arbor, Mich., 1959), 96–97).

6. Burke, *Reflections*, 55. The quotes that follow in this paragraph are on pp. 89, 53, 86, 91, and 56.

7. Smith, *The Theory of Moral Sentiments*, 232. For Burke's relations to Smith, see 26–28.

8. *Correspondence of the Rt. Hon. Edmund Burke, Between the Year 1744 and the Period of his Decease in 1797*, 4 vols., ed. Charles William, Earl Fitzwilliam, and Lt. Gen. Sir Richard Brooke, K.C.B. (London, 1844), Vol. III, 145.

9. Burke, *Reflections*, 69.

10. For my own early attempt to deal with the political paradoxes of Burke, see "The Conservative Revolution of Edmund Burke," *Review of Politics* XX, No. 1 (Jan. 1958), 21–33. For a recent attempt to deal with Burke as a complex, ambivalent person, see Isaac Kramnick, *The Rage of Edmund Burke: Portrait of an Ambivalent Conservative* (New York, 1977).

11. One scholar who does emphasize the similarities between Burke and Rousseau is Annie A. Osborn, *Rousseau and Burke* (New York, 1964).

12. Although, typical of his age, Rousseau often meant the male sex when he refers to "Man" or "Men," i.e., the human species, my capitalization of these terms is definitely meant to indicate the entire species.

13. A very good edition of the first two "Discourses" in English is that edited by Roger D. Masters, *The First and Second Discourses* (New York, 1964). Another handy edition is that of the Everyman's Library (London, 1947).

14. Jean-Jacques Rousseau, *Emile, or On Education*, tr. Allan Bloom (New York, 1979), 276, 83, and 277. This is an excellent translation. In speaking of Man as "king of the earth," Rousseau here reminds us of that side of Robinson Crusoe's social nature (see Chapter 2).

15. Jean-Jacques Rousseau, *The Social Contract and Discourses* (London, 1947), 163.

16. Rousseau, *Emile*, 221. The next quote is on p. 105. Rousseau, speaking of the solitary Man (in this case, is it properly man?), may well have had in mind the Biblical Adam before he was joined by Eve. Cf. T. H. Huxley's treatment of Adam as a "solitary man" who would quickly learn from nature, i.e., would come to shape his conduct "by the observation of the natural consequences of actions" ("A Liberal Education," quoted in U. C. Knoepflmacher, *Religious Humanism and the Victorian Novel* (Princeton, 1965), 33). In a different direction, cf. Carlyle's comment on the solitary state being one of wretchedness, Chapter 4. For actual observations on so-called "wild children," i.e., solitaries from early on, see Werner Stark, *The Social Bond* (New York, 1976), Vol. I. He quotes, for example, one observer of a feral child: "sensible . . . only of the crudest wants of animal nature, occupied with nothing but the taking of his food . . ." (118).

17. Rousseau, *Emile*, 185.

18. *Ibid.*, 214.

19. Kant uses the phrase "unsocial sociability" in his *Idea for a Universal History from a Cosmopolitan Point of View* (1784). By this phrase, expounded

in his short Fourth Principle, he means Man's drive to enter the social state as well as his resistance to that tendency; the latter threatens continually to dissolve society. These two tendencies of Man—to associate himself and to isolate himself—are, for Kant, innate. Because of the mutual struggle which consequently arises among all Men, Man avoids falling into a dull "Arcadian" life of harmony and happiness. "Man wants concord but nature knows better what is good for his kind; nature wants discord" (*The Philosophy of Kant*, ed. Carl J. Friedrich (New York, 1949), 121).

20. Rousseau, *Emile*, 357.

21. *Ibid.*, 43. The quote that follows is on p. 65.

22. *Ibid.*, 43.

23. Rousseau, "A Discourse on the Moral Effects of the Arts and Sciences," in *The Social Contract and Discourses*, 120–21.

24. Rousseau, *Emile*, 189. A comparison with Georg Simmel is in order here. See Chapter 9.

25. Rousseau, *Emile*. Cf. Carlyle's similar statement, quoted in Chapter 4, this book, and Marx's statement in *The Economic and Philosophic Manuscripts*, "Assume man to be man and his relationship to be a human one: then you can exchange love only for love . . ."; in short, not for purchase (*The Marx-Engels Reader*, ed. Robert C. Tucker, 2nd ed. (New York, 1978), 105.

26. Rousseau, "A Discourse on the Origin of Inequality," in *The Social Contract and Discourses*, 223.

27. Rousseau, *Emile*, 59 and 216. This notion of physical degeneracy in the cities is often portrayed in the early nineteenth century as being a result of the malignant effect of industrialization, as it sucks people off the land and into the city. It also figures at the end of the century and the beginning of the twentieth, for example, in psychological works on youth, as in G. Stanley Hall, *Adolescence*, 2 vols. (New York, 1904).

28. Rousseau, *Emile*, 194.

29. Rousseau, *The Social Contract and Discourses*, 11, 12, and 15.

30. *Ibid.*, 15.

31. *Ibid.*, 469.

32. Thomas McFarland, *Romanticism and the Forms of Ruin* (Princeton, N.J., 1981), 46.

33. M. H. Abrams, *Natural Supernaturalism: Tradition and Revolution in Romantic Literature* (New York, 1971).

34. Wordsworth, *Prelude*, III, 81–82, and VII, 725–26.

35. See Arthur O. Lovejoy, *The Reason, The Understanding and Time* (Baltimore, 1961).

36. Wordsworth, Sonnet XXXIII, lines 1–3, in *The Poetical Works of Wordsworth*, 259. The quote that follows is from Sonnet XXXVI, lines 4–8, *Ibid.*, 269.

37. Wordsworth, *Prelude*, VII, 115–18. The next quote is from this same work, I, 6–8.

38. Quoted in A. S. Byatt, *Wordsworth and Coleridge in Their Time* (London, 1970), 78 and 115.

39. Wordsworth, Sonnet XLV, lines 1–2 and 5, in *The Poetical Works,* 282.

40. Wordsworth, *Prelude,* XIII, 209 and 217–20. The next quote is from *The Excursion,* Book III, 915–18.

41. Wordsworth, *The Excursion,* IV, 961–64. In his "A Poet's Epitath," Wordsworth attacked the scientist as having a "pin-point of a soul," but removed the phrase at Charles Lamb's suggestion (Russell Noyes, *William Wordsworth* (New York, 1971), 83).

42. Wordsworth, *Prelude,* III, 61–63.

43. Wordsworth, "The Tables Turned," line 1, in *The Poetical Works,* 481.

44. Wordsworth, Preface to the "Lyrical Ballads," in Eugen Weber, ed. *Paths to the Present* (New York, 1960), 25.

45. Personal communication. In a very different vein, Thomas McFarland calls attention to "a radical paradox" in Wordsworth: as his contemporaries and others have perceived, he was both the supreme egoist, writing, as Hazlitt put it, "as if there were nothing but himself and the universe," and "emphatically the poet of community," as another critic observed (McFarland, *Romanticism and the Forms of Ruin,* 137–38). The beggar, it might be noted, also carries other connotations; as Russell Noyes comments, political economists and politicians "saw begging as a social nuisance, but Wordsworth did not want to see the state push the beggars off the road into the 'House misnamed Industry'" (*William Wordsworth,* 38).

46. Wordsworth, *The Poetical Works,* 205.

47. Wordsworth, *Prelude,* I, 1–5. The next two quotes are from the Preface to the "Lyrical Ballads," Weber, *Paths to the Present,* and "Tintern Abbey," lines 38–39, in *The Poetical Works,* 206.

48. Wordsworth, *Prelude,* XIV, 70–72 and 108–18.

49. *Ibid.,* VII, 512 and 524–28. The next quote is from X, 477–80.

4. The Lament: Prophets and Novelists

1. James Anthony Froude, *Thomas Carlyle: A History of the First Forty Years of His Life, 1795–1835,* 2 vols. (New York, 1882), II, 299. The quote starting "Vain hope . . ." is from II, 167, and the other two quotes in this paragraph are from "Past and Present," in Thomas Carlyle, *Sartor Resartus Heroes Past and Present* (London, 1910), 24.

2. "Signs of the Times," in *Thomas Carlyle: Selected Writings,* ed. Alan Shelston (Harmondsworth, England, 1980), 84. The quotes following are also from this source, pp. 77 and 64. In fact, the historian might argue that Carlyle's nineteenth century was more religious than the enlightened eighteenth century, if only in a kind of reaction.

3. Froude, *Thomas Carlyle,* II, 267. The quotes that follow are on p. 279.

4. *Ibid.*, 145.

5. See Chapter VIII in *Sartor Resartus*.

6. Froude, *Thomas Carlyle*, II, 179. The quote that follows is on p. 96.

7. *Sartor Resartus*, 46–47. See also Charles Dickens's *Hard Times* for his handling of the theme of wonder.

8. Tony Tanner, *The Reign of Wonder: Naivety and Reality in American Literature* (Cambridge, Eng., 1977), 6.

9. "Chartism," in *Thomas Carlyle: Selected Writings*, 188–89. The quote that follows is from "Past and Present," in *Sartor Resartus*, 13.

10. In *Sartor Resartus*, 83.

11. *Ibid.*, 82. "Tool-using animal" is from p. 27.

12. "Past and Present," in *Sartor Resartus*, 49. The quote that follows is from *Sartor Resartus*, 65.

13. *Sartor Resartus*, 115.

14. Froude, *Thomas Carlyle*, I, 78. The quotes that follow are from pp. 214, 310–11, and 187–88.

15. "Past and Present," in *Sartor Resartus*, 58.

16. *Ibid.*, 99. The quotes that follow are on pp. 136 and 138.

17. "Past and Present," in *Sartor Resartus*, 132. The quote that follows is on p. 160.

18. "Chartism," in *Thomas Carlyle: Selected Writings*, 159. The quote that follows is from Froude, *Thomas Carlyle*, II, 67.

19. "Chartism," in *Thomas Carlyle: Selected Writings*, 155.

20. *Ibid.*, 155–56.

21. Russell Noyes, *William Wordsworth* (New York, 1971), 48.

22. For Carlyle's way to his "novel," *Sartor Resartus*, see G. B. Tennyson, *Sartor Called Resartus: The Genesis, Structure, and Style of Thomas Carlyle's First Major Work* (Princeton, N.J., 1965). As Patrick Brantlinger points out, "In his essay called 'Biography,' Carlyle says that fiction is merely 'mimic Biography' and that genuine biography is to be preferred, especially to 'froth Prose in the Fashionable Novel.' Fiction, Carlyle continues, 'partakes . . . of the nature of *lying* . . .'" (*The Spirit of Reform: British Literature and Politics, 1832–1867* (Cambridge, Mass., 1977).

23. Quoted in Sheila M. Smith, *The Other Nation: The Poor in English Novels of the 1840s and 1850s* (Oxford, 1980), 44.

24. Benjamin Disraeli, *Sybil, or The Two Nations* (Harmondsworth, England, 1954), 301.

25. Cf. Kathleen Tillotson, *Novels of the Eighteen-Forties* (Oxford, 1954 and 1956), 78. For other treatments of the industrial novels, see Deidre David, *Fictions of Resolution in Three Victorian Novels: North and South, Our Mutual Friend, Daniel Deronda* (New York, 1981); Catherine Gallagher, *The Industrial Reformation of English Fiction: Social Discourse and Narrative Form 1832–1867* (Chicago, 1985); and Brantlinger, *The Spirit of Reform*.

26. Charles Kingsley, *Alton Locke: Tailor and Poet* (New York, 1983; orig. pub., 1850), 27.

27. Cf. David, *Fictions of Resolution*, 6.

28. Elizabeth Gaskell, *Mary Barton: A Tale of Manchester Life*, ed. Stephen Gill (Harmondsworth, England, 1970), 126.

29. *Ibid.*, 109.

30. In her characterization of Gaskell's realism, Catherine Gallagher says, "The 'real' reality for her does not lie behind human behavior in a set of scientific laws; it is on the very surface of life, and although it is often obscured by conventional modes of perception, it can be adequately represented in common language" (*The Industrial Reformation of English Fiction*, 65). For an overall, and brilliant, critical interpretation of *Mary Barton*, see Gallagher's Chapter 3, "Causality versus Conscience: The Problem of Form in *Mary Barton*."

31. Gaskell, *Mary Barton*, 460.

32. Elizabeth Gaskell, *North and South*, ed. Dorothy Collin (Harmondsworth, England, 1970), 122.

33. *Ibid.*, 296.

34. *Ibid.*, 168. The next three quotes are from pp. 169 and 525.

35. Benjamin Disraeli, *Sybil, or The Two Nations* (Harmondsworth, England, 1954), 73.

36. *Ibid.*, 145, 170 and 118.

37. *Ibid.*, 179 and 145.

38. *Ibid.*, 190. The irony is that while Disraeli speaks here of the "expiring idea of Home" one of the major characteristics of the Victorian period was its idealization of the family.

39. *Ibid.*, 380.

40. In fact, the effort to establish such a secret society was undertaken somewhat later by Cecil Rhodes; his chosen race was the Anglo-Saxon.

41. Hannah Arendt, *The Origins of Totalitarianism* (New York, 1958), 71. See pp. 68–79 for her overall treatment of Disraeli's racism. See, too, Isaiah Berlin, "Benjamin Disraeli, Karl Marx and the Search for Identity," in Berlin, *Against the Current* (New York, 1982).

42. Benjamin Disraeli, *Coningsby*, ed. by Thom Braun (Harmondsworth, England, 1983), 271.

43. Hitler, incidentally, might have taken a line in some of his speeches directly from Disraeli, who in the General Preface to the collected edition of his novels in 1870 proclaimed "the general influence of race on human action being universally recognized as the key to history" (quoted in the introduction by Thom Braun, *Coningsby*, 16).

44. George Eliot, *Felix Holt, The Radical*, ed. Peter Coveney (Harmondsworth, England, 1972), 29, 81 and quoted on p. 26.

45. For Eliot's life, see Gordon S. Haight, *George Eliot: A Biography* (New York, 1968), and Margharita Laski, *George Eliot and Her World* (London, 1973).

46. Thus, for example, in Eliot's novel, *Middlemarch: A Study of Provincial Life* (1872), Dorothea, believing that Mr. Casaubon's synoptical tabula-

tions, "The Key to All Mythologies," will unlock the portals to a past religious tradition, hopes that it will also offer "a binding theory which could bring her own life and doctrine into a strict connection with that amazing past and give the remotest sources of knowledge some bearing on her actions" (New York, 1964), Chap. 10, p. 86).

47. As she has her character Tertius Lydgate in *Middlemarch* say, "I find myself that it is uncommonly difficult to make the right thing work: there are so many strings pulling at once" (480). Reflecting this conception, the novel moves, as one critic so well puts it, through "the controlled motions of an unusually large number of characters, linked either by genealogical ties, or by those intricate causal 'relations' George Eliot calls the 'irony of events'" (U. C. Knoepflmacher, *Religious Humanism and the Victorian Novel* (Princeton, N.J., 1965), 72).

Suzanne Graver, *George Eliot and Community* (Berkeley, 1984), also makes this awareness of the tangled web central to her book, anticipating the point of view I am taking here. In addition, she notes the connection to the work of Tönnies, which I will take up later, though I shall do it in a more extended context. John Killham, "The Idea of Community in the English Novel," *Nineteenth-Century Fiction* 31, No. 4 (March 1977), anticipates us both in mentioning Eliot and Tönnies in the same breath, but does not carry out his comparison to any extent, being more interested in detailing his differences with Raymond Williams on the idea of community.

48. Eliot, *Felix Holt*, 614–15.

49. *Ibid.*, 615. Eliot also is aware of "connections" in its earlier, social sense as when in the very first chapter of *Middlemarch* she speaks of how "the Brooke connections, though not exactly aristocratic were unquestionably 'good . . .'" (9).

50. Quoted in Raymond Williams, *Culture & Society 1780–1950* (Garden City, N.Y., 1960), 117.

51. See Joseph Butlin, "The Pacification of the Crowd: From 'Janet's Repentance' to *Felix Holt*," *Nineteenth-Century Fiction* 35, No. 3 (Dec. 1980). Also, Peter Gay, "On the Bourgeoisie: A Psychological Interpretation," in *Consciousness and Class Experience in Nineteenth-Century Europe*, ed. John M. Merriman (New York, 1979), is a suggestive article. Gay's *The Bourgeois Experience*, Vol. 1: *Education of the Senses* (New York, 1984), in contrast, is disappointing, especially on the theoretical side, and, given its subject, unexpectedly dull. Yet one more such volume *(The Tender Passion)* has already appeared, and three more are to come! As critic Paul Johnson has observed (*Commentary*, June 1984), about Volume 1, "at bottom this book is a lot of miscellaneous information chasing a subject." That Gay, however, can write elsewhere compellingly and cogently, see his *Freud: A Life for Our Time* (New York, 1988).

52. Eliot, *Felix Holt*, 366. Eliot's fear of the mass became translated, in part, into a loss of faith in activist reform and the substitution for it of a

generalized belief in an amorphous "progress." Thus, Patrick Brantlinger writes, "Nowhere is the idea of the transformation of the idea of reform into progress and progressive evolution more strikingly registered than in George Eliot's novels" (*The Spirit of Reform*, 8). Philosophically, one might add, Eliot would have been inspired in this direction by Carlyle, Comte, Spencer, and others.

53. Eliot, *Felix Holt*, 29. The quotes that follow are from *Middlemarch*, 601, and *Letters*, I: 162, quoted in Basil Willey, *Nineteenth Century Studies: Coleridge to Matthew Arnold* (New York, 1966), 218.

54. Eliot, *Daniel Deronda*, ed. Barbara Hardy (Harmondsworth, England, 1967), 63 and 69.

55. *Ibid.*, 383 and 167.

56. *Ibid.*, 502.

57. Graver, *George Eliot and Community*, 10. Cf. the quote from Erasmus Darwin given in Chapter 2, footnote 24.

58. Eliot, *Daniel Deronda*, 413.

59. *Ibid.*, 507–8.

60. Gwendolin's utterance is in *Daniel Deronda*, 48. Eliot's remark is in Laski, *George Eliot and Her World*, 103, where an account is also given of Eliot's friendship with Deutsch. Eliot also knew Balfour, author of the future Balfour Declaration, but it is not clear what influence, if any, he had on her in regard to the Jewish Question (see further, Knoeplfmacher, *Religious Humanism and the Victorian Novel*, 123). Also, on the sources of inspiration for Eliot's "Jewish" interests, see William Baker, *Some George Eliot Notebooks* . . . , Vol. I, MS 707 (Salzburg Studies in English Literature, Salzburg, Austria, 1976).

61. Eliot, *Daniel Deronda*, 592, 587, 413, and 587. Ezra Cohen, in whose house Mordecai lives, and who deals in watches and jewelry, might well be the prototypic Jewish "huckster"—interestingly enough, Eliot applies that term only to his counterpart of "the purest English lineage" (443)—but is presented instead as simply a vulgar but warm-hearted family man and member of society.

62. *Ibid.*, 424 and 802. Writing to Harriet Beecher Stowe, Eliot declared, "There is nothing I should care more to do, if it were possible, than to rouse the imagination of men and women to a vision of human claims in those races of their fellow-men who must differ from them in customs and beliefs" (quoted in Gillian Beer, *Darwin's Plots: Evolutionary Narrative in Darwin, George Eliot and Nineteenth-Century Fiction* (London, 1983), 199. Thus, the bonds of community are to stretch across all of humanity. In this light, Eliot's "racism" can be seen as another form of Christianity (even embracing the Jews).

63. Graver, *George Eliot and Community*, 27.

64. *The Works of George Eliot* (Edinburgh and London, 1885), Vol. 12: *Essays*, 189–90 and 193.

65. *Ibid.*, 295 and 223. It is a nice touch to observe that Riehl, so to speak, anticipated a return of the favor when he claimed that the time had come when statesmen should add novels to their program of instruction, meaning that fiction might be a better means of grasping the reality of community than intellectual or legal forms; in his comments on "socialen Romans" he instanced especially Walter Scott and Eugene Sue (*Die Bürgerliche Gesellschaft* (Stuttgart und Tübingen, 1851), 18–20).

66. Eliot, *Essays*, 209 and 208.

67. Gordon S. Haight, *George Eliot: A Biography* (New York, 1968), 271. On the country-city theme, cf. Raymond Williams, *The Country and the City* (New York, 1973).

68. See Lynn Barber, *The Heyday of Natural History* (London, 1980), for a description of the craze. In *Mary Barton*, Job Legh, an ordinary workman of Manchester, is depicted as a devotee of natural history, and Gaskell, remarking that factory hands often have their Newton's *Principia* open at the loom, adds, "It is perhaps less astounding that the more popularly interesting branches of natural history have their warm and devoted followers among this class" (*Mary Barton*, 75). Eliot herself, in her *Notebooks*, entered three pages of close observations on clouds and two pages on trees (lime, ash, and elm), whose detail would make any natural historian feel at home. See Joseph Wiesenforth, "George Eliot's Notes for ADAM BEDE," *Nineteenth-Century Fiction* 32, No. 2 (Sept. 1977), 144–48.

69. Quoted in F. O. Matthiessen, *American Renaissance* (New York, 1941), 15–16. In his first book, *Nature* (1836), Emerson declared that "The use of natural history is to give us aid in supernatural history: the use of the outer creation, to give us language for the beings and changes of the inner creation . . . ," which suggests that, at bottom, his conception is more in line with Carlyle's than with the later George Eliot's. The danger of regarding human beings as a subject for natural history can be illustrated by a remark of Thomas Jefferson, where he says, "To our reproach, it must be said that though for a century and a half we have had under our eyes the races of black and red men, they have never yet been viewed by us as subjects of natural history" ("Notes on the State of Virginia," in *The Portable Thomas Jefferson*, ed. Merrill D. Peterson (Harmondsworth, England, 1983, 192)). Although Jefferson was pro-Indian, others used his natural history approach—Indians were "vermin"—to justify exterminating them. One wonders, too, whether Jefferson would have also wished to view whites as "subjects of natural history." In any case, he never did.

70. Eliot's remark about Emerson is quoted in Laski, *George Eliot and Her World*, 32. The quotes from *Adam Bede* (Harmondsworth, England, 1980) are on pp. 294 and 308. It is entirely appropriate that the great "naturalist" Charles Darwin read *Adam Bede* on its appearance and, in his book lists, marked it "excellent" (Gillian Beer, *Darwin's Plots* (London, 1983), 266, n. 4). Eliot did not return the favor. On first reading Darwin's *Origin* she wrote

in her journal, "We began Darwin's work on The Origin of Species tonight. It seems not to be well written: though full of interesting matter, it is not impressive, from want of luminous and orderly presentation" (Beer, *Darwin's Plots*, 156).

71. There is also the danger that mere natural history, a kind of literary realism, based on impersonal observation, might "over-distance" us from the phenomena, as discussed earlier. In fact, however, Eliot went beyond natural history in her idea of science, and thus of social science. As Sally Shuttleworth points out, Eliot moved from natural history to experimental physiology as the source of her scientific inspiration, with a consequent effect on her narrative structure as well as her social vision. Hence *Adam Bede* represents the concrete observation of natural history, while *Daniel Deronda* represents the stress on imagination and "fiction" (the term supplied to Eliot by G. H. Lewes) required by the organismic theories of experimental physiology (Sally Shuttleworth, *George Eliot and Nineteenth-Century Science*, Cambridge, England, 1984). See also, George Levine, "George Eliot's Hypothesis of Reality," *Nineteenth-Century Fiction* 35, No. 1 (June 1980), for an elegant anticipation of some of Shuttleworth's ideas.

72. In addition to Riehl's own work, cf. George Mosse, *The Crisis of German Ideology* (New York, 1964), 19–23.

73. It is worth noting that, as R. Jackson Wilson tells us, ". . . the first American books to carry the word 'sociology' in their titles were defenses of slavery" (*In Quest of Community: Social Philosophy in the United States* (New York, 1968), 24). The books were Henry Hughes's *A Treatise on Sociology, Theoretical and Practical*, and George Fitzhugh's *Sociology for the South*, both appearing in 1854. Even in America, however, future work in sociology scanted the racial bond.

74. Charles Kingsley, *Alton Locke* (New York, 1983), 103.

75. Quoted in Gallagher, *The Industrial Reformation of English Fiction*, 132 and 135. For the persistence of the stereotype of the Jew as the proprietor of dress shops, subjecting or luring Christain girls into slavery, see Edgar Morin, *Rumour in Orleans*, tr. Peter Green (New York, 1971), where an account is given of a 1960s' outbreak of an hysterical reaction. Gareth Stedman Jones, in more sober tones, describes the growth of the sweating industry and the Jewish role therein in *Outcast London* (Harmondsworth, England, 1984; orig. 1971).

5. Fictions and Facts

1. Martineau's first tale (33 others followed) appeared in 1832 and "within a few weeks sold thousands of copies; by 1834 the monthly sale of the series had reached ten thousand" (Mark Blaug, *Ricardian Economics* (Westport, Conn., 1973; orig. pub. 1958), 129). (Blaug claims that Dickens's

novels had a sale of only two or three thousand copies, though this is obviously off the mark.) As for Martineau's first "illustration," "Life in the Wilds," it is a "tale" of a group who is left in the wilds of South Africa after an attack by Bushmen (whose actions are justified by the author), without tools, food, etc., and who have to learn to survive and find their way back to the making of artifices *and* the construction of society solely through their own efforts. In my view, it is a direct counterpart of *Robinson Crusoe*, only in the nineteenth century and with a group instead of a single individual as its protagonist; it is also very readable, especially at the level of children. (See Harriet Martineau, *Illustrations of Political Economy*, No. 1: *Life in the Wilds: A Tale* (Boston, 1832).

2. Charles Dickens, *Hard Times*, eds. George Ford and Sylvere Monod (New York, 1966), 303. For the importance of *Hard Times* first appearing in *Household Words*, and an analysis of its readership and its expectations, see Joseph Butwin, "*Hard Times:* The News and the Novel," *Nineteenth-Century Fiction* 32, No. 2 (Sept. 1977), who asserts that "the reader who meets the novel in the journal comes away with a quite different impression of the meaning of the fiction than the reader of the hard-cover volume called *Hard Times for the Times*" (174). As for the actual debate over accident legislation and the arguments pro and con, see Anthony Howe, *The Cotton Masters 1830–1860* (Oxford, 1984), 188.

3. Dickens, *Hard Times*, 304.

4. Igor Webb, *From Custom to Capital: The English Novel and the Industrial Revolution* (Ithaca, N.Y., 1975), 177. Such a reading of Jane Austen is not an obvious one; indeed, it was not my own first reading. However, books such as Marilyn Butler, *Jane Austen and the War of Ideas* (Oxford: 1975) and Julia Prewitt Brown, *Jane Austen's Novels: Social Change and Literary Form* (Cambridge, Mass., 1979), make the persuasive case that Jane Austen was really an author very much concerned with the social changes going on around her. Butler also emphasizes how Austen's awareness grew and was more openly exhibited in her later novels. Austen, for Butler, was on the conservative side of the "War of Ideas," and thus closer in spirit to our lamenters than to the breakers. Brown, emphasizing Austen's attention to the "War of the Sexes," places a more radical gloss on her novels, or at least their feminist effects. See, too, Irene Tayler, "Afterword: Jane Austen Looks Ahead," in *Fetter'd or Free?: British Women Novelists, 1670–1815*, eds. Mary Anne Schofield and Cecilia Macheski (Columbus, Ohio, 1985), 426–33.

5. Black is quoted in David McCloskey, "The Rhetoric of Economics," *Journal of Economic Literature* XXI (June 1983), 503.

6. Dickens, *Hard Times*, 218 and 219.

7. Even today, many neo-classical economists proceed in their work as if rational, profit-maximizing economic Man were a reality instead of a theoretical model and/or prescription.

8. Henry Sumner Maine, *Ancient Law* (Gloucester, Mass., 1970; orig. pub. 1861), 305 and 46.

9. *Ibid.*, 163.

10. *Ibid.*, 353.

11. Quoted in Theodore M. Porter, "The Mathematics of Society: Variation and Error in Quetelet's Statistics," *British Journal for the History of Science* 18 (1985), 51.

12. Quoted in Theodore M. Porter, "A Statistical Survey of Gases: Maxwell's Social Physics," *Historical Studies in the Physical Sciences* 12:1 (1981), 80. For an account of the early development of statistics that emphasizes its political purpose, which is presumably to introduce a form of science— envisaged by its originators, John Graunt and Willian Petty, as a new version of Hobbes's Leviathan authority—that would serve in place of what otherwise would be passion, interest, faction, and party, see Peter Buck, "Seventeenth-Century Political Arithmetic: Civil Strife and Vital Statistics," *ISIS* 68, No. 241 (1977), 67–84.

13. Quoted in Steven Marcus, *Engels, Manchester, and the Working Class* (New York, 1974), 66. For more on "Filthy Lucre" in a psychological vein, see Norman Brown, *Life Against Death* (New York, n.d.; orig. pub. 1959), Part Five. Note that Edwin Chadwick and other Utilitarian-inspired reformers were at the forefront of the sanitation movement in the 1830s, and thus active at the time Tocqueville was writing.

14. Peter Laslett, *The World We Have Lost* (London, 1965), 22 and 31.

15. W. D. Rubinstein, "Wealth, Elites and the Class Structure of Modern Britain," *Past and Present* (Aug. 1977), 99. Cf. R. S. Neale, "Class and Class-Consciousness in Early Nineteenth-Century England: Three Classes or Five?," *Victorian Studies* (Sept. 1968), who argues for five classes: Upper, Middle, Middling, Working A, and Working B Class; nevertheless, he joins Rubinstein in dividing the middle class into two.

16. Rubinstein, "Wealth, Elites and the Class Structure of Modern Britain," 107, and John Foster, *Class Struggle and the Industrial Revolution* (New York, 1974), 104. For an excellent review of Foster's important book, see Gareth Stedman Jones, *Languages of Class: Studies in English Working Class History, 1832–1982* (Cambridge, England, 1983), 25–75.

17. For more on this general topic, see especially Martin J. Wiener, *English Culture and the Decline of the Industrial Spirit, 1850–1980* (Cambridge, England, 1981), and Arnold Thackray, "Natural Knowledge in Cultural Context: The Manchester Model," *American Historical Review* 79, No. 3 (June 1974). Howe, *The Cotton Masters, 1830–1860*, claims that his sample, while investing in land, did so only in relatively small numbers (about 11%), and more for purposes of financial return than for status reasons (29–32). He does not believe that many of them (he estimates at most 20%) chose to leave their mills for landed existence (44). Between them, Wiener and Howe present an interesting case study in the use of literary, i.e., subjective, materials and statistical and prosopographical materials.

18. Howe, *The Cotton Masters*, studies 351 textile masters, on whom

information is available, out of an estimated total of 1,500 partners in textile mills in 1835 rising to approximately 4,000 by 1860. His data undermines the myth of the self-made cotton magnate, while recognizing a few such individuals; more typical, for example, is the fact that of the 48 masters who entered the trade between 1800–1819, "twenty-three were the sons of cotton entrepreneurs" (9). Howe's book is a mine of detailed information, though his wider focus is on the cotton master's role in politics and society. On the self-made cotton master, cf. Jones, *Languages of Class*, 38, who makes the same point as Howe.

19. Gareth Stedman Jones, *Outcast London: A Study in the Relationship Between Classes in Victorian England* (Harmondsworth, England, 1984; orig. pub. 1971), raises a number of interesting questions in this regard. On his account, London, basically a pre-industrial city (for its economic and geographical situation was initially inappropriate for the introduction of steam-powered factory production), was driven, instead, to the sweating system, especially in the garment industry. Here, with the prevalence of "casual labor," the worst features of the "cash nexus" were to be encountered. Here, we are faced with a demoralized working class, separated from its middle-class employers (and upper-class patrons). Jones speaks of "the immense geographical gulf which had grown up between the rich and poor of London . . . nowhere had the process of segregation been carried further than in London" (247). Ironically, the orderly Lancashire operatives were held up as a model in comparison to the disorderly London mob (243). The solution proposed at the time is one familiar to us: the rich, declared contemporaries, should come to know and involve themselves more with the poor (229); as one member of a wealthy Whig family put it, the need was for the "substitution of human sympathy . . . for the cash nexus" (258). This is the world depicted in such novels as Charles Kingsley's *Alton Locke*. It is Dickens's world, too. Yet, dominated as it apparently is by the cash nexus, it is not really the world of industrial capitalism and the factory (though certainly affected powerfully by it). In fact, it may have been the *absence* of the industrial factory that made for the worst cash-nexus features of mid-Victorian England.

20. Sidney Pollard, *The Genesis of Modern Management: A Study of the Industrial Revolution in Great Britain* (Cambridge, Mass., 1965), 161 and 6–7. This is a seminal book, giving attention to an important side of the Industrial Revolution often overlooked.

21. W. Cooke Taylor, *Notes of a Tour in the Manufacturing Districts of Lancaster* (1842), 4–6, quoted in E. P. Thompson, *The Making of the English Working Class* (New York, 1966), 190–91.

22. Benjamin Love, *The Handbook of Manchester* (Manchester, 1842), 100.

23. Quoted in Patrick Joyce, *Work, Society and Politics: The Culture of the Factory in Later Victorian England* (New Brunswick, N.J., 1980), 134.

24. Robert Owen, *A New View of Society and Other Writings* (London, 1949), 96, and Frontspiece.

25. See Neil McKendrick, "Josiah Wedgwood and Factory Discipline," *Historical Journal* IV (1961), reprinted in *The Rise of Capitalism*, ed. David Landes (New York, 1966), 67.

26. See John Seed, "Unitarianism, Political Economy and the Antinomies of Liberal Culture in Manchester, 1830–50," *Social History* 7, no. 1 (January 1982), 8.

27. Reach is quoted in Howe, *The Cotton Masters*, 46, and Taylor in David Roberts, *Paternalism in Early Victorian England* (New Brunswick, N.J., 1979), 179.

28. Jones, *Languages of Class*, 28, 29, 50, 36 and 70.

29. Alexis de Tocqueville, "Memoir on Pauperism" (1835), in *Tocqueville and Beaumont on Social Reform*, ed. Seymour Drescher (New York, 1968), 18. For a fuller discussion of this subject, see Howard Newby, "The Deferential Dialectic," *Comparative Studies in Society and History* 17 (1975), and Jones, *Outcast London*, Chapter 13, "The Deformation of the Gift: The Problem of the 1860s."

30. E. P. Thompson, "Eighteenth-Century English Society: Class Struggle Without Class?," *Social History* 3, No. 2 (May 1978), points out that "paternalist values are [always] seen as 'antique'" (137). As Thompson goes on, each generation and each century looks back to an earlier time, discerns it as "paternalist," and laments the declension in values. (A comparison with Williams, *The Country and the City*, on a similar process in regard to the virtues of the "country", is apt here.)

31. Roberts, *Paternalism in Early Victorian England*, is a useful but somewhat frustrating book for our purposes. His model of paternalism—with four basic assumptions, authoritarian, hierarchic, organic, and pluralistic—might seem to rule out utilitarian and other types of cotton masters almost by definition; but then he includes them as paternalists. So, too, after describing the model paternalism of Titus Salt's factory village of Saltaires, with its 3,000 operatives, Roberts remarks, "There were not many Saltaires in Britain. There were not even many Ashworths, Gregs, and Ashtons [other enlightened, paternalistic mill owners]. There were, however, in the United Kingdom, 4,800 cotton and woollen mills, thousands of collieries, and even more thousands of workshops and small manufactures" (180–81). But later in the book he writes, "Just how many landlords, millowners, and clergymen were as conscientious as Carlisle, Salt, and Jerram is not known. Model paternalists no doubt formed a small minority. But the more research I did into paternalism the larger the minority became . . ." (274). Thus, while it is clear that Roberts believes paternalists to be in a minority—in fact, he claims that cruel mill owners were an even larger minority—he offers no real estimate of any of the numbers involved. For a hint at these we have to go to Howe, *The Cotton Masters*, who also gives us some suggestions as to the

waxing and waning of paternalist attitudes over time (e.g., 163; see also 270–73), as well as discussing the masters' philanthropic activities as a form of their paternalism extended from the factory to the urban community (308).

32. Seed, "Unitarianism, Political Economy and the Antinomies of Liberal Culture in Manchester," 20. It must be noted that Seed is studying the Unitarians, whose religion may have encouraged attitudes found in the middle-class family and projected outward in a manner not favored as much by other creeds.

33. Cf. the important article by Thomas L. Haskell, "Capitalism and the Origins of the Humanitarian Sensibility," *American Historical Review* 90, Nos. 2 and 3 (April and June 1985).

34. Cf. Joyce, *Work Society and Politics*, xx. On the other hand, the middle-class encouragement to self-help and self-respect among the working class operated as a mitigating, although contradictory, force. As Howe wisely remarks, "In this, the textile master differed significantly from the paternalist social policy of his European counterparts" (307).

35. Howard Newby, "The Deferential Dialectic," *Comparative Studies in Society and History* 17 (1975), 158.

36. Joyce's thesis is attacked by H. I. Dutton and J. E. King, "The Limits of Paternalism: The Cotton Tyrants of North Lancashire, 1836–54," *Social History* 7, No. 1 (Jan. 1982), 59–74, as "rather too sweeping a generalization"; instead, they argue, employer paternalism failed to develop as desired by many contemporaries, workers were more independent than Joyce allows for, and class warfare therefore more widespread than in his account. Only after 1854, they claim, and really not until the 1870s, was an acceptable accommodation reached.

37. Although Max Weber might not have it so, in fact many of the cotton masters were Anglicans, not Dissenters, and their paternalism was inspired by Anglican Toryism.

38. It may be that this actual social development, and the fading of the cash-nexus metaphor into the background, is the context for Weber's emancipation of sociology from its embrace; or perhaps Weber's theory and the practical development are simply coincidental.

6. Backgrounds and Bridges

1. Thomas L. Haskell, *The Emergence of Professional Social Science: The American Social Science Association and the Nineteenth-Century Crisis of Authority* (Bloomington, Ill., 1977), 1.

2. Especially important in this regard is Gilles-Gaston Granger, *La Mathématique sociale du Marquis de Condorcet* (Paris, 1956). See also my *The Riddle of History* (New York, 1966), Chapter IV, "Condorcet."

3. For a treatment of Tocqueville and Comte in this light (as well as Montesquieu), see, for example, Raymond Aron, *Main Currents in Sociological Thought*, Vol. I: *Montesquieu, Comte, Marx, Tocqueville* trs. Richard Howard and Helen Weaver (New York, 1967).

4. In a private communication, Robert Nisbet claims that Bonald "wrote—somewhere in his *Collected Works*—an essay on the rural family compared with the rural-industrial that is an acceptable imago for not only all of subsequent rural-urban sociology but Gemeinschaft-Gesellschaft as well."

5. It is interesting to observe the debate between equality and racism, mentioned earlier, played out in Tocqueville's correspondence with Gobineau. In Tocqueville's view, Gobineau's "principal idea" is a "sort of fatalism . . . a close relative of the purest materialism" (Alexis de Tocqueville, *"The European Revolution" and Correspondence with Gobineau*, ed. John Lukacs (Garden City, N.Y., 1959), 224 and 227).

6. Alexis de Tocqueville, *Democracy in America*, tr. George Lawrence, ed. J. P. Mayer (Garden City, N.Y., 1969), 507–8. An excellent book, giving the background for Tocqueville's writing of his great work, is James T. Schleifer, *The Making of Tocqueville's "Democracy in America"* (Chapel Hill, N.C., 1980). A very suggestive article is François Furet, "Naissance d'un Paradigme: Tocqueville et le Voyage en Amérique (1825–1831)," *Annales*, 39th Année, No. 2 (Mars-Avril 1984); see especially p. 231 for an interesting comparison of Chateaubriand and Tocqueville.

7. Tocqueville, *Democracy in America*, 552. The next quote is on p. 538.

8. Alexis de Tocqueville, *Recollections*, tr. George Lawrence, eds. J. P. Mayer and A. P. Kerr (Garden City, N.Y., 1971), 79. The quote that follows is on p. 124. A recent book by William M. Reddy, *The Rise of Market Culture: The Textile Trade and French Society, 1750–1900* (Cambridge, England, 1984), calls into question the actual industrialization of France at this time. Reddy's argument is that, in fact, a competitive labor market never emerged, even among factory workers; only the rhetoric of "market culture" came into being at the time.

9. Tocqueville, *Democracy in America*, 12.

10. See, especially, *The Young Hegelians: An Anthology*, ed. Lawrence S. Stepelevich (Cambridge, England, 1983).

11. Quoted in Basil Willey, *Nineteenth Century Studies: Coleridge to Matthew Arnold* (New York, 1949), 225.

12. Quoted in Sidney Hook, *From Hegel to Marx*, 2nd ed. (Ann Arbor, 1962; 1st ed., 1950), 222–23.

13. Karl Marx, *The Communist Manifesto*, any edition.

14. For arguments, however, about Marx's positivism, see the various chapters on this subject in *After Marx*, eds. Terence Ball and James Farr (Cambridge, England, 1984).

15. For a brief sketch of the details of the development of sociology, see,

for example, Steven Lukes, *Emile Durkheim* (New York, 1972), 396–97. For a fuller treatment, see Geoffrey Hawthorn, *Enlightenment and Despair: A History of Sociology* (Cambridge, England, 1976), though actually its author appears to despair of sociology. For a more exhaustive account, see *A History of Social Analysis*, eds. Tom Bottomore and Robert Nisbet (New York, 1978). For the story in a single country, France, see Terry Nichols Clark, *Prophets and Patrons: The French University and the Emergence of the Social Sciences* (Cambridge, Mass., 1973).

16. Robert A. Nisbet, *The Sociological Tradition* (New York, 1966), identifies five basic "Unit Ideas of Sociology," of which community is the first (the others are authority, status, the sacred, and alienation). As he remarks, "The most fundamental and far-reaching of sociology's unit-ideas is community" (47). In addressing the overall theme of connections, Nisbet's is an important book to read.

17. The way in which the term "socialist" entered modern discourse is interesting in this regard. Apparently the first to use the term in the vernacular was the Italian Ferdinando Facchinei. Facchinei acquired the term from the Latin, where it had been used by a German Benedictine, Anselm Desing, to describe the current of natural law which, as Franco Venturi sums it up, "placed the *socialitas*, the social instinct of man, at the very base of all natural law. According to the Catholic polemicist, these thinkers, these 'socialists' ended up by removing all religious elements from their vision of society, and by considering every human action solely from the point of view of society, ignoring revelation, religion and the church. He believed that this led the 'socialists' to resemble the 'naturalists,' or even the Hobbesians. . . ." When used in 1765 by Facchinei in regard to his countryman and reformer, Cesare Beccaria, "It no longer referred simply to someone who considered sociability as a constituent and primordial element in man. Inevitably it came to mean a writer who wanted a society of free and equal men, and who had been inspired by Rousseau" (Franco Venturi, *Utopia and Reform in the Enlightenment* (Cambridge, England, 1971), 103–4. See, too, Hans Müller, *Ursprung und Geschichte des Wortes "Sozialismus" und Seiner Verwandten* (Hanover, 1967), 35–36. Incidentally, as Müller tells us, Facchinei was also a Benedictine.

18. Steven Seidman, *Liberalism & the Origins of European Social Theory* (Berkeley, 1983), also gives support for my general thesis; as he remarks, "whereas Anglo-American social theory emerged as part of the triumph of liberal civilization, European social theory was elaborated in the context of the failure of liberalism, and developed, in part, as its critique" (13). Cf. also his statement, "This work presupposes a distinction between a European and Anglo-American theoretical tradition" (6).

Reba N. Soffer, *Ethics and Society in England: The Revolution in the Social Sciences 1870–1914* (Berkeley, 1978), challenges Abrams's and my thesis. She claims that "Modern social science developed before World War I. . . .

The role of the English in this development has been either totally ignored or summarily dismissed" (1) (Abrams's book appeared in 1968; he hardly seems "summarily" to dismiss the English theorists). While admitting that "J. W. Burrow has provided a remarkable interpretation of Victorian social thought in his *Evolution and Society: A Study in Victorian Social Theory* (Cambridge, 1966)," Soffer explicitly disagrees with his conclusion that "'England made no distinctive contribution to the rethinking of the fundamental concepts of social thought at the turn of the century'" (261). Instead, Soffer argues that Alfred Marshall, William James, and Graham Wallas "were unquestionably 'revolutionary'" (3), and carried out a theoretical revolution in the social sciences. Clearly, there is a bit of an apples and oranges problem here—sociology and social science are not synonomous—but even on her own grounds I find Soffer's book weak. One catches the flavor of her thinking from a statement such as "Thinkers such as Weber, Freud, Durkheim, and Croce *succumbed* to a psychological *malaise* that acknowledged, reluctantly, irrational forces underlying even the most rational behavior and institutions. While it can hardly be denied that the Europeans built more formidable theoretical structures than the English, their melancholy revelation of irrationality resulted ineluctably in a deterministic and pessimistic social theory severed from social practice" (italics mine) (1–2). See also Soffer's article, "The Revolution in English Social Thought, 1800–1914," *American Historical Review* 75 (Dec. 1970).

James T. Kloppenberg, *Uncertain Victory: Social Democracy and Progressivism in European and American Thought, 1870–1920* (New York, 1986), is a much more informed and thoughtful book—a truly impressive work of scholarship—whose ideas bear in a general way on our topic. Again, he does not treat of sociology per se, although he devotes much attention to Max Weber, but is concerned to relate social theory, as exemplified, for example, in William James, Wilhelm Dilthey, T. H. Green, and John Dewey, to programs of social democracy and progressivism. Implicitly, therefore, if not explicitly, he is validating the presumably more empirical Anglo-American tradition against the theoretical leanings of Continental sociology (Durkheim is mentioned once in the text, in passing, and Tönnies and Simmel not at all, and Kloppenberg's interest in Weber is as political man as much as theorist). Now, there is no reason for Kloppenberg to write a different sort of book; by the same token, my interests, obviously, lie in a different direction, one which leads me to follow Abrams in his account of British sociology.

19. Philip Abrams, *The Origins of British Sociology: 1834–1914* (Chicago, 1968), 36.

20. On this subject, see also Burrow, *Evolution and Society*.

21. See Clark, *Prophets and Patrons*, for further material on Le Play and his role in French sociology.

22. An excellent book on Hobhouse is Stefan Collini, *Liberalism and Soci-*

ology: L. T. Hobhouse and Political Argument in England 1880–1914 (Cambridge, England, 1979), which places Hobhouse in the context of his times, and shows how in the controversy over "individualiam and collectivism" he pursued his liberalism in a "collective" direction that eventually took the form of an evolutionary sociology. Unlike Abrams, Collini sees Hobhouse as part of the problem, and not a propitious starting point, then aborted, for the development of British sociology. Collini's work, incidentally, further confirms my argument for the necessary jump across the Channel in order to pursue connections into sociology. See also his "Sociology and Idealism in Britain 1880–1920," *Archives Européenes de sociologie* XIX (1978).

23. See J.Y.D. Peel, *Herbert Spencer: The Evolution of a Sociologist* (New York, 1971).

24. Talcott Parsons, *The Structure of Social Action*, Vol. I (New York, 1968), 3.

7. Revolutionary Sociology: Engels and Marx

1. The standard biography is Gustav Mayer, *Friedrich Engels* (London, 1936), an abbreviated translation of the original two-volume work. See also, Stephen Marcus, *Engels, Manchester, and the Working Class* (New York, 1974), useful for a sketch of Engels's life and a literary analysis of Engels's *The Condition of the Working Class in England in 1844* (1845).

2. For a beginning of this re-examination, see John M. Sherwood, "Engels, Marx, Malthus, and the Machine," *American Historical Review* 90, No. 4 (Oct. 1985); G. Stedman Jones, "Engels and the History of Marxism," in *History of Marxism*, Vol. I, ed. Eric Hobsbawn (Bloomington, Ind., 1982); Terrell Carver, *Engels* (New York, 1981); and Norman Levine, *The Tragic Deception: Marx contra Engels* (Santa Barbara, Calif., 1975). Carver and Levine tend to see Engels as having perverted and diverted the pure stream of Marxism, while the other authors depict Engels in a much more positive light.

3. *Karl Marx, Frederick Engels Collected Works* (New York, 1976), Vol. 4, 215. (hereafter *MECW*).

4. *Ibid.*, 245–46 and 244.

5. *Ibid.*, 254 and 255.

6. *Ibid.*, 262.

7. The quote from Tocqueville is given in Marcus, *Engels, Manchester, and the Working Class*, 62; that from Carlyle on p. 35 of the same book. In general, see Tocqueville's *Journeys to England and Ireland*, ed. J. P. Mayer (New Haven, 1958), 104–9, for material to compare his and Engels's observations on Manchester.

8. Engels, *Karl Marx, Frederick Engels Collected Works*, 366. Peter Gaskell, no relation to Elizabeth, was a Liberal who deplored the "conditions" as much as did Engels, but proposed reform as the solution. Elizabeth Gas-

kell also read him and, indeed, derived one episode of *Mary Barton*, the murder of a mill owner by John Barton, from her namesake's reportorial account.

9. *MECW*, 4, 309.

10. *Ibid.*, 322.

11. *Ibid.*, 334 and 329.

12. *Ibid.*, 426 and 393. For a different view of the ruling class, as indeed broken into three classes—the upper, middle and middling—see, as previously cited, R. S. Neale, "Class and Class-Consciousness in Early Nineteenth Century England: Three Classes or Five?," *Victorian Studies* XII, No. 1 (Sept. 1968).

13. For a contrasting view, see John Stuart Mill's essay on Arthur Helps, *The Claims of Labor* (1844), where Mill asserts that "The claims of labor have become the question of the day" and, indeed, that the efforts by the middle and upper classes to improve the workers' situation has taken on the aspect of a "new fashion." Mill's point is that neither philanthropy nor paternalism is the proper cure; instead, taking a hard-headed (but not hard-hearted) Malthusian position, he argues that the bourgeoisie's beneficent impulses must be harnessed to correct policy, which should aim at bringing the laborers into a less rather than more dependent position ("The Claims of Labor," in *Dissertations and Discussions*, 5 vols. (New York, 1874), Vol. II, quote on p. 261).

14. *MECW*, 4, 418, 578, and 419. For some incisive comments on Engels's claims, see Sherwood, "Engels, Marx, Malthus, and the Machine."

15. *MECW*, 4, 298, and 525.

16. *Ibid.*, 563–64. See Ferdinand Tönnies, *Karl Marx: His Life and Teachings*, trs. Charles P. Loomis and Ingeborg Paulus (East Lansing, Mich., 1974), 18, for a commentary.

17. *MECW*, 581.

18. Once imbibed by Engels, the "Marxist" doctrine could, it is true, be developed into a "scientific socialism" that was even more rigid than perhaps intended by its original author. On this reading, Engels removed the "humanist" elements of the early Marx in order to give the later nineteenth-century Marxist movement a dogmatic, "scientific" bent beyond that implicit in Marx's own handling of it. See, for example, Leszek Kolakowski, *Main Currents of Marxism*, Vol 1: *The Founders*, tr., P. S. Falla (New York, 1978), 399ff. for a philosophical discussion of the alleged difference between Marx's anthropocentrism and Engels's naturalistic evolutionism.

19. Anthony Giddens, *Capitalism and Modern Social Theory: An Analysis of the Writings of Marx, Durkheim and Max Weber* (Cambridge, England, 1971), 15. On page 18, Giddens himself makes the addition of *The German Ideology*.

20. See, for example, the earlier citation of *The Young Hegelians*, ed. Stepelevic, which also contains a useful bibliography; David McClellan, *The Young Hegelians and Karl Marx* (London, 1969); Sidney Hook, *From Hegel to*

Marx (New York, 1958); and Karl Löwith, *From Hegel to Nietzsche* (Garden City, N.Y., 1967; orig. 1941)).

21. Tönnies, *Karl Marx: His Life and Teachings,* notes this tendency and quotes an American editor of the *Tribune* who wrote to Marx in 1860 about his contributions to the paper: "The only fault . . . you have occasionally exhibited too German a tone of feeling for an American newspaper . . . and too great anxiety for the unity and independence of Germany" (54–55).

22. *The Marx-Engels Reader,* 2nd ed., ed. Robert C. Tucker (New York, 1978), 58.

23. *Ibid.,* 53.

24. See, for example, Marx's writings in 1842 in *MECW,* Vol. 2.

25. *The Marx-Engels Reader,* 64, 65 and 64.

26. See, however, the brilliant essay by Isaiah Berlin, "Benjamin Disraeli, Karl Marx and the Search for Identity," in Berlin, *Against the Current* (New York, 1980). For a suggestive but heavyhanded and non-empathic treatment of Marx's Jewishness, see Gertrude Himmelfarb, "The 'Real' Marx," *Commentary* (April 1985), which is a "review-essay" of my book *The Meaning of Karl Marx* (New York, 1984), where I stress Marx's Protestantism rather than just his Jewishness. Julius Carlebach, *Karl Marx and the Radical Critique of Judaism* (London, 1978) is a full-scale, scholarly treatment of its subject.

27. *The Marx-Engels Reader,* 35 and 43. In the last sentence quoted, Marx has clearly glimpsed the idea of the cash nexus, even though he doesn't use that phrase until, borrowing it from Engels, he will employ a version of it in *The Communist Manifesto.*

28. *The Marx-Engels Reader,* 52.

29. *Ibid.,* 86 and 145.

30. *Ibid.,* 136–37. A problem with Marx's formulation is that "corresponding" quickly becomes "determining," i.e., if two societies are in the same stage of production, etc., they can be assumed to have the same classes, etc.

31. *Ibid.,* 140. For full statements of Marx's materialist interpretation of history, see, for example, Giddens, *Capitalism and Modern Social Theory,* G. A. Cohen, *Karl Marx's Theory of History: A Defense* (Princeton, N.J., 1978), and William Shaw, *Marx's Theory of History* (Stanford, 1978).

32. Giddens, *Capitalism and Modern Social Theory,* 37. Amidst the extensive literature on Marx's theory of class, see Frank Parkin, *Marxism and Class Theory: A Bourgeois Interpretation* (New York, 1979), whose viewpoint is clearly given in its title.

33. Adam Smith, *The Wealth of Nations,* Book I.

34. Marc Bloch, *Feudal Society,* tr. L. A. Manyon (Chicago, 1962), xvii.

35. *The Marx-Engels Reader,* 211.

36. *Ibid.,* 84. A year or so earlier, in a letter (September 1843) to Arnold Ruge, Marx had ridiculed "philosophers [who] have had the solution of all riddles lying in their writing-desks" (*MECW,* 3, 142).

37. See *The Economic and Philosophic Manuscripts* in *The Marx-Engels Reader*, 105.

38. Karl Marx, *Pre-Capitalist Economic Formations*, tr. Jack Cohen, ed. E. J. Hobsbawm (London, 1964), 96.

39. *The Marx-Engels Reader*, 197.

40. *Ibid.*, 491.

8. Academic Sociology: Ferdinand Tönnies

1. Stephen Marcus, *Engels, Manchester and the Working Class* (New York, 1974), 247, quoting Marx-Engels *Werke*, XXX, 343.

2. An essay on color in the Industrial Revolution would serve as a useful background here. Smoke from the factories, for example, is seen as hiding the sun and casting a gray pall on the whole atmosphere in which Man existed. The black or "colorless" clothes of the middle class is in accord with the "deadly" atmosphere of the factories and urban cities. And so forth.

3. Robert Nisbet, *The Sociological Tradition* (New York, 1966), 47.

4. *Ferdinand Tönnies: On Social Ideas and Ideologies*, ed. E. G. Jacoby (New York, 1974), 208. (It is worth noting Tönnies's lingering admiration for the "Natural History" approach here.) Fritz Ringer, *The Decline of the Mandarins: The German Academic Community, 1890–1933* (Cambridge, Mass., 1969) says, ". . . Tönnies himself was never attached to any of the reactionary arguments which others derived from his theory" (167). While this may reflect Tönnies's later position, his own words in *Gemeinschaft und Gesellschaft* would seem to undercut Ringer's sweeping statement. For Tönnies's later views, see, too, Ringer, p. 168.

5. Jacoby, *Ferdinand Tönnies*, 189.

6. For consideration of some of these forces, however, see Terry Nichols Clark, *Prophets and Patrons: The French University and the Emergence of the Social Sciences* (Cambridge, Mass., 1973), and Ringer, *The Decline of the Mandarins*.

7. Mack Walker, *German Home Towns: Community, State, and General Estate, 1648–1871* (Ithaca, 1971). For our purposes, this is a most useful book, and I have mainly followed its account.

8. See the sections on Germany in David S. Landes, *The Unbound Prometheus* (Cambridge, England, 1969). His footnotes give further references, to both German and English texts. Also Theodore S. Hamerow, *Restoration, Revolution, Reaction: Economics and Politics in Germany 1815–1871* (Princeton, N.J., 1958). Certainly, as Hamerow points out, by mid-nineteenth century "The growth of an industrial working class in Germany . . . [was] considerably slower than in England or France" (17).

9. Ferdinand Tönnies and Friedrich Paulsen, *Briefwechsel 1876–1908*, eds. Olaf Klose, Eduard Georg Jacoby, Irma Fischer (Kiel, 1961), 152, 201, and 146. Cf. Arthur Mitzman, *Sociology and Estrangement: Three Sociologists*

of Imperial Germany (New York, 1973), 91 and 92, which first led me to these letters. I offer a long quote from another of these letters to give the full flavor of Tönnies's thought processes and prose at this point in his life. Writing to Paulsen about the "serenity" of the Middle Ages, he declares: "It was just the time of the maturing and flowering of our people. This is increasingly my conviction, especially on the basis of economic considerations. That is romanticism. Yes, it is romanticism. And I am also of the opinion that we must combine romanticism and rationalism into a higher synthesis; that doesn't mean a mixing in actuality as occurred since the 30's toward the end of our entire present era—instead, rationalism must come to the fore, entirely clean and authentically. However, in our theoretical observations— the ethical, sociological and historical-philosophical—we can admit the romantic mode of thinking to the point that we duly appreciate the moral *force* of religion vis-à-vis those which reason has proved valid somewhere in the history of man. I don't here mean rational or sensible religion, that is: religion combined with a fully scientific way of thinking, such as is possible perhaps in the case of individuals. We shouldn't measure the thinking processes of our people—that is, principally people who do physical work—by our own thoughts which evolved from motives developed through a long, complicated educational process. I refer instead to the inimical, indifferent, unscientific actual superstitious religion. True, one can attribute much evil to it, yet one must keep clearly in mind that—albeit in changing forms—it accompanied the historical experience of the life of peoples until now, as long as it rested on healthy and sensible economic and social conditions (at least when so fashioned by its *nucleus*). I mean those very ones that also were destroyed or spoiled or became a lie or subject of ridicule" (Oct. 30, 1879, in *Briefwechsel*, 61). (Whatever smoothness exists in the translation, I owe to Peter Wyden; I might add that after the sentence, "Yes, it is romanticism," the rest of the quotation in the original is *one* sentence, which I have broken up where possible.)

10. Ferdinand Tönnies, *Community and Society* (in German, *Gemeinschaft und Gesellschaft*) tr. and ed. Charles P. Loomis (New York, 1963), 1.

11. For a treatment of Hobbes and the historical context in which he wrote, see Quentin Skinner, "The Context of Hobbes's Theory of Political Obligation," in *Hobbes and Rousseau*, eds. Maurice Cranston and Richard S. Peters (Garden City, N.Y., 1972). The other essays in this collection are also worth reading and supply in their footnotes many of the further references on Hobbes that one might want to pursue. C. B. Macpherson, *The Political Theory of Possessive Individualism: Hobbes to Locke* (Oxford, 1962), and the debate occasioned by it (I find myself skeptical of his assertions) is especially of interest. Tönnies's book, *Hobbes, Leben und Lehre* (Stuttgart, 1896), has remained untranslated into English.

12. Thomas Hobbes, *Leviathan* (Oxford, 1955), 21.

13. Thomas Hobbes, *English Works*, 11 Vols., ed. Sir William Molesworth (London, 1839–45), Vol. VII, 183.

14. Quoted in Ferdinand Tönnies, *Karl Marx: His Life and Teachings*, tr. Charles P. Loomis and Ingeborg Paulus (East Lansing, Mich., 1974), xv.

15. Tönnies, *Community and Society*, 102. The subtitle of the first edition (Leipzig, 1887) is "A Treatise on Communism and Socialism as Empirical Forms of Culture." In the second edition, 1902, this was changed to "Basic Concepts of Pure Sociology." Loomis's translation, inexplicably, does not include the Preface to the first edition, which is concerned with, among other things, rationalism and empiricism, and acknowledges, besides Kant, Comte, Spencer, Schaeffle, A. Wagner, Sir Henry Maine, Bachofen, Morgan, O. Gierke, and Karl Marx as major influences on Tönnies's work.

16. Tönnies, *Karl Marx*, xvi, 81 and 156.

17. Quoted in Mitzman, *Sociology and Estrangement*, 85.

18. Tönnies, *Community and Society*, 1.

19. In Germany, specifically, Tönnies could draw on such previous thinkers as Christian Wolff and Justus Moser, as well as the historical jurists Karl Friedrich Eichhorn and Friedrich Carl Von Savigny (see further Walker, *German Home Towns*, passim).

20. Tönnies, *Community and Society*, 37, 192, 48, and 41. Tönnies's *Gemeinschaft*, incidentally, where members have no identity separate from the whole, reminds us of Rousseau's society of the general will, with the difference that the latter is a modern consensus, whereas Tönnies's society is basically of the past.

21. *Ibid.*, 77 and 65.

22. *Ibid.*, 35.

23. *Ibid.*, 134.

24. *Ibid.*, 127.

25. *Ibid.*, 130.

26. *Ibid.*, 165 and 168. Burke's calculating comment is given in Chapter 3.

27. *Ibid.*, 151.

28. *Ibid.*, 166.

29. *Ibid.*, 173.

30. *Ibid.*, 216.

31. *Ibid.*, 221. For the comment on state socialism, see 217.

32. *Ibid.*, 231. A comparison with Max Weber and his treatment of civilization and charisma (see Chapter 11) is in order here.

33. *Ibid.*, 205.

34. *Ibid.*, 34. For opposition to typology-making of the general kind Tönnies was involved in, see Carlo Antoni, *From History to Sociology: The Transition in German Historical Thought*, tr. Hayden V. White (Detroit, 1959), and my review-essay of this book in *History and Theory* I, No. II (1961), 219–27.

35. Karl Marx, *Capital*, 2 Vols., tr. from 4th Ger. ed., Eden and Cedar Paul (London, 1951), Vol. I, p. 392, n. 2. For interpretations of Vico along the lines set forth here, see my *The Riddle of History: The Great Speculators from Vico to Freud* (New York, 1966), Chapter II, and Isaiah Berlin, *Against*

the Current: Essays in the History of Ideas (Harmondsworth, England, 1982), which reprints two of his essays on Vico.

36. Tönnies and Paulsen, *Briefwechsel,* 58 and 241–242.

37. Quoted from Karl Marx, *Capital,* in Tönnies, *Community and Society,* 233.

38. Cf. *Ferdinand Tönnies: A New Evaluation. Essays and Documents,* ed. Werner J. Cahnman (Leiden, 1973), and Werner J. Cahnman, "Tönnies and Social Change," *Social Forces* 47, No. 2 (Dec. 1968).

39. For an exposition of how Tönnies influenced later sociologists, especially American sociologists—for example, Louis Wirth and Edward Ross both acknowledged Tönnies's formative influence, most obviously in their construction of dichotomies similar to *Gemeinschaft* and *Gesellschaft*—see Thomas Bender, *Community and Social Change in America* (New Brunswick, N.J., 1978), passim and 15–23. Bender, too, sees these theories as offering "a logic of history rather than a historically grounded account of social change" (25).

9. Academic Sociology: Georg Simmel

1. In fact, Simmel preferred the term "sociation," or "societalisation" *(Vergesellschaftung),* as referring to the forming of relationships, rather than the reified term "society" *(Gesellschaft).* Tönnies, incidentally, reviewed Simmel's first book, *On Social Differentiation (Über Sociale Differenzierung. Soziologische und Psychologische Untersuchungen)* (1890), remarking on the "unfinished" nature of the work.

2. *Georg Simmel: On Individuality and Social Forms,* ed. Donald N. Levine (Chicago, 1971), 339 and 147. Here, in the stranger, we have a sociological counterpart of Wordsworth's Cumberland Beggar—but with what a world of difference both as to the content of the role and the evaluation to be placed upon it.

3. This argument is advanced in spite of the view held by many present-day scholars that sociology is a "conservative" reaction; such are the paradoxes of intellectual history. Both views, of course, are partially right.

4. Quoted in *George Simmel,* ed. Lewis A. Coser (Englewood Cliffs, N.J., 1965), 38–39. It should also be said for Schaefer that he was espousing political history versus cultural history, as part of a controversy among German historians at the time, in his attack on Simmel. For the Wilhelmine setting, cf. Fritz Ringer, *The Decline of the Mandarins* (Cambridge, Mass., 1969), and see Barbel Wallisch-Prinz, "A Sociology of Freedom: Georg Simmel's Theory of Modern Society" (Dissertation, Bremen, February 1977), an eccentric but suggestive interpretation of Simmel, seeking to situate him in the context of Wilhelmine society, which he is seen as both representing and transcending.

5. *Georg Simmel*, ed. Coser, 51.

6. For a defense of Simmel as a structuralist, see *A History of Sociological Analysis*, eds. Tom Bottomore and Robert Nisbet (New York, 1978), 590. For the counter-argument, see F. H. Tenbruck, "Formal Sociology," in *Georg Simmel*, ed. Coser, 81ff.

7. *Georg Simmel*, ed. Levine, 336 and 325. (A comparison with Durkheim's *The Divison of Labor* is in order here, for the French thinker talks about the city in similar terms. See Chapter 10.)

As one scholar sums up Simmel's inspirations in this matter, identifying the intellectual roots of his emphasis on evolutionary struggle and increasing specialization, "The *young Simmel* starts out from pragmatism, social Darwinism, Spencerian evolutionism and the principle of differentiation." Then he adds, "Fechner's atomism and Spencer's 'determinate differentiation' lead him . . . to the problem of the individual" (M. Landmann, quoted in David Frisby, *Sociological Impressionism: A Reassessment of Georg Simmel's Social Theory* (London, 1981), 15).

8. Paul Honigsheim, quoted in Arthur Mitzman, *Sociology and Estrangement* (New York, 1973), 32. For details of Simmel's involvement with George and his circle, see Frisby, *Sociological Impressionism*. This book is one of the most interesting recent contributions in English to Simmel studies. Frisby's emphasis is on Simmel as a "modernist," i.e., a part of modernist culture, with its characteristics of fragmentation, impressionism, relativism, etc. (cf. Marshall Berman, *All That Is Solid Melts into Air* (New York, 1982), and Frisby stresses Simmel's use of the feuilleton and essay form to convey the fleeting images of his society (a comparison with Baudelaire is in order here). For an excellent review of Frisby's book, see Harry Lieberson's review essay in *History and Theory* XXIII, No. 2 (1984). Frisby is also the author of a short book, *Georg Simmel* (London and New York, 1984), which is at present the best single overview of its subject.

9. Georg Simmel, *The Philosophy of Money*, tr. Tom Bottomore and David Frisby (London, 1978), 4. This is a brilliant translation. Donald N. Levine, *The Flight from Ambiguity* (Chicago, 1985), Chapter 6, "Ambivalent Encounters: Disavowals of Simmel by Durkheim, Weber, Lukács, Park, and Parsons," is a penetrating examination of how, in fact, Simmel's intellectual estate was handled by some of his heirs. The entire book should be read.

10. Among those who were strongly influenced by Simmel we can name George Lukács, who began a study of his writings in 1904 and then attended his lectures in 1909–10; Walter Benjamin; and, in America, Robert Park, one of the founders of the Chicago school of sociology. Others were Ernst Bloch and Karl Mannheim.

11. As almost every commentator has noted, Simmel was a brillant lecturer whose performances became a social event attended by many highborn non-academics. Needless to say, such popularity did not endear him to many of his academic colleagues.

12. Simmel, *Philosophy of Money*, 82. Of course, it is exactly this assertion that was challenged by the conditions of the early Industrial Revolution, where many observers believed that all the gains of increasing productivity were monopolized or "expropriated" by the capitalist. See p. 84 for Simmel's further discussion of exchange as productive. The notion of "productive" and "unproductive" work runs through the formulations of the early-nineteenth-century classical economists, often to bedevil the subject because it frequently confuses economic and moral judgments. It is in this context that Simmel's comment must be understood.

13. *Ibid.*, 289. Cf. a similar formulation in Albert Hirschman, "Against Parsimony: Three Easy Ways of Complicating Some Categories of Economic Discourse," *Bulletin of the American Academy of Arts and Sciences*, XXXVIII, No. 8 (May 1984).

14. *Georg Simmel*, ed. Levine, 45.

15. Simmel, *Philosophy of Money*, 101 and 146.

16. *Ibid.*, 175.

17. *Ibid.*, 142. In fact, chimpanzees seem to exhibit a similar "intellectuality" as do Men in this regard. In an experiment where poker chips were substituted for food—ten chips, for example, as equal to one banana—the chimps learned to work for the chips as rewards, apparently aware of their later convertibility.

18. *Ibid.*, 102. See Frisby, *Sociological Impressionism*, 23–24 and 72 for the inspiration of Darwin and Spencer on Simmel.

19. Simmel, *Philosophy of Money*, 198.

20. *Ibid.*, 200 and 415.

21. *Ibid.*, 174 and 209.

22. *Ibid.*, 211.

23. *The Sociology of Georg Simmel*, tr. Kurt Wolff (Glencoe, Ill., 1950), 75.

24. *Ibid.*, 77, cf. 76. Also *Georg Simmel*, ed. Levine, 26.

25. Karl Marx, *Pre-Capitalist Economic Formations* (London, 1964), 96. Wallisch-Prinz, *A Sociology of Freedom*, sees Simmel as mainly offering a "complementary commentary to Karl Marx's analysis of capitalism" (4), and emphasizes the "dialectical" tension in Simmel. These are views I cannot share.

26. Simmel, *Philosophy of Money*, 56.

27. *Ibid.* Perhaps the work of the present-day German sociologist Jürgen Habermas can be looked at in these terms. See Thomas McCarthy, *The Critical Theory of Jürgen Habermas* (Cambridge, Mass., 1978). (Simmel, incidentally, in his earlier years had inclined to a mild form of socialism.)

28. Simmel, *Philosophy of Money*, 113–14. Although Simmel's first attempt at a doctoral dissertation was rejected—it was on the psychology and ethnology of music, and condemned by no less an authority than Helmholtz—he did obtain his degree with an accepted dissertation on Kant.

29. *Ibid.*, 283. Cf. 332.

30. See Kant's *Idea for a Universal History from a Cosmopolitan Point of View* (1784).

31. *Georg Simmel*, ed. Levine, 4.

32. *Ibid.*, 7.

33. *Ibid.*, 14–15.

34. *The Sociology of Georg Simmel*, tr. Wolff, 59.

35. "Conflict," in *Georg Simmel*, ed. Levine, especially 74. See, also, *Georg Simmel*, ed. Coser, 11.

36. Simmel, *Philosophy of Money*, 166.

37. For an emphasis, however, on the sensibility side, see Frisby, *Sociological Impressionism;* inasmuch as sociology is a "science" of a very special sort, sensibility, as I have tried to suggest throughout this book, enters into it intrinsically.

10. Academic Sociology: Emile Durkheim

1. For details, see Steven Lukes, *Emile Durkheim: His Life and Work, A Historical and Critical Study* (New York, 1972). On Durkheim's religious background, see especially 44. Lukes's book is fundamental for a consideration of Durkheim's whole life. Also, for a discussion of Durkheim's ideas, as much from the viewpoint of intellectual history as history of sociology, see Dominick LaCapra, *Emile Durkheim: Sociologist and Philosopher* (Chicago, 1985), which gives as well an up-to-date bibliography for those interested in pursuing Durkheim for his own sake. Talcott Parsons's treatment of Durkheim in his *The Structure of Social Action* (New York, 1968) (1937)) is classic, though highly controversial. LaCapra, for example, confesses to "a hidden polemic against the orthodox, liberal-conservative uses made of Durkheim by Talcott Parsons . . ." (ix).

2. The Davy quote is from "Emile Durkheim," *Revue française de Sociologie* I (1960), 6.

3. An excellent and detailed account of the nature of "bourgeois" France and consequent politics is Theodore Zeldin, *France 1848–1945*, 2 vols. (Oxford, 1973), especially Vol. I: Ambition, Love and Politics.

4. Terry Nichols Clark, *Prophets and Patrons: The French University and the Emergence of the Social Sciences* (Cambridge, Mass., 1973), gives a full account of its subject. Clark points out that it was Louis Liard, Director of Higher Education, who, after "an important conversation with Durkheim concerning republicanism, science and secular morality" encouraged him to move toward the social sciences and was instrumental in securing Durkheim's fellowship to study in Germany (see pp. 97 and 163).

5. See Lukes, *Emile Durkheim*, 86–87.

6. Emile Durkheim, "Organisation et vie du corps social selon Schaeffle," in *Revue philosophique* 20 (1885), 85. Reprinted in *Emile Durkheim:*

Textes, ed. Victor Karady, 3 vols. (Paris, 1975), Vol. I, 355–77; the quote cited is on p. 356. Durkheim remarks that Schaeffle's book "est une sorte de statique sociale. Comte n'a consacré à cette partie de la science qu'une leçon de son cours (50e). Spencer s'est surtout occupé de l'évolution des societés. Schaeffle s'est proposé de soumettre à l'analyse les nations actuelles, et de les résoudre en leurs principaux éléments" (355). *Textes* is an invaluable collection of Durkheim's more "occasional" writings: reviews, articles, conference reports, etc., giving summaries of them as well. Vol. I groups the materials on "Eléments d'une théorie sociale," Vol. II on "Religion, morale, anomie," and Vol. III on "Fonctions sociales et institutions"; it also includes a complete bibliography of Durkheim's works.

7. Review of Ludwig Gumplowitz, *Grundriss der Soziologie,* in *Revue philosophique* 20 (1885), reprinted in *Textes,* Vol. I, 344–54; the quote is on p. 344.

8. See Clark, *Prophets and Patrons,* 171–72 and 178. For Durkheim's sociological reviews in *L'Année sociologique,* see *Emile Durkheim: Contributions to L'Année Sociologique,* ed. Yash Nandan (New York, 1980). There is much debate about Durkheim's role in the *Année* group; thus, whereas Clark says Durkheim was authoritarian (185), Philippe Besnard describes his position as simply first among others, with Durkheim "not in any way a master gathering around himself zealous disciples . . ." (*The Sociological Domain:* The Durkheimians and the Founding of French Sociology, ed. Philippe Besnard (Cambridge and Paris, 1983), 17).

9. In Durkheim's review of Simmel's *The Philosophy of Money,* in *Emile Durkheim,* ed. Nandan, we find: ". . . he [Simmel] considers that philosophy is not like the sciences (in the true sense of this word), subject to the usual requirements of proof; its field is undemonstrable. . . . Imagination, personal sensations, would then be rightfully and freely indulged . . . and vigorous demonstrations would be out of place. But, as for ourselves, we confess not to place great value on this type of bastard speculation, whereby reality is expressed in necessarily subjective terms, as in art . . ." (98). Durkheim, in short, agrees with David Frisby's "impressionistic" interpretation of Simmel (see Chapter 9), but places a negative sign upon it. In an important article originally published in Italian, "La sociologia ed il suo dominio scientifico," in *Revista Italiana di Sociologia* 4 (1900), translated into French and reprinted in *Textes,* Vol. I, 13–36 (there is also an English translation in *Essays on Sociology and Philosophy,* ed. Kurt H. Wolff (New York, 1964)), Durkheim devoted a number of pages to his disagreement with Simmel as to the proper domain of sociology. See his further comments in "Sociologie et sciences sociales," *Revue philosophique* 55 (1903), in *Textes,* Vol. I, 138–44. The whole of this essay is reprinted in *Emile Durkheim on Institutional Analysis,* ed. and tr. Mark Traugott (Chicago, 1978). This is a valuable collection of translated articles, with an illuminating introduction by the editor.

10. Clark, however, points out that, in spite of Durkheim's success, ". . . sociology did not attain complete institutionalization: it had no distinct examination or degree sequence, and no lycée posts. Without these foundations for a traditional academic field, the Durkheimians did not dispose of the traditional incentives for recruiting followers. With time, this weakness became disastrous" (*Prophets and Patrons*, 98). Still, even if no longer dominated by the Durkheimians, sociology in France had come to stay.

11. Steve Fenton with Robert Reiner and Ian Hammett, *Durkheim and Modern Sociology* (Cambridge, England, 1984), states that Durkheim "does not offer a theory of how capitalism works, he does not incorporate into his sociology an explicit 'economic' theory of land, labour and capital . . . capitalism was not, for Durkheim, the focal category of analysis" (7). While I agree with the first part of this statement, I disagree with the second: in *The Division of Labor* Durkheim is analysing capitalism directly, though primarily as a social and moral system. Incidentally, Fenton's Chapter 4, "Race and Society: Primitive and Modern," is a valuable treatment of why race failed to play an important role in Durkheim's sociology.

12. Parsons takes the position, though inconsistently, that Durkheim did shift toward the end of his life. H. Stuart Hughes, *Consciousness and Society* (New York, 1958), following on Parsons, has made this view popular. Ronald Fletcher, in his ambitious and sometimes audacious survey, *The Making of Sociology: A Study of Sociological Theory*, Vol. 2: *Developments* (London, 1971), takes an opposing view (265). For the general question of change in Durkheim's thought, see Anthony Giddens, *Studies in Social and Political Thought* (London, 1977), 236; also his *Capitalism and Modern Social Theory* (Cambridge, England, 1971), 68. Giddens's study of Marx, Durkheim, and Max Weber is most thoughtful and stimulating. Jeffrey C. Alexander, *Theoretical Logic in Sociology*, Vol. II (Berkeley and Los Angeles, 1982), deals especially well with the various strands and strains in Durkheim's thought and has the added virtue of studying the early writings with great care; as a history of the formation of Durkheim's sociological ideas this book offers an impressive model.

13. LaCapra, *Emile Durkheim*, 57. Robert Nisbet gives an intelligent exposition of Durkheim as a conservative; see his *The Sociological Tradition* (New York, 1966), his edited *Emile Durkheim* (Englewood Cliffs, N.J., 1965), and *The Sociology of Emile Durkheim* (New York, 1974).

14. Emile Durkheim, *Socialism and Saint-Simon*, tr. C. Sattler, ed. Alvin W. Gouldner (Yellow Springs, Ohio, 1958 (1928)), 19. The lectures were first published posthumously in 1928 as *Le Socialisme*, ed. Marcel Mauss (Paris). See further Lukes, *Emile Durkheim*, Chapter 12.

15. Durkheim, *Socialism and Saint-Simon*, 7.

16. Emile Durkheim, *The Division of Labor in Society*, tr. George Simpson (New York, 1964), 32.

17. *Ibid.*, 73 and 36. Durkheim's statement is reminiscent of Bentham's

conflation of what is and what should be, though in different terms. A closer look at Durkheim's life and works suggests a certain ingenuousness to his value-free claim, as stated here. His advancement was partly due to his suitability as a professor in the effort to secularize French education, and his work fitted with the leanings of the "liberal" sector of French politics. As Clark, *Prophets and Patrons*, puts it, ". . . republicanism, Dreyfusard ideology, and the emergence of the new social sciences became combined as a single effort" (174). (In another mood, Durkheim did declaim against a value-free science; see Clark, 168.) The fact is that Durkheim's sociology is as much affected by his "values" as are the literary writers whom we have considered earlier by theirs; what is different is that his attempt at "science" causes him to try to be value-free in his work, with what success must be judged by each reader. A comparison with Weber's rather different value-free approach is appropriate (see Chapter 11).

18. For further discussion of this point, not necessarily in agreement with my argument, cf. Giddens, *Studies in Social and Political Theory*, 265 ff., and Fletcher, *The Making of Sociology*, 322ff. A selection of Durkheim's writings, in translation, emphasizing his concern with morality, or what its editor calls "civil religion," is *Emile Durkheim on Morality and Society*, ed. with an introd. by Robert Bellah (Chicago, 1973). Ernest Wallwork, *Durkheim: Morality and Milieu* (Cambridge, Mass., 1972) argues that "many of the distinguishing characteristics of Durkheimian sociology derive from his interest in moral philosophy" (vii), and goes on to interpret him as a philosophical naturalist.

19. In *Emile Durkheim on Institutional Analysis*, ed. Traugott, 46.

20. *Ibid.*, 40. Cf. 275 and 56.

21. Quoted in Lukes, *Emile Durkheim*, 139. The quote following is from *The Division of Labor*, 41.

22. *Revue philosophique* 27 (1889); I use the translation in Lukes, *Emile Durkheim*, 146.

23. Parsons, *The Structure of Social Action*, 343. Cf. Alexander, *Theoretical Logic in Sociology*, for a more subtle handling of this general problem.

24. *The Division of Labor*, 106 and 278. Further on primordial ties, see Edward Shils, "Primordial, Personal, Sacred and Civil Ties," *British Journal of Sociology* 8 (1957), 130–45.

25. *The Division of Labor*, 131.

26. Cf. Steven Lukes, *Individualism* (Oxford, 1973), for the general context of Tocqueville's use of the term; and our Chapter 2 for an earlier discussion of individualism.

27. Giddens, *Capitalism and Modern Social Theory*, 116.

28. *The Division of Labor*, 175. For the sexual division of labor, see p. 56.

29. For a discussion of Durkheim's rejection of a Comte-like philosophy of history, see Georges Davy, *L'Homme et le fait social et le fait politique* (Paris, 1973), Chapter VI, "L'Explication sociologique et le recours à l'his-

toire" (originally published as an article in 1949). In fact, Durkheim in practice sometimes fell victim to the ideas embodied in a conjectural philosophy of history.

30. *The Division of Labor,* 267. Cf. Simmel's similar view, Chapter 9.

31. Raymond Aron, *Main Currents in Sociological Thought,* trs. Richard Howard and Helen Weaver, 2 vols. (Garden City, N.Y., 1970), Vol. II, 23.

32. *The Division of Labor,* 1.

33. I have not even mentioned that part of Durkheim's *The Division of Labor* that deals with the shift from "repressive" law, in mechanized society, to "restitutive" law, in organic society, and from penal to civil or contract law. This, too, is derived openly from the Englishman Sir Henry Maine's classic work, *Ancient Law* (1861). Durkheim's only real addition is to note that contracts, too, must be sanctioned by the moral sentiment of society; thus, they do not substitute for such a code, but merely constitute a particular expression of an existing one.

34. Quoted in Lukes, *Emile Durkheim,* 147.

35. *The Division of Labor,* 129–30.

36. *Ibid.,* 172 and 168.

37. Quoted in Lukes, *Emile Durkheim,* 237.

38. For details, see *ibid.,* 477ff. It is well to remember that field work does not, in itself, solve all the problems of methodology. See, for example, the controversy over Margaret Mead's *Coming of Age in Samoa,* as discussed in Derek Freeman, *Margaret Mead and Samoa* (Cambridge, Mass., 1983), a book that itself has given rise to a great deal of further controversy.

39. See especially *Primitivism in 20th Century Art,* ed. William Rubin, 2 vols. (New York, 1984).

40. Emile Durkheim, *The Elementary Forms of the Religious Life,* tr. Joseph Ward Swain (New York, 1961), 17 and 257–58.

41. *Ibid.,* 52.

42. The totem as the origin of religion, however, is no longer accepted in most quarters. Note, too, that Sigmund Freud had written his *Totem and Taboo* (1912–13) about the same time Durkheim was writing *The Elementary Forms,* but see Claude Lévi-Strauss, *Totemism,* tr. Rodney Needham (Boston, 1963), for a general critique.

43. Durkheim, *The Elementary Forms,* 389.

44. *Ibid.,* 471. Cf. Lukes, *Emile Durkheim,* 231ff.

45. Quoted in Lukes, *Emile Durkheim,* 339.

46. See, however, Raymond Aron's sharp disagreement: "It seems to me absolutely inconceivable to define the essence of religion in terms of the worship which the individual pledges to the group, for in my eyes the essence of impiety is precisely the worship of the social order. To suggest that the object of the religious feelings is society transfigured is not to save but to degrade that human reality which sociology seeks to understand" (*Main Currents in Sociological Thought,* 66).

47. Durkheim, *The Elementary Forms*, 475.

48. Quoted in Lukes, *Emile Durkheim*, 339. Cf., however, Giddens, *Studies in Social and Political Theory*, who argues that "Durkheim's theory of moral authority is . . . far from being the rationale for authoritarianism which it is often portrayed as being" (261).

49. Durkheim, *The Elementary Forms*, 409. In fact, of course, Durkheim realized that "It is only in society that there are superiors, inferiors and equals" (173). A comparison with Simmel's ideas about subordination and superordination is in order here.

50. Durkheim, *The Elementary Forms*, 270 and 271. On pp. 364–65, however, Durkheim discussed the potential for confusion in this connecting manner of thinking. I might add that sometimes the desperate need to connect metastasizes into a compulsion. We make connections that are not really there, but are only imagined. Such is the paranoid state of mind. As Thomas Pychon defines paranoia in his novel, *Gravity's Rainbow*, it is "nothing less than the onset, the leading edge of the discovery that *everything is connected*" (quoted in Tony Tanner, "Paranoia, Energy, and Displacement," *Wilson Quarterly* II, no. 1 (Winter 1978), 144). So, too, is the conspiratorial imagination, which can turn an innocent meeting into an established connection, whose ramifications can be seen as going outward to a plot. Such "connection" is a form of false order, which, in fact, disorders the social world.

The opposite of seeing connections everywhere is the sense that nothing is connected, which leaves the world equally disordered. Much less disordering, but certainly frustrating, is when one points out a palpable connection in science or society or a person who says, "I don't see it."

51. Durkheim, Preface to Vol. II (1897–98), *L'Année sociologique*, translated in *Essays on Sociology and Philosophy*, ed. Wolff, 351.

52. I quote here from the translation in *Emile Durkheim*, ed. Yash Nandan, 54.

53. Durkheim, *The Elementary Forms*, 466.

54. *Ibid.*, 29, 357, and 494.

55. "The Dualism of Human Nature and Its Social Conditions," in *Essays on Sociology and Philosophy*, ed. Wolff, 338–39. The comparison that immediately springs to mind is with Sigmund Freud, *Civilization and Its Discontents* (1930).

11. Academic Sociology: Max Weber

1. Talcott Parsons saw part of what was happening: "The central interest of Weber, as of Pareto, was in 'economic' problems, the explanation of the phenomenon of modern capitalism. But as he soon realized that economics alone is incapable of solving his problems, he pushed further on to develop

a science of sociology" ("Economics and Sociology: Marshall in Relation to the Thought of His Time," *Quarterly Journal of Economics* XLVI, No. 2 (Feb. 1932), 343).

2. Among those most prominent in arguing for convergence are Talcott Parsons, *The Structure of Social Action* (New York, 1937), and Jeffrey C. Alexander, *Theoretical Logic in Sociology*, 4 vols. Vol. 3: *The Classical Attempt at Theoretical Synthesis: Max Weber* (Berkeley, 1983).

3. The quotation is from Marianne Weber, *Max Weber: A Biography*, tr. Harry Zohn (New York, 1970), 90. This non-judgmental position is akin to that of Freud and psychoanalysis. Thus, in discussing infantile and "perverted" sexuality, Freud remarked, "The sexual activities of children have hitherto been entirely neglected and though those of perverts have been recognized it has been with moral indignation and without understanding" (*The Standard Edition of the Complete Psychological Works of Sigmund Freud*, 38, *An Autobiographical Study*).

4. In Weber, *Max Weber*, 677.

5. For an in-depth treatment of Weber's methodological positions, emphasizing his indebtedness to Heinrich Rickert, see Thomas Burger, *Max Weber's Theory of Concept Formation: History, Laws and Ideal Types* (Durham, N.C., 1976). Burger argues that Weber was not interested in methodology as such but rather in its service in answering the question of "What is it that makes the writing of history a justifiable undertaking?" (xv). For a short, penetrating discussion of Weber's "Verstehen" method, value-free inquiry, and related issues, see Frank Parkin, *Max Weber* (New York, 1982), Chapter I. In general, this little book offers a most stimulating account and critique of Weber's leading ideas, written with verve and assertiveness. The work of Weber himself most pertinent here is *The Methodology of the Social Sciences*, eds. E. A. Shils and H. A. Finch (New York, 1949).

6. In Weber, *Max Weber*, 114. In general, for Weber's life the biography by his wife Marianne is essential, though uncritical. Arthur Mitzman, *The Iron Cage: An Historical Interpretation of Max Weber* (New York, 1970), in spite of its title, is equally a psychological interpretation, and a good one. See my review-essay in *History and Theory* X, No. 1 (1971), 90–107, where I take a more favorable position than Mitzman to Weber's attempt at a value-free science. *For Max Weber: Essays in Sociology*, eds. H. H. Gerth and C. Wright Mills (New York, 1958), which has an introduction on "The Man and His Works," should also be consulted. Unfortunately, Weber's *Jugendbriefe* (Tubingen, 1936), covering letters from August 1876, when the twelve-year-old boy writes to his mother, Helene, to September 1893, has not yet been translated into English.

7. The quote from Mommsen is from his *Max Weber and German Politics 1890–1920*, tr. Michael S. Steinberg (Chicago, 1984; 2nd ed. Tubingen, 1974), 26. Weber's own statement is quoted in David Beetham, *Max Weber and the Theory of Modern Politics* (Cambridge, England, 1985 (1974)), 219.

One might note that Weber described Chinese culture, and especially Confucianism, as opposed to any form of the breakdown of connections and thus the impersonalization necessary for the development of rational capitalism. See Alexander, *Theoretical Logic in Sociology*, 39 for details.

8. For this address, see *For Max Weber*, eds. Gerth and Mills, 363ff.

9. In Weber, *Max Weber*, 356. Alexander, *Theoretical Logic in Sociology*, 130, claims that Weber never created a school à la Durkheim; while this is true in the literal sense, the *Archiv* obviously helped Weber secure spiritual followers, even if not immediately, who can then be said to form a Weberian school.

10. See Martin Green, *The Von Richthofen Sisters* (New York, 1974), which deals with Else and Frieda von Richthofen, Otto Gross, Max Weber, and D. H. Lawrence. We need, also, to recall Georg Simmel's similar involvement with the George circle.

11. Max Weber, *Economy and Society*, eds. Guenther Roth and Claus Wittich, 2 vols. (Berkeley, 1978), Vol. I, 601. This is a splendid and dedicated work by the editors.

12. *For Max Weber*, eds. Gerth and Mills, 11 and 22. Cf. Weber, *Max Weber*, 518 and 522.

13. The political context for the development of Weber's views is dealt with in two excellent books, previously cited: Mommsen's *Max Weber and German Politics 1890–1920* and Beetham's *Max Weber and the Theory of Modern Politics*. The two, however, disagree in emphasis. Mommsen stresses Weber's nationalist leanings, while Beetham stresses his liberal commitment. Beetham, seeing Weber as a revisionist, reformulating liberalism, argues that "Weber's thought thus stands much more at the starting point than at the conclusion of a series of developments in the theory and practice of liberal democracy in the era of mass politics and bureaucratic organisations; it is much more as a precursor than as an 'epigone' that he should be understood" (7).

14. Max Weber, *The Protestant Ethic and the Spirit of Capitalism*, tr. Talcott Parsons (New York, 1958), 17. The quote that follows is on p. 27.

15. *Ibid.*, 224.

16. For an introduction to the controversy, which easily leads to further references, see *Protestantism, Capitalism, and Social Science: The Weber Thesis Controversy*, ed. Robert W. Green, 2nd ed. (Lexington, Mass., 1973).

17. Weber, *The Protestant Ethic*, 80.

18. *Ibid.*, 180.

19. *Ibid.*, 181. The phrase "iron cage" originally comes from John Bunyan's *Pilgrim's Progress* (see the edition edited by Roger Sharrock, (Harmondsworth, England, p. 65). Weber's phrase is actually "ein stahlhartes Gehäuse"—literally a housing hard as steel—which Talcott Parsons has translated as an "iron cage." It is interesting to note that Matthew Arnold, who can be considered a late-nineteenth-century lamenter, described the

English middle class as having "entered the prison of Puritanism" in the seventeenth century and "having had the key turned upon its spirit there for two hundred years" ("Equality" (1878), in *The Portable Matthew Arnold*, ed. Lionel Trilling (New York, 1949), 595). Arnold is mentioned by Weber as one of his precursors in discerning the relationship between the Protestant Ethic and capitalism.

20. Weber, *Economy and Society*, 612, 613, and 623. Weber makes the general point in *The Protestant Ethic* only in a footnote, where he notes that Jewish capitalism was "speculative pariah capitalism" and not central to the development of mainstream industrial capitalism (271). For an interesting treatment of Sombart and his attempt to place German capitalism and technology in a positive light by freeing it from Jewish "commercialism," see Jeffrey Herf, *Reactionary Modernism: Technology, Culture, and Politics in Weimar and the Third Reich* (Cambridge, England, 1984), Chapter 6, "Werner Sombart: Technology and the Jewish Question." As Herf points out, "Aware of Weber's work on the Protestant ethic and the spirit of capitalism, Sombart wrote: 'Puritanism is Judaism'" (138). Herf's book, in general, describes one way that a given society, Nazi Germany, sought to deal with the connections problem as it continued to work itself out in the twentieth century and to reconcile pastoralism and technology, *Gemeinschaft* and *Gesellschaft*.

21. Gunter Abramowski, *Das Geschichtsbild Max Webers* (Stuttgart, 1966), 12, calls Weber's *Economy and Society* his "chief sociological work." Alexander, *Theoretical Logic in Sociology*, however, reminds us that fully to understand Weber as a sociologist, we must take into account all of his writings, and not focus solely on any one part of his corpus (see especially 16–22). For our purposes, however, *Economy and Society* does take on a special importance. A useful summary of Weber's overall work and theories is Reinhold Bendix, *Max Weber: An Intellectual Portrait* (Garden City, N.Y., 1962).

22. On this subject see Guenther Roth and Wolfgang Schluchter, *Max Weber's Vision of History: Ethics and Methods* (Berkeley, 1979); Wolfgang Schluchter, *The Rise of Western Rationalism: Max Weber's Developmental History*, tr. with introd. by Guenther Roth (Berkeley, 1981); and the various relevant chapters in Wolfgang J. Mommsen, *The Age of Bureaucracy: Perspectives on the Political Sociology of Max Weber* (Oxford, 1974).

23. Max Weber, "Socialism," in *Max Weber: The Interpretation of Social Reality*, ed. with introd. by J.E.T. Eldridge (New York, 1980 (1971)), 205.

24. A sampling of authorities will give us the flavor of the discussions on the Marx-Weber problem. One of the earliest contributors, Karl Löwith, compared Weber's "disenchantment" thesis (i.e., that capitalism rationalizes everything) with Marx's analysis of alienation as a result of capitalist appropriation (*Max Weber and Karl Marx* (London, 1982; orig. pub. 1932)). Marianne Weber claims that "Weber expressed great admiration for Karl

Marx's brilliant constructions and saw in the inquiry into the economic and technical causes of events an exceedingly fruitful, indeed, a specifically new heuristic principle that directed the quest for knowledge into entire areas previously unilluminated. But he not only rejected the elevation of these ideas to a Weltanschauung, but was also against material factors being made absolute and being turned into the common denominator of causal explanations" (*Max Weber*, 335). Anthony Giddens, *Capitalism and Modern Social Theory*, says, "Weber undoubtedly had a general acquaintance with Marx's writings at an early stage in his career; but other influences were far more important" (193). Tom Bottomore, in a review of Weber's *Gesamtausgabe*, asserts that Weber "shows no real knowledge of Marx's theoretical work" other than *The Communist Manifesto*, and, asking whether Weber the social scientist stands above the melee of the Weimar Republic, answers, "I think not. His analysis of capitalism, socialism and democracy is thoroughly partisan and it deserves a more severely critical scrutiny than has even yet become the fashion" (*Times Literary Supplement*, April 19, 1985, pp. 29–30). Bryan S. Turner, *For Weber: Essays on the Sociology of Fate* (Boston and London, 1981), believes that Weber had only "a very partial understanding of Marx's complex view of economic relationships . . ." (20). And so it goes.

Cf. Mitzman, *The Iron Cage*, 180–88 for a brief discussion and 324 n.3 for a further bibliography of the literature on Marx and Weber. Of outstanding importance on this topic is *A Weber-Marx Dialogue*, eds. Robert J. Antonio and Ronald M. Glassman (Lawrence, Kans., 1985); I found the essays by Gerd Schroeter, Steven Kalberg, Lawrence A. Scaff and Thomas Clay Arnold, and Guenther Roth of especial interest.

25. *For Max Weber*, eds. Gerth and Mills, 35, and Weber, *Economy and Society*, 70 and 499.

26. The first quote is from Julius I. Loewenstein, *Marx Against Marxism*, tr. Harry Drost (London, 1980; orig. pub. 1970), 115, and the second from Alexander, *Theoretical Logic in Sociology*, 33.

27. Weber, *Economy and Society*, 1192–93.

28. *For Max Weber*, eds. Gerth and Mills, 280.

29. Weber, *Economy and Society*, 4.

30. *Ibid.*, 927. Among the summaries of Weber, see Giddens, *Capitalism and Modern Social Theory*, Part 3 and Aron, *Main Currents in Sociological Thought* (Garden City, N.Y., 1970), Vol. II, his section on Weber.

31. Beetham, *Max Weber and the Theory of Modern Politics*, 23.

32. In Weber, *Max Weber*, 222. The quote following is from Weber, *Economy and Society*, 39.

33. *For Max Weber*, eds. Gerth and Mills, 78.

34. Weber, *Economy and Society*, 93.

35. *Ibid.*, 202. For what follows, see also 938–39.

36. *Max Weber*, ed. Eldridge, 209.

37. Weber, *Economy and Society*, 1401.

38. In Weber, *Max Weber*, 416, and Weber, *Economy and Society*, 1402.

39. *Economy and Society*, 959 and 225.

40. In *Max Weber*, 416. The quotation that follows is from *Economy and Society*, 1403.

41. *Economy and Society*, 18.

42. *Ibid.*, 585. See also 654, 226, and 584.

43. *Ibid.*, 937, 936, and 637.

44. *Ibid.*, 112.

45. *Ibid.*, 243.

46. *Ibid.*, 244 and 1179.

47. *Ibid.*, 244.

48. See, for example, John Owen King III, *The Iron of Melancholy* (Middletown, Conn., 1983), Chapter 6.

49. *Economy and Society*, 245.

50. *Ibid.*, 1117 and 245.

51. Tom Bottomore points out that "Michels, who was Weber's close friend and had an intimate knowledge of his political views, explained his own conversion to fascism in 1922 by reference to the idea of a great charismatic leader and later wrote of Mussolini that he was 'the modern prototype of what Max Weber meant to be understood by a charismatic leader'" (*Times Literary Supplement*, April 19, 1985, p. 29).

Michels's point is suggestive, but I doubt if it is accurate. Cf. Mommsen, *The Age of Bureaucracy*, especially his chapter on "The Theory of the Three Pure Types of Legitmate Domination and the Concept of Plebiscitarian Democracy."

52. *Economy and Society*, 1391. For one analysis of this persistence, see Charles Meier, *Recasting Bourgeois Europe* (Princeton, N.J., 1975).

53. Gunter Abramowski, *Das Geschichtsbild Max Webers* (Stuttgart, 1966), 14.

12. Conclusions and Evaluations

1. I might add that the power of "sympathy" is not to be dismissed. For example, great political leaders, and not just great thinkers such as Engels and Marx, may find inspiration for their mission in a profound sense of sympathy. Thus, Jawaharlal Nehru tells about his reaction to seeing poverty in India at first hand, saying, "I was filled with shame and sorrow . . ." (Nehru, *Toward Freedom* (Boston, 1963), 56–57). So inspired, he reached out to the masses, and, as one scholar puts it, Nehru "learned to strike the deep chords in Indian humanity; he took to the crowd, and the crowd took to him" (B. R. Nanda, *The Nehrus: Motilal and Jawaharlal* (New York, 1963), 341).

2. As Gareth Stedman Jones so well puts it, "When historians, on the

lookout for some grander conceptual framework within which to situate their research, move out from a narrow empiricism into a theoretical eclecticism, they may easily find themselves tumbling down all manner of slippery paths, which they had had no prior intention of descending" (Gareth Stedman Jones, *Languages of Class*, (Cambridge, England, 1983), 79). See the entire chapter (pp. 76–89) for Jones's handling of the sociological concept of "social control" as an example of the historian's difficulties.

3. See Chapter 7.

4. Cf. E. P. Thompson, "Time, Work-Discipline, and Industrial Capitalism," *Past and Present*, No. 38 (Dec. 1967). Also, Gunnar Myrdal, "The 'Soft State' in Underdeveloped Countries," in Myrdal, *The Challenge of World Poverty* (New York, 1970), for the need of developing nations for the kind of discipline we used to take for granted in the industrialized West.

5. One might note that, in 1980, for example, one out of nine American workers was employed in a late shift.

It should also be noted that the clock had earlier become a symbol of order in a world that had been experiencing chaos—the Hundred Years' War, the Catholic-Protestant Wars, the subsequent modern revolutions—and that had been searching for new forms of order. We can call this development the Horological Revolution, involving especially Huygen's pendulum clock, and taking place around the period 1660–1760. We have mentioned the way the new time discipline in the factories imposed a strain; we must also acknowledge that such discipline gave meaning and structure to both cosmic and daily life for many, whose lives now went regularly, like "clockwork." See David S. Landes, *Revolution in Time: Clocks and the Making of the Modern World* (Cambridge, Mass., 1983), for an intriguing history of the development of the clock and its meaning for modern civilization.

6. An unexpected reality has been given to this vignette by a recent news story. It concerns S. M. Otieno, a successful lawyer in Kenya, himself of the Luo tribe, who married a woman of another tribe, the Kikuyu, an unusual step in itself. On his death, his wife claimed his body for burial in Nairobi, but his Luo tribesmen insisted that "tradition" required his body to be buried in tribal grounds. In court, the issue between "modern" and "traditional," and individual and tribal, loyalties dramatically played itself out, with the court deciding for the tribe in the end (see the *New York Times*, Feb. 25 and May 16, 1987).

7. John Rawls, *A Theory of Justice* (Cambridge, Mass., 1971). The Quaker reformer John Woolman, in 1746, had put it in more traditional language: "How should I approve of this conduct [he was writing about slavery] were I in their circumstance and they in mine? (Quoted in Thomas L. Haskell, "Capitalism and the Origins of the Humanitarian Sentiment, Part 2," *American Historical Review* 90, No. 3 (June 1985), 564).

8. For Pakistan, see Richard Reeves, "Reporter at Large," *The New Yorker*, Oct. 1, 1984, p. 52. For the Soviet Union, see the *New York Times*,

Aug. 25, 1985, p. 14. Though not so obvious in the latter country, but certainly present in many of the other developing nations, a complication exists: in addition to the pressures of industrialization many of these countries must come to terms with the alien forces of Westernization, imposing yet another strain.

9. One scholar, the anthropologist Alan Macfarland, has called community "one of the controlling myths of our time." As he continues, quoting another writer, "the concept of 'community' is to sociology what 'culture' is to anthropology." Yet, Macfarland concludes, a satisfactory definition of community in sociological terms "appears as remote as ever" ("History, Anthropology and the Study of Communities," *Social History* 5 (May 1977), 632 and 633).

10. *The Concept of Community: Readings with Interpretations*, eds. David W. Minar and Scott Greer (Chicago, 1969), ix.

11. Robert Nisbet, *The Sociological Tradition* (New York, 1966), 47.

12. We can look, for an example, at the United States, where one historian calls our attention to community breakdown—or a perception thereof—repeating itself in the 1650s, 1690s, 1740s, 1780s, 1850s, 1880s, and 1920s. (See Thomas Bender, *Community and Social Change in America* (New York, 1978), 51.) "Declension" or "devolution," as historians sometimes characterize it, is thus a constant reality, with "progressive" and "conservative" periods succeeding one another.

One may also raise a question such as whether Puritan communities, to take that example, were any less communal because they were established on a contractual basis—the convenant—rather than (or in addition to) traditional customs brought from England. Further, is not an "add-on," and not just an either/or, possible? Thus, local community members, at the time of the American Revolution, were able to take on a national membership while retaining a local one. In short, there tends to be more, far more, in history than is dreamed of in the narrow concept of community.

Subject Index

Name Index